COOKING WITH THE RIGHT SIDE OF THE BRAIN

COOKING WITH THE RIGHT SIDE OF THE BRAIN

VICKI RAE CHELF

AVERY PUBLISHING GROUP INC.

Garden City Park, New York

Cover Design: Vicki Chelf , Rudy Shur, and Janine Eisner-Wall
Cover Photograph: Alan Ulmer
Original Illustrations: Vicki Chelf
In-House Editors: Karen Price Heffernan, Marie Caratozzolo

Library of Congress Cataloging-in-Publication Data

Chelf , Vicki .
    Cooking with the right side of the brain : creative vegetarian
cooking / Vicki Chelf .
        p.   cm.
    ISBN 0-89529-431-1
    1. Vegetarian cookery.   I. Title.
TX837.H79   1989
641.5′636—dc20   89-17807
                                                                CIP

Printed in the United States of America

10   9   8   7   6   5   4   3   2

Contents

Preface

Feeding ourselves in a harmonious way is what vegetarian cooking is all about. This is done by following the natural rhythms of the seasons with our menu choices, paying heed to what our bodies need to function at their best, and choosing foods that are simple and economical and do not over-tax the ecosystem with their production. Vegetarianism is also about non-violence—realizing that we do not need to kill other creatures to achieve radiant health.

As much as I believe in the benefits of a vegetarian diet, preaching its virtues does not interest me. I feel that it is far more effective to let the food speak for itself. A well-prepared vegetarian meal is so delicious that all its other merits seem secondary.

In the sixteen years that I have been a vegetarian, I have had many teachers. The first was my mother, Hazel Chelf, who set an example by being such a good cook herself. The students in my cooking classes and the clients at "Le Pommier Fleuri" in Ste-Agathe, Quebec have also been valuable teachers. They have tried and tasted my recipes as well as shared recipes of their own. Two very special friends who have inspired me with their glowing beauty, spiritual awareness, and culinary knowledge are Dominique Biscotti and Isabelle Depelteau. Another friend who has been an inspiration with his inventiveness and his positive attitude is Stephen Bertrand. I would like to thank Alan Ulmer for the beautiful cover photograph. Thanks also to Rudy Shur, Diana Puglisi, and Karen Heffernan at Avery who, with their great work, have enabled me to share my culinary experiences in such a lovely book.

Introduction

About ten years ago, my lifelong desire to become a self-supporting artist led me into the realm of cookbook writing. I reasoned that since no one would hire an untrained and inexperienced illustrator, I would create something for myself to illustrate. Everyone seemed to enjoy my cooking and I was frequently copying recipes for friends; therefore, the natural choice for the project was a cookbook. There was no question as to what kind of cookbook, because the cooking that I know and love is vegetarian whole foods cuisine.

At that time, my husband and I were living in the Laurentian Mountains in the Canadian province of Quebec. Eighty percent of Quebec's population is French-speaking, but there were no good vegetarian cookbooks available in French. Therefore, there was a real need for the kind of book that I intended to write.

For three years, my spare time was spent working on the cookbook. I kept a notebook in the kitchen and wrote down recipes as I made them. I also spent one whole summer working on the illustrations.

Finding a publisher was easy, but my plan backfired. The publisher loved my book (it became a best-seller for him), but he didn't feel that the illustrations were professional enough to print.

Heartbroken as I was, there was no time for nursing a bruised ego, because the launching of the book was the beginning of what became a busy career. With more optimism than money, I opened a natural foods store. I also started teaching up to three different cooking classes a week. One thing led to another, and I ended up producing three more books and adding a small vegetarian restaurant to the store.

Working with the public and teaching about healthful eating was very rewarding. It gave me the opportunity to witness, time after time, the wonderful physical and spiritual transformation that occurs when one changes one's diet from standard, high-fat, processed foods to pure and simple vegetarian fare.

There was one factor, however, that kept me from being totally happy with my success. I no longer had the time to do artwork. Therefore, after five years of running my small business, I gave it up to move to the United States and study art.

As a student, I supported myself by teaching cooking. Before long the classes became very popular and people were asking me to translate my books to English.

This book, however, is not a translation of any of my French books. Even though it contains many of the same recipes, it is very different. Over the years I have derived much joy and satisfaction from trying out new ideas and being creative. I am not the type of person who will follow the same routine over and over again just because it works. After seven years of teaching cooking classes, I still have not developed a regular program. There is always something different to try.

There are other factors, too, that help to keep me creative. I often forget to bring an "important" ingredient to the class, or buy the wrong thing. A lack of the proper utensils, combining the wrong two mixtures, and other such "goof-ups" are so common in my classes that quick improvisation is always the order of the day. In spite of the things that might seem to be going against me, the food always turns out great—and my students learn that cooking is a whole lot easier than they'd thought. They also learn that they, too, can be creative cooks.

In this book I have tried to incorporate some of the ambiance of my cooking classes (minus the "goof-ups") in order to illustrate the fact that there is no single "right" or "wrong" way to cook. Each individual has to find what works best for her or him.

Being a good cook takes a little knowledge along with a lot of intuition and the confidence to use it. A good cook also realizes the simple basic truth of why we cook and why we eat. She is able to prepare food that is not only a delight to taste and see, but that nourishes and strengthens the body as well.

This book will help you to become a good cook—as opposed to someone who "just follows recipes." It is not intended to be used only by vegetarians or persons who wish to become vegetarians. It is designed for people who recognize that a pure and balanced diet is essential for good health and who would like to find practical, delicious, and creative ways to incorporate healthful eating into their lifestyle.

1. GETTING STARTED

Do you know about the right and left sides of the brain? Here is a brief and simplified version of how the human mind works: the right side of the brain controls thoughts and actions that are creative, intuitive, spontaneous, and artistic, whereas the left side controls our more logical, concise, analytical, and scientific thinking. When most of us were growing up, our schooling encouraged the left side of our intellect, while ignoring, or repressing, our right or creative side. Thus, most of today's adults have lost a good deal of their innate artistic confidence and the freedom and joy of expression that accompanies it. This unbalanced type of education (which, thankfully, is changing) turns out brilliant mathematicians and business people who cannot dance or stir-fry zucchini.

There is a book called *Drawing on the Right Side of the Brain,* and one about writing with the right side of the brain, so let's try cooking with the right side of the brain!

Your intellect may be a terrible cook, but your intuition instinctively knows what your body needs and likes. So if you do not know how to handle a particular culinary problem, just relax. Take a few minutes and listen to that wise little voice inside of you. If one uses fresh, whole foods in a respectful manner, it is practically impossible to turn out a disaster.

If a recipe calls for a vegetable that is out of season, add something you have on hand. Try substituting millet or buckwheat for rice, or a tahini sauce for a cheese sauce. If a recipe uses an herb or spice you don't care for, omit it and add something you like. Just be sure to allow for changes in cooking times, or differences in the liquid content of the substituted ingredients. Sometimes, the result may not be quite as good as

expected, but often you may be pleasantly surprised to find that you like the new version even better than the original!

Experimenting will help you to learn what you can and can't do in cooking. This knowledge will give you the confidence you need to create masterpieces of your own. *We are all creative;* it is just that most of us are unaccustomed to using our creativity, and therefore, afraid.

A great chef was once explaining to some admirers how he made one of his prize recipes. "First you add ⅛ teaspoon of salt and ½ teaspoon of nutmeg. Sift it three times with ¾ cup of flour. Slowly stir in ⅔ cup of milk and heat to

195° . . . '' —and so on, he recited to his listeners, who were greatly impressed by the scientific exactness of his trade. "Then," he added, "when the temperature is exact, add a big glob of molasses!"

If ten cooks were concocting the same dish from the same recipe, it is very likely that they would each end up with a slightly different finished product . . . some, undoubtedly, more successful than others. Success comes with knowing your ingredients and how to use them. Using the proper kitchen equipment is also important. Following are suggestions intended to help you achieve satisfactory results with the recipes in this book.

- The first time you try a recipe, follow it as written. This will let you know what kind of dish is intended. The next time, you may wish to make changes to suit your own taste and needs. Having prior experience with a recipe will greatly facilitate your experimentation.
- Any recipe in this book may be easily doubled or cut in half without adverse effects. Just remember, if something is doubled, it will take longer to bake, and if it is cut in half, it will take less time.
- An approximation of how many persons a recipe will serve is always given, but, of course, this depends on who is eating and what else is being served. Be aware that a six-foot-two-inch marathon runner will probably eat twice as much as a five-foot-two-inch sedentary office worker. Also, remember that a main dish accompanied by a cheese sauce will serve more people than the same recipe served plain, or with a lighter sauce.
- For baked dishes, always preheat the oven, unless the recipe states otherwise. When timing a baked dish, keep in mind that ovens vary, so *check your dish occasionally* (unless you are making a souffle!), and make any needed adjustments.
- If a recipe calls for an ingredient you are unfamiliar with, you may look it up in the Glossary of Ingredients, starting on page 4.
- In many cases, there are suitable alternatives to ingredients that you do not have on hand. (See "How to Substitute Ingredients" on pages 15-18.)

- Recipes using tofu may have to be slightly adjusted to obtain the desired consistency. The reason for this is that the water content of tofu varies between producers and between batches. Therefore, if a recipe such as a dip, soup, or salad dressing is too thick, add more liquid. If it is too thin, add more tofu.
- The amount of flour needed in a recipe can vary. For example, in very humid weather, you may need more flour for a pie crust, crackers, or bread. Also, if you measure one cup of flour, then stir it, you will have from one-quarter to one-third cup more flour after stirring. All of the recipes in this book call for unstirred flour, right out of the bag.
- The amount of oil used in a recipe for frying or sautéing can sometimes be decreased. You need just enough oil to keep the food that you are cooking from sticking. Food has a tendency to stick more to one type of pan than to another. Therefore, if you feel that a recipe calls for more oil than you need, feel free to try the recipe with a little less oil.
- The herbs called for in these recipes (except for parsley, which is always available fresh) are always dried, unless otherwise stated.
- If you wish to avoid most of the cholesterol in eggs, you may substitute two egg whites for one whole egg in recipes.
- Soymilk, cashew milk, and dairy milk can be used interchangeably in most recipes. However, sweetened soymilks that contain vanilla are not good in savory dishes. For example, a béchamel sauce made with these slightly sweet milks tastes terrible.
- In vegetable cookery, so many factors determine the optimal cooking time that it is impossible to be very precise. The size you cut the veggies, their freshness, the type of pan used, the degree of heat used, and individual taste differences all make to-the-minute, scientific exactness impractical. Cooking times are indicated to give you a good idea of how long something will take, but, at the same time, it is important to use your own judgment. *Look at the food you are cooking, not at your watch, to see when your recipe is done.* Common sense is your most precious resource in being a good cook.

There are no absolutes in cooking. Something is always coming up. We lack an ingredient . . . the oven is not working . . . the pan is not the proper size. A happy and not-too-serious cook who is willing to adapt to any given situation is certainly going to be the most successful.

Bon appetit, and have fun!

THE INGREDIENTS WE USE

As I was working on this book, a nice woman came to me asking for some vegetable recipes. Not an unusual request, considering that this is a vegetarian cookbook. Wanting to oblige, I began leafing through the recipes, looking for a few that the average person would not find too exotic. About halfway through, I began to panic. There were practically no "normal" recipes in the book (at least I couldn't find them at the time). Almost every recipe contained one ingredient or more that would be considered strange. After searching and searching, I was relieved to finally come up with enough recipes to keep me from feeling like an extraterrestrial being.

When she left I began to reflect upon the situation. The foods we use in vegetarian cooking are the same foods that have nourished mankind since the beginning of time. Why is it that so many people are unfamiliar with them? How is it that we have come so far from our roots? The food we eat is as essential to life as the air we breathe. Why do we know so little about it?

The foods used in vegetarian cookery are grains, legumes, and simple products made from them, as well as vegetables, fruits, nuts, seeds, moderate amounts of eggs and dairy products, and a few herbs and spices. People in most parts of the world still depend on these foods. It is we, in the industrialized nations, who eat so differently. In the cooking classes that I teach, it is hard to find someone who is able to recognize a grain of wheat. Barley, buckwheat, and rye seem even more strange. Not to mention the staple foods of other cultures, such as tofu, tempeh, shoyu, or hijiki. On the other hand, who in the United States does not know what Tang, Twinkies, or Pop Tarts are?

If the results of this ignorance were not so pathetic, the situation would almost be comical. However, heart disease, cancer, strokes, diabetes, and many other forms of suffering all stem from a lack of knowing how to feed ourselves. Since most of us buy food as a plastic, wrapped product, it is easy to forget just how essential it is. We need to remember that we can help food to grow, but we cannot actually create it. When I speak of respecting food or of using food in a respectful manner, I mean being aware of the fact that there is a higher power that gives it life and makes it grow. When you really stop and think about it, which is stranger: a bowl of brown rice and tofu, or a bowl of multicolored Pac-Man cereal?

The inset on the following pages is a list of some vegetarian staples, many of which are not in current use in the standard North American kitchen. The list includes descriptions of these foods and suggestions for their uses.

GLOSSARY OF INGREDIENTS

Adzuki beans. These are also called aduki beans or azuki beans. They are small, dark red beans (similar in size to mung beans) that have been cultivated for centuries in China, Japan, Korea, and other Far Eastern countries. They are also grown in the United States, and are available at most natural foods stores and Asian markets here. Adzukis are especially good when cooked with kombu, the sea vegetable.

Agar-agar. No one will have trouble introducing this versatile sea vegetable into their family diet. It is odorless, tasteless, and colorless. Agar-agar (often called just *agar* in this book) is used as a jelling agent to make desserts, aspics, jams, etc. There are thousands of wonderful ways to employ agar-agar in the vegetarian kitchen. It is frequently used in the dessert section of this book to make pies and other treats. *See also* Kanten.

Used in aspics, agar is good for persons who are watching their weight, because it provides bulk without adding a lot of calories. It also aids digestion and is cleansing to the system.

In natural foods stores we usually see agar in the form of feather-light bars or flakes. It usually is sold in packages of two bars.

Alfalfa Seeds. These are tiny brown seeds used for growing alfalfa sprouts. Often considered to be a grain, but actually a legume, alfalfa was originally grown in North Africa. It is now widely cultivated in various parts of the world. Over 27 million acres in the United States alone are devoted to alfalfa each year, and organically grown alfalfa seed is easily found in most natural foods stores.

Alfalfa

Amaranth. Composed of tiny round grains, amaranth is packed with nutrition. An ancient grain that is being newly discovered, amaranth contains about 16 percent protein and is rich in the essential amino acid lysine.

Impressive as the qualities of amaranth are, it is still not widely available. However, a commercially produced amaranth cereal is sold in most natural foods stores.

Amaranth flour can be used in pancakes and added to baked goods. It does not contain gluten and will not make a very light yeast bread if used alone. Amaranth grains can be popped like popcorn.

Amasake. Literally, sweet sake, amasake is made from rice that has been inoculated with koji (a special type of bacteria) and allowed to ferment in a warm place for several hours. As the rice ferments, it becomes delectably sweet and soft. Amasake is used in making desserts and beverages. It may also be eaten plain or with fruit. Amasake can be purchased in most large natural foods stores, or made at home.

Arame. Arame resembles finely textured hijiki, but it is actually from a larger plant that is cut into thin strands. The next time that you stir-fry vegetables, add an exotic touch with some *Arame Condiment* (see page 246). It is truly delicious.

Arame

Arrowroot. The tuberous root of a tropical plant, arrowroot is dried and ground into a fine powder. Arrowroot may be substituted for cornstarch, measure for measure, or cornstarch may be substituted for arrowroot. Many health-oriented cooks prefer arrowroot to cornstarch because it is produced by a fairly simple, traditional method, whereas cornstarch is chemically bleached and treated. Arrowroot is also a *whole* food (made from the entire root) while cornstarch is a *fractured* food (made from the isolated, starchy part of the corn kernel).

Baking Powder. The best type of baking powder to use is one that does not contain aluminum. Recent studies have found high levels of aluminum in the brains of persons with Alzheimer's and Parkinson's diseases. Aluminum has also been linked to bone degeneration and kidney dysfunctions. One piece of a cake made from aluminum baking powder can contain from five to fifteen milligrams of aluminum.

One brand of baking powder that does not contain aluminum is Rumford brand. Rumford contains calcium phosphate, bicarbonate of soda, and cornstarch. It is probably harmless when used on occasion by healthy persons.

Barley. A delicious grain with a chewy texture and a sweet, nutty flavor, barley was cultivated in China over 2,000 years ago and is perhaps the oldest cereal food.

Organically grown barley that has been only lightly pearled (hulled) may be purchased in natural foods stores. Barley flour is also available in the larger stores.

Bran. Bran is the fibrous top layer that is just under the hull of any grain. The most commonly sold type of bran is wheat bran. However, oat bran and rice bran (rice polish) are also available. Bran is a very popular item in natural foods stores. It is bought by persons who wish to increase the amount of fiber in their diets. The vegetarian diet, however, is naturally high in fiber, making the supplementary use of bran unnecessary.

Brown Rice. *See* rice.

Buckwheat

Buckwheat. A traditional ingredient in Russian and Ukrainian cuisines, buckwheat is also used in French Canadian cooking. People who eat macrobiotically consider it the most "yang"* of grains, and its unique, hearty flavor is especially welcome during the winter months. This grain is highly nutritious and is really worth getting to know.

Buckwheat is almost always grown organically. It actually nourishes the soil and thus needs no fertilizer Insecticides are infrequently used on buckwheat, as they are said to lower its yield.

---

*"Yin and Yang" are Japanese (macrobiotic) ideas. Yin means energy or movement that has a centrifugal or outward direction and results in expansion. Yin foods are these that are acidic and contain potassium and sugar. Yang represents energy or movement that has a centripetal or inward direction. Yang foods are alkaline and contain sodium.

When buckwheat is toasted it is referred to as *kasha*. Whole, untoasted buckwheat is known as buckwheat *groats*, and cracked buckwheat is called buckwheat *grits*. Buckwheat can also be ground into flour. Buckwheat pancakes are delicious.

Bulghur (or bulgar). Bulghur wheat is whole wheat that has been cracked, partially cooked, and then dried. Bulghur cooks very rapidly and comes in handy when you are in a hurry.

Burdock. A hardy plant that grows wild throughout the United States. The long, dark burdock root is delicious in soups, stews, and sea vegetable dishes, or sautéed with carrots. It is highly valued for its strengthening qualities. The Japanese name for burdock is *gobo*.

Burdock Root

Carob. Although carob does not taste exactly like chocolate, it is an excellent food in its own right, and merits being appreciated as such. Carob chips can be found in natural foods stores. Make sure to find out the ingredients contained in carob chips before you buy them. Some brands are made mostly out of sugar and saturated fat. See the next entry for more information on carob.

Carob Powder or Carob Flour. A rich-tasting, dark brown powder made from the dried pods of the honey locust tree, carob is usually employed as a healthful alternative to chocolate. It contains less fat than chocolate and because of its natural sweetness (as opposed to chocolate's natural bitterness) less sweetener is needed when carob is substituted for chocolate in a recipe. Furthermore, carob does not contain oxalic acid, as does chocolate. Oxalic acid combines with calcium present in food to form a compound that the body can't absorb—it makes the calcium unavailable to the body.

Chick Peas. Often called garbanzo beans or ceci, chick peas were originally cultivated in the Middle East, where they are still considered a staple food item. They are also widely cultivated in India and throughout the Western Hemisphere. Chick peas are available at most natural foods stores. Use them to make the Middle Eastern spread hummus, and in salads, meatless loaves, dressings, and breads.

Chick Peas

Couscous. Couscous is a staple of Tunisian and Moroccan cuisine. The light and quick-cooking couscous sold in North America is not a whole food. It is made from wheat that has been stripped of its germ and bran. Bulghur wheat is more nutritious and less expensive than couscous, and can usually be substituted in recipes.

Daikon. The daikon is a long, white radish. Freshly grated raw daikon is especially helpful in the digestion of oily foods. Dried daikon, sold in shredded form, is particularly good cooked with kombu and seasoned with tamari soy sauce. Soaking dried daikon before use brings out its natural sweetness.

Daikon Radish

Dry Active Yeast. Used for leavening purposes, dry active yeast is made up of living microorganisms that are in a dormant state. Fresh cake yeast may be substituted for dry active yeast, tablespoon for tablespoon. Inactive food yeasts, such as torula, brewer's, and nutritional yeasts are useless for leavening and should not be confused with fresh cake yeast or dry active yeast. For more information on using yeast in baking, see page 70.

Dulse. This mild-tasting sea vegetable is very easy to use. Just wash it carefully (sometimes there are small shells clinging to it) and add it to whatever you wish. Dulse can be used raw as an ingredient in salads. It is also good with potato and corn dishes.

Durum Wheat. A very high-protein variety of wheat that is used for making pasta.

Gluten. An elastic protein substance found in grains. Wheat contains more gluten than other grains. Several types of meat analogues are made from wheat gluten. *See also* Seitan.

Gluten Flour. This is a fine, greyish flour made from wheat gluten. A small amount of this flour added to any yeast bread recipe will make a lighter bread.

Hard Wheat. A high-protein variety of winter wheat used for making bread flour.

Hijiki. A dark brown sea vegetable that turns black when dried. It has a spaghetti-like consistency, a stronger taste than arame, and is very high in calcium and protein. The hijiki sold in the United States is imported from Japan or harvested off the coast of Maine.

Kanten. A jelled dessert made from agar-agar. It can include melon, apples, berries, peaches, pears, amasake, adzuki beans, or other items. Usually served chilled, it is a cool, refreshing alternative to conventional gelatin.

Kelp. There are many varieties of this sea vegetable. Kombu and arame are both in the kelp family. Kelp is usually ground into a powder and used as a seasoning and nutritional supplement. Powdered kelp may be used as a salt substitute. It has a dark color, however, which may unattractively change the color of some dishes.

Koji. A bacteria culture (similar to yogurt culture) that is used to make miso and amasake. Koji is sold in the larger natural foods stores. Instructions for using koji are included in the package.

Kombu. Kombu is a wide, thick, dark green sea vegetable that is sold in strips about six inches long. These strips are easy to use. Just rinse a strip and add it to a pot of soup, stew, rice, beans, or any other slow-cooking dish. (If kombu is added to a quick-cooking dish, it should first be soaked for twenty minutes.) Kombu more than doubles in size when it is cooked, and like all sea vegetables, it enriches whatever it is cooked with.

Kombu

Kudzu (also called kuzu). This soothing and easily digested starch is made from the root of the kudzu plant. In Japan, kudzu is used both as a food and as a medicine. Its culinary uses include thickening sauces and making jellies and puddings. Kudzu is also used in the manufacture of a special type of delicate noodle.

Kudzu may be substituted for arrowroot in recipes. The proportions for using kudzu powder in cooking, as given by William Shurtleff and Akiko Aoyagi in *The Book of Kudzu* (Avery Publishing Group), are as follows:

For a thin sauce, use 2 teaspoons kudzu powder per cup of liquid;

For a thick sauce, use 1 tablespoon kudzu powder per cup of liquid;

For jellies, use 2½ tablespoons kudzu per cup of liquid.

Legumes. A general term for peas and beans, these often-overlooked foods are rich in proteins and complex carbohydrates, and offer many valuable vitamins and minerals as well. Alfalfa and buckwheat, which are used like grains, are actually legumes.

Lentils. These small beans are native to Central Asia, and have a round, flat shape. Organically grown green and red lentils are available at most natural foods stores. Lentils are high in protein and are terrific in soups, stews, and casseroles.

Lentils

Malt. A natural sweetener made from sprouted barley. It can be purchased either in syrup form or as a powder. Malt is less sweet than honey or maple syrup and is preferred by many persons because the body metabolizes it more slowly than other sweeteners.

Maple Syrup. A natural sweetener with an exquisite flavor, maple syrup is made in the spring. The sap of maple trees is collected and then boiled for several hours until it becomes sweet and thick. Maple syrup is a very concentrated food; forty gallons of sap are needed to make one gallon of syrup. Use it sparingly.

Millet. Millet is light, fluffy, and mild tasting. It is also highly nutritious and is said to be the most alkaline (acid-neutralizing) of cereals. Millet is a staple of northern China, Korea, and parts of Africa. It can be substituted for rice in almost any recipe. Make sure to buy hulled millet for cooking, because unhulled millet has a very hard shell and is suitable only for sprouting.

Uncooked millet can be ground into a flour in a blender for use in pancakes or crepes, or used as a breakfast cereal. Leftover cooked millet is good with fruit and yogurt or soymilk for breakfast. *Millet Cream* (see page 26) or cooked millet, blended with a little stock, can be used to thicken a soup and give it a rich, dairy-like quality.

Miso. A savory fermented paste made from soybeans and/or grains, sea salt, and koji. Miso is mainly used as a base for soups and sauces; however, it can also be used to season patés, dips, salad dressings, and all sorts of other dishes.

The numerous varieties of miso run from a sweet white or yellow through hearty reds to a dark and pungent chocolatey brown. Yellow miso is mild and

does not alter the color of foods that it is mixed with. It is especially nice for seasoning yellow vegetables, cream soups, and mock dairy dishes. Dark miso is fermented for a longer time and is a bit saltier and stronger-flavored. It is good in hearty winter soups and in grain dishes. White miso and barley miso are the ones that I use the most, because I like their mild flavor.

Miso is highly esteemed in Japan for both its culinary uses and its medicinal properties. Miso soup is the traditional Japanese breakfast, and macrobiotic healers recommend easily digestible miso broth for a variety of ailments. To preserve the benefits of the "friendly bacteria" that miso contains, it should be added at the end of cooking, or after the dish is cooked. Miso should never be boiled. *See also* Natto Miso.

Mochi. A traditional Japanese confection made from sweet rice (*see* Rice), mochi is made by cooking the rice and then pounding it until it becomes very smooth and sticky. This paste is spread out into slabs and allowed to partially dry.

Mochi can be purchased in most of the larger natural foods stores, where it is usually kept in the frozen foods section. Cook mochi by pan-frying or baking it according to the directions on the package. As the mochi cooks it puffs up impressively. It is crisp and crunchy on the outside and sticky and moist on the inside. I enjoy mochi for breakfast with the *Apple-Tahini Sauce* on page 249.

Muesli. A cereal consisting of mixed grains, fruit, and nuts, muesli was designed by a Swiss doctor as an ideal breakfast.

Mung Beans. Mung beans are most commonly known in their sprouted form as Chinese bean sprouts. They are second only to alfalfa in popularity for home growing. These sprouts have been used widely by people in the Far East for centuries. The small, green-colored seeds are available at most natural foods stores and Oriental groceries.

Mung sprouts are a good source of protein, especially the amino acid methionine, which may have a calming effect on the body. They are also rich in vitamin C, and contain healthful stores of the minerals iron and potassium. Use mung sprouts in salads, sandwiches, soups, meatless loaves, and marinated vegetables. Mung beans may also be cooked without sprouting, like any other type of bean.

Mung Beans

Natto. This is a very high-protein and easy-to-digest food made from soybeans that have been inoculated with beneficial bacteria and allowed to ferment for twenty-four hours. Natto is not yet well-known in the West; however, it can be bought in Japanese grocery stores.

Natto Miso. A delicious sweet and salty condiment made from barley, soybeans, koji, kombu, sea salt, and ginger. As the fermentation time for natto miso is shorter than for the other types of miso, the grains and strips of kombu that it contains are still whole and not broken down into a paste. Natto miso is usually served alongside salads or other dishes. It can also be lightly spread over bread for use in sandwiches, or added to stir-fries or grain dishes. Natto miso is not used as a soup base.

Nori. Nori is the sea vegetable used in making sushi. It is sold in thin, flat, rectangular sheets. Toasting nori brings out its flavor. Just hold it over the flame of a candle or gas burner for a few seconds, moving it slowly so that it doesn't burn, until it turns a dark emerald green. The toasted nori can then be cut with scissors into strips, or crumbled with your hands to be used as a garnish for soups and grains or vegetable dishes. Pretoasted nori may be purchased in some natural foods stores. A classic and attractive way to use nori is in *Nori Maki* (page 108).

Nori Sheet

Nut Butters. While peanut butter is the most familiar, nut butters can be made with any type of nuts. They are good with bread or toast and can also be used in sauces, patés, and main dishes. Nut butters can be purchased ready-made in natural foods stores or made fresh at home (see the recipe for *Almond Butter* on page 103). Nut butters should be kept refrigerated.

Nutritional Yeast. An excellent food supplement, nutritional yeast is very rich in B vitamins and protein, but low in calories. Nutritional yeast is intended for use as a food and it has an appealing flavor. Don't confuse it with brewer's yeast or torula yeast, both of which taste terrible. Neither should nutritional yeast be confused with dry active yeast or fresh cake yeast, which will·cause great discomfort if eaten raw.

The best way to use nutritional yeast is in your daily cooking. It adds flavor and nutrients to soups, sauces, stews, mock meat dishes, and salads. You may also want to try keeping a small container of nutritional yeast on the table (perhaps in a pretty sugar bowl that you no longer use) so you can sprinkle it on your salads. It is surprisingly good. Persons who are not accustomed to taking yeast will possibly have some difficulty in digesting it in the beginning. Therefore, when you first start using it, use very small quantities (about one teaspoon per serving) and then work your way up to a tablespoon or more.

Nuts. In vegetarian cooking, nuts are employed in a variety of imaginative ways. Not only are they used in baking and desserts, but in main dishes such as veggie burgers and meatless loaves as well. They are also used in soups, salads, salad dressings, and sauces. In some recipes, the high fat content of nuts enables them to replace less nutritious and more concentrated fats, such as butter and oil.

Always refrigerate shelled nuts, because they will go rancid very quickly if they are kept in a warm place, and when nuts become rancid, they are both bad-tasting and bad for you. Chopped or broken nuts are less expensive than whole or half nuts, but they will become rancid more easily.

Oats. Whole grains of oats take a long time to cook. This is why oats are almost exclusively used in their rolled form. Rolled oats, or oatmeal, are made by running whole oats through heavy metal rollers to flatten them out. This makes them much faster-cooking without destroying their nutritive properties.

The few times that I have had oatmeal for breakfast in restaurants have made me understand why more people do not enjoy this wonderful cereal. The way it is usually prepared is so loathsome that I can readily sympathize with anyone who does not like it! If your image of oats is an insipid, sticky paste, please give it one last try (with *real* oatmeal, not that instant stuff!) before abandoning it forever. (See recipe on page 25.)

Oatmeal is usually used in sweet dishes such as porridges, cookies, granolas, and desserts. But there is no need to stop there. Oatmeal is a great filler for meatless loaves, patties, and other vegetarian main dishes. In fact, it is surprising just how many ways it can be used. Oat flour can be used in pancakes, muffins, and breads. To make oat flour, just grind some oatmeal in a blender.

Oils. Those oils that are extracted by low heat and mechanical means are the best quality. Cheaper oils are extracted by chemical solvents and/or very high heat. An oil that is completely odorless, flavorless, and colorless has been highly filtered and treated. It is not as nutritious as the darker, stronger-flavored oils.

My favorite oil for just about everything except sweet foods is olive oil. The strong flavor of high-quality olive oil provides a wonderful seasoning whenever it is used. Unrefined corn oil is good in breads and in grain dishes, and safflower oil is good for frying. For desserts, pancakes, crepes, and delicately flavored dishes, it is preferable to use a more refined and milder-flavored oil rather than olive oil, because the strong taste of an unrefined oil will dominate the dish.

The best place to buy a good-quality oil is in a natural foods store. Always read the labels carefully and buy an oil that has been mechanically rather than chemically extracted. Oils should be kept in the refrigerator.

Okara. This is the fibrous residue that is left over from the fabrication of tofu or soymilk. Okara can be used in making croquettes, meatless loaves, and numerous other dishes.

Peanut butter. Health-conscious cooks use only good-quality, natural peanut butter that contains peanuts and nothing else.

Quinoa. Known as the "mother grain" of the Incas, quinoa (pronounced "keenwa") is currently being discovered by North American whole foods enthusiasts. It is higher in protein, calcium, and iron than other grains, and is a very hardy plant to grow. Quinoa is also quick-cooking and has a delicious, mild flavor.

For information on quinoa and recipes using it, write to the Quinoa Corporation, P.O. Box 7114, Boulder, Colorado 80306, or telephone (303) 444-9466.

Rice. The rice called for in the recipes in this book is whole, unpolished brown rice. Not only is it more nourishing than white rice—it tastes better as well.

In the large natural foods stores there are many varieties of unpolished rice. Each type has its own distinguishing characteristics, so it's fun to try them all. Below is a brief description of some of the different types available.

Brown Basmati Rice, although usually found only in its white, polished form, is occasionally available in natural foods stores. Used in East Indian cooking, it is light, fluffy, and especially fragrant.

Long Grain Brown Rice is lighter and fluffier than most other varieties, and is good in salads, as a side dish, as a bed for vegetables in curries, etc.

Medium Grain Brown Rice has qualities that are in between those of long grain and short grain.

Short Grain Brown Rice has a richer and nuttier flavor than long grain rice, and more of a tendency to be sticky. It is good in casseroles, sushi (nori-maki), desserts, patties, etc.

Sweet Rice is also called glutenous rice. With very short, almost round grains, it is a very sticky rice with a slight crunch and subtly sweet flavor. This rice is used to make mochi. It is also good for sushi, amasake, desserts, and croquettes.

Wehani Rice has a dull burgundy color and gives off an aroma similar to popcorn as it cooks. It is a new hybrid developed by Lundberg Family Farms in California and is well worth trying.

Brown Rice Flour lends a wonderful crispness to cookies, crackers, tempura batters, etc.

There are both organic and nonorganic varieties of rice. Organically grown rice is more expensive, but it tastes much better than the cheaper varieties. It is also cleaner, because it contains fewer hulls. *See also* Wild Rice.

Rice Syrup (often called yinnie syrup). A thick, sweet syrup made from rice, sometimes with the addition of barley malt. It is made by fermenting the rice with koji, straining it, and then boiling the remaining liquid until it thickens. Rice syrup is less sweet than honey. Like malt, it is metabolized more slowly than other sweeteners. Rice syrup may be used to replace honey in some recipes.

Roasted Sesame Oil. A richly flavored oil that is used, just a few drops at a time, in seasoning Chinese and Japanese cooking.

Rye. Although rye berries (whole grains of rye) can be cooked, they are usually ground into flour. In my opinion there is nothing better than a dark and pungent loaf of sourdough rye bread made from whole rye flour. Most commercially produced rye breads, however, are made primarily with refined wheat flour. A small amount of rye flour is added for flavor, and molasses is added to give the bread its characteristic color.

Rye flour is usually associated with chewy dark bread, but that doesn't necessarily mean that the flour, or the products made from it, are whole grain. Rye flour can be (and usually is, unless otherwise stated) just as refined as white flour. Therefore, buy your rye flour from a natural foods store and carefully read the labels on rye breads and crackers.

Sea Salt. Sea salt is obtained from the evaporation of sea water and is used in these recipes either in its granular form or as an ingredient of tamari, shoyu, or miso.

Meat and fish are naturally much higher in sodium than the vegetables and grains used in vegetarian cooking. So are all commercially processed foods. Since these high-sodium foods are avoided in this book, I feel that the moderate use of sea salt in the recipes is not excessive. It is the salt shaker or the tamari bottle on the table that is more likely to be abused.

I prefer sea salt over regular salt because it contains trace minerals that are lacking in regular salt. Another advantage of sea salt is that it does not contain the chemicals that are added to table salt to keep it pouring freely. If your sea salt lumps together, put a few grains of rice in the salt shaker to absorb the excess moisture and remedy the problem.

Sea Vegetables. These are any of a variety of marine plants used as food. Sea vegetables are a source of vitamins, minerals, and trace elements. (For more information on sea vegetables, see the inset on pages 157.)

Seeds. Similar to nuts in their nutritional content, seeds are used in much the same ways in vegetarian cooking. Seeds, like nuts, should always be kept refrigerated.

Seitan. A high-protein meat analogue made from wheat gluten. Like most vegetarian foods, seitan is low in fat, contains no cholesterol, and is less expensive than meat.

While new to most of us, seitan and gluten have been used in the Orient for centuries. Seitan is the Japanese name for wheat gluten that has been cut into small pieces and cooked in a seasoned broth. Gluten is the English name for any product made from wheat gluten. However, recently it has become popular to use the word seitan for any gluten product. Gluten is a very high-protein food. One cup of raw gluten contains seventy-two grams of protein. You can make seitan in fairly large quantities and freeze it. The frozen seitan may be used as needed to supplement other protein foods such as beans, soy products, or dairy products.

Sesame Butter. This is a rich preparation made from unhulled, roasted sesame seeds that have been ground into a paste. Sesame butter and tahini can be used interchangeably in recipes. *See also* Tahini.

Shiitake Mushrooms. These mushrooms are used in Japanese cooking. Dried shiitake mushrooms can be purchased in natural foods stores and Oriental markets. Shiitake are also available freshly grown in some parts of the United States. Either type can be used to flavor soup stocks or vegetable dishes. These mushrooms are said to help the body to discharge excess animal fats.

Shitake Mushroom, Fresh

Shitake Mushroom, Dried

Shoyu. A natural Japanese soy sauce, shoyu is made from soybeans, water, wheat, and sea salt. Shoyu is often misnamed "tamari," but they are not exactly the same product. Shoyu contains wheat and tamari does not. The methods of making the two sauces also differ. Although shoyu and tamari are both high-quality products, shoyu is less expensive. They can be used interchangeably in most recipes; however, in certain recipes the richer flavor of tamari is preferable.

Silken Tofu. A very soft and custardy type of tofu that is available in most of the larger natural foods stores. Silken tofu is exquisite served cold with a salad dressing on a bed of fresh greens. *See also* Tofu.

Soft Wheat. This food is lower in protein than hard wheat, but is ideal for making pastry flour. Both spring and winter varieties are grown.

Sorghum. A staple grain in Africa and parts of Asia, sorghum is also grown in the southern United States. In this country it is not eaten as a grain. The stalks of the plant are used to make sorghum syrup and the grains are used as animal feed.

I did not give recipes or cooking methods for sorghum, because it is not even available in most natural foods stores. But I did want to mention it because it is such an important grain in other parts of the world.

Sorghum Syrup. A sweetener made from the stalks of the sorghum plant. In many recipes, sorghum can be used to replace other sweeteners.

Sourdough Starter. Sourdough is a fermented batter of flour and water and is used as leavening in bread recipes. It reacts much more slowly than yeast and gives breads a distinctive sour flavor. Sourdough bread is said to be more healthful than yeast bread because the long fermentation of the dough renders certain nutrients in the grains easier for the body to assimilate. In addition, many people appreciate the fact that the microorganisms in sourdough are not commercially refined. See page 82 for directions on how to make your own sourdough starter.

Soybeans. While difficult to digest if cooked whole, this versatile legume is the source of a variety of traditional natural foods, including miso, natto, shoyu, soymilk, tamari, tempeh, and tofu. Soybeans are an outstanding source of protein—they are 38 percent protein.

Tahini. This is a paste made from hulled, unroasted sesame seeds. A staple in Mideastern cuisine, tahini is high in fat, protein, and calcium. It is delicious spread on bread or crackers, or when made into dips, salad dressings, or sauces. Store tahini in the refrigerator.

Sesame Seeds

Tamari. (Also called wheat-free tamari.) A natural Japanese soy sauce that is a by-product of traditional miso-making. Tamari is darker in color and richer in flavor than shoyu (which is often misnamed tamari). Tamari and shoyu are both fermented for up to two years in wooden kegs. The cheap commercial soy sauces on the market can in no way compare with their fine flavor.

Tempeh. A traditional food from Indonesia, tempeh is made from partially cooked, split, and hulled soybeans that are inoculated with a special bacteria and incubated for about twenty-four hours. During the incubation, a white, fluffy mold develops around the beans, holding them together to form a slab. Tempeh has a firm but tender texture and a very likable flavor. It is high in protein and easy to digest. Tempeh is the richest known vegetable source of vitamin B_{12}.

The only drawback to tempeh is that it is very perishable and must be used within a few days after it is made, or else frozen. Unlike tofu, tempeh must be cooked before it is eaten. It is not necessary to thaw frozen tempeh before cooking it. Cook tempeh by pan-frying, baking, broiling, or steaming. A number of recipes in this book use this versatile soyfood.

Tofu. A staple of both Chinese and Japanese cuisines, tofu has become very popular in the West over the past few years. Nutritionally, tofu's virtues are no secret. It is high in protein, low in calories, rich in calcium, and easy to digest. It is low in fat and contains virtually no cholesterol. Tofu is also very convenient to use. But it is the culinary wizardry that tofu performs so well that gives it the reputation of being a "miracle food." Tofu can be transformed into an amazingly wide variety of scrumptious dishes, from protein-rich main dishes to creamy desserts.

To make tofu, whole soybeans are soaked for eight to ten hours. They are then ground into a purée. This purée is pressed through a cloth to extract the soymilk from the pulp. The milk is cooked and a coagulant (traditionally, nigari, which is extracted from sea salt) is added to cause the milk to curdle. The curds are carefully ladled away from the whey and placed in a mold where they are pressed until they are firm. The resulting tofu is stored in cold water. Tofu is available in natural foods stores and even in some supermarkets (read the labels carefully to avoid unwanted additives). Tofu may also be made fresh at home.

When refrigerated, freshly made tofu will keep for over two weeks if the water is changed daily. When tofu is no longer fresh, it will develop an unpleasant, sour odor and perhaps a pink or yellow color. Very fresh tofu is especially mild and sweet. For making desserts, try to use the freshest tofu available.

Tofu may be frozen, but freezing alters its texture considerably. Frozen tofu becomes firm and spongy, and its color darkens slightly. Use frozen tofu in mock meat dishes where a firm texture is desirable (see page 198). *See also* Silken Tofu.

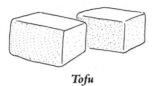

Tofu

T.V.P. (Textured Vegetable Protein). This high-protein convenience food is made from soy beans. T.V.P. is used in spaghetti sauces, chili, veggie burgers, sloppy joe mixes, etc., to give a meaty texture. Because of the high-tech nature of processing this food, I do not make it a regular part of my diet. However, it can really come in handy at times.

Umeboshi. This is a salty pickled plum used as a condiment in Japanese cuisine. It is good in sauces and salad dressings, and it can be purchased either in the form of whole, unpitted plums or as a paste. Umeboshi is valued both as a food and a traditional medicine. It is said to be a good remedy for hangovers and other ailments that stem from excesses in food or drink.

Umeboshi Plum

Umeboshi Vinegar. A salty, sour vinegar made from umeboshi plums, this vinegar is diluted with water and used in sweet and sour sauces, salads, salad dressings, etc.

Wakame. This long, thin, green sea vegetable is used in making soups, salads, and vegetable dishes. High in protein, iron, and magnesium, wakame has a sweet taste and delicate texture and is especially good in miso soup.

Wakame

Wheat. The grain most commonly used in North America today, wheat surpasses all other grains in its versatility. Whole wheat berries can be sprouted, cooked, or ground into flour. The endless variety of breads, cakes, pastries, pastas, and other items that can be made with wheat flour is astounding. A very convincing mock meat dish called seitan is made out of wheat gluten. The wheat flour used in the recipes in this book is, of course, whole wheat flour. With a little practice, one can successfully make almost anything with whole wheat flour that can be made out of white flour. When one becomes accustomed to eating whole grain baked goods, white flour products seem pasty and flavorless.

Whole wheat flour (and all flours made from whole grains) can easily become rancid. Rancid flour has an unpleasant, strong taste and odor. It is not good for you, either. Therefore, buying large quantities of whole grain flours is not a wise practice. It is best to buy the flour you need every week or two and keep it in airtight containers in the refrigerator.

Whole Wheat Berries. These are whole, unground grains of either soft or hard wheat. Wheat berries may be sprouted, cooked, or ground into flour. (Hard winter varieties are best for sprouting.)

Whole Wheat Bread Flour or Whole Wheat Flour. Flour made from hard wheat. It is higher in gluten (protein) and thus makes lighter-textured breads.

Whole Wheat Pastry Flour. Flour made from soft wheat. A low-gluten flour that makes more tender pastries than bread flour.

Wild Rice. Not really a rice at all, but a tall aquatic grass. It is harvested in Canada and the northern United States. Much of this rice is grown by native North Americans in these areas. Don't let its price keep you from using it occasionally. Think of it as a treat, like lobster for vegetarians! We can all use a little luxury for special occasions, and this is a very healthful luxury at that. See page 181 for instructions on how to cook wild rice.

SHOPPING IN NATURAL FOODS STORES

A first-time visit to a natural foods store can be overwhelming. Strange-looking items, brand names that you have never heard of, and a reputation for being expensive all can intimidate the uninitiated shopper. Below are a few suggestions for making shopping in a natural foods store a little easier.

- Just because something is labeled "natural" or "preservative-free" does not mean that it is a wholesome food. Products labeled "natural" often contain sugar, saturated fats, white flour, high amounts of sodium, and other ingredients that a health-conscious person may not care to eat. Don't assume that just because you're in a natural foods store, every food is natural and whole. Read the list of ingredients, just as you would in a supermarket.
- Staple items sold in natural foods stores, such as flours, grains, beans, and tofu, are always a good buy. They are inexpensive and loaded with nutrition. It is the processed "natural" foods that are expensive. If you are on a budget, it is no great loss nutritionally to drop the "natural" chips, frozen pizza, or fancy juices from your shopping list. And by avoiding these items, you will have more money to spend on fresh produce and staples.
- Bulk herbs and spices sold in natural foods stores are usually much less expensive than the packaged ones sold in supermarkets.
- In general, bulk items are less expensive than packaged ones. However, this is not always the case, so it is sometimes worth the time to compare prices.

KITCHEN TOOLS

You don't need a lot of fancy equipment to be a good cook. However, there are a few basic tools that I find myself using almost daily. If you have them it will probably make your cooking easier and more enjoyable. They are listed below.

Blender. A blender is great for grinding nuts and small quantities of grains (for making quick-cooking breakfast cereals). It is also good for soups, purées, salad dressings, dips, and more. A blender is better than a food processor for foods that require an especially smooth and silky texture. It is also better for blending small quantities. I use both a blender and a food processor and find that each one has its advantages and disadvantages. However, for someone who does not wish to spend much money on kitchen equipment, I recommend a blender over a food processor.

Cutting boards. I use two cutting boards: one for onions and strong-flavored vegetables and the other for fruits and milder foods.

Fine wire mesh strainers. A strainer is important for washing grains and beans.

Food processor. The main function of a food processor in my home is that of a large blender. Food processors allow one to blend foods in a single batch that would have to be done in two or more batches in a blender. They will also blend foods that have a consistency that is too thick for a blender to handle. Another advantage of a food processor is that it can be used for grinding dried fruits and sprouted grains, which a blender cannot do very well.

For chopping, slicing, grating, or shredding, I rarely use a food processor. If you are fairly adept with a knife, it is faster by hand (considering the time that it takes to clean the machine). If you are looking for a gadget to do shredding, slicing, etc., the best device that I have found is a manually operated nonelectric food processor made by Health Craft (see page 15). It is faster, more efficient, and much easier to clean than an electric food processor.

Garlic press. If you do not buy a good garlic press it is not worth a penny. Shop around and make sure to get one that works.

Knives. Good, sharp knives are indispensable. However, they need not be numerous or expensive. There are three different knives that I use for just about everything: a serrated bread knife with a long, stainless steel blade; a small, good-quality paring knife with a sharp, pointed blade; and a Japanese vegetable knife that has a thin, wide blade and a squared-off end. These Japanese vegetable knives are available in most of the larger natural foods stores for under ten dollars.

Salad spinner. A salad spinner is a handy gadget that will help you get your greens clean and dry.

Figure 1.1. Japanese Vegetable Knife

Other utensils. There are things that most well-equipped kitchens have, such as measuring cups and spoons, a vegetable steamer, a colander, a rolling pin, mixing bowls in assorted sizes, a large ceramic mixing bowl for bread making, wooden spoons, a wire whisk, a slotted spoon, a metal spatula, a rubber spatula, and so on.

Of course, you will also need an assortment of good-quality cookware. The pots and pans that I use most frequently include a ten-inch cast iron skillet, a four-quart cast iron kettle, a two-quart pan, and a saucepan. I also use bread or loaf pans, pie plates, cake pans, a deep casserole dish with a cover, a seven-by-eleven-inch glass baking dish, muffin tins, and cookie sheets. An electric slow-cooking pot (a crockery cooker) is not really necessary, but is very handy for cooking beans when you are not at home. Like a crockery cooker, a pressure cooker is not really necessary, but it can be a real time-saver when you use it. I use my stainless steel pressure cooker often.

COOKWARE

Good-quality cookware is worth the investment because it will last a lifetime. The quality of cookware is determined not only by its construction but also by the materials from which it is made. Below is a brief review of some different materials used in today's cookware.

Aluminum. Although aluminum is the best heat conductor, the metal is toxic. When foods are cooked in aluminum cookware, they absorb minute amounts of aluminum. Over a long period of time this may cause many health problems.

Carbon Steel. Carbon steel is a better heat conductor than stainless steel, but it rusts and discolors very easily. In addition, food has more of a tendency to stick to carbon steel than to cast iron.

Cast Iron. Just as foods cooked in aluminum absorb some of the aluminum, foods cooked in cast iron absorb iron. For example, one 100-gram serving of spaghetti sauce prepared in cast iron cookware may contain 87.5 milligrams of iron compared to only 3 milligrams when cooked in a glass vessel. Since iron is essential for good health, cooking in cast iron can be an easy way to increase your daily intake of iron. Cast iron cookware is inexpensive and very versatile. Its main drawback is the fact that it rusts easily if not properly cared for. Large cast iron pots can be quite heavy.

To "season" a new cast iron pan, brush the inside of the pan with a generous coat of oil. Place the pan in the oven and bake at 350°F for about fifteen minutes.

Enamelware. Colorful and attractive enamel cookware is good while it lasts. Unless you buy very high-quality enamelware, however, it will easily chip.

Glass. With glass cookware, you can readily see how your food is coming along. Besides this, its only real advantage is that the same cookware can be used in the oven and on top of the stove, and can be placed in the refrigerator as well.

Stainless Steel. Stainless steel cookware is easy to clean and care for, but not always easy to cook with, as food has a tendency to stick to it.

Teflon and Other Nonstick Surfaces. The chemical coating on this type of cookware scratches easily and may flake off into food. In addition, it may give off toxic fumes when exposed to high heat. For these reasons, I do not recommend nonstick cookware.

"Waterless" Cookware. Of all the types that I am familiar with, waterless cookware is definitely the best. It has an aluminum core for good heat conduction, but the aluminum is covered on both sides with five coats of surgical-quality stainless steel. It cooks vegetables without added water or fat, and is excellent for cooking grains and other foods. It saves energy, too, because you can stack the pans one on top of the other to cook several dishes on one burner. This cookware can even be used for baking potatoes, cakes, muffins, etc., on top of the stove. This line is really amazing! Because it must be demonstrated to be appreciated, it is not for sale in most stores. For more information on waterless cookware you may contact Health Craft at 8012 West Waters Ave., Tampa, FL 33615, or call toll-free 1-800-443-8079.

Woks. Almost everyone who becomes interested in natural foods cookery wants to have a wok. For cooking large stir-fry dishes there is nothing better. In my opinion, the best wok is a simple, nonelectric one made from carbon steel. It has the disadvantage of rusting very easily if not properly dried after it is washed, but it cooks better than a stainless steel wok. Food has a greater tendency to stick in the stainless steel woks. Aluminum and nonstick coated woks (such as Teflon or Silverstone) are not recommended. An electric wok is fun because it allows you to cook at the table while entertaining; however, the temperature is easier to control on a nonelectric wok. A handy accessory that comes with some woks is a steamer rack.

HOW TO SUBSTITUTE INGREDIENTS

When you are following a recipe there may be times when you do not have or do not wish to use a specific ingredient. Should you run out and buy the missing component or abandon the recipe? Frequently the dilemma can be simply resolved with some discriminating substitutions of ingredients. Of course, any change in the recipe will make it somewhat different; however, the results may please you more than the original. This little bit of improvisation will give your meal a personal touch. That's what creative cooking is all about.

Following are some suggestions for substituting ingredients that will give you opportunities to exercise your inventiveness as well as the chance to experience some new taste treats. These suggestions may also save you from running to the store in a hurried panic for some "special" ingredient.

VEGETABLES

The possibilities of substituting one vegetable for another in recipes are so extensive that precise rules are impossible. But it's not difficult to do. Just keep the following suggestions in mind and you should not have any problems.

- The most important factor to consider is your own taste. You know better than anyone else what you like. Use discretion when you want to add, subtract, or exchange a vegetable in a recipe.
- Take into consideration the cooking times of the vegetables that you wish to substitute. For example, if you are exchanging kale for spinach in a recipe, remember that kale takes longer to cook and may have to be precooked.
- Be aware of the moisture content of the vegetables that you are substituting. If you substitute a juicy vegetable such as a tomato for a dry vegetable like a potato or vice versa, you can be assured of a too-dry or too-watery dish unless you adjust the other ingredients as well.
- Don't forget flavor. Some vegetables add more flavor to recipes than others. Therefore, if you substitute a mild-tasting vegetable for a vegetable with a stronger taste, you may end up with a bland dish, unless you compensate by adjusting the seasonings.
- Leafy vegetables decrease in volume as they cook. Therefore, you cannot substitute a cup of a raw vegetable that remains approximately the same size when it cooks—such as carrots, green beans, broccoli, etc.—for a cup of raw greens. You can, however, substitute a cup of cooked greens for a cup of a compatible cooked vegetable.
- Also consider the texture and starch content of the vegetables that you are substituting. A starchy vegetable may not work so well in a grain dish in which a crisp, juicy vegetable would be delicious. The opposite can also hold true. Sometimes a starchy vegetable is needed in a recipe to make it satisfying.

DAIRY AND EGGS

Listed below are some ideas for substituting nondairy foods for various dairy products. Also listed are ideas for exchanging high-fat dairy products for low-fat dairy products.

Butter. In my opinion neither butter nor margarine is a healthful food; therefore, I have learned to do without them. Here are some suggestions:

- To season vegetables, a bit of olive oil, mixed with some yellow miso and perhaps some herbs or pressed garlic, more than compensates for a lack of butter.
- *Mock Sour Cream* (see page 132) is delicious on baked potatoes. A slice of sharp cheddar cheese melted under the broiler is also good. For a real treat, try blending a packet of miso soup mix with some cottage cheese and yogurt and serving it over potatoes. It's really great! If you want to completely avoid using dairy products, the *Tahini-Miso Sauce* on page 245 is very nice over baked potatoes.
- In sandwiches, mashed avocado is a marvelous substitute for both butter and mayonnaise. If desired, add a little lemon juice, minced parsley, and/or pressed garlic to the mashed avocado.
- Make garlic bread with olive oil, pressed garlic, and tamari. It is delicious.

Buttermilk. In place of a cup of buttermilk in baking you can use one cup of soymilk with two teaspoons of lemon juice added to it. Another substitution for one cup of buttermilk is three-quarters cup yogurt mixed with one-quarter cup water or milk.

Cheese. There is a nondairy soy cheese on the market that is surprisingly good. It is especially tasty on tomato dishes like pizza and spaghetti and on casseroles because it actually melts like cheese. This soy cheese can be purchased in the larger natural foods stores.

- To replace a cheese topping on a casserole or another baked dish try a generous sprinkling of sesame seeds, or a mixture of sesame seeds and seasoned bread crumbs drizzled with a little olive oil.
- A tahini sauce, yeast gravy, or tofu sauce can often be used in place of a cheese sauce with delectable results.

Eggs. To avoid most of the cholesterol in eggs, substitute two egg whites for one whole egg in your recipes.

- Nut butters or tahini can be used instead of eggs as a binder in vegetable croquettes and meatless loaves.
- Try the tofu quiches in this book.

Milk. Substitute an equal amount of soy or cashew milk for dairy milk. Flavored soymilks may be used in desserts and on cereals, but make sure to use plain soymilk for all other dishes.

- Instead of a traditional béchamel sauce or white sauce, make the same kind of sauce with cashew milk (see *Cashew Béchamel* on page 243) or with soymilk. Be careful not to use a soymilk that contains vanilla. Sometimes even soymilks that are labeled "plain" contain vanilla, which tastes awful in a béchamel.
- Another way to make a creamy base for casseroles, soups, or stews is to blend (in a blender or food processor) some cooked rice, millet, or potatoes with enough water to make a creamy consistency. Season to taste with some white miso and a dash of cayenne. For more richness, add a handful or so of raw cashews. Make sure that you blend the mixture until all the ingredients are smooth. Add this cream to the desired dish.

Yogurt. I have made delicious yogurt with regular yogurt culture and homemade soymilk. The commercial soy yogurts that I have tried were not very good. This probably has to do with their lack of freshness.

GRAINS

In many recipes grains can be used interchangeably. For example, a casserole calling for rice could also be made with millet, bulghur, or perhaps even pasta. Again, you know what you like, and if you think something might be good, try it!

White All-Purpose Flour. When substituting whole wheat flour for white flour in any recipe (apart from yeast breads) you may use whole wheat pastry flour or soft wheat flour. Use one cup, minus two tablespoons, of either type of flour in place of one cup of white all-purpose flour. For yeast breads, use whole wheat bread flour or hard wheat flour in place of white all-purpose flour.

When one becomes accustomed to eating baked goods made from whole grains, similar foods made from white flour seem rather insipid by comparison. However, if you are new to natural foods and do not like the results of whole grain baking, try replacing half of the white flour in a recipe with whole wheat flour.

Wheat Flour. There are several other flours that can be used in place of whole wheat or white flour in baking. Although some will give excellent results, do not expect to duplicate the results given with wheat. A mixture of rye, oat, and rice flours is good for making quick breads and muffins. Rice flour and oats can be used to make cookies. Cornbread and corn muffins can be made totally out of cornmeal or corn flour and crepes and pancakes can be made out of almost any type of flour. If you would like further information on wheatless or glutenless baking, a good book is *Baking for Health*, by Linda Edwards (Avery Publishing Group, 1987).

SALT

Tamari and miso can both be substituted for salt in most recipes. Use white miso in light-colored dishes and tamari or dark miso in dishes where the dark color is not undesirable. As a general rule, one teaspoon of salt in a recipe is equal to two tablespoons of miso or four tablespoons of tamari. By substituting tamari or miso for salt you are adding flavor; therefore, not as much sodium is required to make your dish tasty. If a recipe calls for one teaspoon of salt, it may taste bland with one-half teaspoon of salt; however, two tablespoons of tamari may give it enough flavor to make up for the decrease in sodium.

Other substitutes for salt include kelp powder and herb and vegetable seasonings. These are sold in powder form in natural foods stores. Liquid vegetable and yeast extracts that are sold in natural foods stores can be used to replace tamari.

In many recipes the addition of Parmesan or Romano cheese, olives, or pickles will add enough flavor and sodium to make additional salt unnecessary. To decrease the need for salt in your cooking, be generous with herbs and spices and use only fresh ingredients that are at their peak of flavor.

In cake and pastry recipes, salt can be omitted without adversely changing the end result.

HERBS AND SPICES

Herbs and spices can often be substituted for one another. There is no right or wrong way to use them—it is a matter of taste. However, if you are not familiar with the various seasonings, you may not know where to begin. Below is a list of frequently employed herbs and spices with suggestions for their use. If you are following a recipe and lacking one of the seasonings, perhaps you can use this list to help you find a substitute. Once you become accustomed to the unique properties of herbs and spices, I'm sure that you will discover your own favorite ways to use them.

Basil. This fragrant herb may be used generously in anything that contains tomatoes or corn.

Bay Leaves. Good in soups, stews, spaghetti sauces, and dishes containing beans or beets. Add whole leaves to your recipe and remove them before serving.

Caraway Seeds. Use sparingly in sauerkraut and rye bread, and in cabbage, turnip, and cheese dishes.

Cayenne. Cayenne pepper is extremely hot. Use it sparingly in anything that you wish to give a piquant taste.

Celantro. Wash and chop fresh celantro like parsley, and use it with beans, corn, avocados, or in any Mexican-style dish. It is also a nice, pungent addition to a curry dish.

Celery Seed. A little goes a long way. Good in salads, salad dressings, soups, veggie burgers, and meatless loaves.

Chili Powder. A mixture of herbs and spices that may be used in Mexican-style dishes.

Chives. Use generously when a mild onion

flavor is desirable. Especially nice in egg and dairy dishes, in sauces, and for garnishes.

Cinnamon. Good in desserts, cookies, cakes, puddings, cereals, and breads. Cinnamon goes especially well with apples.

Cloves. Use sparingly in desserts, cakes, cookies, fruit dishes, etc. A dash of cloves in a spaghetti sauce is delicious.

Cumin. Use in curries, bean dishes, and Mexican-style food.

Curry. Curry powder is a mixture of several spices. There are many varieties of curry powder that may be purchased in stores that specialize in East Indian foods. Use curry in grain and vegetable dishes.

Dill Seed. Use sparingly with cucumbers, pickles, potatoes, carrots, and cabbage.

Dill Weed. Similar in flavor to dill seed but much milder. It may be used more liberally than dill seed.

Garlic. Garlic can enhance Italian-style dishes, casseroles, soups, stews, pasta and grain dishes, bean dishes, vegetables, and salads. (I enjoy garlic in almost everything except desserts!) Garlic powder is also a poor substitute for fresh garlic; however, if you wish to use it, one-eighth teaspoon equals one small clove of garlic.

Ginger. Use in desserts and Oriental-style dishes. Fresh ginger is marvelous when combined with garlic. To use fresh ginger root, just wash it and grate it on the finest holes of a grater. Peeling is not necessary.

Mustard. Use mustard powder or prepared mustard in sauces, cheese dishes, salads, salad dressings, potato salad, and dips.

Nutmeg. Enlivens desserts, sauces, spinach, parsnips, carrots, Brussels sprouts, and broccoli.

Oregano. A good seasoning for Italian foods, soups, stews, beans, and tomatoes.

Paprika. Use for eggs, potatoes, salads, and cheese dishes.

Parsley. Fresh parsley is always available. It is mild-tasting and nutritious, so you can use it generously in almost any vegetable, bean, dairy, or grain dish.

Rosemary. Good in omelettes, dried bean dishes, salads, and soups. Rosemary also complements potatoes, green beans, and peas.

Sage. Sage is rather strong-tasting, so use it with discretion. It is delicious in veggie burgers and meatless loaves.

Savory. Use in potato dishes, cabbage, green beans, soups, casseroles, etc.

Tarragon. Wonderful in almost any vegetable dish, especially those with beets or marinated vegetables. Also good in sauces and salads.

Thyme. Use in hearty grain dishes, cheese dishes, veggie burgers, meatless loaves, soups, and stews.

SUGAR AND OTHER SWEETENERS

Any of the following sweeteners can be used to replace one cup of sugar in a recipe:

- 3/4 cup fruit concentrate
- 1/2 cup honey
- 3/4 cups barley malt
- 3/4 cup maple syrup
- 1 3/4 cups rice syrup
- 1/2 cup molasses

When replacing sugar with a liquid sweetener, reduce the liquid (milk, soymilk, water) content of the recipe by one-quarter cup. If the recipe contains no liquid other than the sweetener, increase the flour by one-quarter cup.

I find most standard dessert recipes too sweet for my taste; therefore, I usually add less sweetener than the recipe calls for. The addition of fruit, especially dried fruit such as dates and raisins, will decrease the need for more concentrated sweeteners in recipes. In fact, there are several dessert recipes in this book that are sweetened with fruit alone.

MISCELLANEOUS

Listed below are some additional foods that you may wish to use substitutes for.

Cocoa. Use an equal amount of carob powder.

Jams and Jellies. Fruit butters or fruit-sweetened jams.

Gelatin. For one ounce of gelatin, use one bar agar-agar or four tablespoons agar-agar flakes.

Thickeners. For one tablespoon cornstarch, use one tablespoon arrowroot powder.

For one tablespoon white flour, use one-half tablespoon arrowroot or one tablespoon whole wheat pastry flour.

Vinegar. For one-half tablespoon of vinegar, substitute one tablespoon lemon or lime juice.

WEIGHT CONTROL

Not so very long ago, carbohydrates (starches) were thought to be poor-quality foods that caused weight gain. Because of this false notion, people deprived themselves of potatoes, bread, grains, and pastas while they ate excessive amounts of fatty and cholesterol-laden meats. More recently it has been demonstrated that a high-protein diet is not only unhealthy, but is not a very effective means of achieving permanent weight loss either. Most high-protein animal foods are also high in fat, and of all the things we can eat, fat is the highest in calories.

In a balanced vegetarian diet, you get the optimal amount of protein, and significantly less calories are taken from fat. Therefore, vegetarians eat larger amounts and are more satisfied with fewer calories. On a varied vegetarian diet consisting of whole foods, you may eat your fill at regular meals without gaining weight. The vegetarian diet, which is rich in complex carbohydrates, keeps your energy level high between meals. This helps to eliminate the desire for snacking.

Another plus on a balanced vegetarian diet is that in eating fresh, whole foods you will be improving your overall health. Setting your goal for good health, rather than a certain weight, is a positive attitude that may help you to remain at your desired weight once it is achieved. In fact, the value of making a sincere and disciplined effort to improve your health is not limited to solving weight problems. Your hair will shine, your nails will be strong, your eyes will sparkle, and your skin will glow with a radiance that comes only from genuine vitality.

I'm sure that you are aware of the important role that exercise plays in both health and weight reduction. Diet will not do it alone. So if you are not on a regular exercise program, do yourself a favor and start one today! When I was the owner of a natural foods store, I met numerous individuals who were absolute fanatics about the food they ate. However, many of these people did not exercise, and they looked anything but healthy.

In order to prove how delicious and satisfying a vegetarian reducing diet can be, I've made up menus for one week using recipes from this book. Since each day's menu is just over 1,000 calories, you may add your choice of an additional fruit or vegetable each day without having too many calories. You may also substitute seasonal fruits or vegetables for the ones in the menus if they are out of season. Just make sure that the calorie content of the fruit or vegetables that you substitute is about the same as the ones in the menu.

All in all, the main things to avoid when trying to lose weight are fat, sweets, and snacks. Avoid nuts, avocados, desserts, muffins and sweet breads, and dried fruits. Get in a habit of eating your bread without butter or margarine and use only small amounts of not-too-rich salad dressings. In the reducing menus, I've used the *Lemon-Shoyu Dressing* because it is one of my favorites (and I already had the calories counted for it). However, most of the salad dressings in this book are relatively low in calories and can be used. The exceptions are *Sandra's Sweet French Dressing*, page 134, and the *Homemade Mayonnaise* on page 132. For maximum nutrition, eat lots of vegetables and whole grains, tofu, beans, low-fat dairy products, and fruit. Also, drink plenty of water between meals. If you drink fruit juice instead of water, it is surprising how fast the calories can add up.

One last word on weight control. Sometimes we become overweight not because we don't know how to eat a balanced diet, but because we are unhappy with some aspect of our lives. If this is the case for you, there is no amount of discipline that will help you to control your appetite. You must go further and find out the cause of this unhappiness. When the necessary changes are made, your weight will very likely take care of itself.

READY, SET, GO!

With a little bit of knowledge about your natural and whole foods ingredients, and the essential kitchen equipment in hand, you're ready to get started. And once you start cooking, you'll start to become a good cook. The recipes in the rest of this book will guide you along the way, as you prepare healthful and delicious vegetarian dishes for yourself and your family.

SEVEN-DAY REDUCING MENU

SUNDAY

Breakfast

1/2 recipe *Rice Cream*, (page 26), *228 calories*
1 cup fresh strawberries, *45 calories*
1 cup plain low-fat yogurt, *144 calories*

Total calories *417*

Lunch

1 recipe *Tofu Salad* (page 120),
    served on 1 cup romaine lettuce

Total calories *263*

Dinner

1/2 recipe *Beans and Rice* (page 40),
    with oil and avocado omitted, *348 calories*
Green salad of 4 cups Boston lettuce, *32 calories*
2 tablespoons *Lemon-Shoyu Dressing (page 130),*
    20 calories

Total calories: *400*

Total Calories for the Day **1,080**

MONDAY

Breakfast

1/2 cup leftover cooked rice, *116 calories*
    mixed with 1 1/2 tablespoons raisins, *40 calories*
    1 grated apple, *61 calories*
    and 1 cup plain low-fat yogurt, *144 calories*

Total calories: *361*

Lunch

1 serving (1/6 of total) *Hearty Miso
    Vegetable Soup* (page 54), *105 calories*
2 slices whole wheat bread or toast,
    spread with tahini, *198 calories*

Total calories: *303*

Dinner

1/4 *Carrot-Tofu Quiche* (page 206), *217 calories*
Green salad of 4 cups Boston lettuce, *32 calories*
2 tablespoons *Lemon-Shoyu Dressing* (page 130),
    20 calories
1 steamed artichoke with *Lemon-Shoyu Dressing,*
    54 calories

Total calories *323*

Total Calories for the Day: **987**

TUESDAY

Breakfast

1 seven-grain sprouted English muffin,
    toasted and spread with 1 tablespoon peanut
    butter, and topped with 4 sliced pitted prunes,
    319 calories
1 small apple, *61 calories*

Total calories: *380*

Lunch

¼ recipe *Cucumber-Yogurt Salad* (page 117), *196 calories*
1 slice *Sourdough Rye Bread* (page 83), *100 calories*

Total calories *296*

Dinner

⅓ recipe *Potatoes and Kale a la Grecque* (page 231), with olive oil omitted, *392 calories*
1 sliced ripe tomato, *27 calories*

Total calories: *419*

Total Calories for the Day: **1,095**

WEDNESDAY

Breakfast

½ recipe *Scrambled Tofu* (page 32), *150 calories*
2 slices whole wheat toast, *112 calories*
1 cup freshly-squeezed orange juice, *111 calories*

Total calories: *373*

Lunch

1 whole wheat pita bread stuffed with ¼ cup (⅛ recipe) *Sprouted Hummus* (page 104), and 1 cup alfalfa sprouts

Total calories: *374*

Dinner

1 portion *Spinach Squares* (page 229), *178 calories*
1 medium baked potato, seasoned with 2 tablespoons *Instant Yogurt Dressing* (page 133), *120 calories*
Salad made from 1 cup grated carrots, 2 tablespoons *Lemon-Shoyu Dressing* (page 130), and 2 tablespoons minced parsley, *70 calories*

Total calories: *368*

Total Calories for the Day: **1,115**

THURSDAY

Breakfast

1 *Buckwheat Crepe* (page 30), stuffed with a mixture of 1 cup sliced fresh peaches and ½ cup plain low-fat yogurt

Total calories: *253*

Lunch

1 serving *Corn and Lentil Soup* (page 52), *198 calories*
1 slice *Sourdough Rye Bread* (page 83), *100 calories*

Total calories: *298*

Dinner

¹/₄ recipe *Tempeh Loaf* (page 217), served with ¹/₄ recipe *Sauce Orientale* (page 245), *343 calories*
1 medium stalk broccoli, *47 calories*
Salad made from 1 cup grated carrots, *46 calories*

2 tablespoons *Lemon-Shoyu Dressing* (page 130), *20 calories*

Total calories: *456*

Total Calories for the Day: **1,007**

FRIDAY

Breakfast

¹/₂ recipe *Oat, Apple, and Raisin Pancakes* (page 29), topped with a mixture of ¹/₂ cup plain low-fat yogurt and ¹/₂ cup fresh strawberries

Total calories: *421 calories* for pancakes made with 2 large eggs and skim milk

Lunch

Tofu, Tahini, and Miso Sandwich (page 66), topped with ¹/₂ cup alfalfa sprouts

Total calories: *289*

Dinner

¹/₄ recipe *Tabouli* (page 122), with oil decreased from ¹/₄ cup to 3 tablespoons or less, served on a bed of 3 cups Boston lettuce, topped with ¹/₂ cup chick peas, and garnished with 1 sliced ripe tomato

Total calories: *463*

Total Calories for the Day: **1,173**

SATURDAY

Breakfast

¹/₂ recipe *Muesli* (page 31), *306 calories*
¹/₂ cup blueberries, *45 calories*

Total calories: *351*

Lunch

¹/₂ cup low-fat ricotta cheese, mixed with 2 tablespoons minced scallions, and served on a bed of 2 cups Boston lettuce with 2 tablespoons *Lemon-Shoyu Dressing* (page 130), *210 calories*
1 slice whole wheat bread, *56 calories*

Total calories: *266*

Dinner

¹/₂ recipe *Oilless "Stir-Fried" Vegetables* (page 141), *177 calories*
¹/₃ recipe *Ginger Tofu (page 199), 146 calories*
1 cup cooked millet, *190 calories*

Total calories: *513*

Total Calories for the Day: **1,130**

Tempting Oat and Apple Pancakes *(page 29)* Topped with Strawberry Preserves.

Glorious Maple-Oat Bran Granola *(page 31)* to Start Your Day.

Sensational Scrambled Tofu *(page 32)* with Peppers and Mushrooms.

Wake Up to Buckwheat Crepes with Cherry Sauce *(page 30)*.

2. *BREAKFASTS*

What could be more wonderful than waking up to a celebration of the earth's goodness in the delectable form of strawberries, cherries, and other fresh, seasonal fruit? Using the pure and simple gifts of nature, we can create a myriad of irresistible morning menus.

When our eating habits follow the seasons, it is impossible to become bored. Nature changes the menu for us, from spring's sweet strawberries and summer's succulent peaches to the blueberries of early fall. In winter we welcome heartier fare, such as hot cereals, dried fruits, and of course, apples. We can supplement our fruit and cereals with soymilk, dairy milk, or yogurt, a variety of nuts and seeds, and some occasional farm-fresh eggs. The possibilities for wholesome breakfasts are endless.

Oatmeal is a good breakfast cereal, but have you ever tried buckwheat and cornmeal sweetened with figs? Or millet cream cooked with dried apricots and topped with homemade yogurt and chopped nuts?

Pancakes can be made with many different types of flour. For variations in flavor and texture, why not try pancakes made from millet flour, barley flour, cornmeal, or rice flour? They are all delicious.

Don't forget homemade breads and muffins. Who can resist these? But rather than drenching them in butter or over-sweet jam, try some nutritious almond or apple butter. (Recipes for breads and muffins are in Chapter 5.)

For those of you who do not eat a good, substantial breakfast because you are afraid of gaining weight, take a look at the following comparison:

Standard North American "Light" Breakfast

2 slices enriched white bread (toasted), *124 calories*

1 tablespoon butter, *102 calories*

1 tablespoon jam, *54 calories*

2 cups coffee, *10 calories*

2 tablespoons cream, *58 calories*

1 tablespoon sugar, *46 calories*

Total calories: *394*

Nourishing Breakfast

1 cup cooked oatmeal, *140 calories*

1 cup plain yogurt made from skim milk, *127 calories*

1 medium-sized peach, *38 calories*
1½ tablespoons raisins, *40 calories*
1 cup unsweetened herbal tea, *0 calories*
Total calories: *345*

Besides having fewer calories than the standard quick breakfast, the nourishing breakfast contains 19 grams of protein, 1,316 I.U. of vitamin A, and 432 milligrams of calcium. It is also much lower in fat and higher in fiber.

A good breakfast need not be time-consuming. Most of the breakfast recipes in this book take only a few minutes to prepare, and when you see how much better you feel after a nutritious, low-fat breakfast, you will agree that it's well worth the effort.

BREAKFAST SUGGESTIONS

At our house, we like to eat fruit for breakfast and vegetables at our two other meals. We do not eat desserts, except for special occasions, but with breakfasts like these we do not miss them. The following are some suggestions for filling, wholesome breakfasts.

Morning Fantasy. Oatmeal, rice cream, millet cream, or any other hot cereal is a marvelous base for a satisfying breakfast. Cook your cereal with some raisins or other dried fruit so that it will be naturally sweet. Place the cereal in a shallow bowl and surround it with two or three different types of fresh seasonal fruit. Top it with a sprinkling of chopped nuts and a dollop of plain yogurt.

Oriental Tropique. Bake or pan-fry a piece or two of mochi (available in the frozen foods section of the larger natural foods stores). At the same time, bake or pan-fry a sweet, ripe plantain (cooking banana). The mochi is done when it puffs up and becomes crisp. The plantain is done when it is soft and golden brown. When you buy plantains, make sure to choose very ripe ones, because when they are unripe they are starchy and not very sweet. Serve the mochi and plantain with slices of ripe papaya or mango (or any other fruit that is in season where you live). Top it with the *Apple-Tahini Sauce* on page 249. Baked mochi is also good spread with almond, peanut, or apple butter. This is our favorite breakfast. My husband and I save it for weekends when we have the time to spend over a leisurely morning meal.

Alpine Delight. Follow the recipe for *Muesli*, page 31. Vary the fruit and change it around any way you like. If you do not wish to make your own muesli, there are some good ones available at natural foods stores.

East Meets West. Try *Scrambled Tofu* (page 32), with whole grain toast and half a grapefruit.

Country Style. For a country-style breakfast, make any of the pancake or crepe recipes in this book, but instead of smothering the pancakes in butter and syrup, try them with a fresh fruit salad and a little plain yogurt. This chapter contains three basic crepe recipes and simple breakfast crepe recipes appearing on pages 28-30. Chapter 10 contains several more main-dish crepe recipes and how-to instructions for cooking crepes.

Hearty Sandwich. Generously spread a toasted whole grain English muffin with peanut or almond butter; top with raisins or pitted prunes. On top of the dried fruit place thick slices of apple, banana, or fried plantain.

Special Treat. Bake any of the muffin recipes in this book and enjoy the muffins with a glass of hot or cold soymilk and some seasonal fruit.

OAT, WHEAT, OR RYE PORRIDGE

Rye flakes and wheat flakes can be found in natural foods stores. They are rolled rye and wheat—similar to rolled oats.

1 cup rolled oats, rye flakes, or wheat flakes (or a mixture)
2 cups water
Raisins or other dried fruit, to taste

Serves: 2–3
Time: Quick method, 3–5 minutes;
      Slow method, 20 minutes

Quick Method: Place the cereal, water, and fruit in a small saucepan. Bring to a boil. Stirring constantly, cook until the mixture thickens.
Slow Method: Boil the water. Add the cereal and fruit. Reduce the heat to low and cover. Cook, stirring occasionally, for about 20 minutes.

PEANUT BUTTER OATMEAL

If your children do not like hot cereal, try this! This is not as fattening as one might think. The whole recipe, including an apple, contains approximately 450 calories.

1 cup water
1/3 cup rolled oats
2–3 chopped, pitted dates or 2 tablespoons raisins
2 tablespoons crunchy peanut butter
1 apple, grated

Serves: 1–2
Time: About 8 minutes

1. Place the water, rolled oats, and dried fruit in a small saucepan. Bring to a boil. Reduce heat and simmer, stirring occasionally, for about 5 minutes.
2. Add the peanut butter and mix well.

3. Serve with grated apple. Top with a dollop of plain yogurt if desired.

APPLE OATMEAL

The slow cooking of this simple dish makes it especially delicious.

1 cup rolled oats (do not use instant or quick-cooking oats)
2 cups water
2 small apples, washed and cut into bite-sized pieces
1/4 cup raisins
Pinch of cinnamon (optional)

Serves: 2–3
Time: 22 minutes

Place all ingredients together in a saucepan. Cover and cook over low heat for 20 minutes, stirring occasionally.

CORN AND BUCKWHEAT PORRIDGE

Corn and buckwheat are a nice cereal combination. The sweetness of the corn mellows out the stronger taste of the buckwheat.

1/4 cup cornmeal
1/4 cup buckwheat grits
2 cups water
4–6 black figs or other dried fruit (optional)

Serves: 2
Time: 8 minutes

1. Place all the ingredients in a saucepan and mix well. Bring to a boil while stirring constantly.
2. Reduce the heat and cook, stirring constantly, until porridge thickens (3–5 minutes).
   Serve with fresh fruit and yogurt or soymilk.

RICE CREAM

| ½ cup brown rice |
| 2 cups water |
| ¼ cup raisins or other dried fruit (optional) |

Serves: 2
Time: 12 minutes

1. Wash and drain the rice. Place the rice in an unoiled skillet or pan and stir over medium-high heat until it begins to brown and give off a nutty aroma.
2. Transfer the rice to a blender and grind it to a flour.
3. Place the ground rice in a saucepan along with the water and the raisins. Mix well. Bring to a boil, then lower the heat and cook, stirring constantly, until the mixture thickens (3–5 minutes).

VARIATION

*   *Sesame Rice Cream*: Add 2 tablespoons sesame seeds to the rice as you are toasting it. Proceed as indicated.

MILLET CREAM

Millet cream is wonderful cooked with dried apricots and served with yogurt and sliced banana.

| ½ cup millet |
| 2 cups water |
| ¼ cup raisins or other dried fruit (optional) |

Serves: 2
Time: 12 minutes

1. Wash and drain the millet. Place it in an un-oiled skillet or pan and heat it for a few minutes, stirring constantly, to dry it off. Then transfer the millet to a blender and grind it to a flour.
2. Place the ground millet in a saucepan along with the water and the raisins. Mix well. Bring to a boil, then lower the heat and cook, stirring constantly, until mixture thickens (3–5 minutes).

EASY COOKED WHEAT

If you would like to have a hearty bowl of hot cereal ready when you wake up in the morning, try this.

| 1 cup soft wheat berries |
| Water |
| 2½ cups boiling water |

Yield: About 4 cups cooked cereal
Time: Soak 8 hours; leave overnight; prepare in about 3 minutes.

1. Wash the wheat berries and drain them in a wire mesh strainer. Place the wheat in a medium-sized bowl and cover it with water. Cover the bowl with a cloth and let the wheat soak for about 8 hours.
2. At night, after the wheat berries have soaked for 8 hours and before going to bed, heat a quart-sized insulated container such as a thermos (preferably one with a wide opening) by rinsing it with boiling water. Drain the wheat and place it in the container, add the 2½ cups

of boiling water, and close the container.

3. Place it on its side and leave it all night long. When you get up the next morning, the wheat will be cooked and still warm. Serve with soymilk or yogurt and some fresh or dried fruit.

Cooked wheat may be used in meatless loaves and croquettes instead of other cooked grains. It can also be mixed with rice or millet for use in a variety of recipes.

MILLET FLOUR PANCAKES

½ cup millet flour
1 egg
½ cup buttermilk
½ teaspoon baking powder

Serves: 2
Time: About 12 minutes

1. Place all the ingredients in a blender and blend until smooth.
2. Drop the batter by the ¼ cup onto a hot, lightly oiled skillet. Cook each pancake until bubbles appear on the top. Turn over and cook until done.

VARIATION

• Wash ½ cup millet and use it instead of millet flour. Blend all ingredients in a blender until a smooth batter is formed.

ORANGE-BANANA CORN CAKES

For a real tropical treat, serve these with orange blossom honey and slices of fresh papaya. Do not try to make large pancakes with this batter, because they may fall apart.

1 cup cornmeal
½ teaspoon baking powder
1 banana
3 eggs
⅓ cup orange juice
1 teaspoon grated orange peel
Pinch of nutmeg

Yield: 8 small pancakes
Serves: 2–4
Time: 12–15 minutes

1. In a medium-sized bowl, mix together the cornmeal and the baking powder.
2. In a separate bowl, mash the banana and beat in the eggs, one at a time. Add the orange peel, orange juice, and nutmeg. Mix well. Add the cornmeal mixture and beat well.
3. Drop the batter by the ¼ cup onto a hot, oiled skillet. Cook each pancake until bubbles appear on the top and the bottom is brown. Turn over and cook until done.

SWEET BREAKFAST CREPES

Crepes for breakfast—sounds exotic, doesn't it? Actually, crepes are not that difficult to make, and are a nice departure from the usual breakfast fare. Also see the other crepe recipes in this chapter, and see page 218 in Chapter 10 for detailed directions on making crepes.

Sauce Suggestions

Any fruit sauce, *Tofu and Cashew Cream* (page 274), *Apple-Tahini Sauce* (page 249), a dollop of yogurt, apple butter, malt syrup, maple syrup, rice syrup, honey, etc.

Fillings

- Fresh strawberries, raspberries, or blueberries, mixed with yogurt.
- Grated raw apple mixed with raisins and chopped nuts. Grated raw apple may also be mixed with yogurt.

- Hot cooked apples sweetened to taste with raisins, honey, malt syrup, etc., and seasoned with a sprinkling of cinnamon.
- Sliced banana mixed with chopped pineapple and freshly grated coconut. Serve with an orange sauce such as *Orange Date Sauce* (page 248).
- Ricotta cheese thinned with a tablespoon or so of milk, sweetened to taste with honey, flavored with vanilla, and then mixed with fresh pitted cherries or berries.
- Sliced bananas served with a raisin or an orange sauce such as *Orange Date Sauce* (page 248).
- Sliced raw peaches with a pinch of clove or cinnamon, mixed with *Tofu and Cashew Cream* (page 274) or with yogurt.
- Applesauce sprinkled with grated cheese. Roll the crepes up and bake them at 375°F for about five to ten minutes, just to melt the cheese.

KATHY'S RICE BATTER CAKES

Kathy says that this recipe is well loved in her house because it is so versatile. She adapted it from a 1939 cookbook on Creole cookery.

3/4 cup whole wheat pastry flour
2 teaspoons baking powder
1/4 teaspoon sea salt (optional)
1 egg, well beaten
1/2 cup skim milk or soymilk
1 tablespoon honey, malt syrup, or maple syrup
1 cup cooked brown rice

Yield: About 16 small pancakes
Time: 12–15 minutes

1. In a medium-sized bowl, mix together the pastry flour, baking powder, and salt.
2. Beat in the remaining ingredients in the order listed above. Continue to beat until the batter is well mixed.
3. Drop the batter by the heaping tablespoon onto a hot, oiled skillet. The batter will be thick, so press it down with the back of your spoon to make pancakes that are about 3–4 inches in diameter. Cook the cakes until they are brown on the bottom, then turn them over and cook on the other side.

Serve these rice batter cakes for breakfast with your favorite fruit sauce or syrup. They are also good at dinner when you are out of bread. Kathy doubles the recipe and freezes half. When they're needed, she pops the frozen cakes into the toaster or oven until hot. She also spreads them with peanut butter to make "pancake sandwiches" for her kids.

OAT, APPLE, AND RAISIN PANCAKES

Pleasantly sweet without any added sweetener. Although this batter is thick, the grated apple keeps the pancakes light and tender. However, if the batter sits for a while and becomes too thick, add a little more liquid.

$1/3$ cup rolled oats
$1/4$ cup whole wheat pastry flour
$1/2$ teaspoon baking powder
Pinch of cinnamon (optional)
3 small or 2 large eggs
$1/4$ cup milk or apple juice
2 tablespoons raisins
1 cup grated apple

Serves: 2
Time: 12–15 minutes

1. In a medium-sized bowl, mix together the rolled oats, flour, baking powder, and cinnamon.
2. Beat in the eggs and the milk or apple juice. Add the raisins and the grated apple. Mix well.
3. Spoon one-fourth of the mixture at a time onto a hot, lightly oiled skillet. Using a spatula, spread the batter out to a thickness of about $1/3$ of an inch. Cook over medium-high heat until bubbles appear and the surface begins to dry out. Turn over and cook until done.

VARIATION

• Substitute $1/3$ cup cooked brown rice for the rolled oats.

MILLER'S PANCAKES

These pancakes are especially good because the wheat that they contain is freshly ground in the blender. The simplicity of this recipe makes it ideal for children. They enjoy seeing the whole wheat berries transformed into pancakes right before their eyes. If the batter becomes too thick, add a little water to thin it.

1 cup soft wheat berries
1 cup buttermilk
2 eggs
$1/2$ teaspoon baking powder (optional)

Serves: 4
Time: 12–15 minutes

1. Wash the wheat thoroughly and place it in a blender along with the other ingredients. Blend until the batter is very smooth and the wheat is finely ground.
2. Drop the batter by the $1/4$ cup onto a hot, oiled skillet. Cook over medium-high heat until the pancakes are brown on the bottom; then turn them over and cook until done.

RICE FLOUR CREPES

Delicately flavored and paper-thin, these crepes will turn breakfast into a gourmet delight. For how-to instructions on cooking crepes, see page 218 in Chapter 10.

$1/2$ cup brown rice flour
$1/2$ cup whole wheat pastry flour
3 medium eggs
$1/2$ cup milk, soymilk, or water (more if needed)
1 tablespoon maple syrup (optional)
$1/2$ teaspoon natural vanilla extract

Yield: 6 crepes
Serves: 3
Time: 10 minutes

1. Combine the flours in a medium-sized bowl. Add the eggs and mix well. Add the remaining ingredients and beat until smooth.
2. Drop about $1/4$ cup of batter onto a hot, oiled

skillet. Tilt the skillet in a circular motion to distribute the batter thinly and evenly over the bottom. Cook the crepe briefly and then turn it over. Place the cooked crepe on a plate. Drop another ¼ cup of batter onto the skillet and cook as before. Repeat until all the batter is used. (Oil the skillet as needed; it doesn't have to be oiled for each crepe.) If the batter thickens as it sits, add a little more milk or water.

3. As you cook the crepes, stack them one on top of the other on the plate and cover them with a clean dishtowel to keep them warm.

4. Place a large spoonful of your choice of filling on each crepe and roll it up. Serve with pure maple syrup or the sauce of your choice. See page 28 for filling suggestions.

VARIATION

•   If desired, these crepes can be made entirely out of either wheat or rice flour. If you wish to use the crepes as an entrée or appetizer, omit the maple syrup and vanilla.

OAT CREPES

These crepes are very thin and mild flavored. Crepe cooking instructions appear on page 218.

⅓ cup rolled oats
⅓ cup plain or vanilla soymilk drink (Can be purchased in a natural foods store. Dairy milk or water may be substituted, if desired.)
1 egg

Serves: 1–2
Time: 12–15 minutes

1. Place all the ingredients in a blender and blend until smooth. The batter will be thin.

2. Drop the batter by the ¼ cup or less onto a hot, lightly oiled skillet or crepe pan. Cook over medium-high heat until set and golden brown on the bottom. Turn over and cook briefly on the other side.

BUCKWHEAT CREPES

¼ cup buckwheat flour
1 large egg
⅓ cup milk or water

Yield: 2 large crepes (See page 218 for how-to instructions.)
Serves: 1–2
Time: 12 minutes

1. Combine the flour, egg, and milk or water in a small bowl. Beat the mixture with a fork until the lumps are gone.

2. Heat a small amount of oil in a skillet and pour in half of the batter. Tilt the skillet to one side and rotate it to evenly distribute a thin, even layer of the batter over the bottom.

3. When the bottom of the crepe is golden brown, turn it over and cook it briefly. Place the cooked crepe on a plate. Repeat with the rest of the batter. (You may not need to oil the skillet the second time.)

    Serve with apple butter, maple syrup, or a fruit sauce. This crepe is also good stuffed with grated apples or an apple-yogurt mixture.

MUESLI

An old-time favorite among health enthusiasts, slightly revised. This is my preferred breakfast in warm weather.

¼ cup rolled oats
¼ cup oat bran
2 tablespoons raisins
2 tablespoons chopped walnuts
1 slice of lemon peel (to make about ½–1 teaspoon grated)
6 ounces plain soymilk drink (can be purchased in a natural foods store)
1 grated apple
Fresh, seasonal fruit as desired (strawberries, peaches, pitted cherries, grapes, blueberries, etc.)

Serves: 1–2
Time: 10 minutes

1. Place the rolled oats, oat bran, raisins, walnuts, and grated lemon peel in a blender. Grind to a coarse flour.
2. Transfer the ground cereal mixture to one to two bowls (depending on how many persons you are serving), and pour the soymilk over it. Mix well and let sit for about 5 minutes while you prepare the fruit.
3. Add the fresh fruit, mix well, and serve.

NOTE: Wheat germ, corn germ, or extra oatmeal may be substituted for the oat bran, if desired.

VARIATION

- *Tropi Muesli:* Substitute 2 or 3 dates for the raisins and grated coconut for the walnuts. Use a sliced banana and a ripe mango for the fruit. This is wonderful!

MAPLE-OAT BRAN GRANOLA

Store-bought granola cannot compete with the fresh crispness of homemade granola. Fresh, grated coconut is so good that it is worth the extra effort. However, unsweetened dried coconut may be substituted if desired. If you do not like coconut, substitute another type of nut, such as chopped cashews or pecans.

1 pound rolled oats
2 cups oat bran
1 fresh coconut, grated
½ cup sunflower seeds
¼ cup sesame seeds
1 cup almonds, whole or sliced
⅓ cup oil
½ cup maple syrup
1½ cups raisins or other chopped dried fruit

Yield: 11-12 cups granola
Time: 40 minutes

1. In a large bowl, mix together all the ingredients except for the dried fruit. Use your hands for mixing if necessary.
2. Spread a thin layer (about ½ inch thick) of the mixture on an unoiled cookie sheet. Bake at 350°F for 20 minutes, or until golden brown. Stir occasionally during the baking to assure even browning.
3. When the granola is browned, remove it from the oven and add the dried fruit. Mix well. Let cool before storing. Store in covered glass jars in the refrigerator.

SCRAMBLED TOFU

Quick and easy.

7 ounces firm tofu
Pinch of sea salt or 1 teaspoon tamari, to taste
Pinch of paprika, to taste
Pinch of tumeric, to taste (optional)
1 tablespoon minced parsley
1 tablespoon fresh chives, or 1 teaspoon dry chives

Serves: 1–2
Time: 5–7 minutes

1. Crumble the tofu with your hands and mix it with the other ingredients in a small bowl.
2. Heat about 1 teaspoon of oil in a skillet. Add the tofu mixture and stir over medium-high heat for a few minutes until thoroughly heated.
3. Serve with whole grain toast.

VARIATIONS

- Omit the tumeric and add one or more beaten eggs to the tofu mixture. Cook until eggs are set, stirring constantly as if you were making ordinary scrambled eggs.
- Sauté about ¼ cup of diced green or red pepper, sliced mushrooms, etc. Then add the tofu to the sautéed veggies and cook until thoroughly heated.
- Add half of a chopped ripe tomato to the tofu mixture. Heat thoroughly but do not cook the tomato too long or it will become very soft.

ROCKY MOUNTAIN TOAST

Children love this!

1 thick slice whole grain bread
1–2 teaspoons oil (as needed)
1 egg
Pinch of sea salt (optional)

Serves: 1
Time: 7 minutes

1. Carefully cut a hole about 3 inches in diameter out of the center of the slice of bread. Save both the slice of bread and the cut-out portion.
2. Heat the oil in the skillet. Place the slice of bread in the skillet and place the "hole" beside it.
3. Break the egg into the cut-out center of the bread. Cook over medium heat until the egg is set enough to turn over.
4. Carefully turn both the slice of bread and the "hole" over with a spatula and cook briefly on the other side.

Serve the toast with the "hole" on the side, and use it to dunk into the center.

3. VEGETARIAN-STYLE FAST FOOD

Many would-be vegetarians are put off by vegetarian cooking's reputation for requiring lengthy preparation. Others are able to follow a vegetarian diet when they have plenty of time, but are unable to continue when their work schedule becomes more demanding. This is a shame, because during these stressful periods of our lives the body's need for a good balanced diet is accentuated. It is only through proper nutrition and a healthful lifestyle that we can keep our energy level high and function to our maximum. The little bit of time spent on health care is nothing compared to the hours and the days that can be lost in illness or fatigue resulting from a poor diet.

Preparing wholesome meals is certainly more time-consuming than eating fast food; however, when one becomes adept at vegetarian cooking, it is much quicker than one might think.

The recipes in this chapter are all designed to be made in under thirty minutes from start to finish. Some of them have been chosen because of their ease of preparation, others because of their rapid cooking time. With many of the recipes you can make a satisfying meal in about twenty minutes. Not a gourmet meal, mind you, but a simple, tasty, and nutritious meal. In vegetarian cooking (as in standard cooking) there are lots of tricks and short cuts that will help you save time. Following is a list of some of these tips that have helped me to become and remain an active and healthy vegetarian. They should be useful to you, too.

- Every time you cook whole grains or dry legumes, cook more than you need. This is of utmost importance for rapid vegetarian cooking. In fact, many of the recipes in this section rely on the precooked grains and beans that you'll have on hand. (See Chapter 10 for how to cook grains and legumes.)

- Lightly season your precooked grains with sea salt and store them in a clean, tightly covered container in the refrigerator. They will keep for about one week.

- An easy way to reheat cooked rice or other cooked grains is to place a little bit of water (about one-quarter cup for each two cups of cereal) in a pan. Heat the water and then add the cooked grains. Stir for a minute over medium-high heat. Cover and steam over low heat for about three minutes more, or until heated through. Cereals reheated this way are not sticky.

- Another way to reheat cooked grains is to steam them over boiling water in a vegetable steamer. (This way is a little more troublesome because it gives you an extra utensil to wash.)
- If you have cooked more beans than you can use in a week, freeze them. Here are two methods:

  —Drain the beans well and place them in a plastic bag. Close the bag with a twist tie and put it in the freezer. When you are ready to use the beans, just shake as many as you want right out of the bag directly into the soup, stew, or whatever it is you are cooking. There is no need to thaw the beans before use.
  —After allowing them to cool, place the beans, with the liquid from cooking them, in a plastic container with a lid. Freeze. Thaw by immersing the container in hot water.

- Always keep plenty of tofu on hand. It is a ready-to-eat, high-protein food. During the times that I've been too busy to cook, tofu has been a real lifesaver. Tofu with some whole grain bread and vegetables can make a perfectly nourishing quick meal.
- Most sprouts need little or no cooking. Add some to your salad, soup, or sandwich for high-powered, quick nutrition. (Large beans that are sprouted for just two or three days require longer cooking.) See the section on sprouting in Chapter 9 for more information.
- Homemade sauerkraut is ready to eat right out of the jar. Uncooked kraut is high in vitamin C and an aid to digestion, so serve it often, especially in winter. See the recipe on page 144.
- Keep some soaked hijiki or some *Arame Condiment* (page 246) in the refrigerator. (It will keep for about a week.) You can add it to stir-fried dishes at a moment's notice to lend an exotic touch—not to mention an abundance of vitamins and minerals. See page 157 for more information on sea vegetables.
- Dulse and nori are nutritious sea vegetables that can be used without much preparation. See page 157 for more details.
- Bulghur wheat takes less than fifteen minutes to cook. Use it when you don't have time to cook other grains. Millet, buckwheat, and quinoa are also quick-cooking. They take about twenty minutes.
- To save time, use a thick slice of whole grain bread or toast instead of cooked grain as a bed for vegetables, beans, or tofu in a sauce.
- To make bread crumbs, place a slice or two of whole grain bread in a blender. Blend at high speed until the desired texture.
- When you buy some Parmesan or Romano cheese, grate the whole piece and store it in the refrigerator. A little grated Parmesan or Romano will instantly add flavor and protein to salads, pasta dishes, soups, etc.
- Make extra salad dressing so that you will always have some on hand. For an easy dressing see the *Bottomless Salad Dressing with Marinated Garlic* on page 131.
- Make a whole meal out of a salad. See pages 112-114 for ideas on making complete meal salads.
- Eat leftover steamed vegetables cold in salads. It saves time and helps retain the nutritional value of the vegetables.
- Make up a double batch of *Sprouted Hummus* (page 104) or any other bean dip. Keep as much as you will use within a week in the refrigerator and freeze the rest in one-cup portions.
- Keep the kitchen tools and utensils that you use most frequently out where you can reach them.
- Learn how to use a good Japanese vegetable knife (see the illustration on page 14). With a little practice, you can learn to chop vegetables faster than if you were using a food processor, considering the time that it takes to clean the food processor. It is surprising how much time you can save by having sharp knives.
- To clean a blender, put some warm soapy water in it and turn it on.
- To clean a burned pot, put some water and baking soda in it. Bring the water to a boil; then lower the heat and simmer for about half an hour.
- The most helpful object in my kitchen for preparing quick meals is my stainless steel pressure cooker. It allows me to cook delicious soups, stews, or vegetables in just minutes. If you have a pressure cooker, you'll find it very comforting when you get home late and hungry some cold evening!

There is no need to be afraid of a pressure cooker. It is very safe if you follow the manufacturer's instructions. Here are a few tips on using pressure cookers.

—Do not fill a pressure cooker more than two-thirds full.
—Never go away and leave a pressure cooker on high heat. Always watch it carefully.
—Do not use it to cook split peas or other broken beans.
—Soups made in a pressure cooker need about ¼ less liquid than soups made in an ordinary pot.
—Do not try to force the lid of a pressure cooker open while the pressure is still up. Let it cool down either on its own or under running water before trying to open it.

• An electric slow-cooking pot is another helpful utensil for the busy cook. It's ideal for cooking beans. See page 186 for details.
• If you know that you are going to be especially busy, wash and thinly slice a variety of vegetables to last for a few days. Store them sealed in plastic bags in the refrigerator, keeping the quicker-cooking vegetables in one bag and the slower-cooking vegetables in another bag. When you get home from work, just heat up your wok. You can have stir-fried vegetables in a matter of minutes. See the recipe for *Oilless "Stir-Fried" Vegetables*, page 141.
• Before you begin cooking, make a mental plan of how you are going to proceed. Consider which foods take the longest to cook and use the time while these slow foods are cooking to make sauces or salads. Being organized in this way can cut down considerably on food preparation time.
• Be confident. Learn how to cook without measuring. After you have tried most recipes once, you should then be able to do them your own way. There is no mystery or secret to good cooking. The main thing is to begin with pure, wholesome ingredients and use them in a respectful manner.

SUMMER GRAIN PILAF

A light and subtly sweet grain dish that can easily be made into a complete meal.

2 tablespoons olive oil
1 cup chopped onions
2 stalks celery, chopped
2 medium carrots, sliced
1 teaspoon basil
½ teaspoon thyme
1 cup millet, washed and drained
2 ¼ cups boiling water or stock
½ teaspoon sea salt, to taste (optional)
2 cups corn, cut off the cob

Serves: 3–4
Time: 25 minutes

1. Heat the olive oil in a large skillet. Add the onion, celery, carrots, basil, and thyme. Sauté for 2–3 minutes.
2. Add the millet and stir over medium-high heat for 2–3 minutes more. Remove the skillet from the heat and add the boiling water. Add the salt, if desired. Stir once, cover, and return the skillet to the heat. Reduce the heat to low and simmer for about 15 minutes.
3. After the millet has cooked for about 15 minutes, add the corn. Do not stir. Cover immediately and simmer for another 5 minutes, or until the liquid is absorbed. Toss the pilaf lightly with a fork before serving.

VARIATIONS

To make this recipe into a main dish, do one of the following:

• Serve with a protein-rich sauce such as the *Spicy Peanut Sauce* on page 246, the *Tofu and Peanut Sauce*, page 244, or the *Easiest Cheese Sauce*, page 242.
• Serve with some pan-fried tempeh or baked tofu.
• Sprinkle with grated cheese.

Any of the above variations is good served with a green salad. If you are serving this dish with a sauce, it does not need the salt.

BULGHUR WITH SPINACH

Tasty, easy, and nutritious.

10 ounces fresh spinach (1 package)
1 tablespoon olive oil
½ cup chopped onion
½ cup bulghur wheat
¼ teaspoon dill seed
¾ cup skim milk
¾ cup grated Parmesan cheese, or more to taste

Serves: 2–3
Time: About 20 minutes

1. Wash the spinach and dry it in a salad spinner or between towels. Coarsely chop the spinach and set it aside.
2. Heat the olive oil in a large skillet or heavy kettle. Add the onion and sauté for 2–3 minutes. Add the bulghur and stir over medium heat for a minute more. Add chopped spinach, mix well, and add the dill seed and the milk. Mix and cover.
3. Reduce the heat and simmer gently for 10–12 minutes, or until the liquid is absorbed. Mix well and place on serving plates.

   Sprinkle each serving generously with the Parmesan cheese.

BULGHUR WITH ZUCCHINI

Quick, easy, and good.

2 tablespoons olive oil
1 medium onion, chopped
3 cloves garlic, minced
2 medium-sized zucchini, scrubbed and sliced
1 cup bulghur wheat
1 teaspoon basil
1½ cups boiling water
1½ cups canned tomatoes
¼ cup tomato paste
⅓–½ cup sliced pitted black olives
Finely grated provolone cheese

Serves: 3
Time: About 20 minutes

1. Heat the oil in a large skillet. Add the onions and garlic. Sauté for a few minutes.
2. Add the zucchini and stir over medium heat for about 3 minutes; then add the bulghur and basil and stir for a minute more.
3. Pour the boiling water over the vegetable-bulghur mixture. Stir once and cover. Lower the heat and simmer, without stirring, for 10–15 minutes, or until the water is absorbed.
4. Add the tomatoes, tomato paste, and olives. Mix well. Place on individual plates and sprinkle with finely grated provolone.

   Serve with a green salad.

BULGHUR-PEANUT PILAF

1 tablespoon olive oil
1 cup chopped onion
3 cloves garlic, minced
3 cups carrots, cut into matchsticks
1 teaspoon thyme
1/2 teaspoon cumin
1 cup bulghur
1 3/4 cups water or vegetable stock
1/2 teaspoon sea salt
2 cups snow peas
1/2–2/3 cup roasted, unsalted peanuts

Serves: 3–4
Time: 20 minutes

1. Heat the oil in a large skillet. Add the onions, garlic, carrots, thyme, and cumin. Stir over medium-high heat for a minute or two. Reduce the heat, cover, and let cook for about 3–5 minutes more.
2. Raise the heat to high and add the bulghur. Stir for a minute. Lower the heat, add the water and salt, stir once, and cover. Let simmer over low heat for about 10 minutes more.
3. Add the snow peas and cover. Do not stir. Cook for about 3 minutes, until the peas are bright green and the liquid is absorbed. Add the peanuts. Toss and serve.

DOMINIQUE'S HUNGARIAN TOFU

Dominique was my best friend when we lived in Canada. She has been a vegetarian since she was seventeen years old and she runs marathons as a hobby.

2 tablespoons oil
1 medium onion, thinly sliced
4 medium-large (or 6 small) carrots, cut into thin matchsticks
1 pound tofu, crumbled
4 cups wheat sprouts (Soft wheat berries sprouted for 3 days. See page 124.)
1/2 teaspoon dill seed
1 teaspoon thyme
1 cup water
2 tablespoons arrowroot
2 tablespoons shoyu or tamari

Serves: 4
Time: 20 minutes

1. Heat the oil in a large skillet or wok. Add the onion and the carrots. Stir over high heat for 2–3 minutes, then lower the heat. Cover and cook, stirring occasionally, until the vegetables are almost tender.
2. Add the tofu, wheat sprouts, dill, and thyme. Cook over medium-low heat, stirring occasionally, for about 5 minutes.
3. Mix together the water, arrowroot, and shoyu. Pour the liquid mixture over the tofu and vegetables. Stir and cook until the sauce thickens.

PASTA AND LENTIL SPROUT QUICKIE

Surprisingly good!

1 tablespoon olive oil
1 small onion, chopped
1 small zucchini, quartered and sliced
³/₄ cup lentil sprouts (see pages 124-125 for instructions on growing your own sprouts)
1 teaspoon basil
1¹/₄ cup canned tomatoes with their juice
1 cup whole wheat pasta shells

Serves: 2
Time: 20 minutes

1. Heat the oil in a heavy kettle. Add the onion and sauté for a couple of minutes. Add the zucchini, lentil sprouts, and basil. Sauté for 2–3 minutes more.
2. Add the tomatoes and pasta shells. Cover and simmer until the shells are cooked (about 10 minutes). Stir occasionally and add more tomato juice if the mixture becomes too dry and begins to stick.

VARIATION

• You may add all sorts of other vegetables to this basic recipe. Green peppers, mushrooms, celery, garlic, etc. may all be added at the same time as (or in place of) the zucchini.

WHEAT AND LENTIL SPROUTS

If you have some sprouts on hand, this will make an almost-instant meal. See pages 124-125 for instructions on growing your own sprouts.

1 tablespoon oil
1 small onion, chopped
1 red pepper, chopped
1–2 cloves garlic (to taste), minced
¹/₂ teaspoon thyme
1 cup lentil sprouts (sprouted for 3 days)
2 cups wheat sprouts (sprouted for 2 days)
¹/₄ cup water
1 tablespoon barley or rice miso, or to taste
2 tablespoons chopped parsley

Serves: 2
Time: 15 minutes

1. Heat the oil in a skillet. Add the onion, red pepper, garlic, and thyme. Sauté for a few minutes.
2. Add the sprouts and stir over medium-high heat for a couple of minutes. Add the water, cover, and cook over low heat until the sprouts are tender but still a bit crisp.
3. Remove the skillet from the heat and stir in the miso and chopped parsley. Mix well and serve accompanied by a green salad.

VARIATION

• Add other vegetables to this stir-fry if desired. Broccoli and carrots are good choices.

Quick and Easy Soy Burger *(page 41)* with All the Fixings.

Palate–Pleasing Pasta with Vegetables *(page 42)*.

Hearty T.V.P. Chili with Corn Tortilla Chips *(page 44)*.

South-of-the-Border Beans and Rice *(page 40)* with Steamed Asparagus *(page 139)* and Garden-Fresh Tomatoes.

EGGPLANT AND CHICK PEAS IN YOGURT-TAHINI SAUCE

2 tablespoons olive oil
1 medium onion, chopped
1 green pepper, diced
½ medium eggplant, cubed
2 cloves garlic, minced
1 teaspoon cumin
1 teaspoon basil
¼ teaspoon celery seed
1¼ cups cooked chick peas

SAUCE

2 tablespoons lemon juice
3 tablespoons tahini
¼ cup yogurt
2 tablespoons tamari, or to taste
½ cup chopped parsley

Serves: 2–4
Time: 20 minutes

1. Heat the oil in a large skillet. Add the onion and pepper and sauté for a couple of minutes. Add the eggplant, garlic, cumin, basil, and celery seed. Stir over high heat for a minute or two. Lower the heat, cover, and cook until the eggplant is tender, stirring occasionally.
2. Add the chick peas and stir over medium heat until the mixture is thoroughly heated.
3. In a small bowl, mix together the ingredients for the sauce. Remove the skillet from the heat and stir in the sauce. Warm over low heat but do not cook.
4. Serve over whole grain pasta, rice, or millet, accompanied by a big green salad.

VARIATION

- Almost any vegetable can be substituted for the eggplant. Broccoli and squash are very good.

CARROTS, TOFU, AND HIJIKI IN MISO BROTH

For a quick meal that is very nourishing, yet light, serve this dish with some whole grain bread.

1 tablespoon oil
1 carrot, cut into thin matchsticks
½ cup chopped onion
1 or more cloves garlic, minced
¼–⅓ cup soaked and washed hijiki
½ teaspoon thyme
1 cup water
1 cup tofu, cut into ½ inch cubes
1–1½ tablespoons miso, to taste
1 tablespoon nutritional yeast (optional)

Serves: 1–2
Time: 15 minutes

1. Heat the oil in a skillet and sauté the carrots, onion, and garlic for a couple of minutes. Add the hijiki and thyme. Stir, cover, and reduce the heat to medium-low. Cook, stirring often, until the carrots are just tender (about 5 minutes).
2. Add the water and tofu. Bring to a boil, cover, and simmer for a minute or two.
3. Remove the skillet from the heat and add the miso and yeast. Mix well.
   Serve in shallow bowls.

SWEET AND SOUR TEMPEH WITH VEGGIES

Quick and easy, but at the same time colorful and exotic enough to serve to guests.

2 tablespoons oil, or as needed
1/2 pound tempeh, cut into cubes
1 medium onion, chopped
2 stalks broccoli, with flowerets cut into bite-sized pieces and stems peeled and cut into matchsticks
2–3 carrots, scrubbed and cut into matchsticks
2 cloves garlic, minced
1 teaspoon thyme

SAUCE

2 umeboshi plums or 2 teaspoons umeboshi paste
1 1/2 cups water or vegetable stock
2 tablespoons arrowroot
3 tablespoons tamari
1 teaspoon honey
Dash of hot sauce (optional)

Serves: 2–3
Time: 25–30 minutes

1. Heat the oil in a wok or a large skillet. Stir-fry the tempeh until it is golden brown (about 10 minutes).
2. Add the vegetables, garlic, and thyme. Stir, cover, and cook over medium heat (stirring occasionally) until the vegetables become tender but still crisp (about 10 minutes). If the vegetables seem to be getting too dry, you may add about 1/4 cup of water.
3. If you are using the whole plums to make the sauce, remove and discard the pits and blend the plums in a blender with the other sauce ingredients. If you are using the paste, just mix the sauce ingredients together in a small bowl. Pour the sauce over the tempeh-vegetable mixture. Stir and cook till sauce thickens.

    Serve over rice, millet, or whole grain pasta.

VARIATION

* Substitute a 10-ounce cube of firm tofu for the tempeh. Or substitute 1 tablespoon of lemon juice or 1/2 tablespoon vinegar for the umeboshi. Adjust the other seasonings to taste.

BEANS AND RICE

If you have some precooked beans and rice, it takes only minutes to prepare a "south-of-the-border" style feast. This recipe is an old standby at our house.

2 cups cooked pinto or red kidney beans, with enough of their cooking liquid to make them juicy
2 tablespoons shoyu, or to taste
1 teaspoon basil
1 teaspoon chili powder
1/2 teaspoon cumin
1/4 teaspoon oregano
Dash of cayenne or your favorite hot sauce (optional)
1 or more cloves garlic, pressed
2 fresh ripe tomatoes, chopped (when in season)
1–2 tablespoons olive oil (optional)
3 cups cooked brown rice, warmed

GARNISHES

3 scallions, chopped
1/4 cup chopped parsley
1 red or green pepper, chopped
1/2–1 avocado, sliced

Serves: 3–4
Time: 15–20 minutes

1. Mix together beans and spices. Simmer for about 10 minutes. Add chopped tomato and simmer for a minute more. Stir in olive oil, if desired.
2. Spoon warm rice onto the individual serving plates and cover with the bean mixture. Make a beautiful arrangement of the garnish ingredients over each portion. Serve with a large green salad.

TOFU AND MUSHROOMS IN TAHINI-MISO SAUCE

This easy recipe can be the basis of many quick meals, because almost any vegetable can be substituted for the ones listed here.

2 tablespoons oil or less, as needed
1 large onion, chopped
2–3 cloves garlic, minced
1 red pepper, diced
2 cups sliced mushrooms
1 teaspoon thyme
2 tablespoons whole wheat pastry flour
1/4 cup tahini
1 1/3 cups water
10–16 ounces tofu, cut into 1/2-inch cubes
3 tablespoons miso
2 tablespoons nutritional yeast
3 tablespoons chopped parsley
1 tablespoon lemon juice
Cooked rice, millet, or pasta

Serves: 3
Time: 20 minutes

1. Heat the oil in a large skillet. Add the onion and the garlic. Sauté for a couple of minutes; then add the pepper. Continue sautéing until the onions are almost tender.
2. Add the mushrooms and the thyme. Cook until the mushrooms are done.
3. When the vegetables are cooked, add the flour and mix well. Then stir in the tahini and mix again. Gradually add the water. Keep stirring until the sauce boils.
4. Add the tofu and cook, stirring gently, for a minute or two. Remove the skillet from the heat. Add the miso and remaining ingredients and mix well.

     Serve over a bed of cooked rice, millet or pasta. If you are really in a hurry, serve this dish over whole grain toast. Accompany it with a green salad.

QUICK AND EASY SOY BURGERS

1 1/2 cups mashed tofu
3/4 cup T.V.P. (textured vegetable protein)
2 tablespoons peanut butter
1–2 cloves garlic, pressed
3 tablespoons minced parsley
1/4 cup minced onion
1/2 teaspoon thyme
1/4 teaspoon sage
2 tablespoons tamari
2 tablespoons oil, or as needed

Yield: 7 or 8 small burgers
Serves: 3–4
Time: 20 minutes

1. Mix together all ingredients (except for the oil) in a large bowl, using your hands to mix if necessary. Allow mixture to sit for about 10 minutes so that the T.V.P. will absorb the moisture from the tofu.
2. Shape the mixture into 7 or 8 small patties that are about 1/2 inch thick. Press the patties firmly between your hands to make sure that they hold together.
3. Heat the oil in a skillet and cook the patties over medium-low heat until they are brown on the bottom. Turn them over and brown on the other side.

     Serve the burgers on whole grain hamburger buns or on lightly toasted whole grain English muffins. Add your favorite trimmings.

VARIATIONS

The students in my cooking classes have been very creative with this recipe. Here are two of their variations.

• *Soy Loaf:* Mix all ingredients (except oil) and allow the mixture to sit for about 10 minutes. Then pack the mixture into an oiled loaf pan. Spread the top of the loaf with 2 tablespoons of tomato paste. Bake at 350°F for about 30 minutes, or until firm.

- *Baked Soy Burgers*: Prepare the patties as indicated above, but rather than frying them in oil, bake them on a well-oiled cookie sheet at 350°F until firm and brown (about 20 minutes).

VEGETARIAN SLOPPY JOES

This is another one of those recipes that will probably vary a little every time you make it, depending on what is in your refrigerator.

1 tablespoon olive oil
1½ cups chopped onion (1 large onion)
2–3 cloves garlic, minced
1 teaspoon basil
¼ teaspoon celery seed
½ cup bulghur wheat
⅓ cup T.V.P. (textured vegetable protein)
1½ cups boiling water
½ cup sliced pitted black olives
¾ cup tomato sauce
1 large or 2 small fresh tomatoes, chopped
Chopped parsley
Finely grated Romano cheese

Serves: 2–3
Time: About 20 minutes

1. Heat the olive oil in a large skillet. Add the onion, garlic, basil, and celery seed. Sauté until the onion is translucent.
2. Add the bulghur and the T.V.P. Mix well, then add the boiling water. Cover and simmer over low heat for about 15 minutes, or until the water is absorbed.
3. Add the black olives, tomato sauce, and chopped tomato. Cook until the dish is thoroughly heated. Garnish with parsley, and place a bowl of grated Romano cheese on the table for garnish. Serve with a salad.

VARIATION

- Sauté your choice of the following vegetables along with the onion: finely chopped celery, diced green or red pepper, and/or sliced mushrooms.

- Omit the black olives and/or the Romano cheese and season to taste with tamari.

PASTA WITH LIMA BEANS AND VEGETABLES

1 tablespoon oil
2 cups chopped mixed vegetables (onions, celery, broccoli, red pepper, etc.)
2 cloves garlic
1 teaspoon thyme
½ teaspoon savory
2 cups whole wheat macaroni (such as elbows, shells, or spirals)
1 cup cooked lima beans
¾ cup water or vegetable stock
1 tablespoon arrowroot
2 tablespoons tahini
2 tablespoons lemon juice
2 tablespoons shoyu or tamari

Serves: 2
Time: 20 minutes

1. Heat the oil in a wok or large skillet. Add the mixed vegetables and spices and stir-fry until the vegetables become tender, but still crisp.
2. While the vegetables are cooking, boil a large kettle of water. Drop the pasta into the water and cook until tender.
3. Add the lima beans to the cooked vegetables.
4. Drain the pasta and add it to the vegetable-bean mixture.
5. In a small bowl, mix together the water, arrowroot, tahini, lemon juice, and shoyu. Pour this sauce over the mixture in the skillet. Cook, stirring gently, until the sauce thickens.

   Serve with a green salad.

Peasant Meal

This is too simple to be a recipe, but it is something that we often rely on when there is not much time for cooking. Of course, for this dish to be quick, you must have some cooked beans on hand.

Season a pot of well-cooked beans (any kind) with some tamari, garlic, herbs, and perhaps some olive oil. When the beans are well-cooked, their cooking liquid should thicken into a sauce. If the cooked beans are dry, add enough water or vegetable stock to make them juicy. If the cooking liquid is too thin, either cook longer (uncovered), or (if the beans are tender) remove some of the beans from the pot and mash them with a fork. Return them to the pot and stir.

Place one or two slices of whole grain bread, toast, or cornbread on individual serving plates. Pour a ladle full of beans over the bread. Top with chopped parsley and scallions.

Serve with a big green salad, sliced tomatoes, and avocado. Sauerkraut is also a good accompaniment.

WHEAT AND LIMA BEANS

This dish cooks all day in an electric slow-cooking pot, and is ready to eat when you get home. The garlic does not get cooked very much and therefore has a strong taste. I prefer it this way. However, if you do not relish the taste of raw garlic, omit it and sprinkle some chopped scallions over the dish as a garnish instead.

1 cup dry baby lima beans or large lima beans
1 cup soft wheat berries
3 cups water
1 bay leaf
2 tablespoons tamari
2 cloves garlic, pressed
1/2 cup minced parsley, or less to taste
1 tablespoon olive oil

Serves: 3–4
Time: Soak overnight; prepare in 5-10 minutes; let cook all day without supervision.

1. Wash and pick over the beans. Place them in a medium-sized bowl, cover with water, and let soak overnight.
2. In the morning, drain the beans and place them in an electric slow cooking pot. Wash the wheat and drain it through a wire strainer. Place the wheat in the cooker with the beans and add the water.
3. Cover the pot and turn it to high; cook for about 1 hour. Then turn it to low and cook for about 8 hours more. If you want this dish to cook faster, cook it on high for about 4 hours.
4. When the beans and wheat are well-cooked, add the tamari and garlic. Let cook a few minutes more (you can use this time to make a salad).
5. Add the parsley and the olive oil. Mix well and serve. If the dish is too dry, add a little extra water. It should be like a thick stew.

VARIATION

• Some cooked vegetables may be added to this stew just before serving. Also, any leftover *Wheat and Lima Beans* can be easily made into a soup. Add some cooked vegetables, water, and tamari to taste. Heat and serve.

REFRIED BEANS

The kidney beans used in this recipe should be purchased dry and soaked overnight. One cup of dry kidney beans, soaked overnight and cooked in about 3 cups of water, will yield 2½–3 cups of beans. The beans may also be sprouted for a day or two, if desired. See pages 124–125 for information on growing your own sprouts at home.

2½ cups cooked red kidney beans or pinto beans
¼ cup cooking liquid from beans
2 tablespoons olive oil
1½ cups chopped onion
1 green pepper, diced
1 teaspoon basil
½ teaspoon oregano
1–2 teaspoons cumin, to taste
1 teaspoon chili powder
2 tablespoons tamari
1–2 teaspoons hot sauce or cayenne, to taste

Serves: 3–4
Time: 20 minutes

1. Using a potato masher, mash the beans with their cooking liquid. Set aside.
2. Heat the oil in a large skillet. Add the onion and sauté for 2–3 minutes. Add the green pepper and sauté until tender. Add the mashed beans and mix. Add the remaining ingredients to taste, and mix well. Reduce the heat and simmer, stirring often, for 5–10 minutes, or until the mixture has thickened a little bit and the flavors have blended.

     Serve with tortillas or rice, accompanied by sliced ripe tomatoes, guacamole, and a green salad. This mixture will stuff about 10 tortillas.

NOTE: If you do not have cooked beans on hand for this recipe or for *T.V.P. Chili,* you may use canned beans. There are many brands that contain only beans, water, and salt. Read the label and choose carefully.

T.V.P. CHILI

2 tablespoons olive oil
1 large onion, chopped
3 cloves garlic, minced
1–2 stalks celery, chopped
1 red or green pepper, diced
2 cups red kidney beans, cooked
1 cup liquid from cooking beans
2 cups canned tomatoes with their juice
½ cup T.V.P. (textured vegetable protein)
2 tablespoons tamari
3 bay leaves
1 teaspoon basil
1 teaspoon cumin
1 teaspoon chili powder
½ teaspoon cloves
Cayenne or hot sauce to taste

Serves: 4
Time: 25 minutes

1. Heat the oil in a skillet. Add the onion, garlic, and celery. Sauté for a few minutes. Add the green or red pepper and sauté until almost tender.
2. Place the cooked beans, liquid from cooking them, tomatoes, T.V.P., and seasonings in a large kettle. Bring to a boil. Lower the heat and simmer for a few minutes.
3. Add the sautéed vegetables to the bean mixture and simmer for about 10 minutes to blend the flavors.

     Serve with corn tortillas or whole grain bread and a big green salad. This chili is also good served over rice.

CHINESE STEAMED EGGS

An exquisitely simple dish with a fine, custard-like texture.

The steamer can be any cooking utensil that allows the bowl to sit upright while not touching the bottom of the pan. A wok that has a wire rack that fits in the bottom is ideal. Or, alternatively, you can place some chopsticks in the bottom of a large kettle and set the bowl of eggs on the chopsticks.

3–4 eggs
Water
1–2 teaspoons oil
A few drops of roasted sesame oil, to taste
1/4 cup minced onion
1 clove garlic, minced
Tamari to taste

Serves: 2
Time: 20 minutes

1. Break the eggs into a large measuring cup. Pour the same quantity of water as there are eggs into the cup. (For example: 1/3 cup water for 1/3 cup eggs.) Beat with a fork. If desired, add a small pinch of salt. Transfer the beaten eggs to a bowl that can be heated.
2. Place about 1 1/2 inches of water in the bottom of a pot. Place a vegetable steamer in the pot and place the bowl inside. Bring the water to a boil. Cover and steam over medium-low heat for 12–15 minutes, or until the eggs are set. Do not open the steamer for the first 10 minutes of cooking.
3. While the eggs are cooking, heat the oils in a small frying pan and sauté the onion and garlic until tender. Remove the pan from the heat and mix the sautéed onion with a little tamari, to taste.
4. After 10 minutes or so, open the steamer to check the eggs. When they are ready, top with the tamari-seasoned onions. Serve with some brown rice and stir-fried veggies.

BLACK-EYED PEA AND OAT CASSEROLE

Make and bake this dish in an ovenproof skillet.

2 tablespoons olive oil
1 medium onion, chopped
1/2 green pepper, diced
1/2 teaspoon grated fresh ginger
1/2 teaspoon thyme
1/4 teaspoon cumin
1 cup rolled oats
1 cup water
2 tablespoons shoyu or tamari
1 1/2 cups cooked black-eyed peas
1/2 cup whole grain bread crumbs

Serves: 2–3
Time: 25 minutes

1. Heat the oil in an ovenproof skillet. Add the onion and stir-fry for a couple of minutes. Add the pepper, ginger, thyme, and cumin. Sauté until the vegetables become tender, but are still crisp.
2. Add the oats and cook, stirring constantly until the oats are lightly toasted.
3. Mix together the water and the shoyu or tamari. Pour this mixture over the vegetable-oat mixture in the skillet. Stir.
4. Remove the skillet from the heat and top it with the cooked beans. Sprinkle the casserole with bread crumbs.
5. Bake at 350°F for about 15 minutes. Then broil for a minute or two to brown the top.
   Serve this casserole with a big salad.

INCA DÉLICE

This makes a light and nourishing summer meal. It uses silken tofu. Silken tofu is a very soft, custardy, mild-flavored tofu that comes in cardboard containers. It is different from the regular tofu that is used in most of the recipes in this book, because it does not need any preparation to be delicious.

2 cups water
1 cup quinoa
1–2 tablespoons oil
1 large carrot, scrubbed and cut into matchsticks
1–2 cloves garlic, minced
¼ pound snow peas, cleaned
3 scallions, chopped

SAUCE

¼ cup tahini
2 tablespoons white miso
Juice of ½ lemon
¼ cup water, approximately
10-ounce package silken tofu

Serves: 2
Time: 25 minutes

1. Wash the quinoa and drain it through a wire strainer. Place the quinoa in a pan with the water. Cover and bring to a boil.
2. Reduce the heat and simmer for about twenty minutes or until the water is absorbed. While the quinoa is cooking, prepare the vegetables.
3. Heat the oil in a skillet. Add the carrot and the garlic. Stir for a minute and then reduce the heat to medium. Cover and cook until the carrot begins to get tender.
4. Add the snow peas and the scallions. Stir and cook until the vegetables are tender, but still slightly crisp. While the vegetables are cooking, prepare the sauce.
5. To make the sauce, place the tahini and the miso in a small bowl. Add the lemon juice and mix well.
6. Slowly stir in enough water to achieve the desired sauce consistency. Whip with a fork until smooth.

1. Cut the tofu into small cubes.
2. When the quinoa is done, divide it between two serving plates. Arrange the vegetables over the quinoa. Pour the sauce over the vegetables and top with the tofu. Serve immediately.

OMELETTE IN A CRUST

This dish is satisfying, tasty, and quick to make.

1–2 tablespoons oil, as needed
1 small onion, minced
1½ cups bread crumbs
4 eggs
½ teaspoon thyme
½ teaspoon sea salt
¼ cup milk or water

Serves: 2–3
Time: 15 minutes

1. Heat the oil in a 10-inch skillet and sauté the onion for a minute or two.
2. Add the bread crumbs. Mix well and distribute the bread crumbs evenly over the bottom of the skillet.
3. Beat together the eggs, thyme, salt, and milk or water. Slowly pour the egg mixture over the bread crumbs. Cook over medium-low heat until the eggs are set.
4. Fold the omelette over, cut it into two portions, and serve.

VARIATIONS

- Sauté some mushrooms with the onion; sprinkle some grated cheese over the egg mixture.

4. *SOUPS AND SANDWICHES*

Traditionally, soup recipes were created out of necessity—the need to feed large, hungry families with what little food was on hand. Therefore, a "right" or "wrong" way to make soup does not exist. More than any other area of cuisine, soup making is a field where you can really let your imagination and the right side of your brain run full range. It is an opportunity to clean out your refrigerator and use up all the odds and ends of food that are too good to throw away, yet too small to use for anything else.

In day-to-day cooking, I use the basic ideas represented in recipes in this book over and over, but quite frankly, I don't know if I've ever made the exact same soup recipe more than once. The same ingredients, in the same proportions, just never seem to turn up in my refrigerator a second time, and no matter how good a certain soup may be, it never seems to be worth the trouble of running out to buy special ingredients. There is always a way to make something just as good with whatever is on hand. Using the right side of your brain, you can harness your creativity and come up with some exciting new recipes. Of course, if you are just learning to cook, or just learning to cook vegetarian style, I advise you to follow the recipes just as they are written for the first time. Later, when your confidence and understanding of the foods we use become more developed, you will surely wish to change the recipes around to suit your own taste and needs.

Changing a recipe is easier than you might think. For example, take the recipe for the non-dairy *Cream of Onion Soup* on page 57. By substituting mushrooms for some of the onions, you can make a delicious cream of mushroom soup. By substituting chopped celery for most of the onions, you can make a cream of celery soup.

Below is a list of tips intended to help you to make the kind of soups that are a pleasure both to eat and to serve.

- A good soup starts with a flavorful stock. Therefore, it is helpful to always save a little bit of water that is left over from steaming vegetables. To keep this cooking liquid from going bad before you can use it, store it in a plastic bowl in the freezer. Keep the bowl tightly covered and add more stock every time you have some, until you have enough to use. By saving this cooking liquid and using it to replace all or part of the water in a recipe, you are adding vitamins and minerals as well as flavor to your soup.

- If a soup is too thick for your taste, just add some liquid. Depending on the kind of soup you are making, the liquid can be water, vegetable stock, tomato juice, soymilk, nut milk, or dairy milk. After you have added the liquid, taste the soup and adjust the seasoning if necessary.

- If a soup is too thin, there are several ways to thicken it. Here are a few suggestions:

  —Mix a little flour with some cold water to make a paste. Add it to the hot soup and stir for a couple of minutes while the soup simmers. Do not use more than three or four tablespoons of flour to thicken a large pot of soup, because if you add too much you will end up with an enormous quantity of gravy. If your soup is still too thin, add some more flour paste.

  —Blend some leftover rice or millet in a blender with enough soup stock to make a cream. Add this to the cooked soup. A rich-tasting cream will be the result.

  —A handful or so of cashews mixed with some soup stock in a blender is another way to turn a clear soup into a rich cream. Make sure that the cashews are blended well, or the soup will not be creamy enough.

  —Starch water that is left over from making seitan thickens when it is cooked. If you're feeling adventurous, you may wish to try using it to thicken a soup.

  —A cooked potato, blended in the blender with some stock and added to the soup, will also thicken it nicely. In some recipes, sweet potatoes can be used.

- To accompany a meal, a light soup is usually preferred. Sometimes soup is not really too thin—it just needs some seasoning or garnish. Some suggestions that will help you to "spice up" a bland soup are included below.

  —When you need to add some flavor to a dull soup, tamari and miso are wonder workers.

Use tamari or dark miso in clear soups and tomato-based vegetable soups, and use white or yellow miso in cream soups.

  —A tablespoon or so of lemon juice or vinegar will awaken the flavors in a bean soup.

  —A little olive oil added to a soup at the end of cooking adds both flavor and richness. A few drops of roasted sesame oil enhances tamari- and miso-based soups.

  —Don't forget the herbs. Almost any soup will profit when it has a bay leaf or two simmering along with the other ingredients. Basil is good in a soup that contains tomatoes or corn. Savory enhances bean soups and potato soups. Thyme is a nice addition to hearty grain or root vegetable soups; tarragon is good in borscht (beet soup) and vegetable soups; and a pinch of nutmeg will complement most cream soups. If you make a point of experimenting a little with herbs you will learn which ones you like and how to use them.

- For blender soups, do not blend green vegetables with red or orange vegetables, because you will end up with an unattractive brown purée. Cook the two colors separately and blend only one (leaving the vegetables of the other color in chunks); the result will be a very pretty soup. See the *Sprouted Pea Soup* on page 51 for an example of this method.

- When using legumes in a soup, make sure to cook them at least partially before adding the other vegetables.

- A small amount of uncooked pasta may be added to a soup if the soup is not too thick. Add it during the last ten minutes or so of cooking. Precooked pasta (e.g., leftovers) can be added to a cooked soup.

- When a soup contains many different varieties of vegetables, chop the slow-cooking vegetables more finely than the quick-cooking ones. This ensures that they will both be done at the same time.

- As with other foods, soups should be as visually appealing as they are good-tasting. This can be achieved by not overcooking the soup (which dulls the color of the vegetables) and by garnishing. Listed below are some garnish ideas:

—A sprinkling of fresh herbs adds flavor as well as eye appeal. Herbs to use as garnish include parsley, basil, dill weed, fennel, chives, and scallions.

—Cream soups look nice with a dusting of paprika or nutmeg.

—Herb croutons will add interest both in texture and appearance.

—A dollop of cold white yogurt in a steaming hot soup makes an intriguing garnish.

—Grated Parmesan or Romano cheese is a garnish that will bring even the most insipid soup to life.

—For a touch of elegance, sprinkle some finely chopped nuts over a cream soup.

• To make a simple soup into a satisfying meal, serve it with a big, beautiful salad and some nutritious whole grain bread. If the soup you are serving contains a source of protein, this is all you need to make a meal. If not, serve a sandwich made with one of the spreads or patés in this book, or some good-quality cheese along with the bread.

The following recipes include warm, hearty soups for those cold winter evenings and cool, light soups that are so refreshing. They make delicious lunches—I hope you enjoy them as much as I do.

FRENCH ONION SOUP

The tamari and miso make a rich-tasting and healthful substitute for the usual beef broth.

2 tablespoons olive oil
½ teaspoon roasted sesame oil (optional)
4 cups chopped onion
1 teaspoon thyme
2 bay leaves
½ teaspoon rosemary
4 cups water or vegetable broth
2 tablespoons tamari
2 tablespoons dark-colored rice or barley miso

Serves: 4–6
Time: 40 minutes

1. Heat the oils in a large, heavy kettle. Add the onion, thyme, bay leaves, and rosemary. Sauté over very low heat for at least 30 minutes, stirring occasionally. The trick to making a good onion soup is in cooking the onions very slowly so that they become almost sweet.

2. Add the water and tamari. Bring the soup to a boil. Reduce the heat and simmer for about 5 minutes. Remove the kettle from the heat and add the miso. (Miso should never be cooked.) If desired, the miso may be diluted with a little of the broth from the soup before you add it to the kettle.

VARIATION

• Make the recipe above and place the soup in individual ovenproof soup bowls. Toast 4–6 slices of whole wheat bread, and trim it so that it will fit into the bowls. Float a slice of bread in each bowl of soup and sprinkle it with grated Gruyère cheese.

Place the bowls of soup under the broiler. Broil for a few minutes, until the cheese is bubbly and beginning to become golden brown. Serve immediately.

LENTIL SOUP

Easy, inexpensive, and nourishing, lentil soup has become a vegetarian classic.

½ cup dried lentils
4½ cups water or vegetable stock
1 medium onion
1 stalk celery
1 green pepper
1 medium carrot
3 cloves garlic
2 bay leaves
½ teaspoon savory
3 tablespoons tamari
2 tablespoons olive oil

Serves: 4
Time: 60 minutes

1. Wash and pick over the lentils. Place them in a large kettle along with the water or stock. Cover and bring to a boil. Reduce the heat to low and simmer for about 20 minutes while you prepare the vegetables as follows: chop the onion and celery, cube the pepper, slice the carrot, and mince the garlic.
2. Add the vegetables, garlic, bay leaves, and savory to the kettle. Simmer for about 20 minutes. Add the tamari and continue to simmer for about 10 more minutes, or until the vegetables and the lentils are both tender.
3. Add the olive oil. Serve with some homemade bread and a big green salad.

SPLIT PEA AND BARLEY SOUP

½ cup split peas
¼ cup barley
8 cups water or vegetable stock
1 large onion, chopped
1 medium carrot, sliced
1 stalk celery, chopped
1 teaspoon basil
4 tablespoons yellow miso, or to taste
¼ cup chopped parsley
2 tablespoons olive oil

Serves: 6
Time: 1 hour, 20 minutes

1. Wash the peas and the barley and place them both in a large kettle with the 8 cups of water or vegetable stock. Cover and bring to a boil. Lower the heat and simmer for about 1 hour, or until the peas are tender
2. Add the onion, carrot, celery, and basil and simmer until the vegetables are tender.
3. Remove the kettle from the heat and add the miso, parsley, and olive oil. Stir until the miso is dissolved.

SOUPE PROVENCALE
(Garlic Soup)

Don't be afraid to try this amazingly mild-flavored soup. Besides being delicious, it has the bonus virtue of being able to knock a cold right out!

1–2 tablespoons oil
1 teaspoon roasted sesame oil (optional)
2 bulbs garlic (about 30 cloves)
1 medium onion, sliced
4 cups water or vegetable stock
1 large potato, scrubbed and cut into cubes
3 bay leaves
½ teaspoon thyme
4 tablespoons shoyu, or miso to taste
Pinch of cayenne

Serves: 4
Time: 50–60 minutes

1. Smash each clove of garlic with the handle of a knife to make removing the skin easier. Remove the skin and chop the garlic.
2. Heat the oils in a heavy kettle; add onion and garlic. Sauté over very low heat for about 20 minutes or until well cooked.
3. Add the water, potato, bay leaves, and thyme. Bring to a boil, then reduce heat and simmer until the potato is tender. Remove the kettle from the heat and add the shoyu or miso; then add the cayenne to taste.

    For a wonderful peasant-style meal, serve with a hot, crusty loaf of whole grain bread (preferably sourdough), a small round of baked Brie, and an enormous green salad.

SPROUTED PEA SOUP

This recipe tastes like the traditional split pea soup, but it has two advantages; it cooks faster, and is much easier to digest.

1 cup whole peas, bought dried and sprouted for 3 days (see page 124)
4 cups water or vegetable stock
4 bay leaves
2 tablespoons oil
1 large onion, chopped
2 carrots, thinly sliced
2 stalks celery, chopped
1 teaspoon sea salt
1 teaspoon savory

Serves: 4
Time: 50 minutes

1. Place the sprouted peas, water, and bay leaves in a large kettle. Bring to a boil, lower heat, and simmer, covered, until the peas are tender (about 30–40 minutes).
2. While the peas are cooking, sauté the onion, carrots, and celery until tender.
3. Remove the bay leaves from the cooked peas. In a blender, blend the peas with their cooking water until smooth and creamy.
4. Return pea purée to the kettle. Add sautéed veggies, salt, and savory. Simmer for a couple of minutes.

    Serve with whole grain bread and a big green salad for a simple but hearty meal.

CORN AND LENTIL SOUP

1 cup dried lentils
4 cups water
1 medium onion, chopped
1 green or red pepper, chopped
3 cups tomatoes (canned or chopped fresh)
2 cups corn (cut off the cob, or frozen)
1 or more cloves garlic, minced
1 teaspoon savory
1 teaspoon basil
3 tablespoons tamari
2 tablespoons olive oil (optional)
Grated Parmesan cheese (optional)

Serves: 6
Time: 50–60 minutes

1. Wash the lentils and cook them in the 4 cups of water for 30–40 minutes.
2. Add the vegetables, herbs, and tamari. Simmer for about 20 minutes, or until the vegetables are tender. Add olive oil, if desired.

   Serve with whole grain bread and a green salad for a good, simple meal. Place a bowl of grated Parmesan cheese on the table to be sprinkled on the soup, if desired.

LIMA BEAN SOUP

1 cup dried baby lima beans
4 cups water or vegetable stock
1 cup chopped onion
1½ cups chopped celery
1 green pepper, diced
1 teaspoon basil
1 can (28 ounces) tomatoes
Tamari or shoyu to taste
1–2 tablespoons olive oil

Serves: 4–6
Time: Soak beans 8 hours or overnight; cook 1 hour, 45 minutes.

1. Wash and pick over the beans. Place them in a bowl with enough water to cover and let them soak for 8 hours.
2. Drain the soaked beans and place them in a large kettle with the 4 cups of water or vegetable stock. Cover and bring to a boil. Reduce the heat and simmer until the beans are tender (about 1½ hours).
3. Add the onion, celery, green pepper, basil, and tomatoes. Simmer until the vegetables are tender.
4. Remove from the stove and add the tamari and olive oil.

   Serve with some whole grain bread and a green salad.

KALE, CABBAGE, AND WHITE BEAN SOUP

This soup, is hearty, flavorful, and very nutritious. This is a rather thick soup; if you prefer a thinner soup, just add some more water.

1 cup dried baby lima beans
5 cups water
1 strip kombu, 6 inches long (see the inset on sea vegetables, page 157)
1½ cups chopped onion
3 cups chopped kale
2 cups finely chopped cabbage
1 teaspoon savory
1–2 tablespoons lemon juice, to taste
¼ cup miso, or to taste (barley miso is good, as is yellow or white miso)

Serves: 4–6
Time: Soak beans 8 hours or overnight; Cook 1 hour, 30 minutes–2 hours.

1. Wash the lima beans and place them in a medium-sized bowl. Add enough water to cover, with about 1½ inches more water than beans, and soak for at least 8 hours.
2. Drain the soaked beans and place them in a large kettle with 5 cups of water. Cover the kettle and bring to a boil. Lower the heat and simmer the beans for about 1 hour, or until tender.
3. Rinse the strip of kombu and put it in the kettle with the beans. Add the chopped onion, kale, cabbage, and savory. Cover and simmer for about 30 minutes more, or until the vegetables are tender.
4. Remove the kettle from the heat and add the lemon juice and the miso. Remove the kombu and either discard it or chop it into bite-sized pieces and return it to the soup. Mix well and serve with some whole grain bread.

VEGETABLE GUMBO

When used in a soup, okra loses its undesirable texture and becomes very delicious. This recipe makes a large kettle of soup; you may wish to cut it in half.

½ cup barley
6 cups water or vegetable stock
1 large carrot, sliced
1½ cups chopped onion
3–4 cloves garlic, minced
1½ cups green beans, broken into ½-inch pieces
2 cups finely chopped white cabbage
3 bay leaves
3 cups canned tomatoes or finely chopped fresh tomatoes
2 tablespoons tamari, or to taste
1½ cups corn, cut off the cob
2 cups sliced okra
1 teaspoon basil
2–3 tablespoons olive oil (optional)

Serves: 6–8
Time: 1 hour, 50 minutes

1. Wash the barley and place it in a large kettle with the 6 cups of water or stock. Cover and bring to a boil. Reduce the heat and simmer for about 1½ hours.
2. Add the carrot, onion, garlic, green beans, cabbage, bay leaves, tomatoes, and tamari. Cover and simmer until the vegetables are almost tender.
3. Add the corn, okra, and basil. Simmer for about 15 minutes more, or until the okra is cooked.
4. Add the olive oil, if desired. If the soup is too thick for your taste, add some water or tomato juice. Add more tamari to taste, if you wish.

HEARTY MISO VEGETABLE SOUP

Vary the vegetables in this soup according to what is in season and what you have on hand. If you have some leftover cooked noodles, they are a very good addition to this soup.

1–2 tablespoons oil
½ teaspoon roasted sesame oil
1 medium onion, chopped
1–2 stalks celery, cut into thin diagonal slices
2 medium carrots, cut into matchsticks
2 medium parsnips, cut into matchsticks
1½ cups corn, cut off the cob
6 cups water or vegetable stock
¼ cup miso (barley miso, rice miso, and yellow miso are all good)

Serves: 4–6
Time: 15–20 minutes

1. Heat the oils in a large kettle. Add the onion, celery, carrots, and parsnips. Sauté the vegetables until they begin to get tender.
2. Add the corn and pour the water over the vegetables. Cover and bring to a boil. Reduce the heat and simmer for a few minutes, or until the vegetables are tender.
3. Remove the kettle from the heat and add the miso. Dilute the miso with a little of the soup stock to make mixing it easier, if desired. Mix well.

VARIATION

- Before you begin to sauté the vegetables, soak a 6-inch strip of wakame for about 20 minutes. Rinse the wakame and chop it into bite-sized pieces (removing the tough mid-rib). Add the wakame to the soup at the same time that you add the corn.

MELTING POT STEW

An unusual but very tasty dish—actually more like a thick soup than a stew.

4½ cups sprouted pinto beans, soaked 8 hours and sprouted for 2 days (see page 124)
4 cups water
2 tablespoons olive oil
1 carrot, diced
1 medium onion
½ teaspoon caraway seed
1½ cups sauerkraut (see page 144 for how to make your own sauerkraut)
1½ cups grated sharp Cheddar cheese
¼ cup fresh minced parsley
3 scallions, chopped

Serves: 6–8
Time: 1 hour, 20 minutes

1. Place the sprouted beans and the water in a large kettle. Cover and bring to a boil. Reduce the heat and simmer until the beans are very tender (about 1 hour).
2. Heat the oil in a skillet. Add the carrot and onion; sauté until almost tender. Add the caraway seeds and the sauerkraut and sauté for about 5 minutes more, stirring occasionally.
3. Add the sautéed mixture to the cooked beans and simmer for a few minutes. Add the cheese and stir until it is melted. Just before serving, add the parsley and scallions.

Serve with some Sourdough Rye bread (see page 83).

TRACEY'S CREAM OF BROCCOLI SOUP

This soup is good served hot or cold.

2 tablespoons oil
1 1/2 cups chopped onion
1 bay leaf
1 medium green pepper, diced
5 cups chopped broccoli
1 teaspoon sea salt, or to taste
2 1/2 cups vegetable stock
2 cups skim milk
1/2 cup yogurt
1/2 teaspoon thyme
Dash of cayenne, to taste
Pinch of allspice
1 teaspoon tamari, or to taste
4–5 scallions, finely chopped

Serves: 4–6
Time: 30 minutes

1. Heat the oil in a large, heavy kettle. Add the onion and bay leaf. Sauté until the onion is translucent.
2. Add the green pepper, chopped broccoli, salt, and stock. Cover and cook for about 10 minutes or until the broccoli is tender, but still bright green. Discard the bay leaf and purée the vegetable mixture in a blender or food processor. (In a blender this will have to be done in about 3 batches.) Blend until smooth, adding some milk to make the blending easier, if necessary.
3. Return the purée to the kettle and stir in the remaining milk and the yogurt. Mix well. Add the thyme, cayenne, allspice, and tamari to taste. Reheat the soup if necessary, but do not boil. Garnish with chopped scallions just before serving.

YELLOW SQUASH SOUP

A very pretty soup.

1/2 cup uncooked millet
2 tablespoons oil
1 cup chopped onion
3 cloves garlic, minced
1 1/2 carrots, cut into thin matchsticks
3 cups diced yellow squash
3–3 1/2 cups water or vegetable stock (to desired consistency)
1/2 cup frozen peas
1/4 cup yellow miso
2 scallions, finely chopped

Serves: 4–5
Time: 25–30 minutes

1. Place the millet in a wire strainer and rinse it. Place the wet millet in a saucepan and stir over medium heat or a few minutes to dry it. Grind the millet to a powder in a blender and set aside.
2. Heat the oil in a large, heavy kettle. Add the onion, garlic, and carrots. Stir for a minute or two, turn the heat to low, and cover. Cook, stirring occasionally, until the carrots begin to get tender. Add the squash and stir for a couple of minutes. Cover and cook, stirring occasionally, until all the vegetables become tender but are still slightly crisp.
3. Add the millet flour to the sautéed veggies and mix well. Pour a small amount of the water (or stock) into the kettle and stir to form a paste. Continue stirring while you slowly add the remaining water. Add the peas and simmer for a minute.
4. Transfer about 1/2 cup of the soup to a measuring cup or small bowl. Add the miso and stir until the miso is diluted. Remove the kettle of soup from the heat and add the diluted miso. Mix well. Garnish with chopped scallions just before serving.

CREAM OF LEEK SOUP (Nondairy)

In the late fall or early winter, when all other garden vegetables are frozen, the hardy leek will remain green. Try to use fresh tofu in this soup, because it has the mildest flavor.

2 large leeks with their green tops (about 7 cups chopped)
2 large baking potatoes (about 2½ cups diced)
5 cups water or vegetable stock
1 teaspoon savory
1 teaspoon thyme
1 cup mashed tofu
½ cup whole raw cashews
Pinch of nutmeg
Pinch of cayenne
2 teaspoons sea salt (or less to taste), or ¼ cup yellow miso (or to taste)

Serves: 6
Time: 40 minutes

1. Wash and chop the leeks (see page 155). Scrub and dice the potatoes. Place the prepared vegetables in a large kettle. Add 4 cups of the water, the savory, and the thyme. Cover the kettle and bring to a boil over high heat. Reduce the heat to medium-low and simmer for about 20 minutes, or until the potatoes are tender.
2. While the potatoes and leeks are simmering, place the tofu, cashews, and the remaining 1 cup of water in a food processor or blender. Blend until the mixture is very smooth and creamy.
3. Pour the cashew cream into an empty kettle. When the potatoes and leeks are tender, blend them (along with the liquid from cooking them) in the blender or food processor until smooth and creamy (this will have to be done in more than one batch, because the blender will not hold all of the soup at once).
4. Mix the potato-leek cream with the cashew-tofu cream and reheat if necessary, but do not boil.

5. Add the nutmeg and cayenne to taste. Then add the salt or miso to taste. (If you are adding miso, first remove the kettle from the heat.) Mix well.

CREAM OF FENNEL SOUP

If you are lucky enough to have some fresh fennel, try this delicately flavored soup.

2 cups chopped fennel bulb
2 cups chopped cauliflower
2 cups scrubbed and diced potatoes
1 small onion, chopped
4 cups water
¼ cup finely chopped fennel tops
1 teaspoon sea salt, or to taste
Finely chopped pecans

Serves: 6
Time: 30 minutes

1. Place the chopped fennel bulb and cauliflower in a large kettle. Add the potatoes, the onion, and the water. Cover and bring to a boil. Lower the heat and simmer until the vegetables are tender (about 20 minutes).
2. Blend the cooked vegetables in a blender or food processor until they are smooth and creamy. This will have to be done in about three batches if you are using a blender.
3. Add the fennel tops and the salt. Mix well. Place the soup in individual serving bowls and lightly sprinkle with finely chopped pecans.

VARIATION

- For a richer soup, cook the vegetables in 2 rather than 4 cups of water; then add 2 cups of milk when blending.

Lunch

Lunch does not have to be confined to sandwiches. Hot or cold soup is always nice, and so is a salad. Among the salads that lend themselves particularly well to lunch boxes are cooked vegetable salads such as the *Marinated Vegetable Medley* on page 122, the *Low-Fat Potato Salad* on page 114, and the *Broccoli and Cauliflower Salad* on page 120. Grain-based salads such as *Tabouli* (page 122), *Pasta and Chick Pea Salad* (page 116), and *Arame Rice Salad* (page 118), are also good for lunch.

My lunches often consist of leftovers from the night before. In fact, I often make more than we need for dinner, just to have something left over for lunch.

When you are packing a lunch box, don't forget to add the little extras that will make lunch more pleasant—packages of raw veggies, olives, or nuts, a miniature bottle of salad dressing, etc. Natural convenience foods that can enhance your lunch include miso soup mixes, instant soba noodles, rice cakes, and individual packages of soy milk drinks. For an occasional treat, add some homemade cookies, muffins, or candy to your lunch box, but make sure to bring along enough to share!

If keeping your lunch fresh is a problem, you can buy one of the small coolers that are usually used for six-packs of canned beverages. They are reasonably priced and are available in most department stores.

JANUARY VEGETABLE SOUP

½ cup chopped onion
2 cups finely chopped white cabbage
1 cup scrubbed and sliced parsnips
1 large carrot, scrubbed and sliced
1 cup diced rutabaga (Peel if waxed. The rutabaga should be cut into smaller pieces than the other vegetables, because it takes longer to cook.)
2 cups water
½ teaspoon thyme
1 teaspoon sea salt, or less to taste
½ cup grated sharp Cheddar cheese, or more to taste
2 cups skim milk

Serves: 4
Time: 30 minutes

1. Place the chopped vegetables, water, thyme, and salt in a large kettle. Cover and bring to a boil. Lower the heat and simmer for about 20 minutes or until the vegetables are tender.

2. Stir in the cheese and milk. Stir over medium heat until the cheese is melted, but do not boil.

   This soup is delicious with sourdough rye bread. (See page 83.)

CREAM OF ONION SOUP (Nondairy)

2 tablespoons oil
4 cups chopped onion (see page 159 for how to chop onions easily)
1 teaspoon thyme
½ teaspoon nutmeg
3 bay leaves
½ cup uncooked millet
⅔ cup raw unsalted cashews
4 cups water or vegetable stock
1 teaspoon sea salt, or yellow miso to taste

Serves: 4–6
Time: 30 minutes

1. Heat the oil in a large kettle. Add the onion, thyme, nutmeg, and bay leaves. Sauté very slowly until the onions are tender.
2. Wash the raw millet. Place it in a skillet and stir it over high heat for a few minutes until it is dry. Using a blender, grind the millet into a powder (a food processor will not work).
3. Place the millet flour in a small saucepan and slowly stir in 1 cup of water. Bring to a boil and stir until mixture thickens. Return the millet to the blender along with 1 more cup of water and the cashews. Blend until very smooth and creamy, adding more water if necessary.
4. Pour the millet-cashew cream over the cooked onions in the kettle. Add the remaining water and bring to a boil, stirring constantly. If the mixture becomes too thick, add more water. Add the salt or yellow miso to taste (remove the kettle from the heat first, if you are adding miso). Mix well.

VARIATION

- Replace part of the onions with chopped celery and/or mushrooms. If using mushrooms, add them after the onions and celery are almost cooked.

SWEET POTATO AND CHEESE SOUP

This unusual soup is very good—especially if you like sweet potatoes as much as I do!

2 medium sweet potatoes (3 cups diced)
1 large onion, chopped
2 cups water
1/2 teaspoon nutmeg
3–4 teaspoons Dijon mustard
1 cup sharp Cheddar cheese, grated and lightly packed
1/2 cup skim milk (approximately)
1 teaspoon sea salt, or yellow miso to taste

Serves: 4–6
Time: 30 minutes

1. Place the sweet potatoes, onion, and water in a large kettle. Bring to a boil. Lower the heat and simmer until tender.
2. Transfer the cooked vegetables and the liquid to a food processor or blender and blend until creamy. In a blender, this will have to be done in two or three batches.
3. Return the creamed mixture to the kettle. Add the nutmeg, mustard, and cheese. Stir over medium heat until the cheese is melted. Add as much milk as needed to achieve the desired consistency. Season to taste with either sea salt or yellow miso. If you are adding miso, first remove the kettle from the heat; mix well to blend the miso.

SPROUTED RED BEAN CREAM

Nourishing and easy to digest. This recipe calls for sprouted and cooked kidney beans. The beans should be sprouted 2–3 days and cooked in about 3 cups of water. See pages 124–125 for instructions on growing your own sprouts.

3 cups sprouted and cooked red kidney beans
1 red pepper, chopped
2/3 cup tomato paste
3 or more cups water (you may use all or part of the water from cooking the beans)
2 tablespoons olive oil
1 large onion, chopped
1 teaspoon basil
1 teaspoon cumin
1 teaspoon chili powder
1/2 teaspoon oregano
1/4 cup tamari, or to taste

Serves: 6
Time: 25 minutes

1. In a food processor, place the cooked beans, chopped pepper, tomato paste, and enough water to make blending easy. Blend until smooth and creamy. If you don't have a food processor, you may use a blender, but this will have to be done in about three small batches.

2. Heat the olive oil in a large kettle. Add the onion, basil, cumin, chili powder, and oregano. Sauté until the onion is tender.

3. Add the bean purée and the tamari to taste. Then add enough water to achieve the desired consistency. Reheat if necessary.

For an easy meal, serve with whole grain bread or hot tortillas and a big green salad.

CREAM OF CHESTNUT SOUP

Try this scrumptious soup for a special occasion. Don't be in a hurry though—shelling the chestnuts is time-consuming.

1 large onion, chopped
1 large potato, scrubbed and chopped
2 stalks celery, chopped
3 bay leaves
2 cups water
1 teaspoon curry powder
1 teaspoon sea salt
2 cups skim milk (approximately)
1/4 cup chopped parsley

Serves: 4–6
Time: 1 hour

1. Cut an X into each chestnut with a sharp knife. Place the chestnuts in a saucepan, cover with water, and boil for 20 minutes. Let cool. Remove the shells and the brown skins from the chestnuts.

2. Place the onion, potato, celery, bay leaves, and water in a large kettle. Cover and simmer until the vegetables are tender. Discard the bay leaves.

3. To the cooked vegetables, add the curry, salt, the cooked chestnuts, and enough of the milk to blend. Put this mixture into the blender and blend until smooth and creamy. Return the cream to the kettle and add more milk to achieve the desired consistency. Heat the soup but do not boil. Add the parsley and serve.

CARROT AND RICE CREAM

Simple and satisfying.

3 cups sliced carrots
1 cup chopped onion
2 bay leaves
4 cups water or vegetable stock
2 cups cooked brown rice
4 tablespoons mellow white miso
Pinch of nutmeg (optional)

Serves: 4
Time: 30 minutes

1. Place the carrots, onion, bay leaves, and water or stock in a large kettle. Cover and bring to a boil. Lower the heat and simmer until the vegetables are just barely tender. Remove the bay leaves.

2. Place the cooked vegetables, 1 cup of the rice, the miso, and enough of the stock to blend, in a food processor or blender. Blend until smooth and creamy. In a blender this will have to be done in more than one batch.

3. Pour the purée back into the kettle. Add the remaining cup of rice and a pinch of nutmeg, if desired. Reheat if necessary, but do not boil.

VARIATION

• *Carrot and Rice Cream with Arame*: Follow the above recipe, omitting 1 tablespoon of the miso and the nutmeg. Add 1/2 cup *Arame Condiment* (page 246) to the purée just before serving.

NEW BRUNSWICK CHOWDER

The dulse in this soup gives it a flavor similar to that of clam chowder.

2 tablespoons olive oil
2 cups chopped onion
1 cup chopped celery (2 stalks)
2 cups sliced mushrooms
1 teaspoon basil
1 teaspoon savory
1 cup dry dulse (see the inset on sea vegetables, page 157)
2 cups corn, cut off the cob and lightly steamed
3 cups skim milk
1 teaspoon sea salt, or to taste

Serves: 4
Time: 30 minutes

1. Heat the oil in a large, heavy kettle. Add the onions and celery. Sauté until almost tender.
2. Add the mushrooms, basil, and savory. Continue to sauté while you prepare the dulse.
3. Wash, drain, and chop the dulse. Add the chopped dulse to the other vegetables in the kettle. Sauté until the mushrooms are cooked.
4. Blend together the corn and milk in a blender to obtain a creamy consistency. Pour the corn cream into the kettle and salt to taste. Reheat but do not boil.

VARIATION

• Sauté the onion and celery. Add the mushrooms, herbs, dulse, and corn. Cover and cook, stirring occasionally, until the vegetables are tender. Stir in 5 tablespoons whole wheat pastry flour and mix well. Slowly stir in the milk; then add salt to taste. With this method, you do not need a blender or food processor.

CHILLED BUTTERMILK AND SCALLION SOUP

A cool, light soup for a hot afternoon. Try to use a very fresh and mild tofu for this recipe. Tofu sometimes varies in its moisture content. If you use firm tofu, 1/2 cup may be all you need.

1 cup buttermilk
Juice of one small lemon
1/4 teaspoon sea salt, or to taste
1/2 cup alfalfa sprouts
5 scallions, chopped
1 cup mashed soft tofu (approximately)
Whole wheat croutons

Serves: 3
Time: 10 minutes

1. Place the buttermilk, lemon juice, salt, sprouts, 3 chopped scallions, and 1/2 cup of the tofu in the blender. Blend until creamy. Blend in as much of the remaining tofu as necessary to obtain the desired consistency.
2. Sprinkle with the remaining scallions and top with whole wheat croutons.

CHILLED CUCUMBER-YOGURT SOUP

Very refreshing!

3 medium cucumbers
1 cup yogurt
1½–2 tablespoons lemon juice
2 tablespoons yellow miso
2 tablespoons fresh mint or 1 teaspoon dry mint
2–3 scallions, finely chopped
½ teaspoon dill seed
½ cup cold water
¼ cup finely chopped walnuts or pecans

Serves: 4
Time: 10-15 minutes

1. Peel the cucumbers if they are waxed; other-wise, just wash them well. Slice 2 cucumbers into large chunks and place them in a blender or food processor. Add the yogurt, lemon juice, yellow miso, and mint. Blend until very smooth and creamy. If you are using a food processor, make sure you blend the mixture long enough to make it smooth.
2. Pour the mixture into a bowl and add the chopped scallions, dill seed, and cold water. Grate the remaining cucumber and add it to the mixture. Chill for at least 1 hour before serving.
3. Sprinkle the soup with the chopped nuts just before serving.

CREAMY GAZPACHO

5–6 ripe medium tomatoes, sliced into large pieces
1 cup yogurt
Juice of one small lime
2 tablespoons minced onion
1 teaspoon honey
1 tablespoon white miso
½ cup cold water or vegetable stock
½ green pepper, very finely chopped
½ cucumber, grated
½ teaspoon basil

Serves: 4
Time: 10–15 minutes

1. Blend together the first seven ingredients in a blender or food processor until smooth and creamy.
2. Pour the purée into a large serving bowl. Add the green pepper, cucumber, and basil. Mix well and chill for at least 1 hour before serving.
3. Sprinkle each serving with *Parmesan Croutons*, page 91.

CLAIRE'S BORSCHT

4 large beets, scrubbed and grated
1 onion, minced
1 teaspoon tarragon
5 cups water or vegetable stock
2 tablespoons lemon juice
1 tablespoon honey
1 teaspoon sea salt
1 egg, beaten
4 medium potatoes, scrubbed, diced, and boiled until tender

GARNISH

Yogurt
Grated cucumber (if the soup will be served cold)

Serves: 6
Time: 45 minutes

1. Place the grated beets, onion, tarragon, and water in a large kettle. Cover and bring to a boil. Reduce the heat and simmer for about 30 minutes.
2. Add the lemon juice, honey, and salt. Simmer for about 5 minutes more.
3. Remove the kettle from the heat and slowly pour in the beaten egg while vigorously stirring the soup.
4. Place some of the boiled, drained potatoes in each serving bowl. Pour some soup over the potatoes. Garnish with a big dollop of yogurt.

NOTE: This soup may be served hot or cold. For a hot soup, make sure that the potatoes are hot, but for a cold soup, you can use either hot or cold potatoes. If you are serving the soup cold, it may be garnished with grated cucumber as well as yogurt. Sourdough rye bread is a wonderful accompaniment to this soup.

WINTER FRUIT SOUP

Serve hot or cold for breakfast or dessert.

1 cup raisins
1 cup pitted prunes
1/2 cup currants
2 cups water
1 cinnamon stick
3 cups unsweetened apple juice
1/2 cup unsweetened grape juice

Serves: 6–8
Time: Soak overnight; 10 minutes to prepare.

1. Place the dried fruit in a bowl. Cover with 2 cups of water, add the cinnamon stick, and let soak overnight.
2. The next morning, place the soaked fruit, cinnamon stick, and water in a pan. Cover and bring to a boil. Lower the heat and simmer for about 5 minutes. Add the juice. Reheat the soup to serve it hot; chill if serving cold. This soup will keep well for one week in the refrigerator.

VARIATION

- Instead of soaking the fruit overnight, it may be gently simmered in the water for about 20 minutes.

SCANDINAVIAN APPLE SOUP

Serve this soup hot or cold, for breakfast or for dessert. If you are serving the apple soup for breakfast, omit the wine and honey. Dissolve the arrowroot in apple juice and use apple juice to replace part of the water.

4 apples, washed but not peeled
4 cups water
1 teaspoon lime peel, finely grated
2/3 cup raisins
2 tablespoons arrowroot
1/2 cup white wine or apple juice
1 teaspoon cinnamon
3 tablespoons honey, or to taste

Serves: 4–6
Time: 20 minutes

1. Cut the apples into small cubes. Place the apples, water, lime peel, and raisins in a large kettle. Bring to a boil, lower heat, and simmer, covered, for about 5 minutes.
2. Dissolve the arrowroot in the wine or apple juice. Slowly stir the arrowroot mixture into the kettle containing the simmering apples. Add the cinnamon and simmer about 5–10 minutes more. Add honey to taste.

NOTE: Apple soup is delicious served hot and garnished with a large dollop of yogurt. If you wish to serve this soup as a dessert, you might like to mix the yogurt with some vanilla and honey to taste.

TOFU DUMPLINGS

Soft tofu is best for this recipe. If you are using a very firm tofu, add about 2 tablespoons of water to the blended mixture.

1 cup mashed tofu
2 tablespoons olive oil
1/2 teaspoon sea salt
1 cup whole wheat pastry flour
1 1/2 teaspoons baking powder

Serves: 4
Time: 15–20 minutes

1. Place the tofu, olive oil, and salt in a food processor or blender. Blend until smooth and creamy.
2. In a medium-sized bowl, mix together the flour and baking powder. Add the tofu cream. Using a fork, combine the two mixtures. Knead lightly with your hands to form a dough that will hold together.
3. Pinch off pecan-sized pieces of the dough and drop them into a large pot of gently simmering soup, stew, or cooked beans in their cooking liquid. Cover and cook, without stirring, for 10 minutes.

YOGURT DUMPLINGS

1 cup whole wheat pastry flour
1 1/2 teaspoons baking powder
1/4 teaspoon sea salt
3 tablespoons oil
1/3 cup yogurt

Yield: About 20 dumplings
Serves: 4
Time: 30–35 minutes

1. In a medium-sized bowl, mix together the flour, baking powder, and sea salt. Stir in the oil; mix with a fork. Add the yogurt and mix just enough to combine the ingredients. Do not overmix.

2. Drop the dough, about 1 tablespoon at a time, into a pot of simmering soup, stew, or beans. The dumplings will float on the surface as they cook. They will also double in bulk, so make sure that there is enough room in the pot to allow them to expand. Cover and cook at a gentle simmer, without stirring, for 20 minutes.

SIGI'S BREAD DUMPLINGS

This simple recipe comes from a German friend. It is easy to make and a good way to use up extra bread.

2¹/₂ cups soft whole grain bread crumbs
2 eggs, beaten

Yield: About 15 walnut-sized dumplings
Serves: 4
Time: 15 minutes

1. In a medium-sized bowl, mix together the bread crumbs and the eggs. Using your hands, shaped the mixture into balls the size of small walnuts. Press firmly so that they hold together well.
2. Drop the balls into a simmering soup, broth, stew, or kettle of beans. Cover and cook over medium-low heat (simmering gently) for 10 minutes. Do not stir the dumplings while they are cooking.

VARIATION

• Add the herbs of your choice to the egg and bread crumb mixture. Dried chives are especially good.

MILLET CHEESE BALLS

These millet cheese balls will turn a soup or stew into a hearty meal.

1¹/₂ cups cooked millet
1 cup grated sharp Cheddar cheese
2 scallions, finely chopped
1 egg
¹/₂ cup whole wheat pastry flour

Yield: About 20 walnut-sized balls
Serves: 3–4
Time: 20 minutes

1. Place all the ingredients in a bowl and mix them well. Using your hands, shape the mixture into walnut-sized balls.
2. Drop the balls into a large pot of simmering soup, stew, or beans. They will float on the surface. Cover and cook, without stirring, for 15 minutes.

   Serve with a green salad.

Sandwiches

Using the recipes in this book, along with a little of that right-side imagination, it is possible to make a different kind of sandwich almost every day. With an interesting variety of breads and some cleverly selected garnishes, a brown bag lunch can become an intriguingly delectable experience.

There is just one warning. Don't be surprised when your coworkers or fellow students start asking for samples and recipes, because unless you eat in total isolation, this will surely happen! Here are some suggestions for making sandwiches, followed by a few recipes.

- Don't be content with sandwiches made on the same old sliced whole wheat bread day after day. There are so many wonderful varieties of whole grain breads available today that it is a shame not to try them. Homemade bread is always great for making sandwiches because it has a special freshness that is hard to find in purchased breads. (Chapter 5 has recipes for a variety of homemade breads.)
- For a delightful change, try a *Chapati* (East Indian flat bread—see page 90) spread with *Hummus* (page 104). Top it with some shredded lettuce or sprouts and roll it up. Wrap the sandwich in wax paper to hold it together.
- Instead of peanut butter and jelly, try peanut butter sprinkled with raisins or chopped dates and topped with sliced banana or apple.
- Use *Almond Butter* (page 103) or other types of nut or seed butters instead of peanut butter.
- Leftover meatless loaves such as the *Almond Loaf* (page 224), *Wheat Loaf* (page 194), or *Lentil-Carrot Loaf* (page 190), are good cold in sandwiches. So are leftover veggie burgers such as the *Tempeh Patties* on page 216. Try the leftover patties or burgers on a whole grain English muffin.
- Other recipes that are good in sandwiches include: *Tofu "Fish" Sticks* (page 200), *Ginger Tofu* (page 199), and *Baked Peanut Tofu* (page 200). When you make one of the marinated and baked tofu recipes, cut some of the tofu into one or two sandwich-sized pieces and bake these along with the smaller pieces. Use them for lunch the next day.
- Seitan (page 193) is good in sandwiches.
- Any of the paté recipes in this book will make a tasty sandwich filling. Chapter 6 will give you many good ideas. Spread the bread with some Dijon mustard or homemade mayonnaise, if desired, before spreading the paté. Garnish with some lettuce, watercress, sliced dill pickles, or tomatoes, etc.
- Leftover cooked beans of any kind can be mashed with a bit of olive oil, minced parsley, tamari or miso, and finely chopped raw veggies to make a sandwich spread.

The following recipes make appealing vegetarian sandwiches. Use your creativity to come up with your own unique combinations!

- *Avocado Delight*. Mash half of a small avocado with a little lemon juice. Add some minced parsley and mix well. Spread the avocado purée on a slice of whole grain bread. Spread another slice with Dijon mustard. Place a thin slice of cheese and some watercress or lettuce on one of the slices of bread. Top with the other slice. This is great!
- *Avocado Reuben*. Place two slices of whole grain rye bread in a toaster oven. Toast on one side. Turn the bread over and place a slice of cheese on one slice of bread. Spread the other slice with mustard, then place a generous layer of mashed avocado and sauerkraut on the mustard. Place the two slices of garnished bread back in the toaster oven and broil until the cheese is melted. Cover the avocado-garnished bread with the cheese-garnished bread and serve.
- *Avocado, Tomato, and Sprouts*. Spread mustard on a slice of whole grain bread and top this with mashed avocado, sliced tomato, and sprouts.
- *Croque Monsieur*. Lightly toast one side of a nice, thick slice of whole grain bread under the broiler or in a toaster oven. Turn the bread over and place it on a cookie sheet. Place slices of tomato, green or red pepper, mushroom, and onion, along with a handful of sprouts, on the bread. Top with a thin slice of cheese and broil until hot and bubbly.
- *Croque Sante*. Lightly toast one side of a thick slice of whole grain bread under the broiler or in a toaster oven. Turn the bread over and place it on a cookie sheet. Top with a slice of cheese. Sprinkle with pumpkin seeds, sunflower seeds, and chopped scallions. Broil until golden and bubbly.
- *Minute Pizza*. Lightly toast an English muffin, pita bread, or a slice of whole grain bread. Spread with tomato sauce, top with grated cheese, and broil.
- *Summer Sandwich*. Mix a generous amount of *Soyannaise* (page 133) with some chopped cucumber and scallions. Use this mixture to stuff a whole wheat pita bread. Garnish with sliced tomatoes and lettuce.

TOFU, TAHINI, AND MISO SANDWICH

This sandwich tastes better than it sounds! In fact, it was my favorite lunch for one whole winter when I was going to art school.

2 slices whole grain bread
1 tablespoon tahini (approximately)
1 teaspoon miso, or to taste
1 large slice of tofu, about ½ inch thick
Alfalfa sprouts or lettuce

Serves: 1
Time: 5 minutes

1. If you have access to a toaster at lunchtime you may toast the bread; if not, it is also good untoasted. Spread one slice of bread generously with tahini. Spread the other slice with a light coat of miso (remember that the miso is salty, so don't use too much).
2. Place the slice of tofu and a generous serving of alfalfa sprouts or lettuce between the two slices of bread.

CUCUMBER-WATERCRESS SANDWICH

1 whole grain pita bread
Soyannaise (page 133)
½ medium cucumber, sliced
6 sprigs of watercress, or as desired

Serves: 1–2
Time: 5 minutes

1. Cut the pita bread in half and carefully open up the pockets.
2. Generously spread a thick layer of soyannaise inside each pita half. Cover with a layer of cucumber slices and then add as much watercress as will fit in the pockets.

SUPER-QUICK TEMPEH BURGER

These are square, rather than round, burgers. Round, seasoned tempeh burgers can be bought in most of the larger natural foods stores. If you use these seasoned burgers, omit the miso in this recipe.

A small amount of oil, as needed
2 ounces of tempeh
1 whole wheat English muffin
Miso or tamari

GARNISHES
A paper-thin slice of Bermuda onion
Good-quality prepared mustard
Prepared horseradish
Alfalfa sprouts
Slices of ripe tomato
Crisp leaves of lettuce
Pickle slices

Serves: 1
Time: 5–10 minutes

1. Heat the oil in a skillet and slowly cook the tempeh until it turns brown on one side. (If the tempeh is frozen, you can cook it without thawing.) Turn the tempeh over and cook it on the other side. Tempeh must be well cooked, so do not rush the cooking; keep the burner on medium-low.
2. Lightly toast the English muffin and spread one half with a very thin coat of miso. If you do not have miso, brush the tempeh with tamari instead.
3. Place the tempeh on the muffin and add your choice of garnishes.

HOT TOFU SANDWICH

Want something warm, nutritious, tasty, and *quick*? Try this!

1 large slice of tofu, about ½ inch thick
2 teaspoons miso, or less to taste
2 tablespoons tahini
1 tablespoon nutritional yeast
2 tablespoons hot water (approximately)
1 clove garlic, pressed (optional)
1 thick slice of whole grain bread
Chopped parsley

Serves: 1
Time: 5 minutes

1. Place the slice of tofu under the broiler of a toaster oven or regular oven. Broil for a few minutes, until it begins to brown. Turn tofu over and brown on the other side.
2. While the tofu is cooking, mix together the miso, tahini, and yeast. Slowly stir in enough water to make a sauce. Add the garlic, if desired, and mix well.
3. Place the bread under the broiler with the tofu and toast it on both sides.
4. Place the toast on a plate and top with the hot tofu. Pour the sauce over the sandwich. Garnish with chopped parsley, if desired.
5. Serve with a green salad.

PARMESAN EGG SANDWICH

Eggs play only a small role in my diet. However, about once a month I enjoy an egg dish like this easy and nourishing sandwich.

1 teaspoon oil
1 egg
2 tablespoons finely grated Parmesan cheese
2 slices whole grain bread, toasted
1 leaf romaine lettuce

Serves: 1
Time: 7 minutes

1. Heat the oil in a skillet. Break the egg into the pan and pierce the yolk with a fork. Sprinkle the Parmesan over the egg.
2. Cook for a minute or two and then turn over and cook until the Parmesan is golden brown.
3. Place the egg between two slices of whole grain toast and garnish it with the lettuce.

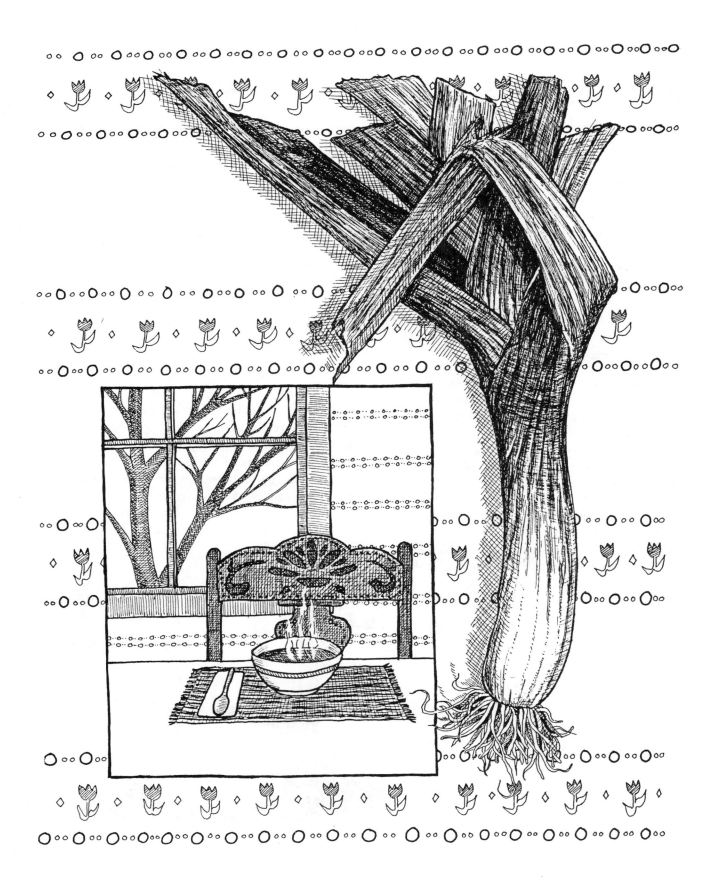

5. *BREADS, MUFFINS, & PIE CRUSTS*

Today, every health-conscious person knows the importance of eating good-quality bread. Nevertheless, it is rare to find someone who makes his or her own. Bread making is considered time-consuming, difficult, and ever-so-lightly mysterious (sometimes it works and sometimes it doesn't). However, with a better knowledge of the bread-making process, you will find that turning out a perfect loaf of whole grain bread is easier and less time-consuming than you may have imagined.

With whole wheat bread available in stores, you may not feel the need to make your own. However, there are advantages to making homemade bread:

- Truly good commercial breads are sometimes hard to find—and they are usually expensive.
- The quality of the ingredients used in making bread can be assured when it's homemade. We have the choice of buying organically grown grains instead of those that were produced by standard methods.
- Making our own bread allows us to use the freshest ingredients possible. The freshness of the ingredients used in bread making is very important. (Whole grain flours go rancid very quickly. Therefore, it is best to find a store that grinds its own whole grain flour. Buy it in small quantities and keep it in a sealed container in the refrigerator.)
- Making our own bread gives us more control over what ingredients and how much of them we use. Many commercial breads use more salt, sweetener, and oil than necessary—not to mention unnecessary ingredients such as dough conditioners and preservatives.
- No store-bought bread can compete with the delicious taste of a freshly baked loaf of home-

made bread. Until you know what it is, you do not know what you are missing.
- Once you understand the simple process of bread making, it becomes a very relaxing, satisfying, and almost therapeutic activity. The natural and rhythmic movement of kneading the dough is a meditative sort of procedure that seems to bring us closer in touch with our own true nature and our earthly roots.

The inset shows a sample bread recipe. For someone who understands bread making, this recipe provides more than enough information.

However, for the novice, most bread recipes are rather vague. Therefore, I have broken this recipe down and analyzed it in detail to give you an idea of the function of each ingredient and why each step is done. Also included are some tricks and tips that even the more experienced baker may find helpful. You should note that some of these breads call for gluten flour. This can be found in most natural foods stores.

Basic Bread, Analyzed

BASIC BREAD

½ cup warm water
Drop of honey
2 tablespoons dry active yeast
2 cups warm water
¼ cup oil
¼ cup honey
2 teaspoons sea salt
¼ cup gluten flour
7 cups whole wheat bread flour (approximately)

Yield: 2 loaves
Time: 3½ hours

1. Place the ½ cup of warm water, the drop of honey, and the yeast in a small bowl. Let this sit for 10 minutes to dissolve the yeast.
2. In a large bowl, mix together the 2 cups of warm water, oil, honey, salt, and the dissolved yeast mixture. Add the gluten flour and about 3 cups of the whole wheat flour. Beat with a wooden spoon for about 100 strokes. Add as much of the remaining flour as necessary to make a kneadable dough.
3. Turn the dough out onto a well-floured surface and knead in enough flour to make a smooth dough that is not sticky.
4. Place the kneaded dough in a large, oiled bowl. Oil the top of the dough. Cover the bowl with a clean, damp cloth and let it sit in a warm place until the dough doubles in bulk. Punch down.
5. Shape the dough into 2 loaves and place the loaves in 2 well-oiled loaf pans (4½ x 8½ x 2½ inches). Bake at 350° for 45 minutes.

THE INGREDIENTS

½ cup warm water: To dissolve the yeast. The water should not be hot or cold, but warm (around 100°F). If the water is too hot (120°F and over), it will kill the yeast, and if it is too cold, the yeast will work very slowly.

A drop of honey: Food for the yeast. Malt, maple syrup, molasses, rice syrup (yinnie syrup), or sorghum may be substituted for the honey.

2 tablespoons dry active yeast: The leavening agent. Yeast is a microorganism of vegetable origin. Dry active yeast is alive, but in a dormant state. Like all living things, yeast has certain needs that must be met before it can grow and flourish. Its needs are moisture, food, and warmth. When provided with these things, the sleeping yeast "wakes up" and rapidly begins to grow. As the yeast multiplies, it creates carbon dioxide. It is this gas that makes the bread rise.

Two tablespoons of yeast is equal to 2 packages. If you bake bread often, the least expensive way to buy yeast is in bulk at a natural foods store. Dry active yeast may be stored in the refrigerator for several months.

Fresh cake yeast may also be used in any bread recipe; in fact, most bakers prefer it. Some bakeries will sell fresh yeast if you ask for it. Its only disadvantage is that is doesn't store as well as dry active yeast. Fresh yeast may be kept in the refrigerator for 2 weeks, or in the freezer for 2 months. For 1 tablespoon of dry active yeast, substitute 1 small cake or 1 tablespoon of fresh yeast.

Do not try to substitute nutritional yeast, torula yeast, or brewer's yeast for bread yeast, because these yeasts are inactive.

Carrot, Raisin, and Oat Bran Muffin *(page 88)* with Sliced Almond Topping.

Scrumptious Corn Muffin *(page 89)* with Fresh Strawberry Jam.

From Left to Right, Luscious Whole Wheat *(page 92),* Oatmeal *(page 96),* and Peanut Butter *(page 96)* Pie Crusts.

Oatmeal Bread *(page 81)* Fresh from the Oven.

Raisin Cinnamon Swirl Bread *(page 76)* Makes Any Meal Special.

2 cups warm water: Bread is basically flour and water. The water holds the flour together. Make sure that the water is lukewarm (around 100°F).

¼ cup oil: Makes a more tender bread. If desired, however, the oil may be decreased or left out completely. The result will be slightly different, but the bread will still be good.

¼ cup honey: As stated above, honey is food for the yeast. If desired, you may decrease the amount of honey (or other sweetener) in this recipe to as little as 1 tablespoon, or increase it to as much as ⅓ cup, and still make a good loaf of bread.

2 teaspoons sea salt: Without salt, bread just doesn't taste right. It is very bland and seems to be missing something. However, if you are on a low-sodium diet and you wish to decrease or leave out the salt, you can.

¼ cup gluten flour: Gluten is the protein of the wheat. It is a sticky, elastic substance that helps you to make a light-textured bread that does not crumble when sliced. If you do not care for an especially light bread, you may leave out the gluten flour and still get excellent results.

7 cups whole wheat bread flour: Bread flour is a high-gluten flour, whereas pastry flour is a low-gluten flour. The quantity of flour can never be exact in a bread recipe due to factors such as the humidity in the air and the moisture content of the flour. For the best quality bread, use flour that is freshly ground from organically grown wheat.

NOTE: If you want your bread to rise as quickly as possible, all ingredients (except for the warm water) should be at room temperature.

THE METHOD

STEP 1

Place the ½ cup of warm water, the drop of honey, and the yeast in a small bowl. Let this sit for 10 minutes to dissolve the yeast.

This step is called proofing the yeast. The reason for proofing is that when yeast is old it becomes inactive. If we mix up a large batch of dough with inactive yeast, the result will be disappointing, to say the least. Therefore, to avoid this situation we can "check out" or proof the yeast before adding the other ingredients. If the yeast is active, it will foam up and begin to bubble after a few minutes. If it is inactive it will just sit

there. If this happens, throw it out and get some new yeast.

If you make bread regularly and you are sure that your yeast is good, this step may be omitted. In fact, it has been omitted in most of my recipes. However, if you want to play it safe, it is a good idea to always proof the yeast. If the recipe you are following does not call for proofing the yeast and you wish to proof it, just use ¼–½ cup of the water from the recipe along with a drop of honey. When the yeast has bubbled up, add it back to the recipe.

STEP 2

In a large bowl, mix together the 2 cups of warm water, oil, honey, salt, and the dissolved yeast mixture.

This is to combine the liquid ingredients and to make sure the salt is evenly distributed.

Add the gluten flour and about 3 cups of the whole wheat flour. Beat with a wooden spoon for about 100 strokes.

This is to activate the gluten. It will make the batter smoother and more elastic and help to make a lighter bread.

Add as much of the remaining flour as necessary to make a kneadable dough.

This will take about 2 cups of flour. When the dough is too stiff to stir and begins to pull away from the sides of the bowl it is ready to knead.

STEP 3

Turn the dough out onto a well-floured surface and knead in enough flour to make a smooth dough that is not sticky.

Sprinkle your work surface generously with flour (use at least ½ cup). Place the dough on the floured surface, then sprinkle the top of the dough very generously with more flour.

Now to work! Kneading should be done vigorously and rhythmically. Fold the dough towards you, then push it away. Give it a half turn, fold, and push. Turn, fold, push. Use your body weight to push into the dough and continue the movement, adding as much flour as necessary to keep the dough from sticking. (See Figure 5.1.)

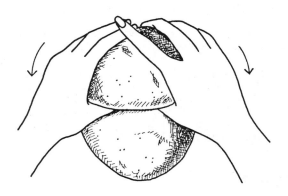

1. Fold the dough.

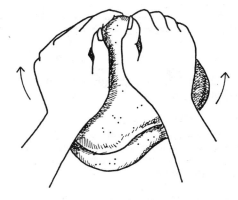

2. Push the folded dough away from you.

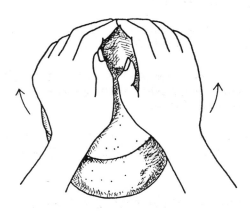

3. Fold the dough toward you.

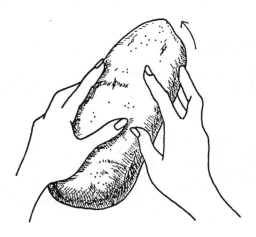

4. The kneaded dough.

Figure 5.1.   Kneading the Bread

A well-kneaded dough makes a light-textured bread that does not crumble when you slice it. When the dough can be kneaded without your having to add more flour, and it does not stick to the work surface or to your hands, it is almost ready. Continue kneading until the dough becomes very smooth and feels satiny (some people say that it feels like an ear lobe). A really good bread usually takes about 20 minutes of kneading. Yes, you can get by with 5–10 minutes of kneading, but the results will not be as good. Don't worry about overkneading; it is practically impossible by hand.

I hope you don't panic at the thought of so much kneading. It can be fun if you let it. Sometimes I put on lively music and knead to the music. If you really knead vigorously, you can get your heart and respiratory rate high enough to give yourself an aerobic workout!

STEP 4

Place the kneaded dough in a large, oiled bowl. Oil the top of the dough. Cover the bowl with a clean, damp cloth and let it sit in a warm place until the dough doubles in bulk.

Use the same bowl that you mixed the dough in. The bowl is oiled to keep the dough from sticking to it and the top of the dough is oiled to keep it from drying out. Covering the bowl with a damp cloth is also to keep the dough from drying out.

The ideal temperature for rising is about 85°F. Therefore, on a warm summer day, room temperature is perfect. However, if your house is cool, the dough will rise faster in a warm place. Some suggested places for letting the dough rise are: over a hot water heater, on top of a refrigerator, in front of a warm, sunny window, under a wood stove, etc. If you are careful not to overheat the dough, you can let it rise in the oven. To do this, turn the oven on as low as it will go for just a couple of minutes. Then turn the oven *off* and place the dough in it. A bowl of hot water in the oven will help to keep it warm without overheating. The main thing to remember is to *avoid putting the dough in a place that is too hot,* because it will kill the yeast. Yeast begins to die around 120° F.

The time required for dough to double in size depends on two things: the temperature of the place where it is rising, and the temperature of the ingredients. If your ingredients were at room temperature when you started to make the bread, and the dough is in an 85° F environment, it should take about 1 hour. However, if the ingredients were cold (just out of the freezer or refrigerator), the process can take up to 3 hours or more. If you place the dough in a cold environment (a cold room, or in the refrigerator) it can take 8 or more hours to double. This can be used to an advantage, if desired. (See "Bread Making for the Busy Cook" on page 74.)

Punch down.

This means just what it says. Hit your big, beautiful dough right in its middle with your fist and watch it fall.

After you have punched down the dough, you may let it rise in the bowl another time. This second rising is not necessary, but it does not hurt the dough; in fact, it seems to make a lighter bread. The dough should double in size in this second rising.

STEP 5

Shape the dough into 2 loaves and place the loaves in 2 well-oiled loaf pans.

When you shape the loaves it is important to get out all the air. Air bubbles left in the dough will make big holes in the bread. There are several ways to shape the dough into loaves. I will explain two of these methods below.

Method 1. Cut the dough into two portions of equal size. Flatten out each piece into a rectangular shape. Roll up the dough very tightly, like a jelly roll (see Figure 5.6.). Pinch together the seam (this will be the bottom of the loaf), then pinch together at each end to seal.

Method 2. Knead the dough for a couple of minutes to eliminate the air bubbles, then cut the dough into 2 portions of equal size. The cut side of the dough will make the bottom of the loaf, and the rounded side will be the top. Hold the dough with the bottom (cut side) facing down. Using both hands, stretch the sides of the dough to form a smooth and round top surface. Then tuck the stretched ends of the dough tightly under at the bottom of the loaf. Pinch together the bottom of the loaf to seal it. (See Figure 5.2.)

Oil the bread pans very generously with a good-quality vegetable oil. The pans that I use are 4½ x 8½ x 2½ inches. If desired, you may sprinkle the oiled pans with cornmeal or oatmeal. This makes the bread look nice, taste good, and helps to keep the loaves from sticking. Place the loaves in the pans.

Bake at 350°F for 45 minutes.

Bake the bread on the middle rack of the oven. After 45 minutes, remove one of the loaves from the pan and tap it on the bottom with your knuckles. If the bread sounds as if it were hollow, it is done. If you are still not sure, you may carefully take a slice from the loaf and examine it. If the bread is not done, place the loaf

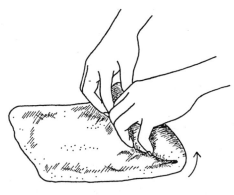

Method 1

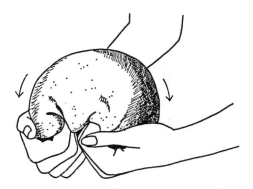

Method 2

Figure 5.2.   Shaping the Dough into Loaves

and the slice back in the pan, and bake for a few minutes more. When you become an experienced baker, you will be able to tell when your bread is done by its smell.

Remove the warm bread from the loaf pans and let it cool on a wire rack before wrapping it.

WHAT DID I DO WRONG?

Every beginning baker will occasionally have a less than perfect batch of bread. Please don't be discouraged, because this is how we learn. It is important, however, to know the reason for your "failure" to keep it from recurring. Listed below are some of the most common complaints of novice bakers and what causes them.

- A crumbly bread that falls apart when sliced.
  —The dough was not kneaded enough.
  —You used pastry flour instead of bread flour.
  —You were improvising and added too much of a low-gluten flour (such as barley flour, rice flour, or cornmeal) to your dough.

- A heavy bread.
  —Any bread that contains grains other than wheat will be heavier than a wheat bread. Sourdough breads are also relatively heavy. This does not mean that the bread is unsuccessful; some breads just have a heavy nature. In my opinion, the best bread you can eat is a hearty sourdough rye. The *Basic Bread* recipe on page 76 yields a very light, whole wheat bread when followed properly. If you have followed each step carefully, kneaded the dough well, and are still not satisfied with the results, try substituting unbleached white flour for half of the whole wheat flour.

- Bread that is too dry.
  —You kneaded too much flour into the dough.
  —You baked the bread too long, at too low a temperature.
  —For an especially moist bread, try the recipe for *Golden Squash Bread* (page 79).

- Sticky, over-moist bread.
  —The bread was not baked long enough.
  —The bread was left in the pans too long after baking.
  —The bread was stored in plastic bags while it was still hot.

- Bread that did not rise.
  —You forgot the yeast.
  —The yeast was old and inactive.
  —You killed the yeast by placing the dough in an environment that was too hot.
  —You killed the yeast by mixing it with water that was too hot.

  —The ingredients you used were cold and you just didn't wait long enough before mixing them.

- The bread rose well, but then fell during baking.
  —You let the dough rise too much before baking. (It should rise no more than double its size.)

- The bread rose and then fell over the sides of the pan like an enormous mushroom.
  —The dough was too soft. Add more flour the next time.

WHAT TO DO WITH A DOUGH THAT WILL NOT RISE

More than once, I have made up a big batch of bread dough, kneaded it for 20 minutes, and then realized that I forgot to add the yeast. If this ever happens to you, there are two ways to keep from wasting all that dough.

1. *Make chapatis*: Follow the recipe for rolling and cooking *Chapatis* (page 90). They are delicious, and they can be used in hundreds of ways. Chapatis may be frozen.

2. *Make pasta*. This works with any 100 percent wheat dough, but may not work with rye or multi-grain doughs. Follow the recipe for rolling, cutting, and cooking *Whole Wheat Egg Noodles*, page 208.

BREAD MAKING FOR THE BUSY COOK

REFRIGERATOR METHOD

If you are too busy to stay around the house waiting for dough to rise, but would still like to enjoy the pleasures of bread making, the refrigerator method for proofing the dough can come in very handy. It allows you to make a batch of bread dough, let it rise once, and then leave it unattended for several hours until you have the time to bake it.

Below are two schedules for making bread by this method; maybe one of them will work for you.

Morning Schedule

Make the bread dough the first thing in the morning. Let it rise once and then punch it down. Shape the dough into loaves. Oil the bread pans well, then sprinkle them with cornmeal or oatmeal. Place the loaves in the pans and sprinkle the top of the loaves with additional cornmeal or oatmeal (this will keep the dough from sticking). Place the loaves in plastic bags that are large enough to allow for the expansion of the dough. Close the bags with twist-ties and place them in the refrigerator. Make sure that the bags are not pulled tightly around the top of the loaves.

Now you may go away and forget about the dough for 8–10 hours. When you get home, remove the dough from the refrigerator and take it out of the plastic bags. It should be doubled in bulk. Place the dough in the oven and bake at 350°F for 45 minutes as usual. You will have fresh bread for dinner!

Evening Schedule

Make the bread dough a couple of hours before going to sleep at night. Let it rise once and punch it down. Shape the dough into loaves. Prepare the loaves for rising as indicated above, and let them rise all night while you sleep. When you wake up place the loaves in the oven and bake at 350°F for 45 minutes. You will have fresh bread for breakfast!

BASIC BREAD

½ cup warm water
Drop of honey
2 tablespoons dry active yeast
2 cups warm water
¼ cup oil
¼ cup honey
2 teaspoons sea salt
¼ cup gluten flour
7 cups whole wheat bread flour (approximately)

Yield: 2 loaves
Time: 3½ hours

1. Place the ½ cup of warm water, the drop of honey, and the yeast in a small bowl. Let this sit for 10 minutes to dissolve the yeast.
2. In a large bowl, mix together the 2 cups of warm water, oil, honey, salt, and the dissolved yeast mixture. Add the gluten flour and about 3 cups of the whole wheat flour. Beat with a wooden spoon for about 100 strokes. Add as much of the remaining flour as necessary to make a kneadable dough.
3. Turn the dough out onto a well-floured surface and knead in enough flour to make a smooth dough that is not sticky.
4. Place the kneaded dough in a large, oiled bowl. Oil the top of the dough. Cover the bowl with a clean, damp cloth and let it sit in a warm place until the dough doubles in bulk. Punch down.
5. Shape the dough into 2 loaves and place the loaves in 2 well-oiled loaf pans (4½ x 8½ x 2½ inches). Bake at 350° for 45 minutes.

NOTE: The inset on pages 70-75 analyzes this recipe for the benefit of the novice baker.

RECIPES USING BASIC BREAD DOUGH

With the recipe for *Basic Bread* it is easy to make all of the following variations. Each of these variations uses one-half of the recipe for *Basic Bread*. Therefore, you can have one regular loaf for sandwiches and toasting as well as one specialty bread.

RAISIN BREAD

½ recipe Basic Bread *dough*
³⁄₄–1 cup raisins

Yield: 1 loaf
Time: 3½ hours

1. Follow the *Basic Bread* recipe (see left column) up until the final rising.
2. Knead the raisins into the dough. Shape into a loaf. Let rise and bake as usual.

RAISIN CINNAMON SWIRL

½ recipe Basic Bread *dough*
³⁄₄–1 cup raisins
2 teaspoons cinnamon

Yield: 1 loaf
Time: 3½ hours

1. Follow the recipe for *Basic Bread* (see left column) up until the final rising. Knead the raisins into the dough.
2. After you have added the raisins roll the dough out into a ½-inch-thick rectangle. If you first let the dough rest for 10 minutes, this will be easier. Sprinkle the dough very generously with cinnamon.
3. Roll it up very tightly, like a jelly roll. Pinch together the edges. Let rise and bake as usual.

CHEESE ROLLS

½ recipe Basic Bread *dough*

1½ cups grated sharp Cheddar cheese

1 teaspoon paprika

Yield: 13–15 rolls
Time: 3½ hours

1. Follow the recipe for *Basic Bread* (page 76) up until the final rising.
2. Roll or press the dough into a rectangle that is approximately 10 x 15 inches. Sprinkle the cheese over the surface of the dough and then sprinkle with paprika. Roll the dough up very tightly and pinch together the edges to seal it. (See Steps 1 and 2 in Figure 5.3.)
3. Cut the roll of dough into pieces 1 inch thick and place them in a well-oiled 10-x-11-inch cast iron skillet or well-oiled shallow baking dish (about 7 x 11 inches). (See Steps 3 and 4 in Figure 5.3.) Cover the rolls lightly with a damp cloth and let them rise until they double in bulk. Bake for 20–25 minutes at 350°F.

DELICIOUS ONION ROLLS

½ recipe Basic Bread *dough*

1 tablespoon oil

2½ cups chopped onion

½ teaspoon sea salt

1 teaspoon basil

½ teaspoon oregano

½ teaspoon thyme

2 tablespoon dry onion flakes (optional; for extra flavor)

Yield: 13–15 rolls
Time: 3½ hours

1. Follow the recipe for *Basic Bread* (page 76) up until the last rising.
2. Heat the oil in a skillet. Add the onion, salt, basil, oregano, and thyme. Sauté the onions until they are very tender and have been re-

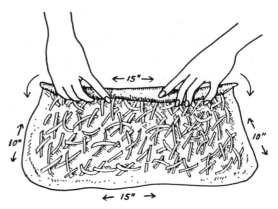

1. Roll up the dough.

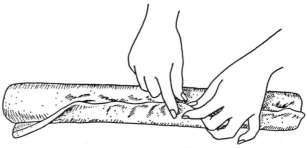

2. Pinch the edges.

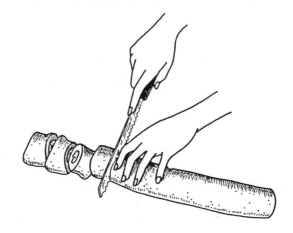

3. Cut the dough into 1-inch pieces.

4. Place the rolls in a skillet.

Figure 5.3   Making Rolls

duced in size. Let cool to lukewarm.

3. Roll or press the dough into a rectangle that is approximately 10x15 inches. Spread the sautéed onion mixture evenly over the surface of the dough. Sprinkle with the 2 tablespoons dry onion flakes, if desired. (Refer to Step 1 in Figure 5.3.) Roll the dough up very tightly and pinch together the edges to seal it, as seen in Step 2.

4. Cut the roll of dough into slices 1 inch thick (see Step 3) and place them either in a well-oiled cast iron skillet that is 10 inches in diameter or larger, (see Step 4), or in a shallow baking dish (about 7 x 11 inches). Cover the rolls with a damp cloth and let them rise until they double in bulk. Remove cloth and bake at 350°F for 20–25 minutes.

SESAME CLOVERLEAF ROLLS

½ recipe Basic Bread *dough*

⅓ cup sesame seeds (or more as needed)

Yield: 12 large rolls
Time: 3½ hours

1. Follow the recipe for *Basic Bread* (page 76) until the final rising.

2. Cut the dough into 36 pieces of equal size. Cover the pieces of dough with a damp cloth to keep them from drying out. Remove one piece of dough at a time and roll it into a ball. Roll each ball in sesame seeds and place it in a well-oiled muffin tin. (Make sure to oil around the top of the muffin tin because the rolls will rise over the sides.)

3. Place 3 balls of dough in each muffin cup. Cover with a damp cloth and let rise until double in bulk. Bake the rolls at 350°F for 20 minutes.

CINNAMON-PECAN STICKY ROLLS

½ recipe Basic Bread *dough*

¾ cup raisins

2 teaspoons cinnamon

3 tablespoons oil

1 cup chopped pecans

¼ cup plus 2 tablespoons malt syrup

Yield: 13–15 rolls
Time: 3½ hours

1. Follow the recipe for *Basic Bread* (page 76) up until the final rising.

2. Knead the raisins into the dough. Cover the dough with a damp cloth and let it rest for 10 minutes.

3. Roll or press the dough into a rectangle that is approximately 10x15 inches. Sprinkle the surface of the dough with cinnamon; then drizzle it with 2 tablespoons of malt. Roll the dough up very tightly and pinch together the edges to seal it. (See Steps 1 and 2 in Figure 5.3.) Cut the roll of dough into pieces 1 inch thick, as in Step 3.

4. Oil the sides and the bottom of a 10- or 11-inch cast iron skillet with the 3 tablespoons of oil. Sprinkle the nuts over the bottom of the pan. Drizzle the malt over the nuts. Place the pieces of dough on top.

5. Cover the rolls with a damp cloth and let them rise until they double in bulk.

6. Remove the cloth and bake at 350°F for 20–25 minutes. Loosen the rolls from the sides of the pan with a knife and turn them out onto a plate to serve.

GOLDEN SQUASH BREAD

This is one of my favorite yeast breads because it is light and moist.

2 cups grated winter squash or pumpkin (raw)
2 cups hot water
¼ cup honey
¼ cup oil
1 tablespoon sea salt
2 tablespoons dry active yeast
¼ cup gluten flour
7¼ cups whole wheat bread flour (approximately)

Yield: 2 loaves
Time: 3½ hours

1. In a large bowl, mix together the grated squash, hot water, honey, oil, and salt. Add the yeast and let it sit for about 10 minutes (until the yeast is dissolved).
2. Add the gluten flour and 1½ cups of the bread flour. Beat 100 strokes. Gradually stir in enough of the remaining flour to make a kneadable dough.
3. Turn the dough out onto a generously floured surface and knead in enough of the remaining flour to make a smooth, elastic, and nonsticky dough. (To make a really good bread, this dough needs about 20 minutes of kneading.)
4. Place the dough in a lightly oiled bowl. Turn the dough over to oil the top and cover with a damp cloth. Let the dough rise until doubled in bulk. Punch down. If desired, let the dough rise a second time and punch down.
5. Shape the dough into 2 loaves. Place the loaves in well-oiled bread pans. Let the loaves rise until they double in bulk, then bake at 350°F for 50 minutes. Remove the bread from the pans and let it cool on wire racks.

BREAD CRUMB BREAD

This economical bread has a very good texture. It is a great way to use up stale bread.

3 cups warm water
3 tablespoons dry active yeast
¼ cup honey
¼ cup oil
1 tablespoon sea salt
2 cups whole grain bread crumbs
½ cup gluten flour
8 cups whole wheat bread flour (approximately)

Yield: 2 large loaves
Time: 3½ hours

1. Mix together the first 6 ingredients. Let the mixture sit for about 15 minutes.
2. Add the gluten flour and enough of the bread flour to make a kneadable dough. Knead in enough of the remaining flour to make a smooth and not-too-sticky dough. This should take at least 10 minutes of kneading.
3. Place the dough in an oiled bowl, cover with a damp towel, and let it rise in a warm place until it has doubled in bulk. Punch down.
4. Shape the dough into 2 loaves. Place the loaves in oiled loaf pans and let them rise till doubled in bulk. Bake at 350°F for 45–50 minutes.

POTATO BREAD

Potato Bread is good for making sandwiches because it slices well and the loaves are large. This recipe is also a good way to use up leftover mashed potatoes.

2 cups water left over from cooking potatoes
1½ cups unseasoned mashed potatoes, at room temperature
3 tablespoons dry active yeast
2 tablespoons honey
¼ cup oil
2 teaspoons sea salt
⅓ cup gluten flour
7–8 cups whole wheat bread flour

Yield: 2 large loaves
Time: 3½ hours

1. If the water from the potatoes is cold, heat it to lukewarm. If it is hot, let it cool to lukewarm. If you do not have enough water from cooking the potatoes, add plain water to yield 2 cups. Pour the water into a large bowl.
2. Add the mashed potatoes, yeast, and honey to the water. Let the bowl sit for about 10 minutes to dissolve the yeast.
3. Add the oil, salt, gluten flour, and about 2 cups of the whole wheat flour. Mix well and beat about 100 strokes. Add enough of the remaining flour to make a kneadable dough.
4. Turn the dough out onto a floured surface and knead in enough of the remaining flour to make a dough that is smooth, firm, and not sticky. For best results, knead for about 20 minutes.
5. Place the kneaded dough in a large, oiled bowl. Oil the top of the dough and cover it lightly with a damp cloth. Let it rise in a warm place until it has doubled in bulk. Punch down. If desired, let the dough rise a second time. If not, shape it into 2 loaves for the final rising.
6. Place the loaves in well-oiled bread pans and let them rise in a warm place until they double in bulk. Bake at 350°F for 55 minutes. Remove the bread from the pans and let it cool on racks.

VARIATION

- If you prefer smaller loaves of bread, divide the dough into 3 small loaves rather than 2 large ones. Bake the small loaves for 45 minutes.

AVOCADO BREAD

Avocado replaces the oil in this bread.

1 cup mashed ripe avocado (at room temperature)
¼ cup honey
2 cups warm water
2 tablespoons dry active yeast
1 tablespoon sea salt
7½ cups whole wheat bread flour (approximately)

Yield: 2 loaves
Time: 3½ hours

1. Mix together all the ingredients except for the whole wheat bread flour. Let the mixture sit for 10 minutes.
2. Stir in enough flour to make a kneadable dough. Turn the dough out onto a floured surface, and knead in enough of the remaining flour to make a smooth dough that is not sticky. Knead the dough for at least 10 minutes.
3. Place the dough in an oiled bowl. Cover it with a damp cloth and let it rise in a warm place until it has doubled in bulk. Punch down. Let the dough rise a second time, if desired; then punch it down again.
4. Shape the dough into 2 loaves. Place the loaves in oiled loaf pans, and let them rise until doubled in bulk. Bake at 350°F for 45 minutes. Remove bread from pans and cool on racks before storing.

NOTE: ¼ cup gluten flour may be added to this dough if desired. It should be added along with the first batch of bread flour.

OATMEAL BREAD

A moist and subtly sweet version of the basic bread recipe that is well-liked by children.

1½ cups rolled oats
2 cups boiling water
½ cup warm water
2 tablespoons dry active yeast
⅓ cup honey
¼ cup oil
2 teaspoons sea salt
⅓ cup gluten flour
5–6 cups whole wheat bread flour

Yield: 2 loaves
Time: 3½ hours

1. Place the oats in a large bowl and pour the boiling water over them. Let the oats sit for about 10–15 minutes, or until they are warm, rather than hot.
2. While the oatmeal mixture is cooling, place ½ cup of warm water in a smaller bowl. Add the yeast and a drop of the honey. Let this sit for about 10 minutes to dissolve the yeast.
3. Add the remaining honey, the oil, the salt, and the gluten flour to the bowl with the oat mixture. Mix well and add the dissolved yeast.
4. Add about 1 cup of the bread flour and beat 100 strokes. Gradually stir in enough of the remaining flour to make a kneadable dough.
5. Turn the dough out onto a generously floured surface and knead in enough of the remaining flour to make a smooth, elastic dough that is not sticky. Place the dough in an oiled bowl. Cover the bowl with a damp cloth and let the dough rise until it has doubled in bulk. Punch down.
6. Shape the dough into 2 loaves. Oil 2 bread pans and sprinkle them with some dry oats. Place the loaves in the pans and let them rise in a warm place until they double in bulk.
7. Bake at 350°F for 45 minutes. Remove the loaves from the pans and let them cool on a wire rack.

VARIATION

- *Sunflower Oatmeal Bread*: Follow the recipe for *Oatmeal Bread* with the following addition: After the bread has risen once, punch it down and knead in 1 cup of sunflower seeds. Shape the dough into loaves, allow it to rise, and bake as indicated in the recipe.
- *Oatmeal Raisin Bread*: Follow the recipe for *Oatmeal Bread* with the following addition: After the bread has risen once, punch it down and knead in 1 cup of raisins. Shape the dough into loaves, allow it to rise, and bake as indicated in the recipe. This makes a very sweet bread for breakfast or for peanut butter sandwiches.

QUICK YEAST ROLLS

Somewhere between a roll and a muffin, these are very easy to make and have a light, spongy texture.

1 cup milk, water, or soymilk
2 tablespoons dry active yeast
3 tablespoons honey
2 tablespoons oil
2¼ cups whole wheat pastry flour

Yield: 12 rolls
Time: 1½ hours

1. If you are using milk, scald it and then let it cool to lukewarm. If you are using water, just use warm tap water. If you are using soymilk, just heat it to lukewarm—do not scald it.
2. Place the lukewarm milk, water, or soymilk in a large bowl and add the remaining ingredients. Beat with a wooden spoon until the batter is well mixed.
3. Generously oil 12 muffin tins and fill them halfway with the batter. Set the tins in a warm place and let the batter rise until it has reached the top of the tins. Bake at 350°F for 20 minutes.

   Serve warm or at room temperature. These yeast rolls are good for breakfast, or with a soup or salad.

EGG BATTER BREAD

A crusty, no-knead bread with an airy texture. If you are in a hurry, this bread can be made with only one rising, and it is still very good. Just place the batter directly in the oiled bread pan. Let it rise and bake as described below.

1 cup warm water
2 tablespoons dry active yeast
2 tablespoons honey
2 tablespoons oil
1 teaspoon sea salt
3 eggs
3 cups whole wheat bread flour

Yield: 1 loaf
Time: 3 hours

1. Combine the water, yeast, and honey in a bowl. Let the mixture sit for 10 minutes to dissolve the yeast.
2. Put this mixture in a food processor with a blending attachment, or use an electric mixer. Add the oil, salt, eggs, and 1 cup of the flour. Blend well. Gradually add the remaining flour until the batter achieves the consistency of a thick cake batter or a quick bread batter. Stop adding flour and continue to mix the batter for 3–5 minutes longer. This will activate the gluten in the flour.
3. Slowly add as much of the remaining flour as your food processor or mixer can handle. Transfer the batter to a large bowl and add the remaining flour. Use your hands to mix. Cover the bowl with a damp cloth and let the dough rise in a warm place until it has doubled in bulk. Stir the batter down.
4. Pack the dough into a well-oiled and floured bread pan. With wet hands, pack it down and smooth out the top.
5. Let the dough rise until doubled in bulk. Bake at 350°F for 45 minutes.

SOURDOUGH STARTER

In my opinion, the hearty Old World flavor of dark and pungent sourdough bread surpasses even the fanciest pastries or croissants.

2 cups whole wheat or rye flour
2 cups warm water
1 tablespoon dry active yeast
1 clove garlic

Yield: 3 cups
Time: 3 minutes to prepare; 3–4 days to ferment.

1. Mix together all the ingredients in a glass, ceramic, or plastic container. Make sure that the container is large enough to allow the mixture to double without overflowing. Cover the container with a cloth or a piece of plastic that has a hole punched in it.
2. Let the mixture sit in a warm place for 3–4 days. A good place to let the starter ferment is on top of a hot water heater or refrigerator. It should bubble up and fall several times. It should also begin to emit a sour but pleasant aroma. If the starter turns pink or orange, or develops an unpleasant odor, throw it away and start again.
3. After 3–4 days of fermentation, the starter is ready to use. Discard the garlic and use the starter according to your chosen recipe. If you are unable to use the starter immediately, store it in the refrigerator. After one week of storage, the starter should either be used, or fed to keep it active.

    To feed the starter, just mix in a little flour and water (about ½ cup of each). Let the starter sit out of the refrigerator for a few hours. The older a starter gets, the better it becomes, so it is worth it to keep it going.
4. Each time that you use some of your starter, replace it with more flour and water. For example, if you use 1 cup of starter, add about ½ cup of flour and ½ cup of water to replace it. Let the starter sit in a warm place for 3–4 hours before returning it to the refrigerator.

SOURDOUGH RYE

One of the easiest, most healthful, and delicious breads you can make. Don't expect something light and fluffy—this bread is rich and satisfying.

1 cup Sourdough Starter (See page 82)
1 cup warm water
2 tablespoons molasses (or another sweetener)
1 teaspoon sea salt
2 tablespoons oil (optional)
2 cups whole wheat bread flour
2 cups whole rye flour (approximately)
Cornmeal or rolled oats

Yield: 1 loaf
Time: 20–30 minutes to prepare; 8 hours to rise; 1 hour to bake.

1. In a large bowl, mix together the sourdough starter, water, sweetener, salt, oil, and wheat flour. Slowly stir in enough of the rye flour to make a kneadable dough.
2. Turn the dough out onto a tabletop or countertop that has been generously sprinkled with some of the remaining rye flour. Knead in enough of the remaining rye flour to make a dough that is smooth, firm, and not sticky. Take your time, because this bread really profits from a long and thorough kneading.
3. Shape the dough into a loaf and place it in a well-oiled bread pan. To keep the bread from sticking, sprinkle the oiled pan with cornmeal or rolled oats.
4. Place the loaf in a warm place. Cover it lightly with a damp cloth and let it rise for about 8 hours. To keep the cloth from sticking to the dough, sprinkle the top of the loaf with a light coat of additional cornmeal or rolled oats. When the dough has risen enough for baking it will be almost double in bulk.
5. Bake at 350°F for 1 hour. Remove the bread from the pan and let it cool on a rack before storing.

VARIATIONS

- *Caraway Rye*: Knead 1 tablespoon of caraway seeds into the dough.
- *Wheatless Rye*: Omit the whole wheat flour and use only rye flour. A heavier but very flavorful bread will be the result.

SOURDOUGH ENGLISH MUFFINS

½ cup Sourdough Starter (See page 82)
1 cup warm water
1 tablespoon dry active yeast
2 tablespoons oil
2 tablespoons honey
1 teaspoon sea salt
3½ cups whole wheat bread flour (approximately)
¼ cup cornmeal

Yield: 12 muffins
Time: 2 hours

1. Mix the first 6 ingredients together in a large bowl. Let the mixture sit for 10 minutes to dissolve the yeast.
2. Add enough of the flour to make a kneadable dough. Turn the dough out onto a floured surface and knead in as much flour as necessary to make a smooth, elastic dough that is not sticky. Knead for at least 10 minutes.
3. Place the kneaded dough in an oiled bowl. Oil the top of the dough and cover the bowl with a clean damp cloth. Place it in a warm

place and let the dough rise until it has doubled in bulk. Punch down. If desired, you may let the dough rise (and punch it down) a second time.

4. Cut the dough into 12 equal-sized pieces. To shape the muffins, roll each piece of dough into a ball and then flatten it out to a thickness of about ½ inch.

5. Place the muffins on a surface that has been sprinkled with cornmeal; then sprinkle more cornmeal over the tops of the muffins. Let the muffins rise until they double in bulk.

6. Using a spatula, carefully pick up the muffins one at a time and place them in a heavy, unoiled skillet. Cook 3 muffins at a time in the skillet over medium-low heat for 5–7 minutes on each side.

7. To serve, split the muffins in half using a fork. Toast if desired.

VARIATIONS

• English muffins may also be made using the recipe for *Potato Bread* (page 80). Make one or two loaves of regular bread, and shape the remaining dough into English muffins.

• If desired, add ½–1 cup of raisins and 1 teaspoon of cinnamon to the above recipe. Add the cinnamon with the flour and knead the raisins into the dough after the first rising.

PUMPERNICKEL BAGELS

A better bagel would be hard to find.

1 cup warm water
1 tablespoon honey
1 tablespoon dry active yeast
1 teaspoon sea salt
1 tablespoon carob powder
3 eggs
3 cups whole wheat bread flour
2 cups whole rye flour (or less)
2 quarts water
½ teaspoon sea salt
1 egg, beaten with 1 tablespoon water
Caraway, poppy, or sesame seeds

Yield: 12 bagels
Time: 3 hours

1. Mix together the warm water, honey, yeast, salt, and carob powder in a large bowl. Let the mixture sit for 10 minutes to dissolve the yeast.

2. Beat in three eggs. Add the wheat flour and enough of the rye flour to make a kneadable dough.

3. Knead the dough on a floured surface for about 10 minutes. Knead in enough of the remaining rye flour to make a dough that is smooth, elastic, and not too sticky.

4. Place the dough in an oiled bowl. Lightly oil the top of the dough and cover the bowl with a damp cloth. Let the dough rise in a warm place until it has doubled in bulk. Punch down.

5. Knead the dough briefly and then cut it into 12 pieces of equal size. Roll each of the 12 pieces of dough into a ¾-inch-thick strand that is about 6–7 inches long. Pinch the ends of the strand firmly together to form a round bagel (roll out and shape one piece of dough at a time, keeping the others covered with an inverted bowl so they will not dry out).

6. Place the shaped dough on a lightly floured surface in a warm place and cover lightly with a damp cloth. Let the bagels rise until they have doubled in bulk.

7. Place the 2 quarts of water and the ½ teaspoon of salt in a large kettle. Bring to a boil. Carefully pick up the bagels one by one with a spatula and drop them into the boiling water. Boil about 3 bagels at a time for about 3–4 minutes. Turn the bagels over once during the boiling.

8. Pick up the boiled bagels one at a time with a large slotted spoon and place them on a well-oiled cookie sheet.

9. Brush the bagels with the beaten-egg-and-water mixture and sprinkle them with your choice of seeds. Bake at 400°F for 20 minutes.

SLOW-COOKING SPOON BREAD

This spoon bread is especially tender and moist. It is also easy to make. You will need, however, an electric slow cooking pot and an ovenproof container that will fit inside the pot.

1 cup cornmeal
2 teaspoons baking powder
1/2 teaspoon sea salt
2 cups corn, cut off the cob
1 cup buttermilk
2 eggs
1 tablespoon honey or malt syrup
1 cup grated sharp Cheddar cheese

Serves: 4
Time: 2 hours, 45 minutes

Food Processor Method: Place all the ingredients in a food processor and blend.

1. Pour the batter into a lightly oiled ovenproof dish that will fit inside a slow-cooking pot. If you have a tall slow-cooking pot, a 2-pound coffee can will do. In my slow cooker I use a ceramic bowl that is large enough to hold the batter (with about 1 inch of extra space on top). A stainless steel bowl would also work well.
2. Cover the bowl containing the batter with a piece of aluminum foil. Be careful to leave 1–2 inches of space above the batter, because the bread will rise slightly. Poke a few holes into the foil with a fork.
3. Cover the pot with its lid and cook on high heat for 2–2 1/2 hours, or until the bread is set.

Blender Method: In a large bowl, mix together the cornmeal, baking powder, and salt.

1. Place the corn, buttermilk, eggs, and honey in the blender and blend them together. Pour this mixture over the cornmeal mixture. Add the grated cheese and beat just enough to mix well.

2. Then, pour the batter into a lightly oiled, ovenproof dish that will fit inside your slow-cooking pot. Continue to follow directions 1–3 above.

SOUTHERN CORNBREAD

1 1/2 cups cornmeal
1/2 cup whole wheat pastry flour
2 teaspoons baking powder
1/2 teaspoon salt
2 eggs
1/4 cup oil
1 cup buttermilk

Serves: 4–6
Time: 30 minutes

1. Preheat the oven to 375°F. In a medium-sized bowl, mix together the cornmeal, flour, baking powder, baking soda, and salt.
2. In a large bowl, beat together the eggs, oil, and buttermilk. Add the flour mixture to the liquid mixture. Beat just enough to blend well; don't overbeat.
3. Pour the batter into a well-oiled, 9-inch cast iron skillet. To make cornbread with a very crisp crust, heat the oiled skillet in the oven for 3 minutes before pouring in the batter. Bake at 375°F for 20 minutes, or until the center is done.

   Serve hot. A traditional Southern-style meal would consist of cornbread, beans (pinto or black-eyed peas), and some sort of cooked green, such as collards, turnip greens, or kale.

VARIATION

• Add 1 cup of corn cut off the cob and 1 cup grated sharp Cheddar cheese to the batter. Mix well and bake as usual.

ZUCCHINI-PARMESAN QUICK BREAD

A moist and rich loaf that is delicious served with soup or salad.

2 eggs
1/2 cup oil
1/3 cup milk
1 1/2 cups grated zucchini (lightly packed)
2 cups whole wheat pastry flour
3 teaspoons baking powder
3/4 cup grated Parmesan cheese

Yield: 1 loaf
Time: 1 hour, 15 minutes

1. Beat together the eggs, oil, and milk. Add the zucchini and mix well.
2. Sift together the flour and baking powder. Add the Parmesan cheese and mix well.
3. Stir the dry ingredients into the liquid ingredients. Beat just enough to mix well; don't overbeat.
4. Place the dough in an oiled and floured loaf pan. Bake at 350°F for 1 hour, or until a toothpick inserted in the center of the loaf comes out clean. Remove the bread from the pan and let it cool on a wire rack before slicing.

VARIATION

• Use 3/4 cup grated Romano cheese instead of Parmesan in the above recipe.

WHEATLESS ONION QUICK BREAD

Surprisingly light and moist, with a sweet onion flavor.

1 tablespoon oil
2 cups chopped onion
1 cup rolled oats
1 cup brown rice flour
1 cup whole rye flour
3 teaspoons baking powder
1/2 teaspoon baking soda
1/2 teaspoon sea salt
1/4 cup oil
3 eggs
3/4 cup water
1 teaspoon cider or rice vinegar

Yield: 1 loaf
Time: 1 hour, 15 minutes

1. Heat 1 tablespoon of oil in a skillet. Add the onions and sauté over low heat until they are tender. Set aside.
2. Grind the oats in a blender to make a fine flour. Sift together the oat flour, rice flour, rye flour, baking powder, baking soda, and salt.
3. In a large bowl, beat together the 1/4 cup of oil, the eggs, the water, and the vinegar. Stir the flour mixture into the liquid mixture and beat just enough to mix well. Fold in the onions.
4. Transfer the batter to a well-oiled and floured bread pan. Bake at 350°F for 50-55 minutes, or until a toothpick inserted into the center of the loaf comes out clean. Let the bread cool on a rack for at least 15 minutes before slicing.

KENTUCKY HOE CAKES

An old Kentucky hill recipe that my mother still makes a few times a week. *Fresh Corn Cakes* on page 148 is a delicious variation of this recipe.

1 cup cornmeal
2 teaspoons baking powder
¼ teaspoon sea salt
1 egg, beaten
1¼ cups buttermilk

Yield: About 15 small cakes
Serves: 4–6
Time: 12 minutes

1. In a medium-sized bowl, mix together the cornmeal, baking powder, and salt.
2. Add the egg and mix well; then add the buttermilk and beat until the batter is no longer lumpy.
3. Heat a small amount of oil in a skillet. Drop the batter by the heaping tablespoon onto the skillet and cook the cakes over medium-high heat until they turn golden brown on the bottom. Turn the cakes over and brown on the other side.
4. Serve hoe cakes in place of bread. For a real Southern country-style dinner, serve them with pinto beans or black-eyed peas and some cooked collards, kale, spinach, or turnip greens.

BANANA-DATE MUFFINS

Bananas and dates sweeten these muffins.

1½ cups whole wheat pastry flour
3 teaspoons baking powder
1 teaspoon cinnamon
½ cup chopped walnuts
1 cup chopped pitted dates
1 cup bananas, mashed (2 medium)
⅓ cup oil
2 eggs
1 teaspoon lemon juice
½ cup soy milk

Yield: 12 muffins
Time: 30 minutes

1. Sift together the flour, baking powder, and cinnamon. Add the nuts and dates. Mix well.
2. Beat together the bananas, oil, eggs, lemon juice, and milk. Stir the dry ingredients into the wet ingredients. Beat just enough to mix; don't overbeat.
3. Spoon the batter into well-oiled and floured muffin tins.
4. Bake at 350°F for 18-20 minutes, or until a toothpick inserted into the center of a muffin comes out clean.

CARROT, RAISIN, AND OAT BRAN MUFFINS

1 cup whole wheat pastry flour
1 cup oat bran
3 teaspoons baking powder
2 teaspoons cinnamon
1 cup raisins
¼ cup oil
1 egg
1¼ cup apple juice
1 cup grated carrots

Yield: 12 muffins
Time: 25 minutes

1. Mix together the flour, bran, baking powder, and cinnamon. Add the raisins and mix again.
2. In another bowl, beat together the oil, egg, apple juice, and carrots. Add the dry ingredients to the wet ingredients. Beat just enough to blend.
3. Spoon the mixture into oiled and floured muffin tins. Bake at 350°F for 15 minutes or until a toothpick inserted into the center of a muffin comes out clean.

CRANBERRY MUFFINS

1½ cups whole wheat pastry flour
3 teaspoons baking powder
½ cup maple syrup
2 tablespoons oil
2 eggs
¼ cup milk or soymilk
1 teaspoon vanilla
1 cup whole cranberries
½ cup chopped pecans

Yield: 12 small muffins
Time: 25 minutes

1. Sift together the flour and baking powder.
2. In a separate bowl, beat together the maple syrup, oil, eggs, milk, and vanilla.
3. Stir the dry ingredients into the liquid ingredients. Beat enough to blend well, but don't overbeat. Fold in the cranberries and the pecans. Spoon the mixture into well-oiled muffin tins.
4. Bake at 350°F for 15 minutes, or until a toothpick inserted into the center of a muffin comes out clean.

APPLE, DATE, AND OATMEAL MUFFINS

Sweetened with fruit.

1½ cups whole wheat pastry flour
½ teaspoon cinnamon
Pinch of cloves
3 teaspoons baking powder
½ cup rolled oats
1 cup chopped pitted dates
⅓ cup oil
2 eggs
⅓ cup water or milk
¾ cup grated apple (1 medium apple)

Yield: 12 muffins
Time: 30 minutes

1. Sift together the flour, spices, and baking powder. Add the rolled oats and dates and mix well.
2. In a separate bowl, beat together the oil and the eggs. Beat in the milk, then add the apple. Mix well.
3. Stir the flour mixture into the wet mixture. Beat just enough to mix; don't overbeat.
4. Spoon the batter into well-oiled muffin tins. Bake at 375°F for 20 minutes.

CORNY CORN MUFFINS

Subtly sweet, with both fresh corn and cornmeal.

1 cup cornmeal
1 cup whole wheat pastry flour
2 teaspoons baking powder
1 teaspoon baking soda
1 egg
¼ cup oil
¼ cup maple syrup
1 cup buttermilk
½ cup raisins or currants
1 cup corn, cut off the cob

Yield: 12 muffins
Time: 30 minutes

1. In a large bowl, mix together the cornmeal, flour, baking powder, and baking soda.
2. In a separate bowl, beat together the egg, oil, and maple syrup. Add the buttermilk and mix well.
3. Add the dry mixture to the wet mixture. Beat enough to blend, but don't overbeat. Fold in the raisins or currants and the corn.
4. Spoon the mixture into muffin tins that have been oiled and lightly floured. Fill the tins about three-quarters full. Bake at 375°F for 20 minutes. These muffins are especially good served hot.

EGGLESS BANANA MUFFINS

These muffins are soft, moist, and not too sweet.

2½ cups whole wheat pastry flour
2 teaspoons baking powder
2 teaspoons baking soda
1 cup mashed bananas (2 small bananas)
1 teaspoon vanilla
¼ cup honey
½ cup mashed tofu
½ cup chopped walnuts or pecans
½ cup water or milk (approximately) (See note below.)

Yield: 12 large muffins
Time: 30 minutes

1. Sift together the flour, baking powder, and baking soda.
2. Place the bananas, vanilla, honey, and tofu in a blender or food processor. Blend until smooth and creamy.
3. Stir the flour mixture into the cream mixture. Fold in the nuts and add the water or milk. Mix well, but do not overbeat.
4. Spoon the mixture into oiled and floured muffin tins. The tins should be about three-quarters full. Bake at 375°F for 20 minutes, or until a toothpick inserted into the center of a muffin comes out clean.

NOTE: The amount of liquid depends on the consistency of the tofu. If you are using a very firm tofu, it may be necessary to add a little extra liquid. This is supposed to be a rather thick batter, so be careful not to add too much liquid.

GARLIC TOAST

Instead of using butter to make garlic bread, try this. It is better for you, and it's so good!

¼ cup olive oil
6–8 cloves garlic, pressed
2 teaspoons tamari
1 tablespoon finely minced parsley (optional)
10–12 slices whole grain bread

Yield: 10–12 slices
Time: 10 minutes

1. In a small bowl, mix together the oil, garlic, tamari, and parsley.
2. Spread the mixture over sliced whole grain bread. Toast for a minute or two under the broiler or in a toaster oven.
3. Serve hot with soup, vegetable-based main dishes, or salad.
   You may store this garlic mixture in a small covered container in the refrigerator and use it as needed.

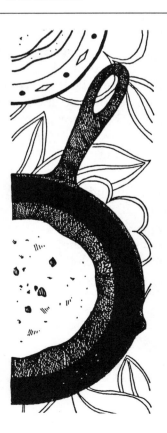

CHAPATIS

These East Indian flat breads are very simple to make. Use them with curries and Indian-style food, as flour tortillas with Mexican food, or as a good basic bread when you want to change from the ordinary.

1 cup water
½ teaspoon sea salt
2½ cups whole wheat bread flour (approximately)

Yield: 10–12 chapatis
Time: 50 minutes

1. Place the water and salt in a large bowl. Gradually stir in enough of the flour to make a kneadable dough.
2. Turn the dough out onto a well-floured surface and knead in enough flour to make it smooth and not sticky. This should take about 5–10 minutes of kneading.
3. Cover the dough with an inverted bowl and let it rest for about 30 minutes. (This is not absolutely necessary, but it makes the dough easier to roll out.)
4. Cut the dough into 10–12 pieces of equal size. Shape each piece of dough into a ball; then press the ball between your hands to flatten it out. Place each flattened ball of dough on a floured surface and sprinkle the top with a little additional flour. Using a rolling pin, roll out each piece of dough until it is very thin (about ¹⁄₁₆ of an inch thick). As you roll the chapatis, try to keep them as round as possible.
5. Heat an unoiled skillet. One by one, cook the chapatis over medium-high heat for about 1 minute on each side. As the chapatis are cooking, use a clean dishtowel to press them firmly down against the bottom of the skillet. This will make them puff up. The chapatis are done when they are lightly flecked with dark brown all over.
6. Stack the cooked chapatis on a plate and cover them with a clean towel to keep them warm.

ESSENE BREAD

This is the wonderful, sticky, sweet, cake-like bread that is sold in natural foods stores, usually in the freezer section. It is rather expensive to buy, but it's cheap to make. If you have a food processor and an electric slow-cooking pot, it is really easy.

2 cups soft wheat berries
1/2–1 cup raisins

Yield: 1 round loaf
Time: 2–3 days to sprout wheat; 15 minutes to prepare; cooks unattended for 10 hours.

1. Sprout the wheat for 2–3 days (see the inset on pages 124–125 for how to sprout grains).
2. Place the wheat sprouts in a food processor. With the blending blade, grind them to a thick paste. Using a spatula, scrape the sides of the food processor occasionally to make sure that all of the wheat gets ground up. Any grains that are left whole will become hard when the bread bakes, so take care to grind them well.
3. Remove the sticky dough from the processor. Place it in a bowl and mix in the raisins. Using your hands, shape the dough into a ball. If the dough is too sticky to handle, lightly flour your hands.
4. Oil a small, ovenproof plate. Sprinkle the plate generously with cornmeal or rolled oats to keep the bread from sticking. Place the loaf on the plate and place the plate in an electric slow-cooking pot. Cover and cook on low for 10 hours. Enjoy—it is sweet and delicious!

VARIATIONS

• Substitute rye sprouts for the wheat sprouts; use other dried fruit in place of the raisins, or omit the fruit altogether; add a pinch of cinnamon and ground cloves if desired.

HERB CROUTONS

1/4 cup olive oil
3–4 cloves garlic, pressed
1/4 teaspoon sea salt
6 slices whole grain bread (you can use stale bread)
1 teaspoon basil
1/2 teaspoon oregano
1/2 teaspoon thyme
1 teaspoon dried parsley
1 tablespoon dried chives

Yield: 4 cups
Time: 30 minutes

1. In a small bowl mix together the olive oil, garlic, and salt. Brush both sides of each slice of bread with the oil mixture. Cut the bread into 1/2-inch cubes and bake on a cookie sheet at 300°F for 15–20 minutes or until dry.
2. Remove the croutons from the oven and mix them with the herbs. Replace them in the oven and bake at 375°F until they are crusty and golden (about 10 minutes). Stir the croutons once or twice during the last 10 minutes of baking to make sure that they brown evenly.
3. Allow the croutons to cool before placing them in containers that can be kept tightly sealed in the refrigerator. These croutons will enliven the flavor of soups and salads.

VARIATION

• *Parmesan Croutons*: Follow the instructions given above, but add 1/4 cup of grated Parmesan cheese along with the mixed herbs.

PIE CRUSTS

A good pie crust is the foundation of a good pie. A crisp and tender crust is easy to achieve with whole wheat pastry flour and unrefined vegetable oil. Therefore, if you use fresh, wholesome ingredients in your filling, it would be a shame to spoil it by using saturated fat and white flour in the crust.

When you become adept at making pie crusts it opens the door to an entire range of possibilities for creative cooking. A whole grain crust is marvelous not only with desserts but with quiches and other main-dish-type pies as well.

Here are a few tips for making successful pie crusts.

- Mix your dough just enough to blend the ingredients, because too much handling will activate the gluten in the flour and make the crust tough.
- If the dough appears too dry to hold together, sprinkle it with water as you are rolling it out.
- If the dough appears too moist, sprinkle it with flour as you are rolling it out.
- To make a round crust with an even thickness, be careful not to roll in only one direction. Roll back and forth, from side to side, and diagonally.

WHOLE WHEAT PIE CRUST

1½ cups whole wheat pastry flour
⅓ cup oil
¼ cup hot water

Yield: 1 double 9-inch crust
Time: 15 minutes to prepare; baking time depends on type of filling used.

1. Place the flour in a medium-sized bowl. Measure the oil and the hot water into a smaller bowl. Do not mix. Slowly pour the oil and water over the flour, mixing with a fork as you pour. Mix just enough to form a dough that will hold together; don't overmix. Divide the dough into 2 portions, one piece slightly larger than the other.
2. Place the larger piece of dough between two sheets of wax paper and roll it out. Lightly sprinkle your work surface with water to keep the paper from slipping.
3. Carefully peel off the top sheet of paper. Pick the dough up by the corners of the bottom paper and place it (paper side up) in the pie pan, as in Step 1 of Figure 5.4. Carefully peel off the paper as seen in Step 2. Fill the crust with the desired filling and roll out the remaining dough. Cover the pie with the top crust. Flute the edges (see Step 3) and cut some holes in the top crust to allow the steam to escape (see Step 4). Bake according to the directions given in the filling recipe you choose.

Proportions for 1 double 11-inch crust:

2¼ cups whole wheat pastry flour
½ cup oil
⅓ cup hot water

Follow the above directions.

POTATO PIE CRUST

This crust is tender, easy to roll out, and has a delicious flavor. You can use this crust for either a 9- or 10-inch pie. A 9-inch crust will be thick, but light and delicious.

1 cup unseasoned mashed potatoes, at room temperature
¼ cup oil
1 cup whole wheat pastry flour
1 teaspoon baking powder
¼ teaspoon sea salt
1 tablespoon or more of water, if needed

Yield: 1 single 9- or 10-inch crust
Time: 15 minutes to prepare; baking time depends on the type of filling used.

1. Whip together the potatoes and oil, using wire whisk or fork.

2. Mix together the flour, baking powder, and salt. Add the flour mixture to the potato mixture. Using a fork or your hands, blend the two mixtures together. Do not overwork. If the dough is too dry to hold together, gradually add a little water. (If your mashed potatoes are fairly moist, you will not need to add any water. However, if they are dry, slowly sprinkle water onto the dough until it is moist enough to hold together.)

3. Roll the dough out onto a piece of wax paper. Sprinkle the counter or tabletop with a few drops of water to keep the paper from slipping, and sprinkle the dough with flour to keep the rolling pin from sticking.

4. Pick up the dough by the edges of the paper and place it (paper side up) in a pie plate (see Step 1 of Figure 5.4). Carefully peel off the paper as in Step 2. Flute the edges of the pie crust (see Step 3) and fill and bake according to the recipe of your choice.

1. Pick up the dough by holding on to the corners of the bottom sheet of wax paper.

2. Carefully peel off the paper.

3. Flute the edges.

4. Cut holes in the top crust to allow steam to escape.

Figure 5.4. Placing the pie crust in the pan

PARMESAN PIE CRUST

A flavorful crust to use with a quiche or vegetable pie. Do not choose a recipe that takes more than 50 minutes to bake when using this crust, because it browns rather fast.

1 cup whole wheat pastry flour
¹/₃ cup grated Parmesan cheese
¹/₄ cup oil
2 tablespoons water (approximately)

Yield: 1 single 9-inch crust
Time: 15 minutes to prepare; baking time depends
     on type of filling used.

1. Mix together the flour and cheese. Slowly stir in the oil; mix with a fork until the oil is incorporated into the flour mixture. Stir in enough water to make a dough that will hold together.
2. Press the dough between your hands to make it hold together and then place it between two sheets of wax paper. Roll out the dough between the wax paper. Sprinkle your work surface with water to keep the paper from slipping.
3. Peel off the top paper. Pick the dough up by the corners of the bottom paper and place it (paper side up) in a 9-inch pie pan (refer to Step 1 of Figure 5.4). Carefully peel off the paper as in Step 2. Flute the edges of the crust (Step 3). Fill and bake according to the recipe of your choice.

VARIATION

*   Use ¹/₃ cup grated Romano cheese instead of Parmesan.

QUICK BREAD CRUMB CRUST

Use this easy crust for any kind of egg or tofu quiche.

2 tablespoons oil
1¹/₂–2 cups fine whole grain bread crumbs (to make fine-textured bread crumbs, grind in a blender)

Yield: 1 single 9-inch crust
Time: 5 minutes to prepare; baking time depends
     on type of filling used.

1. Using 2 tablespoons of oil, generously oil a 9-inch pie pan or 7-x-11-inch casserole dish. Firmly and evenly press the crumbs (1¹/₂ cups for the pie pan, or 2 cups for the baking dish) against the oiled surface.
2. Fill and bake according to the quiche recipe that you are using. The filling will hold the crust together when it is baked.

COCONUT PIE CRUST

Good 'n' easy.

¾ cup whole wheat pastry flour
½ cup rolled oats
½ cup finely shredded unsweetened coconut
¼ cup oil
2 tablespoons water, or as needed

Yield: 1 single 9-inch crust
Time: 25 minutes to prepare and bake.

1. Place the flour, oats, and coconut directly in a 9-inch pie pan. Mix well.
2. Slowly stir in the oil. Mix with a fork to evenly distribute the oil. Gradually stir in enough water to make the mixture hold together when pressed.
3. Press the dough against the sides and bottom of the pie pan. Poke some small holes in the sides and bottom of the crust with a fork to keep it from puffing up.
4. Bake at 375°F for 20 minutes, or until the crust is light brown.

Proportions for 1 single 10-inch crust:

1 cup whole wheat pastry flour
¾ cup rolled oats
½ cup finely shredded unsweetened coconut
5 tablespoons oil
2 tablespoons water, or as needed

Yield: 1 single 10-inch crust
Time: 25 minutes to prepare and bake.

Using these proportions, follow the instructions given above.

VARIATION

• Add 1 teaspoon of cinnamon.

PRESS-IN PIE CRUST

If you don't like to roll out pie crusts, try this one. It is good for quiches and pies that do not need top crust.

1 cup whole wheat pastry flour
¼ cup oil
3 tablespoons water (approximately)

Yield: 1 single 9-inch crust
Time: 10 minutes to prepare; 15–20 minutes to bake.

1. Place the flour in a 9-inch pie pan. Gradually stir in the oil. Mix with a fork until the oil is incorporated into the flour. When the oil is thoroughly mixed in, gradually stir in enough water to make a dough that will hold together when you press it.
2. Using your hands, press the dough evenly against the sides and the bottom of the pan. Take care to nicely flute the edges of the crust (see Step 3 of Figure 5.4). If the crust is to be baked before it is filled, poke little holes in the sides and bottom with a fork. If it is to be filled before it is baked, this is not necessary.
3. Bake according to the filling recipe or at 375°F for 15–20 minutes, until light brown.

OATMEAL PIE CRUST

1 cup whole wheat pastry flour

½ cup rolled oats

¼ cup oil

2 tablespoons water, or as needed

Yield: 1 single 9-inch crust
Time: 25 minutes to prepare and bake.

1. Place the flour and rolled oats directly in a 9-inch pie pan. Mix well.
2. Slowly stir in the oil. Mix with a fork to evenly distribute the oil. Gradually stir in enough water to make the mixture hold together when pressed.
3. Press the dough against the sides and bottom of the pie pan. Poke some small holes in the sides and bottom of the crust with a fork to keep it from puffing up.
4. Bake at 375°F for 20 minutes, or until the crust is light brown.

VARIATION

•   Add 1 teaspoon of cinnamon.

PEANUT BUTTER PIE CRUST

This crust is great with the *Peanut Butter Cream Pie* on page 259. It is also good with any of the banana or carob pies in this book.

¾ cup whole wheat pastry flour

¾ cup peanut butter

3 tablespoons maple syrup

1–2 tablespoons of water, or as needed

Yield: 1 single 9-inch crust
Time: 25 minutes to prepare and bake.

1. Place the flour and the peanut butter in a large bowl. Using a fork or your hands, incorporate the peanut butter into the flour to form crumbs. Stir in the maple syrup and mix well.
2. Slowly stir in enough water to make the mixture hold together well. Transfer the dough to a 9-inch pie pan and press it evenly against the sides and bottom of the pan. Flute the edges of the crust (see Step 3 of Figure 5.4). and poke holes all over the bottom and sides to keep it from puffing up.
3. Bake at 375°F for 15–20 minutes, or until brown.

MAPLE PECAN PIE CRUST

This is similar to the *Oatmeal Pie Crust* and the *Coconut Pie Crust*, but is slightly sweet and a little bit fancier. This crust is especially good with *California Date and Orange Pie* (page 259), *Strawberry Pie* (page 258), and *Carob Cream Pie* (page 262).

1 cup whole wheat pastry flour
½ cup pecans
½ cup rolled oats
¼ cup oil
2 tablespoons maple syrup

Yield: 1 single 9-inch crust
Time: 35 minutes to prepare and bake.

1. Place the whole wheat flour in a 9-inch pie pan. Place the pecans and the oats in a blender and grind to a powder. Combine the pecan-oat mixture with the flour in the pie pan and mix well.
2. Slowly stir in the oil. Mix with a fork until the oil is thoroughly incorporated into the flour mixture.
3. Stir in the maple syrup; mix just enough to blend well and form a dough that will hold together when pressed.
4. Press the dough in an even thickness against the sides and bottom of the pie pan. Poke little holes in the sides and bottom of the crust with the tines of a fork, to keep the crust from puffing up as it bakes.
5. Bake at 375°F for 20–25 minutes or until golden brown. Let the crust cool before filling.

PAPER-THIN PASTRY DOUGH

This dough will keep for about 4–5 days in the refrigerator, and it can be rolled out and filled with all sorts of stuffings. Be creative and see what you can come up with.

1¾ cups whole wheat pastry flour
½ teaspoon sea salt
2 tablespoons olive oil
½ cup water

Yield: Dough for sixteen to eighteen 3-inch-square pastries
Time: 45 minutes

1. Sift together the flour and salt. Incorporate the oil, using your hands to mix. Slowly stir the water into the flour mixture.
2. Turn the dough out onto a lightly-floured surface and knead until it is firm and elastic, adding more flour if necessary. The kneading should take 3–5 minutes. Cover the dough with an inverted bowl and let it rest for half an hour.
3. Roll out the dough and fill as indicated in *Marie-Hélène's Spinach Pastries,* page 109.

6. APPETIZERS, DIPS, & SPREADS

Spreads and patés have the ability to lead a double life. They can be the most practical of practical foods when sandwiched between two slices of whole grain bread and carried to work or to school in a brown paper bag. However, with a different presentation, the very same recipe can be quite at home in an atmosphere of gastronomic elegance.

Take, for example, the *Olive and Almond Paté* on page 105. Spread it thickly between two slices of whole grain bread, top it with a slice of tomato and a handful of alfalfa sprouts, and you have a good, quick lunch. However, if your desire is for something a little fancier, slice the chilled paté into diamond shapes. Place each diamond on a small leaf of fresh, curly lettuce. Top it with a sprig of parsley, surround it with some tiny wedges of cherry tomatoes and some thin tamari-glazed rice crackers, and you have an elegant appetizer.

Many of the spreads in this book can also be used as dips. With a bit of adjusting, even some of the recipes in the chapter—such as *Soyannaise* (page 133), *Tofu-Blue Cheese Dressing* (page 133), and the *Avocado-Yogurt Dressing* (page 134)—can be made into dips. Except for the *Soyannaise*, these dressings will have to be thickened. Do this either by adding more of the firmly textured ingredients or less of the liquid ones.

As I have said so many times before, don't be afraid to experiment. Play around with the recipes. Change a particular type of dish into something different. There is not really much that can go wrong, but there is a lot that can be gained in the way of confidence and artistic pleasure.

TOFU-RED PEPPER SPREAD

The attractive orange color of this spread is so bright that it almost looks artificial!

1 cup mashed tofu
1 small or 1/2 large red pepper
1/3 cup cashews
1/4 cup chopped onion
1 tablespoon yellow miso
1 tablespoon Dijon mustard

Yield: About 1 1/2 cups
Time: 10 minutes

Mix together all the ingredients in a blender or food processor until smooth and creamy. The mixture will thicken slightly when it is chilled. If the spread is too thick, add about a tablespoon of water (as needed); if it is not thick enough, add a little more tofu or cashews.

Use this spread for sandwiches or on rice cakes topped with alfalfa sprouts. It also makes a great dip to serve with crackers or raw veggies.

SAVORY PEANUT SPREAD

Who made the rule that peanut butter sandwiches must be sweet? Here is a spread that is quick to make, nourishing, and a tasty change from peanut butter and jelly.

1/4 cup unsalted peanut butter
1/3 cup minced celery
1/4 cup grated carrots
1/2 teaspoon barley miso
1 clove garlic, pressed (optional)
2-3 tablespoons water, as needed

Yield: Enough for 2 sandwiches
Time: 10 minutes

1. Combine all the ingredients, except for the water, in a small bowl. Mix well. Gradually stir in enough water to make a good spreading consistency.
2. Make sandwiches on whole grain toast or bread and garnish them with lettuce.

BABA GANOUI

This is a traditional Middle Eastern spread or dip made from eggplant.

1 medium eggplant
1/4 cup tahini
2 tablespoons lemon juice, or to taste
1 or more cloves garlic, pressed
1/4 cup minced parsley
1/2 teaspoon sea salt
2 scallions, finely chopped
1 tablespoon olive oil

Yield: Approximately 1 1/2 cups
Time: 1 hour, 15 minutes to prepare; 1 hour to chill.

1. Wash the eggplant and, with a fork, pierce holes all over it.
2. Place the eggplant on a baking sheet and bake it at 350°F for about 1 hour or until it is very soft. Let the eggplant cool for easier handling; then cut it in half and scoop out the flesh. Place the pulp in a medium-sized bowl.
3. Add the remaining ingredients. Mix well and chill.

    Serve with bread (pita bread will provide an authentic flair) or crackers.

VARIATION

- *Vitamin B Spread:* Follow the recipe for *Baba Ganoui*, substituting 2 tablespoons tamari (or to taste) for the sea salt and adding 1/4 cup nutritional yeast to the recipe. This variation yields about 1 1/2 cups of spread.

QUICK TOFU SPREAD

A light but nourishing spread that takes only a few minutes to prepare.

½ cup mashed tofu
1 teaspoon miso (dark barley miso or rice miso is good)
1 tablespoon tahini
1 tablespoon grated onion
¼ cup finely minced celery
1 teaspoon nutritional yeast

Yield: Enough for 1 large sandwich
Time: 5 minutes

Place all the ingredients in a small bowl and mix them together well. Spread on whole grain bread, or use to stuff a whole grain pita. Garnish your sandwich with alfalfa sprouts or lettuce.

VARIATION

- Grated carrots, diced pickles, finely chopped red or green pepper, etc., may be added either in place of or in addition to the celery.

MALTED PEANUT SPREAD

This spread is delicious on toast or mochi.

2 tablespoons good-quality peanut butter
1 teaspoon malt syrup
1½ tablespoons water or fruit juice (approximately)

Serves: 1–2
Time: 5 minutes

Mix together the peanut butter and the malt syrup in a small bowl. Stir vigorously while slowly adding enough water to achieve the desired consistency.

VARIATION

- *Date-Peanut Spread:* Substitute 2 or 3 finely chopped dates for the malt.

MEXICAN SANDWICH SPREAD

Use this spread as a filling for sandwiches or as a dip to serve with corn chips.

1 cup cooked and drained red kidney beans
¼ cup tomato paste
1 tablespoon tamari, or to taste
1 tablespoon lemon juice, or to taste
1 teaspoon basil
1 teaspoon cumin
1 teaspoon chili powder
⅓ cup finely chopped Bermuda onion
2 stalks celery, finely chopped

Yield: 2 cups
Time: 10–15 minutes

Blend together all the ingredients, except the onion and celery, in a blender or food processor. Add the chopped vegetables. Mix well and chill.

For a delicious sandwich, stuff a whole wheat pita pocket with Mexican spread, chopped tomatoes, and shredded lettuce.

Entertaining

Entertaining should be no problem for the vegetarian. It is easy to assemble an outstandingly beautiful table using only wholesome vegetarian foods. Fruits and vegetables, with their exquisite forms and colors, are naturally attractive. When you arrange them to enhance this beauty, the results can be spectacular.

Be creative with the way you display your food. A pumpkin shell makes a great soup tureen, and a hollowed-out melon becomes a bowl for fruit salad. Use flowers, baskets, and whatever else you like to make your table a splendid presentation of nature's gifts.

Specialty bread can create an enticing center of interest. A large impressive braided loaf, hot rolls in various shapes and sizes, garlic breadsticks, and crispy crackers will be admired by everyone. Serve them with dips, spreads, and assorted cheeses.

Savory individual pastries, as well as small wedges of quiches, are always appreciated. Jellied salads and aspics in fancy molds also add appeal.

Don't forget the desserts. A party is the time to go all out. See Chapter 12 for scrumptious desserts that are attractive and not too rich.

Maybe you are already convinced that it is possible to make a great party or buffet serving only vegetarian food. But what about your guests? Most of them are probably not vegetarians—and more than likely, they have not tasted this kind of food before.

This can actually make your party even more fun. There will be endless topics for conversation and lots of questions. Your guests might not know what they are eating, but they are sure to enjoy it. Well-prepared vegetarian food is so good that I have yet to meet someone who did not appreciate a vegetarian buffet (and I've given many).

As more and more people are becoming concerned with health and fitness, rich, heavy food is not as popular as it once was. You may be surprised at how enthusiastically your light and wholesome fare is received. Your guests can have meat and other rich food whenever they wish. However, the occasion to sample a wonderful array of healthful, homemade delicacies is a rare treat. Your guests will love it, and they'll probably be raving about your party for weeks!

GUACAMOLE

1 cup mashed avocado
3 tablespoons lemon juice
2 cloves garlic
1/2 cup finely chopped tomato (1 small)
1/3 cup finely chopped green pepper (1/2 small)
2 tablespoons finely minced onion
1/2 teaspoon cumin
Pinch of cayenne

Serves: 2–4
Time: 10 minutes

1. Place the avocado, lemon juice, and garlic in a blender and blend until smooth. (If you do not have a blender, place the avocado in a medium-sized bowl and mash it with a fork. Press the garlic in a garlic press. Mix the pressed garlic and lemon juice with the avocado.)

2. Place the blended mixture in a medium-sized bowl; add the remaining ingredients and mix well.

Serve as an accompaniment to Mexican-style dishes or other bean dishes.

Tasty Vegetable Paté *(page 104)* for That Special Occasion.

Gorgeous Guacamole *(page 102)* Offers a Touch of Tex-Mex.

Virginia's Cheese Yummies *(page 107)* Will Be a Surprise Treat for Your Guests and Family.

Festive Appetizers Made with Tofu–Red Pepper Spread *(page 100)* and Quick Tofu Spread *(page 101)*.

PARSNIP PATÉ

1 cup parsnips, sliced and scrubbed
½ cup raw cashews
1 cup cooked millet
½ cup mashed tofu
2 tablespoons minced onion
1 teaspoon basil
2 tablespoons minced parsley
½ cup celery, chopped
1 tablespoon water (use the water from cooking the parsnips)
1½ tablespoons shoyu or tamari
1 tablespoon olive oil

Serves: 6–8 as an appetizer
Time: 35 minutes

1. Cook the parsnips in a small amount of water or steam until tender. Drain the cooked parsnips, reserving the water, and mash.
2. Grind the cashews to a powder in the blender.
3. Mix together the millet, tofu, onion, basil, and parsley in a bowl. Add the mashed parsnips and the ground cashews. Mix well.
4. Place the celery, water, shoyu or tamari, and olive oil in a blender and blend to a pulp. Add the celery purée to the bowl containing the millet mixture. Mix well, using your hands if necessary.
5. Mold the paté into an attractive shape directly on a lettuce-covered serving platter. Garnish with parsley sprigs, cherry tomatoes, etc.

    This paté is good served with crackers or bread. It may also be served on a bed of mixed greens and raw veggies as a complete meal salad.

ALMOND BUTTER

A rich and delicious spread to use on bread, rice cakes, or crackers. It is better to use a blender than a food processor in this recipe, because a food processor does not grind the nuts finely enough.

1½ cups raw unblanched almonds
4 tablespoons oil (approximately)

Serves: 1 cup
Time: 25–30 minutes

1. Roast the almonds in a 350°F oven for 20 minutes or until toasted, stirring occasionally.
2. Place ⅓–½ of the nuts at a time in the blender and grind. Slowly add enough oil to make a thick paste. Blend to the desired consistency. Repeat with the remaining nuts.

    Store in the refrigerator.

VARIATION

- Substitute peanuts, cashews, or pecans for the almonds. If using peanuts, do not roast them unless they are raw.

SPROUTED HUMMUS

Hummus is a Middle Eastern specialty. This recipe is a slightly revised version of the original. Sprouting the chick peas before cooking them makes the hummus easier to digest. It also gives it a lighter color and texture. The inset on pages 124-125 has information on growing your own sprouts, and pages 184-186 have information on cooking peas and beans. Of course, if you do not wish to use sprouted beans, you may use regular cooked chick peas with this recipe instead.

2 cups chick peas that have been sprouted for 3 days and cooked until tender, or 2 cups cooked chick peas
1/2 cup tahini
2 tablespoons olive oil
1/3 cup lemon juice, or less to taste
2–3 cloves garlic
1/2 teaspoon sea salt
Liquid from cooking chick peas, as needed
2 tablespoons minced parsley

Yield: Approximately 2 cups
Time: 15 minutes

Food Processor Method:
1. Place all the ingredients (except for the liquid from cooking the chick peas and the parsley) in a food processor. Blend until smooth. If the mixture is too thick (as it probably will be) add as much cooking liquid as needed to achieve the desired consistency.
2. Add the parsley and mix well. Place in a bowl and chill before serving.

Blender Method:
1. Place 1 cup of the chick peas and the remaining ingredients (except for the liquid from cooking the chick peas and the parsley) in a blender. Blend until smooth. Gradually add the remaining chick peas. If the mixture becomes too thick to blend, add enough of the cooking liquid to achieve the desired spreading consistency.
2. Add the parsley and mix well. Place in a bowl and chill before serving.

    Serve with bread or crackers. For a great sandwich, stuff a pita bread with hummus, alfalfa sprouts, and sliced tomatoes. For delectable cañapés, generously spread small cut-out shapes of toasted whole grain bread with hummus, top with a slice of black olive, and sprinkle with minced parsley.

VEGETABLE PATÉ

A mild and not-too-rich paté to serve with crusty whole grain bread. If you are unable to obtain millet flour, you can grind your own in a blender.

2 1/2 cups grated sweet potato (about 1 medium potato)
2 1/2 cups water
2 tablespoons oil
1/4 cup chopped onion
1 teaspoon tarragon
1 teaspoon basil
Pinch of cayenne
1 cup sunflower seeds
1/4 cup tamari
2 tablespoons nutritional yeast
1/4 cup millet flour

Serves: 6
Time: 1 hour

1. Blend together all ingredients in a blender or food processor until smooth. In a food processor this can be done in one operation. However, in a blender it will have to be done in about 3 batches, because the ingredients won't fit into the blender container at the same time.
2. Pour the mixture into a well-oiled and lightly floured 11-x-17-inch baking dish. Bake at 350°F for 40 minutes or until set. Chill before serving. The paté will become firmer when cool. Cut into squares to serve.

1. Place the sunflower seeds in an unoiled skillet and stir constantly over medium-high heat until they become lightly toasted.
2. Place the toasted seeds in a blender along with the oil and the salt. Blend until smooth and creamy.

OLIVE AND ALMOND PATÉ

The taste, texture, and appearance of this paté resemble the French *paté de foie gras*.

1 can (6 ounces) pitted black olives
1 cup water
½ cup almonds
1 tablespoon tamari, or more to taste
½ cup chopped onion
¼ cup whole wheat pastry flour
½ teaspoon thyme
½ teaspoon sage

Serves: 6
Time: 1 hour

1. Blend together all the ingredients in a blender until very smooth. Pour the mixture into an oiled 8-x-8-inch cake pan.
2. Bake at 350°F for 45 minutes or until set. Chill before serving. Cut into squares and garnish with sprigs of parsley.

    Serve with hot, crusty whole grain bread, or with crackers.

SUNFLOWER BUTTER

1½ cups sunflower seeds
4 tablespoons oil
¼ teaspoon sea salt

Yield: 1 cup
Time: 15 minutes

TAMARI ALMONDS

A great party snack.

1½ cups whole raw almonds
2 tablespoons tamari or shoyu

Yield: 1½ cups
Time: 50 minutes

1. Place the almonds in a shallow bowl and sprinkle them with the tamari or shoyu. Stir and let sit for about 30 minutes, stirring from time to time.
2. Place the almonds on an unoiled cookie sheet and bake at 350°F for 20 minutes, removing them from the oven to stir occasionally. The almonds will become crisp as they cool. Let them cool completely before storing them in an airtight container in the refrigerator.

The Visual Presentation of Food

To illustrate the importance of attractively presenting the food one serves, I would like to relate an amusing incident that happened at a cooking class party. At the end of every twelve-week session of cooking lessons, I would have each student bring a dish that he or she prepared at home. Together, we would sample all of these wonderful vegetarian recipes. At one particular dinner almost everyone in the class was in accord about what they thought was the best dish. It was a rather unusual molded vegetable paté. It had a very good flavor and texture, but above all, the dish was presented in a manner that made it visually beautiful. Set on an elegant platter and exquisitely garnished with just the right complementary colors of decoratively carved fresh vegetables, this dish was so tastefully presented that it was truly outstanding.

The cook who was responsible for this superb creation was inordinately humble as everyone raved over her dish. She was also a bit hesitant to tell us exactly how she made it. By the end of the evening, the poor woman was so embarrassed by the praise she was receiving that she broke down and told us the secret of her marvelous recipe. It was a mistake. She had been trying to make a soufflé!

UNCOOKED ALMOND PATÉ

This paté is easy to make, and it lends itself to a very attractive presentation.

1 cup whole raw almonds
1 cup whole grain bread crumbs
1/2 cup mashed tofu
1/2 red bell pepper, diced
1 stalk celery, chopped
1 or more cloves garlic, to taste
2 tablespoons tamari or shoyu
3 tablespoons nutritional yeast
1/2 teaspoon sage
1/2 teaspoon thyme
GARNISH
Thin slices of red pepper
Strips of celery and carrot
Sprigs of parsley

Serves: 6–8 as an appetizer
Time: 15–20 minutes to prepare; 2 hours to chill.

1. Grind the almonds to a very fine meal in a blender. Put the ground almonds and the bread crumbs in a large bowl and mix.
2. Blend together the tofu, pepper, celery, garlic, and tamari in the blender.
3. Place the tofu-vegetable cream in the bowl with the almond-bread crumb mixture. Add the yeast, sage, and thyme. Mix well, using your hands if necessary.
4. Lightly oil an appropriate-sized bowl or mold for the paté. Decorate the sides and bottom of the bowl or mold with strips of red pepper, celery, carrot, and sprigs of parsley.
5. Firmly press the paté into the mold, taking care to keep the garnish in place. If the garnish veggies come higher up in the mold than the paté, just cut off the excess. Chill for at least 2 hours.
6. Unmold the paté onto a serving platter. Make an interesting arrangement of crackers and crisp breads around the platter for an impressive presentation.

This paté is also good as a sandwich filling. Generously spread it on whole grain bread or toast and top with alfalfa sprouts, lettuce, or watercress. It will keep in the refrigerator for at least a week.

VIRGINIA'S CHEESE YUMMIES

Crisp and savory little pastries that resemble cookies in appearance, these were a big hit at a cooking class party.

2 cups grated sharp Cheddar cheese
2 cups whole wheat pastry flour
1 teaspoon sea salt
¼ teaspoon celery seed
¼ teaspoon paprika
½ cup oil
50 pecan halves

Yield: Fifty 1-inch pastries
Time: 25 minutes

1. Place the grated cheese, flour, salt, celery seed, and paprika in a large bowl. Toss lightly with a fork until evenly mixed.
2. Gradually stir in the oil. Stir just enough to mix well, but do not overmix.
3. Shape the dough into small balls. Place each ball on an unoiled cookie sheet. Press a pecan half into each "cookie," flattening out the dough to a ½-inch thickness as you press.
4. Bake at 350°F on the lower rack of the oven for 7 minutes, then bake for 7 minutes more, or until golden brown, on the top rack. Let cool, then store in an airtight container.

ADZUKI-MISO SPREAD

This spread is good with whole grain bread or crackers.

2 cups cooked adzuki beans
2 tablespoons barley miso
2 tablespoons lemon juice
⅓ cup tomato paste
1 teaspoon basil
Liquid from cooking beans, as needed

Yield: 2 cups
Time: 10 minutes

Food Processor Method: Place all ingredients (except for the cooking liquid) in a food processor. Blend till smooth. Add a little of the liquid from cooking the beans, if necessary, to achieve the desired consistency.

Blender Method: Place 1 cup of the beans and the remaining ingredients (except for the cooking liquid) in a blender. Blend until smooth and gradually add the remaining beans. Gradually add liquid as needed to blend and to achieve the desired consistency.

Nori-Maki

This colorful and traditional Japanese dish is not at all difficult to make.

1 cup short grain brown rice
2½ cups water
4 sheets nori
2 tablespoons brown rice vinegar
1 small carrot, scrubbed and cut into thin matchsticks
½ cucumber, cut into matchsticks (peel if waxed)
Shoyu or tamari

Serves: 4–6
Time: 1 hour

1. Wash the rice and place it in a kettle with the water. Cover and bring to a boil. Lower the heat and simmer for about 40 minutes, or until the water is absorbed.
2. While the rice is cooking, briefly toast the nori until it becomes green. This may be done over the burner of a gas stove, a candle, or the burner of an electric stove turned on high. Hold the nori by the edge and quickly pass it over the heat until it turns a dark, translucent emerald green. (Pre-toasted nori may be purchased at some natural foods stores.)
3. When the rice is cooked and still hot, add the vinegar. Mix well.
4. Place one sheet of the toasted nori at a time on a special sushi mat, a woven placemat, or a clean dishtowel.
5. Spread one-quarter of the hot vinegared rice over the nori, leaving a 2-inch border on the two longer sides. Place a row of sliced carrots and cucumber lengthwise down the center of the rice, as shown in Step 1 of Figure 6.1. Sprinkle lightly with shoyu or tamari.
6. Using your mat to help you, roll up the nori into a cigar shape (see Step 2 of Figure 6.1). Press gently as you roll, so the nori roll is firm. Unroll the mat and roll the nori-maki in a sheet of wax paper.
7. Continue this procedure until the remaining sheets of nori are used up. Place the nori rolls in the refrigerator to chill for at least 3 hours. Chilling the nori-maki will make it tender. (It may be made up to a day before serving.)

To serve, slice the nori rolls into 1½-inch rounds using a very sharp knife, as seen in Step 3. Serve with a dipping sauce. The dipping sauce in the tempura recipe on page 234 would be good with this.

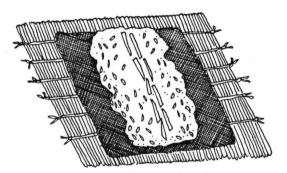

1. The nori-maki, with filling, before it is rolled.

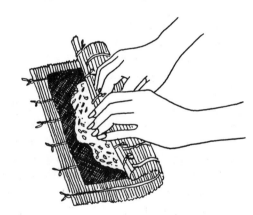

2. Rolling the nori-maki and sushi mat.

3. Slicing the nori-maki.

Figure 6.1. Making Nori-Maki

MARIE-HÉLÈNE'S SPINACH PASTRIES

This recipe is more time-consuming than most of the recipes in this book. However, the time is well spent, because these beautiful little pastries taste as good as they look. They are great for a party.

---

1 recipe Paper-Thin Pastry Dough *(see page 97)*

FILLING
2 packages (10 ounces each) fresh spinach

½ teaspoon sea salt

1 pound cottage cheese

1 egg, beaten

½ cup grated Parmesan or Romano cheese

2 tablespoons olive oil

1 teaspoon basil

½ teaspoon oregano

COATING
1 egg, beaten

1–2 tablespoons sesame seeds

Yield: Sixteen to eighteen 3-inch square pastries
Time: 2 hours

---

1. Wash and drain the spinach well. Let the spinach sit in a clean sink and sprinkle ½ teaspoon of salt over it. Rub the spinach between your hands to distribute the salt thoroughly. Set aside for 1 hour.
2. While the spinach is sitting, follow the recipe for the dough. After kneading, let the dough rest for 30 minutes while you finish the filling.
3. After the spinach has sat for an hour, squeeze it between your hands to press out the excess water. Squeeze out small amounts of spinach at a time until it is all finished.

4. Chop the pressed spinach with a sharp knife and place it in a large bowl. Add the cottage cheese, beaten egg, Parmesan cheese, olive oil, basil, and oregano, and mix well. Set this mixture aside while you roll out the dough as instructed below.
5. After the dough has rested for 30 minutes, cut it into 4 equal-sized pieces. Roll out 1 piece at a time, keeping the other pieces covered with a damp cloth to prevent them from drying out.
6. Roll each piece of dough into a paper-thin square that is about 8 inches on each side after it is neatly trimmed. Take your time in rolling the dough out nice and thin, because this is what makes the pastries so special. Cut each large square of paper-thin dough into 4 squares (4 inches on each side).
7. Place a heaping tablespoon of filling in the center of each of the small squares. Bring the corners of the dough toward the center and press them together to form a pouch. Press together the four seams. Gently place the pastries on a well-oiled cookie sheet; let them sit while you roll out and fill the remaining pieces of dough.
8. When all the pastries are filled, brush them with beaten egg and sprinkle them with sesame seeds. Bake at 350°F for 25–35 minutes, or until golden. Serve either hot or at room temperature.

These pastries are much easier to make and much prettier if you take care to cut the dough into very neat squares. The uneven pieces of dough that you trim off can be kneaded together and rolled back out. If they become too dry, just sprinkle them with a few drops of water. Leftover dough may also be refrigerated and saved for up to 3 days. It can be rolled out and filled with just about anything you like.

7. *SALADS*

THE BASIC GREEN SALAD

A big green salad is a welcome addition to almost any meal. I like to serve my salads "European-style"—after the meal—rather than before the meal in the American manner. Some health experts believe that eating a raw salad before the protein portion of a meal inhibits the digestion of protein. Other experts say the contrary. Which school of thought is right? Who really knows? It is probably not that important anyhow. The main thing is to enjoy your salad and to serve it often!

A good salad need not be elaborate. In fact, the clean taste of a simple green salad is often more appreciated than some fancy mixture. It is quicker and easier to make, too.

Below is a list of tips for making crisp and savory green salads. I'm not going to give you a measured recipe because even the most inexperienced cook is able to make a salad without one!

- A large variety of different types of vegetables is not necessary, but a variety of greens will lend interest, eye appeal, and flavor. What could be more boring than the typical restaurant salad of iceberg lettuce and unripe tomatoes?

  Some salad greens are mild-flavored and may be used as freely as desired. Others have a strong and sometimes bitter flavor. Unless you have a liking for these strong-flavored greens, it is best not to use them as the base for your salad. Don't forget them, though. The stronger-flavored greens are highly nutritious, and when used along with some sweet mild greens, they can be a real taste treat.

  —**Mild-flavored greens.** Boston lettuce, buttercrunch lettuce, Bibb lettuce, leaf lettuce, red lettuce, romaine lettuce, iceberg lettuce, Belgian endive, spinach.
  —**Strong or bitter-tasting greens.** Escarole, curly endive, watercress, dandelion, arugula, parsley, mustard and turnip greens, radicchio.

- Be generous with your portions of raw greens. One cup of lettuce contains eight to ten calories, so eat all you want!
- Wash your greens thoroughly, but quickly, in cool water.

- If you find that you do not always eat a salad because of the time it takes to wash the lettuce, wash the whole bunch right after you buy it. Dry it well and keep it in a tightly closed plastic bag in the refrigerator. It is nutritionally better to wash vegetables just before using them, but when you are in a hurry, prewashed lettuce is a lot better than no lettuce at all.
- A salad spinner is a handy gadget. It will leave your washed lettuce crisp and dry.
- If you don't have a salad spinner, drain your washed greens in a colander. Line a bowl with a clean dish towel, then place the drained greens in it and store them in the refrigerator until serving time.
- Tearing salad greens is often said to be better than chopping them. This is true only if they are torn with a light hand, because when tender greens are roughly torn they become bruised and limp.
- Always add the salad dressing at the last minute and toss the salad lightly. Excessive overmixing will wilt your salad. My favorite dressings for a tossed green salad are the simple *Lemon-Shoyu Dressing* on page 130, the *Bottomless Salad Dressing* on page 131, and the *Miso-Mustard Dressing* on page 132. The thicker, creamier dressings in this book are better poured over individually served salads than with tossed greens.
- If you think that you have made more salad than you can use, serve the dressing on the side. When a green salad has been mixed with dressing it will not be fresh the next day.

Because salads are made of different vegetables mixed together, making them with the "right side" of the brain can be fun. Almost any combination of vegetables works, and pasta, nuts, seeds, tofu, cheese, eggs, rice, or beans can be added to the combination.

Some of my favorite salad recipes are for what I call "Complete Meal Salads." These combine a variety of cooked and raw ingredients, and are often served on a bed of fresh greens. The following section discusses these light and refreshing meals.

THE COMPLETE MEAL SALAD

In warm weather, a salad is often more appealing than a hot meal. However, to make an entire meal out of a salad, it must be well-balanced. A meal consisting solely of raw or cooked vegetables or fruit is not very sustaining, even in summer.

For a salad to be a satisfying meal, it must either contain or be accompanied by both a source of protein and some complex carbohydrates.

Listed below are serving suggestions for the salads in this book that can easily be made into complete meals.

- *Maritime Salad* (page 115). Serve on a bed of lettuce or watercress, and accompany with hard-boiled eggs or a slice of cheese.
- *Corn and Bean Dip Salad* (page 116). Serve over lettuce or other greens.
- *Pasta and Chick Pea Salad* (page 116). Serve on a bed of greens.
- *Summer Rice Salad* (page 117). Serve on a bed of crisp greens. For a little extra protein, sprinkle with chopped nuts or toasted sesame seeds.
- *Easter Salad* (page 118). This salad is lovely when arranged on a bed of alfalfa sprouts and accompanied by a simple assortment of your favorite raw vegetables. Serve with some whole grain bread.
- *Belgian Endive and Walnut Salad with Goat Cheese* (page 119). Serve with some sourdough rye bread for a gourmet lunch.
- *Tempeh Salad or Sandwich Filling* (page 119). Serve over greens with some whole grain bread or on whole grain bread with some greens on the side.
- *Tofu Salad* (page 120). This is a salad that I make often and change every time I make it. Serve it on a bed of greens accompanied by some whole grain bread.
- *Arame-Rice Salad* (page 118). This salad and other grain-based salads are delicious when accompanied by a nice bowl of bean soup.
- *Tabouli* (page 122). Serve on a bed of lettuce. Top with yogurt or some cooked chick peas, and garnish with slices of ripe tomato and cucumber.

- *Summer Picnic Salad* (page 127), *Broccoli and Cauliflower Salad* (page 120), and *Marinated Vegetable Medley* (page 122) all have the potential to be made into a meal when they are served with whole grain bread and some good-quality cheese.

CREATING YOUR OWN COMPLETE MEAL SALAD

Here is a step-by-step guide to assist you in making a nutritious and wholesome complete meal salad. The only thing needed to transform it into a culinary masterpiece is the assistance of your taste, discrimination, and imagination.

Think of yourself as a painter. Your palette is composed of brilliantly colored cooked and raw vegetables. Your canvas is each individual serving plate. The objective of your painting is to produce a harmonious design of tone and texture.

As all painters know, contrast is of primary importance. Without contrasts in color, texture, and form, a painting will be drab or wishy-washy. The same holds true of your edible three-dimensional creations. As an inventive cook, take your awareness of contrast one step further—to the realm of flavors. Since you already know which flavors you enjoy, the task will be to combine them in a sensitive way so that they complement each other.

By focusing your attention on the essentials of color, texture, form, and flavor, you will be able to turn out salads that are not only as beautiful as the ones in food magazines, but are also as fine-tasting as the offerings of any gourmet restaurant.

1. On individual plates, make a bed of lettuce or other mild-flavored greens.
2. Add one or more of the following spicier varieties in a smaller proportion: watercress, curly endive, arugula, escarole, spinach, dandelion, paper-thin shreds of red cabbage, young and tender mustard greens, and/or young beet tops. A small amount of dulse may also be added. Just wash it well and mix it with the other greens.

    The greens should be washed, thoroughly dried, chilled, and torn into bite-sized pieces.

3. Choose a nice, colorful variety of raw or cooked vegetables from the following lists.

RAW VEGETABLES

- Carrots, cut into matchsticks or curls, or grated.
- Snow peas (pea pods) whole, but with the ends pinched off.
- Mushrooms, sliced.
- Cucumbers, thinly sliced or cut into matchsticks.
- Belgian endive, chopped or separated into leaves.
- Tomatoes, sliced or chopped; or cherry tomatoes, whole.
- Mung sprouts, whole.
- Alfalfa sprouts, whole.
- Zucchini, sliced.
- Radishes, sliced.
- Chick peas.
- Cauliflower or broccoli, separated into flowerets.
- Red or green peppers, sliced into rings, or diced.
- Sauerkraut: made from red or white cabbage.

COOKED VEGETABLES

- Peas.
- Beets: steamed or pickled, sliced, diced, or grated.
- Potatoes: sliced or diced and tossed with some *Lemon-Shoyu Dressing* (page 130).
- Rutabagas: lightly steamed and diced or cut into matchsticks.
- Carrots: lightly steamed and sliced.
- Asparagus spears or tips: lightly steamed.
- Artichoke hearts: marinated (see page 128).
- Palm hearts: marinated in *Lemon-Shoyu Dressing* (page 130).
- Green beans: left whole and lightly steamed.

4. Artfully arrange your choice of cooked and raw (or only raw) vegetables over the bed of greens.

5. To make your salad into a satisfying meal, you must now add some protein. Choose one of the following:

- Any type of cooked beans, either plain or marinated in *Lemon-Shoyu Dressing* (page 130).
- Tofu in one of the following forms: made into *Soyannaise* (page 133); cut into cubes and marinated in a mixture of tamari, rice vinegar or lemon, and water; or crumbled and made into *Tofu Salad* (page 120).
- Cold leftover pan-fried or baked tempeh, cut into sticks and sprinkled with tamari.
- Hard-boiled eggs or the marinated eggs from the *Easter Salad* on page 118.
- Good-quality hard cheese, thinly sliced, grated, or cut into cubes or sticks.
- Low-fat mozzarella cheese, grated and tossed with a small amount of *Lemon-Shoyu Dressing* (page 130) and finely chopped parsley.
- Crumbled blue cheese.
- Low-fat cottage or ricotta cheese mixed with finely chopped scallions or chives, parsley, and minced celery.
- Crumbled feta cheese.

6. Now your salad is ready for the finishing touch! Choose one or more of the following garnishes:

- Whole or sliced black or green olives.
- Red onion, sliced into thin rings.
- Nuts or seeds such as walnuts, almonds, pumpkin seeds, sunflower seeds, etc. (Try *Tamari Almonds*, page 105.)
- *Herb Croutons*, page 91.
- Alfalfa sprouts—a mixture of sprouts such as alfalfa, radish, and mustard sprouts (see pages 124-125 for information on sprouting).
- Pickles (either homemade or from the natural foods store).
- Chopped scallions, parsley, dill weed, fennel, etc.
- Toasted nori cut into strips or other shapes (see the section on sea vegetables on page 157).

Take an admiring look at the object of beauty that you have created—because it won't be around for long! Serve your salad with your choice of creamy dressings (see Chapter 8) and some whole grain bread. For a real treat, serve the salad with *Garlic Toast* (see page 90).

LOW-FAT POTATO SALAD

A creamy and colorful potato salad that does not contain mayonnaise or oil. This recipe includes pickles, and you can find pickles that do not contain sugar or preservatives in natural foods stores.

4 cups potatoes, scrubbed and cut into ¹/₂-inch cubes (new potatoes are especially good)
2 cups sliced carrots (2 large)
1 cup fresh or frozen peas
²/₃ cup finely chopped onion
1 cup finely chopped dill pickles
¹/₂ green pepper, finely chopped
4 hard-boiled eggs, finely chopped (optional)
1 cup soft tofu
1 cup yogurt
3 tablespoons Dijon mustard
2 tablespoons white miso
¹/₂ teaspoon dill seed

Serves: 3–4 as a complete meal or 6–8 as a side dish.
Time: 30 minutes to prepare; 1–2 hours to chill.

1. Place the potatoes and the carrots in a large pan with about 1¹/₂ inches of water in the bottom. Cover and bring to a boil. Lower the heat and simmer until the vegetables are almost tender.
2. Add the peas; simmer until the potatoes and carrots are tender but not mushy. Drain the vegetables (reserving any leftover water for future use) and place them in a large bowl.
3. Add the onion, pickles, green pepper, and hard-boiled eggs.
4. In a blender or a food processor blend together the tofu, yogurt, mustard, and miso until smooth and creamy. Combine this cream with the vegetables. Add the dill seed and mix well. Chill before serving.

Serve on a bed of crisp lettuce.

MARITIME SALAD

Potatoes and the sea vegetable dulse combine beautifully in this mineral-packed salad.

5 cups scrubbed and diced potatoes
1 cup finely chopped sweet Bermuda onion
¼ cup olive oil
¼ cup lemon juice
1 teaspoon Dijon mustard
2–4 cloves garlic, pressed
Sea salt, to taste
½ cup washed and chopped dulse (see inset on sea vegetables, page 157)
1½ cups washed and chopped watercress

Serves: 4–6
Time: 30 minutes to cook potatoes;1–2 hours to chill.

1. Place the potatoes in a large pan. Pour about 1½ inches of water into the pan. Cover and bring to a boil. Lower the heat and cook, stirring occasionally, until the potatoes are done. Drain the potatoes, reserving any leftover water for soup or bread making.
2. Place the potatoes in a large bowl. Add the onion and mix.
3. In a small bowl, mix together the olive oil, lemon juice, mustard, garlic, and salt. Pour this dressing over the potato-onion mixture. Mix well and chill for one or two hours.
4. Mix the chopped dulse and watercress with the chilled salad. Garnish with a few sprigs of watercress. This salad will stay fresh for several days.

FRESH CORN SALAD

This salad is excellent with any bean dish. It is used in making *Corn and Bean Dip Salad* (see page 116).

4 small ears sweet corn
½ small red pepper, diced, and ½ small green pepper, diced; or, 1 whole red or green pepper, diced
1 stalk celery, finely chopped
¼ cup finely chopped red onion
⅓ cup dill pickles (pickles that do not contain sugar or preservatives can be purchased at natural foods stores)
½ teaspoon basil
2 tablespoons rice or cider vinegar
½ teaspoon roasted sesame oil or 2 tablespoons olive oil

Serves: 4
Time: 20 minutes to prepare; 30 minutes to chill.

1. Steam the corn until it is tender. Let it cool slightly and cut it off the cob.
2. Place the corn in a large bowl. Add the remaining ingredients and mix well. Chill for at least 30 minutes before serving.

MUSHROOM SALAD

The mushrooms must be very fresh and crisp for this salad.

2 cups sliced mushrooms
½ cup minced parsley
2 tablespoons minced onion or scallions
½ cup Instant Yogurt Dressing (page 133)
2–3 leaves Boston lettuce

Serves: 2–3
Time: 15 minutes

Mix together the mushrooms, parsley, onion, and dressing. Place a clean, crisp leaf of Boston lettuce in the bottom of each individual serving bowl. Top with the mushroom salad.

CORN AND BEAN DIP SALAD

A nourishing but not-too-heavy meal for warm weather.

1 recipe Fresh Corn Salad *(page 115)*
1 recipe Hummus *(page 104), or any other bean dip or spread that you enjoy*
½ head Boston lettuce
1 tomato, sliced
½ cucumber, sliced
Black olives

Serves: 2–3 as a complete meal
Time: If bean dip is already made, 25 minutes to prepare; 30 minutes to chill.

1. Follow the recipes for the corn salad and for hummus. Make sure to add enough oil or cooking water to the bean spread so that it will not be too thick.
2. Wash and dry the lettuce. Tear it into bite-sized pieces and place them on individual serving plates. Top each portion of the lettuce with some *Fresh Corn Salad*. Then top the corn salad with a nice mound of hummus. Use as much of the bean spread as you desire, but you should have a larger quantity of corn than bean spread. (Use any leftover bean spread to make sandwiches.)
3. Surround the mound of bean spread with tomato and cucumber slices, and decorate it with black olives. Serve chilled.

PASTA AND CHICK PEA SALAD

2 cups whole wheat pasta shells
2 cups broccoli flowerets
1 cup cooked chick peas
⅓ cup sweet onion, minced
2 tomatoes, chopped
2 tablespoons olive oil
3 tablespoons lemon juice
1 tablespoon tamari or shoyu
2 cloves garlic, pressed
3 tablespoons tomato paste
1 teaspoon basil
½ teaspoon tarragon

Serves: 2–3 as a complete meal or 4–6 as a side dish.
Time: 30 minutes to prepare; 1–2 hours to chill.

1. Bring a large kettle of water to a boil. Add the pasta and cook until just tender (al dente). Drain and rinse with cold water. Place in a large bowl.
2. While the pasta is cooking, steam the broccoli. Then drain it and place it in the bowl with the pasta.
3. Add the remaining ingredients to the pasta-broccoli mixture and mix gently. Chill and serve on a bed of crisp greens.

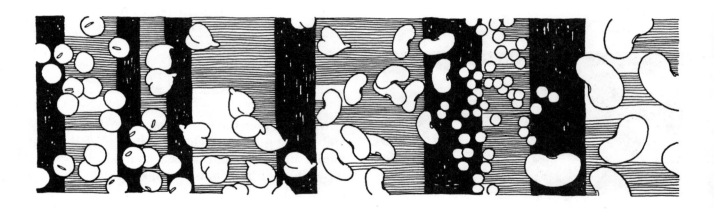

SWEET AND SPICY SALAD

This recipe utilizes a root vegetable called the jicama, which is also known as the Mexican potato. The jicama is delicately flavored and slightly sweet.

1½ cups grated carrot
1½ cups grated jicama (peel the jicama before you grate it)
¼ cup finely chopped parsley
1 scallion, finely chopped
¼ cup finely chopped celery
¼ cup finely chopped green pepper
¼ cup Sandra's Sweet French Dressing (page 134)

Serves: 4
Time: 20 minutes

Combine all the prepared vegetables in a large bowl. Toss with the dressing and place in a smaller bowl to serve.

This salad is a tasty accompaniment to *Super Quick Tempeh Burgers* on page 66. It is also a good salad to take along on a picnic.

CUCUMBER-YOGURT SALAD

2 medium cucumbers
10 radishes, thinly sliced
3 scallions, chopped
⅓ cup chopped parsley
½ cup chopped walnuts
2 cups plain yogurt
½ teaspoon sea salt
½ teaspoon dill seed
Juice of ½ lemon
2–3 cloves garlic (or to taste), pressed

Serves: 4–6
Time: 15 minutes

If the cucumbers are waxed, peel them. If not, just wash them and slice them into very thin diagonal slices.

Mix together all ingredients in a salad bowl.

VARIATION

- The addition of sliced avocado to this salad is delicious.

SUMMER RICE SALAD

SALAD
2 cups cooked long grain brown rice
2 cups cooked sliced carrots
⅓ cup sweet onion, minced
⅔ cup chopped celery
1 red pepper, diced
¼ cup minced parsley
¼ teaspoon celery seed
½ teaspoon tarragon
1 teaspoon basil

DRESSING
1 cup mashed tofu
¼ cup yogurt
2 teaspoons Dijon mustard
¼ cup lemon juice
2 tablespoons yellow miso
2 cloves garlic
2 tablespoons minced onion

Serves: 2–3 as a complete meal or 4–6 as a side dish.
Time: 20 minutes to prepare; 30 minutes to chill (longer if rice is still warm).

1. To make the salad, place the cooked rice, cooked carrots, onion, celery, pepper, parsley, celery seed, tarragon, and basil in a large bowl. Keep the mixture refrigerated while you make the dressing.
2. To make the dressing, place the tofu, yogurt, mustard, miso, garlic, and 2 tablespoons minced onion in a blender or food processor. Blend until very smooth and creamy.
3. Add the dressing to the salad. Mix well and chill.
    Serve on a bed of lettuce.

CARROT-ALMOND SALAD

1/3 cup sliced or chopped almonds
1 tablespoon white miso
2 tablespoons oil
1/2–1 teaspoon Dijon mustard
2 tablespoons lemon juice
2 cups grated carrots

Serves: 3–4
Time: 5–10 minutes

1. Place the almonds in a small cake pan or other oven-safe dish. Bake them at 350°F for about 5 minutes or until they are lightly toasted. Set aside.
2. Mix together the miso, oil, mustard, and lemon juice in a medium-sized bowl. Add the grated carrots and the toasted almonds. Mix well.

VARIATION

- One or two tablespoons of finely minced fresh dill weed would be good in this salad. You may also substitute chopped pecans for the almonds.

EASTER SALAD

You won't believe the color of these eggs!

6–8 small to medium beets
2 cups liquid from cooking the beets
6 hard-boiled eggs
1/4 cup apple cider vinegar
2 tablespoons honey
1 teaspoon tarragon
1 teaspoon sea salt

Serves: 6
Time: 40 minutes to prepare; 3 days to marinate.

1. Scrub the beets. Slice them and put them in a pot with 2½–3 cups of water. Cover and bring to a boil. Reduce the heat and simmer until the beets are tender.
2. Drain, reserving the cooking liquid, and place the cooked beets in a large, wide-mouthed glass jar.
3. Peel the hard-boiled eggs and place them in the jar with the beets.
4. Measure the liquid from cooking the beets. Add more water if necessary to make 2 cups. If you have more than 2 cups of liquid, pour off as much as necessary to make 2 cups. Combine the 2 cups of cooking liquid with the vinegar, honey, tarragon, and salt. Pour this mixture over the beets and eggs. Cover and refrigerate for 3 days before serving.
5. To serve, remove the eggs from the marinade, slice them in half or in quarters, and place them on a nest of alfalfa sprouts and watercress. Arrange the beets in an attractive pattern around the eggs.

ARAME-RICE SALAD

The arame gives this salad an exotic appearance.

1 recipe Arame Condiment (page 246)
3 cups cooked long grain brown rice
1½ cups grated carrots
1 cup chopped raw snow peas, or lightly cooked fresh or frozen green peas
1 cup chopped parsley
2 tablespoons rice vinegar
2 tablespoons oil
1 or more cloves garlic, pressed (optional)
1/4 teaspoon sea salt (optional)

Serves: 4
Time: 15 minutes for Arame Condiment; 10 minutes for salad; 45 minutes to chill.

Drain the *Arame Condiment* and mix with the other ingredients. Chill and serve on a bed of crisp lettuce.

BELGIAN ENDIVE AND WALNUT SALAD WITH GOAT CHEESE

A similar salad is on the menu of a very chic restaurant in Sarasota, Florida. I enjoyed it so much that I created my own lighter version. The cheese used for this salad should be mild, firm enough to slice, and white. It may be purchased in a cheese store or a gourmet shop.

4 medium Belgian endives (4 cups chopped)
1/2 cup chopped walnuts
1/2 cup finely chopped parsley
2 tablespoons olive oil
1/2–1 teaspoon roasted sesame oil, or to taste
1/4 cup lemon juice
1–2 cloves garlic, pressed
2 teaspoons shoyu or tamari
4 ounces goat cheese
A few black olives
A few sprigs of parsley

Serves: 2 as a complete meal or 4 as a side dish.
Time: 15–20 minutes

1. Wash and chop the endive. Place it in a large bowl with the chopped walnuts and parsley.
2. Combine the olive oil, sesame oil, lemon juice, garlic, and shoyu or tamari in a small bowl. Mix well. Pour this dressing over the endive-walnut mixture. Toss lightly.
3. Place the salad on individual serving plates, and crumble the goat cheese over each portion. Garnish with a few black olives and some sprigs of parsley, if desired.

TEMPEH SALAD OR SANDWICH FILLING

8 ounces tempeh
1/4 cup tahini
2 tablespoons olive oil
2 tablespoons lemon juice
2 tablespoons shoyu
1/4 teaspoon thyme
1/3 cup minced onion
1–2 cloves garlic, pressed
1/2 cup grated carrots
2 tablespoons minced parsley

Serves: 2 as a complete meal salad, or makes 4 sandwiches.
Time: 30 minutes to prepare; 1 hour to chill.

1. Chop the tempeh into bite-sized pieces and steam it in a vegetable steamer for about 20 minutes. Transfer the cooked tempeh to a medium-sized bowl.
2. In a separate bowl, mix together the tahini, olive oil, lemon juice, shoyu, and thyme. Pour the mixture over the steamed tempeh. Chill for 1 hour.
3. Add onion, garlic, carrots, and parsley to the tempeh, and mix well.

   Serve on a bed of fresh greens, or use in sandwiches. Leftover salad can be kept refrigerated for 2–3 days.

VARIATION

- The addition of finely chopped celery, dill pickles, or green pepper is good in this salad.

TOFU SALAD

Want a light, nourishing meal fast? Try this easy salad. It has become a regular at our house.

1 cup crumbled tofu
1/3 cup finely chopped celery
1/2 red or green pepper, diced
1 small carrot, grated
2 scallions, chopped
1 tablespoon shoyu, or less to taste
1–2 tablespoons lemon juice, or to taste
A few drops of roasted sesame oil, to taste
1 clove garlic, pressed (optional)
1 tablespoon nutritional yeast

Serves: 1 as a complete meal
Time: 10–15 minutes

Mix together all ingredients. Serve on a bed of lettuce.

VARIATION

• For a different flavor, substitute 1/4 teaspoon sea salt (or to taste) for the shoyu and 1 tablespoon olive oil for the roasted sesame oil. You may also vary the vegetables as desired.

BROCCOLI AND CAULIFLOWER SALAD

4 cups bite-sized broccoli flowerets (from about 1 bundle of fresh broccoli)
2 cups bite-sized cauliflower flowerets (from approximately 1/2 head of cauliflower)
1/4 cup olive oil
2 tablespoons lemon juice
1 tablespoon shoyu or tamari
1 teaspoon prepared horseradish
1 teaspoon Dijon mustard
1/2 teaspoon tarragon
1/4 cup minced onion

Serves: 4
Time: 20 minutes to prepare; 40 minutes to chill.

1. Separately steam the broccoli and the cauliflower for about 5 minutes each, or until they are just barely tender. Place them together in a medium-sized bowl and chill.
2. In a small bowl, combine the oil, lemon juice, shoyu or tamari, horseradish, mustard, tarragon, and onion. Let the mixture stand for about 10 minutes; then pour it over the broccoli and cauliflower. Toss the salad lightly and refrigerate it for at least 30 minutes before serving. Mix the salad occasionally while it is being chilled.

CÉLINE'S ROYAL ASPIC

A beautiful jelled salad that is perfect for a fancy buffet.

4–5 medium beets
2³/₄ cups liquid from cooking the beets
2 bay leaves
1 bar agar torn into small pieces
¹/₄ teaspoon sea salt, or more to taste
3 tablespoons lemon juice
2 tablespoons honey

Serves: 6
Time: 40 minutes to prepare; 2 hours to chill.

1. Scrub the beets and cut them into quarters. Place them in a pot with about 3¹/₂ cups of water. Cover and bring to a boil. Lower the heat and simmer until the beets are tender.
2. Drain the beets, reserving the cooking liquid, and let them cool for easier handling. Grate the beets and measure; you need 2 cups of grated beets.
3. Measure the liquid from cooking the beets. If necessary, add water to obtain 2³/₄ cups of liquid. Place the liquid in a saucepan along with the bay leaves, agar, and salt. Bring to a boil; then reduce the heat and simmer until the agar is completely dissolved. Discard the bay leaves.
4. Combine the dissolved agar mixture with the grated beets, lemon juice, and honey. Pour the mixture into a lightly oiled 4-cup mold. Chill for 2 or more hours to set. Just before serving, unmold the jelly onto a bed of salad greens.

   Serve with *Soyannaise* (page 133). For an especially attractive buffet presentation, serve with *Easter Salad* (see page 118).

VARIATION

- If you wish to serve this aspic with *Easter Salad* (page 118), use the liquid from marinating the salad to form the basis of the aspic. Add more water or cooking liquid as needed and adjust the seasoning to taste. Rather than cooking more beets, you may grate the beets from the salad and use them in the aspic.

SUMMER TOFU

Elegant in its simplicity and very refreshing.

1 bar agar
2 cups water
1 tablespoon honey
1¹/₂ cups mashed tofu (try to use very fresh tofu)

Serves: 4–6
Time: 15 minutes to prepare; 2 hours to chill.

1. Break the agar into small pieces and place them in a small saucepan along with the water. Bring the water to a boil, then lower the heat and simmer until the agar is completely dissolved.
2. While the agar is cooking, blend together the honey and tofu in a blender or food processor until smooth and creamy. Add the dissolved agar mixture to the tofu cream while blending. Continue blending until the two mixtures are thoroughly blended.
3. Pour the cream into a lightly oiled 8-x-8-inch cake pan. Chill for about 2 hours to set.
4. Cut the gel into squares, diamonds, or rectangles, and serve it on a bed of lettuce or watercress. Garnish with slices of ripe tomato and Belgian endive and top with *Tahini-Yogurt Dressing* (page 131).

MARINATED VEGETABLE MEDLEY

A colorful cooked vegetable salad.

2 large sweet carrots (or 3–4 smaller carrots)
3 small red potatoes
1 large stalk broccoli
2 medium yellow squash
½ red onion, thinly sliced and separated into rings
1–2 cloves garlic, pressed
3 tablespoons olive oil
2 tablespoons tamari
¼ cup lemon juice
1 teaspoon basil
½ teaspoon tarragon

Serves: 4
Time: 30 minutes to prepare; 2 hours to chill.

1. Scrub the carrots and the potatoes. Cut them into ¼-inch slices. Wash the squash and the broccoli. Peel the broccoli stems and slice them into rounds. Separate the broccoli flowerets into bite-sized pieces. Halve the yellow squash at its widest point and cut it into ½-inch slices.
2. In a vegetable steamer (the steaming rack of a wok works very nicely), make a layer of sliced carrots and broccoli rounds. Over this, place a layer of potato slices. Top the potatoes with broccoli flowerets and finish with yellow squash slices.
3. Place about 1 inch of water in the bottom of the pan. Cover and bring the water to a boil. Steam the vegetables until they are tender, but still crisp and brightly colored.
4. Transfer the lightly steamed vegetables to a large bowl. Add the remaining ingredients and mix gently. Refrigerate for a couple of hours, or until the salad is chilled. Mix occasionally while salad is chilling, and again before serving.

VARIATION

- Substitute cauliflower for the broccoli, zucchini for the yellow squash, etc.

TABOULI

This Mideastern specialty has become a classic in vegetarian cuisine.

³/₄ cup bulghur wheat
1 cup boiling water
¼ cup olive oil
Juice of 2 small lemons
2 or more cloves garlic, pressed
½ teaspoon sea salt
1 cup finely chopped parsley
¼ cup finely chopped scallions
¼ cup finely chopped fresh mint, or 1 teaspoon dry mint
2 ripe tomatoes, chopped

Serves: 4
Time: 30 minutes to prepare; 1 hour to chill.

1. Place the bulghur in a bowl and pour the boiling water over it. Cover the bowl and let it stand for about 30 minutes. The water should be completely absorbed.
2. Add the olive oil, lemon juice, garlic, and salt to the soaked bulghur and refrigerate for at least half an hour.
3. Add the remaining ingredients, except for the chopped tomatoes, and mix well. Chill.
   Serve on a bed of salad greens and garnish with the tomatoes.

NOTE: To make a complete meal of tabouli, add some cooked chick peas or serve it with a yogurt sauce.

MUNG SPROUT SALAD

Crisp and colorful.

2 cups mung bean sprouts
1 sweet red pepper, diced
1/2 cup cooked corn, fresh or frozen
2 scallions, chopped
2 tablespoons minced parsley
Lemon-Shoyu Dressing *(page 130)*, Bottomless Salad Dressing with Marinated Garlic *(page 131)*, or Oriental Dressing *(page 130)*

Serves: 4
Time: 10 minutes to prepare; 30 minutes to chill.

1. Combine the vegetables in a medium-sized bowl. If the corn is hot, let it cool before mixing it with the other ingredients.
2. Add your choice of dressing, to taste (about 1/4 cup should be good). Chill for 1/2 hour before serving.

SAUERKRAUT, PARSLEY, AND MUSHROOM SALAD

This is a good salad to serve in winter when fresh lettuce is scarce.

1 1/2 cups sauerkraut, in its own juice
1 1/2 cups sliced mushrooms
1 cup chopped parsley
2 cloves garlic, pressed
1/4 cup minced onion
2 tablespoons olive oil
1/2 teaspoon caraway seed

Serves: 4
Time: 10 minutes

Mix together all ingredients.

MARINATED CARROTS

A pretty dish for a buffet.

2 pounds carrots, scrubbed and cut into rounds or diagonal slices
15 ounces (about 2 cups) tomato sauce (use the recipe on page 240, or use a good-quality canned sauce, if desired)
1/4 cup rice vinegar or cider vinegar
1/4 cup honey
1/4 cup oil
1 teaspoon Dijon mustard
1 tablespoon yellow miso
1 medium onion, thinly sliced
1/3 cup minced parsley

Serves: 8–10
Time: 20 minutes to prepare; marinate overnight.

1. Steam the carrots until they are tender but still firm. Place them in a large bowl and chill.
2. In a smaller bowl, mix together the tomato sauce, vinegar, honey, oil, mustard, and miso. Pour this dressing over the cooked carrots. Add the raw onion and mix well. Cover the bowl and let the carrots marinate overnight in the refrigerator.
3. Just before serving, add the parsley, reserving a little bit to garnish the top of the dish. Mix well and place in a serving dish.

Sprouting— a Garden in Your Kitchen

Sprouting is a great activity for anyone who wishes to enjoy fresh, high-quality produce throughout the year. It requires surprisingly little effort, and it does not take up much room in the kitchen. As far as rewards for time, investment, and effort are concerned, sprouting can't be beat. Both children and adults marvel at the miracle of how a few dry seeds can grow into a bouquet of luscious greens in a matter of days.

When seeds are sprouted, their nutritional content (especially vitamin C) is significantly increased, they become easier to digest, and they require less cooking, or none at all. Sprouts are the cleanest food one can eat because while they're growing they must be rinsed two or three times a day. They are also free from pesticides and other additives. Sprouts are crisp and tender; their flavors run from sweet to piquant depending on the kind of seeds sprouted.

Another reward of sprouting is the simple satisfaction that one derives from growing a portion of one's own food. With sprouting, even the busy city-dweller has a chance to participate in the art of food cultivation.

WHAT TO SPROUT

Any whole, unbroken seed can be sprouted. Of course, you will want to use non-chemically treated seeds from edible food plants! Below I will list some of the more popular ones.

Wheat and rye. These make sweet, delicious sprouts, and they are among the easiest to grow.

Beans. The following whole, unbroken dried beans are some of my favorites: chick peas (garbanzos), lentils, kidney beans, pinto beans, adzuki beans, peas, and mung beans.

Alfalfa, clover, radish, and mustard. All of these make wonderful sprouts for salads and sandwiches. Clover is mild-flavored and similar to alfalfa. Radish and mustard are very piquant and are best mixed with alfalfa or clover.

Fenugreek. Fenugreek is spicy and aromatic.

Sunflower. Sunflower sprouts are mild.

There are lots of other seeds that can be sprouted; look for them in your local natural foods store. Always make sure to use seeds that are sold for sprouting or eating, because seeds that are sold for gardening are sometimes treated with chemicals.

Fenugreek

Sesame Seeds

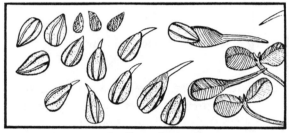

Sunflower Seeds

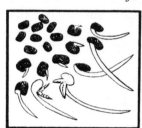

Mung Beans

Lentils

Alfalfa

Almonds

Adzuki Beans   *Kidney Beans*   *Pinto Beans*

HOW TO SPROUT

MASON JAR METHOD

Use this method for small seeds such as alfalfa, mustard, clover, fenugreek, and radish. You will need a quart jar and a piece of cheesecloth or clean nylon stocking big enough to stretch across the opening of the jar.

Begin with two tablespoons of alfalfa seed or a mixture of alfalfa and other small seeds equal to two tablespoons.

1. Place the seeds in the bottom of the glass jar. Add some room temperature water to generously cover the seeds and let them soak for anywhere from four to eight hours. Cut out a piece of cheesecloth or clean nylon stocking of an appropriate size to cover the opening of the jar. Secure the cloth over the opening of the jar with a string or rubber band.
2. After the seeds have soaked for four to eight hours, pour the water out of the jar. The seeds will be caught by the fabric covering the opening and will remain in the jar. If desired, save the water from soaking and use it to water your house plants. They will love you for it!
3. After you have drained the seeds, rinse them thoroughly (do not remove the fabric covering the jar). Then pour out the water and let the seeds drain well. Don't let them stand in water. Just rinse them and immediately pour out the water.
4. Continue rinsing the seeds in this way two or three times a day for four to five days (in warm climates it may take less time) until the sprouts have grown to their optimal length. They should practically fill the jar.

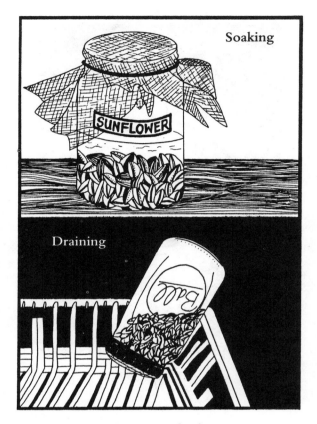

The Jar Method

BOWL AND WIRE STRAINER METHOD

Use this method for growing larger sprouts (beans, grains, and sunflower). It is unbelievably easy, but it works!

1. Place the beans, grains, or sunflower seeds in a bowl that gives them enough room to double without being crowded. About 1 cup is a nice amount to sprout; however, you can use more or less, as you wish. If you are using beans, pick them over and remove any broken ones.
2. Cover the beans or seeds with water and let them soak for eight to ten hours.
3. Drain the soaked beans or seeds through a wire strainer and rinse them under running water. (Save the water from soaking the seeds for your house plants.)
4. Return the rinsed (and drained) seeds back to their bowl. Rinse and drain them as specified above twice a day, for three to five days, or until they have reached the desired length.

Bowl and Wire Strainer Method

SPROUTING TIPS

Here are six essential tips for successful kitchen gardening.

- In my opinion it is not worth the trouble to try to grow mung sprouts that look like the bean sprouts in the grocery store. They always turn brown before they get long enough. When mung sprouts are shorter they are still very good, but they take a little more time to cook.
- Do not sprout wheat or rye for more than two or three days (unless you wish to grow wheatgrass), because they become too fibrous to chew if allowed to grow.
- The most common mistake that people make the first time they try sprouting is that they do not drain the seeds adequately. They leave them standing in water, which causes them to rot.
- If sprouts begin to get moldy, it is because they were not drained well enough or are in a place that is too warm. If only a few of the sprouts in a batch start to mold, you may pick out and discard the moldy ones. Rinse the remaining sprouts well and they will still be good to eat.
- Most books on sprouting recommend growing the sprouts in a dark place. This is not necessary. I keep mine on the kitchen counter so that I will not forget to rinse them, and they do just fine.
- If the sprouts dry up, it is because they were not rinsed frequently enough.

SUGGESTIONS

Listed below are some of my favorite ways to use sprouts.

- Use alfalfa or clover sprouts in sandwiches, as a garnish, and in salads. They are also good blended into soups (see the recipe for *Chilled Buttermilk and Scallion Soup*, page 60).
- For a spicier flavor, mix a small portion of radish or mustard seeds with alfalfa seeds when you sprout them.
- Wheat or rye sprouts can be used as a cold or hot breakfast cereal (or mixed with your favorite cereal). They can also be added to fruit salads, *Tabouli* (page 122), rice or grain dishes, pancake or muffin batters, and bread dough. The divine *Essene Bread* on page 91 is made entirely out of wheat or rye sprouts and is sweet like cake.
- Fenugreek sprouts are good in curries and grain dishes.
- Lentil sprouts cook very quickly. They may be stir-fried with vegetables to make a fast and nourishing entrée. See the recipes for *Wheat and Lentil Sprouts*, page 38 and *Pasta and Lentil Sprout Quickie*, page 38.
- If mung sprouts are long enough they can be stir-fried or added to soups during the last few minutes of cooking. Mung beans can also be sprouted only slightly and cooked like any other beans.

TOFU AND EGG SALAD

4 hard-boiled eggs
1½ cups crumbled tofu
½ cup finely chopped sweet Bermuda onion
½ cup grated carrots
⅔ cup chopped raw snow peas, or lightly cooked fresh or frozen green peas
1 cup yogurt
2 tablespoons Dijon mustard, or less to taste
½ teaspoon sea salt
½ teaspoon dill seed
¼ teaspoon tumeric
1–2 tablespoons lemon juice, or to taste

Serves: 4
Time: 20 minutes to prepare; ½ hour to chill.

If the eggs are hot, chill them for ½ hour or until cool. Mix together all ingredients.

Serve on a bed of crisp greens or use as a sandwich filling.

SUMMER PICNIC SALAD

4 cups wax beans or green beans, broken into 1-inch pieces
1 cup sliced carrots
½ cup minced onion
¼ cup olive oil
2 tablespoons lemon juice
2 tablespoons lime juice
2 tablespoons Dijon mustard
3–4 cloves garlic, pressed
1½ cups snow peas (raw or lightly steamed) cut into bite-sized pieces
1 cup chopped parsley
⅓ cup sliced black olives
½ teaspoon sea salt if needed (depending on the saltiness of the olives)

Serves: 6
Time: 30 minutes to prepare; 1 hour to chill.

1. Steam together the beans and carrots till they are just barely tender.
2. Drain the vegetables and mix them with the onion, oil, lemon and lime juice, mustard, and garlic in a large bowl. Chill for at least 1 hour.
3. Add the remaining ingredients. Toss and serve.

GREEN BEAN SALAD

1 pound fresh green beans
2 tablespoons olive oil
2 tablespoons shoyu or tamari
2 tablespoons Dijon mustard
2 tablespoons lemon juice
2 cloves garlic, pressed
⅓ cup sweet Bermuda onion, cut into very thin slices
⅓ cup sweet red pepper, cut into very thin slices
3 tablespoons minced parsley

Serves: 4–6
Time: 30 minutes to prepare; 2½ hours to chill.

1. Wash the green beans and remove the ends, but leave them whole. Steam until just barely tender.
2. Mix together the oil, shoyu, mustard, and garlic. Drain the steamed beans, and while they are still hot, place them in a large, shallow container and pour the dressing over them. Toss lightly, and chill for about 30 minutes.
3. Add the remaining ingredients and toss gently. Refrigerate for at least 2 hours before serving.

JODY'S CARCIOFI IN SALSA (Dressed Artichoke Hearts)

Most of the marinated artichoke hearts that are sold in stores contain additives. So why not make your own? It takes only a few minutes.

1/4 cup olive oil
2 tablespoons lemon juice
1 tablespoon finely grated onion
1 bay leaf
2 teaspoons tamari, or to taste
16 small fresh-cooked or canned and drained artichoke hearts
1–2 tablespoons minced parsley

Serves: 4
Time: 10 minutes to prepare; 1–2 hours to chill.

1. In a large bowl, mix together the olive oil, lemon juice, grated onion, bay leaf, and tamari. Add the artichoke hearts, toss lightly, and chill for 1–2 hours. Stir the mixture occasionally during this time.
2. Before serving, sprinkle the artichoke hearts with the minced parsley.

PEARL BUCK RADISHES

A certain paragraph in a Pearl Buck novel describes the preparation of a radish dish. It sounded so good that I decided to try it. Here is the result. Whether it is what Ms. Buck intended, I will never know, but it is my favorite way to eat radishes.

10–12 medium to large red radishes
1/4 teaspoon roasted sesame oil
2 tablespoons rice vinegar or cider vinegar
1 tablespoon tamari
3 tablespoons cold water

Serves: 2–4
Time: 10 minutes to prepare; 30 minutes to chill.

1. Wash the radishes. Cut off the stem and the root end. Slice the radishes into paper-thin rounds and place them in a shallow bowl.
2. In a cup or small bowl, mix together the remaining ingredients. Pour this dressing over the sliced radishes. Mix and serve immediately, or if desired, chill for 30 minutes before serving.

MARINATED CUCUMBER SALAD

A cool and light accompaniment to a summer meal. "Iced Delight" tea by Celestial Seasonings works very well in this recipe.

1 1/2 cups water
1 mint tea bag
1 medium cucumber (or 2 small cucumbers)
1 small onion
1/4 cup lemon juice
1/4 teaspoon sea salt

Serves: 4
Time: 10 minutes to prepare; 1 1/2 hours to chill.

1. Bring the water to a boil in a pan. Add the tea bag and steep for about 5 minutes.
2. Remove the bag and place the tea in the refrigerator (or freezer if you are in a hurry) until chilled.
3. Peel the cucumber if it is waxed; otherwise, just wash it well. Slice the cucumber and the onion very thinly and place them in a serving bowl. Combine the lemon juice and sea salt with the chilled tea and pour it over the sliced cucumbers. Place the dish in the refrigerator and let the cucumbers marinate for at least an hour.

8. *SALAD DRESSINGS*

Have you ever stopped to read the list of ingredients on a bottle of salad dressing in the grocery store? Doesn't sound like very nourishing food, does it? Perhaps it goes well enough with rusty iceberg lettuce and anemic tomatoes, but why anyone would wish to pour this stuff on a good salad of beautiful fresh greens is beyond me. Especially when it takes only a few minutes to make a dressing that is as fresh-tasting as the vegetables you'll use it on.

All of the salad dressings in this book are quick to make, and they will keep very nicely in the refrigerator for at least one week. Most of them will keep even longer.

When I make a salad dressing recipe, I not only think of what it will taste like on the salad—I also consider what it will add to the meal nutritionally. Some of these recipes do not contain oil. Instead, they contain a food that is high in oil, such as tahini or avocado. By using foods that are naturally rich in oil rather than the oil itself, you are getting a lot more nutrition for your calories. Most of these dressings are much lower in fat (and therefore calories) than conventional dressings, and the ones that contain tofu or yogurt are high in protein, too.

The *Homemade Mayonnaise* on page 132 and *Sandra's Sweet French Dressing* on page 134 are more like their commercial counterparts than the other dressings in this book. But they do not contain the refined sweeteners and additives that are used in commercial dressings.

As with the other recipes in this book, feel free to change any of these salad dressings to suit your own taste. Add more or less garlic, more or less lemon, etc. Above all, enjoy them with the plea-

sure of knowing that their zest and flavor comes from your own creative combination of nutritious, natural ingredients.

TAHINI-UMEBOSHI DRESSING

This simple and unusual dressing is one of my favorites.

½ cup water
3–4 medium umeboshi plums, pitted, or 3 tablespoons umeboshi paste
¼ cup tahini

Yield: Approximately ¾ cup
Time: 5 minutes

Blend together all ingredients in the blender until smooth and creamy. Serve over a green salad.

NOTE: If this dressing is too thick, add some more water. If the taste is too strong for you, add some extra tahini and some water.

CUCUMBER-UMEBOSHI DRESSING

½ large or 1 small cucumber (about 1 heaping cup, sliced)
¼ cup olive oil
1 teaspoon umeboshi paste, or 2 umeboshi plums, pitted
2 scallions, finely chopped

Yield: About 1 cup
Time: 5–10 minutes

1. If the cucumber is waxed, peel it; if not, just wash it well.
2. Slice the cucumber and place it in a blender. Add the olive oil and the umeboshi paste. Blend until smooth and creamy.
3. Pour the dressing into a small bowl. Mix in the scallions. This dressing is delicious with a green salad or a Complete Meal Salad (see pages 112–114).

LEMON-SHOYU DRESSING

This is the salad dressing that we use most often at our house. It has just 10 calories per tablespoon!

¼ cup lemon juice
¼ cup olive oil
1–2 tablespoons shoyu or tamari
1 or more cloves garlic, pressed
1–2 teaspoons Dijon mustard (optional)

Yield: About ½ cup
Time: 5 minutes

Place all ingredients in a small glass jar. Cover tightly and shake well. Serve on green salads, marinated vegetable salads, even over hot vegetables. It is especially good for dipping artichokes and can be used for marinating cooked beans.

VARIATION

- If you find the flavor of this dressing too strong, you may add some safflower oil or another mild-tasting oil in addition to the olive oil.

ORIENTAL DRESSING

Light, simple, and very tasty. This dressing is good on a green salad or with a bean sprout salad. It is also good over sliced cucumbers and for marinating sliced mushrooms.

¼ cup vegetable oil, or more to taste
¼ cup rice vinegar
½–1 teaspoon roasted sesame oil
2 tablespoons tamari
1 clove garlic, pressed (optional)

Yield: Approximately ⅔ cup
Time: 5 minutes

Place all the ingredients in a small glass jar with a lid. Cover and shake to blend well. Store in the refrigerator.

BOTTOMLESS SALAD DRESSING WITH MARINATED GARLIC

For garlic lovers only!

½ cup mild-flavored oil such as safflower
¼ cup lemon juice, apple cider vinegar, or wine vinegar
2 tablespoons tamari or shoyu
2–3 bulbs garlic (20 or more cloves, as needed to fill the jar)

Yield: About 1½ cup dressing
Time: 20 minutes

1. Combine the oil, juice or vinegar, and the tamari or shoyu in a pint-sized glass jar.
2. Separate the cloves from the bulb of garlic and remove their skins. To make peeling easier, firmly hit (but do not smash) each clove with the side of a knife blade or with the bottom of a glass.
3. Place the peeled garlic in the jar along with the oil mixture. Place a lid on the jar and shake. The salad dressing may be used immediately, if desired (with the garlic strained out, of course). When you use some of the dressing always add more oil, juice or vinegar, and tamari or shoyu. The proportions are not really important; just add the ingredients to taste.
4. Store the dressing in the refrigerator, adding more ingredients whenever the jar begins to get empty. In about 2–3 weeks the garlic will begin to turn light brown and acquire a delicious, not-too-strong flavor. It actually becomes almost sweet. Serve the garlic as a condiment, like pickles or olives. It is unbelievably good!

TAHINI-YOGURT DRESSING

A creamy dressing that can be made as mild or as spicy as you like.

2 tablespoons tahini
2 tablespoons light miso (white or yellow)
2–3 tablespoons lemon juice
¼–⅓ cup yogurt

OPTIONS
1 or more cloves garlic, pressed
¼ teaspoon freshly grated ginger, or more to taste
1 teaspoon Dijon mustard
1 teaspoon prepared horseradish

Yield: About ⅔ cup dressing
Time: 5 minutes

Cream together the tahini, miso, and lemon juice. Add the yogurt and mix well. This makes a very good dressing, but if you enjoy a more piquant flavor, add one or more of the options.

NOTE: Several of the optional ingredients may be combined. The garlic and ginger are good when added to this recipe together; so are the garlic and mustard and the garlic and horseradish. About the only two combinations that are not so good together are ginger-mustard and ginger-horseradish. If this dressing is too thick, add a little water and mix well.

MISO-MUSTARD DRESSING

2 tablespoons white miso
2 tablespoons Dijon mustard
1/4 cup lemon juice
1/4 cup olive oil
1 clove garlic, pressed

Yield: 3/4 cup
Time: 5 minutes

1. In a small bowl, mix together the miso and the mustard.
2. Add the lemon juice, oil, and garlic. Beat with a fork until the mixture is well-blended. Store in the refrigerator in a covered container.

MOCK SOUR CREAM

Just as delicious as the real thing, but not nearly as rich. One cup of *Mock Sour Cream* contains 173 calories and 17 grams of protein. One cup of real sour cream contains 493 calories and 7 grams of protein.

1 cup cottage cheese
1 cup yogurt
1/8 teaspoon sea salt, or to taste
1 teaspoon lemon juice, or to taste
1 tablespoon fresh minced chives, or 1 teaspoon dry chives
1 tablespoon minced parsley

Yield: 2 cups
Time: 5–10 minutes

1. Place the cottage cheese, yogurt, salt, and juice in a blender. Blend until the mixture is smooth and creamy.
2. Add the chives and parsley. Mix well.
   Serve over baked potatoes or other vegetable dishes. This also makes a good low-calorie dip for raw vegetables.

HOMEMADE MAYONNAISE

If you use mayonnaise, it is worthwhile to make your own. Not only is it less expensive, it also is fresher, tastier, and more healthful.

1 egg
2 tablespoons lemon juice
1/2 teaspoon sea salt
1/2 teaspoon mustard powder or 2 teaspoons Dijon mustard
1 teaspoon honey
1 cup mild-flavored vegetable oil (such as safflower)

Yield: Approximately 1 cup
Time: 15 minutes

1. Place the egg, lemon juice, salt, mustard, and honey in a blender. Blend on low speed for a few seconds.
2. When these first 5 ingredients are well blended, remove the small plastic cap from the lid of the blender. Continue to blend on low speed while you very slowly pour a thin stream of oil into the blender. If you pour the oil too fast, the mayonnaise will separate. Continue to slowly pour the oil into the blender until the mayonnaise reaches the desired consistency.
   Store the mayonnaise in a covered glass jar in the refrigerator.

VARIATION

- *Aioli* (Garlic Mayonnaise): Add 3 cloves garlic, or more to taste, when you blend together the first 5 ingredients in the above recipe. Continue to blend while slowly adding the oil as indicated above.

SOYANNAISE

One quarter of a cup *Soyannaise* contains 78 calories and 4.6 grams of protein. It can be used like mayonnaise, but is low-fat and egg-free.

1 cup mashed tofu
2 tablespoons lemon juice
1 tablespoon olive oil
1/2 teaspoon sea salt
1 teaspoon Dijon mustard
1 clove garlic, minced
1/2 teaspoon honey
1 tablespoon water or more, if needed

Yield: Approximately 1 cup
Time: 10 minutes

Blend together all ingredients in a blender till smooth and creamy. If the mixture is too thick, add enough water to achieve the desired consistency. Adjust seasoning to taste.

VARIATION

- *Tofu Dip.* Follow the recipe given above for *Soyannaise* and add one or more of the following ingredients: 2 tablespoons minced parsley; 2 scallions, finely chopped; 1 stalk celery, finely chopped; 1/4 cup chopped black olives; 1/4 cup finely chopped dill pickles; 2–3 tablespoons grated Parmesan cheese.

INSTANT YOGURT DRESSING

1 cup plain yogurt
1 tablespoon lemon juice, or to taste
1/8 teaspoon sea salt, or to taste
1/4 teaspoon tarragon (optional)
1 tablespoon minced parsley
1 clove garlic, pressed

Yield: About 1 cup
Time: 3–5 minutes

Mix together all ingredients.

This dressing is delicious with baked potatoes, green salad, and other salad you might choose to serve it with. It is also good with curries or vegetable-stuffed crepes.

TOFU-BLUE CHEESE DRESSING

This dressing is not nearly as rich as it tastes. It will keep for several days in a covered container in the refrigerator.

1 cup mashed tofu
1 cup yogurt
3/4 cup crumbled blue cheese
3 finely chopped scallions

Yield: 2 1/2 cups
Time: 10 minutes

1. Place the tofu, yogurt, and 1/2 cup of the blue cheese in the blender. Blend till smooth and creamy.
2. Add the remaining cheese and the scallions. Mix well.

CREAMY CUCUMBER DRESSING

Cashews replace the oil in this mild and creamy dressing. This dressing will keep for several days in a covered container in the refrigerator.

1 cup mashed tofu
¼ cup lime juice
1 medium cucumber, sliced (peel the cucumber only if it is waxed)
¼–½ teaspoon sea salt
⅓ cup cashews
2 tablespoons chopped onion
¼–½ teaspoon dill seed

Yield: 2 cups
Time: 10 minutes

Blend together all ingredients in a blender until the dressing is smooth and creamy.

SANDRA'S SWEET FRENCH DRESSING

This recipe comes from one of my students, who has become an expert at converting her family's old favorite recipes to feature natural ingredients.

½ cup honey
1 teaspoon paprika
⅓ cup natural imitation catsup (sold in natural foods stores)
1 teaspoon celery seed
1 teaspoon grated onion
⅓ cup apple cider vinegar
1 cup mild-flavored vegetable oil, such as safflower oil

Yield: Approximately 2 cups
Time: 10 minutes

Place all the ingredients in a blender and blend till smooth. Store in the refrigerator in a covered glass jar.

AVOCADO-YOGURT DRESSING

The lime green color and the exquisite rich, creamy texture of this dressing make it especially nice.

1 medium avocado
3 tablespoons lemon juice
½ cup yogurt
¼ teaspoon sea salt, or to taste

Yield: Approximately 1½ cups
Time: 5 minutes

Blend together all ingredients in a blender.

VARIATION

• Minced onion, scallions, chives, or parsley may be added if desired.

TOMATO DRESSING

1 medium ripe tomato
¼ cup olive oil
Juice of one small lemon
1 tablespoon yellow miso
½ teaspoon basil

Yield: About 1½ cups
Time: 5 minutes

Coarsely chop the tomato and place it in a blender along with the other ingredients. Blend until smooth and creamy. Store in a covered glass jar in the refrigerator.

This dressing is good with green salads or with a Complete Meal Salad (see pages 112–114).

9. *VEGETABLE DISHES*

Today's concern with health and fitness has made us aware of the importance of including an abundance of fresh vegetables in our diet. Considering the nondescript canned mixed vegetables, frozen spinach, anemic tomatoes, and rusty-looking iceberg lettuce that so many Americans grew up on, it is evident that a change is in order. Many of us have sought new ways of preparing vegetables to make them more appealing.

Preparing scrumptious vegetable dishes is easier than you might think. Actually it depends more on the vegetables themselves than on us. If you have ever had a garden, you will know what I mean. Garden-fresh vegetables picked at their peak of ripeness are so good that very little preparation or seasoning is needed to put together a dish that is as delightful to the palate as it is colorful and visually pleasing. To prepare irresistible vegetable dishes, it is essential to start with the finest-quality ingredients.

Always select vegetables that are in season locally. Doesn't it make sense that the foods provided by nature at certain times of the year are the ones that our bodies need at that time? In selecting our foods with regard to their proper season, we are assuring ourselves of fresh foods as well as letting nature create for us an ever-changing menu. In the winter, of course, there are not too many places in the United States where fresh vegetables will grow. However, many vegetables, such as cabbage, pumpkins, winter squash, and root vegetables, keep all winter long. It is these hearty vegetables that are the most sustaining and satisfying during the cold months. Later, when the first tender greens of springtime begin to grow, we are more than ready to cast off our heavy winter fare for their light and clean-tasting goodness.

The best method of acquiring top-quality produce (aside from your own garden) is to buy it from an organic farmer. In most cities today we are lucky enough to have stores or farmer's markets that sell organic produce (vegetables and fruits grown on composted soil without the use of chemical fertilizers or insecticides). Buying organic produce may not be as convenient as running to the corner supermarket, and it may cost a little more, but the rewards are well worth it. Not only does organic produce taste a great deal better than foods grown by standard methods, but buying it gives us the satisfaction of knowing that we are encouraging a renewable system of agriculture that will keep the soil alive and productive for future generations. At the same time we benefit from clean, poison-free food.

Once you have your beautiful fresh vegetables, choose a simple way to prepare them. This chapter begins with a discussion of some different methods of cooking vegetables. Each method has nutritional advantages and disadvantages; therefore, it is wise to use a variety of cooking methods and not to depend solely on one method. Following the cooking methods you will find descriptions of various vegetables including tips on cleaning, preparing, and serving, as well as recipes. Say goodbye to those hard, pale, winter tomatoes forever!

COOKING METHODS FOR VEGETABLES

Boiling. The vegetables are completely submerged in water, the water is heated to a boil, and the vegetables are cooked over a fairly high heat until they are very tender. This was America's favorite method of cooking vegetables until it was discovered that it causes a substantial loss of vitamins, minerals, and flavor.

Modified Boiling. Any type of vegetable can be cooked by this method. It is recommended over the standard type of boiling, especially if the water that is used for cooking the vegetables (the "cooking water") is also used in preparing the meal.

Place the vegetables in a pan with a tight-fitting lid. Pour about one inch of water into the bottom of the pan. Cover and bring the water to a boil. Reduce the heat and simmer until the vegetables are tender. Check occasionally and add more water if necessary.

A tasty and nourishing way to use the cooking water is to make it into a light sauce, using arrowroot to thicken it. To determine how much arrowroot to use, drain the water from the cooked vegetables into a measuring cup. Add more water, or pour some of the water off, if necessary, to obtain the amount of liquid that you desire for the sauce. Measure the cooking water. In 1/4 cup of cold water dissolve one-and-a-half tablespoons of arrowroot for each cup of water that you are using to make the sauce. Return the cooking water to the vegetables and then add the dissolved

arrowroot mixture. Bring to a boil. Cook, stirring gently, for one to two minutes, until the sauce thickens. Season to taste with some tamari or shoyu. (One tablespoon tamari per cup of cooking water, or to taste.) If desired, a little lemon juice, some chopped scallions, or some parsley may also be added.

Steaming. All vegetables lend themselves nicely to steaming. It is probably the most popular method of cooking vegetables among health-oriented people today.

Pour about one inch of water into the bottom of a pan. In the pan, place a rack that will hold the vegetables above the water. Cover tightly and bring the water to a boil. Add the vegetables, cover, and reduce the heat to medium-low. Cook until the vegetables are tender. Check the water level in your pan once during the cooking to make sure that there is enough water.

Although steaming releases less nutrients into the cooking water than boiling does, there is still a nutrient loss. Therefore, the leftover cooking water should always be consumed with the vegetables, or reserved for a sauce or soup.

Pressure Cooking. Pressure cooking vegetables is usually discouraged because it is so easy to overcook the vegetables. Very quick-cooking vegetables, such as snow peas, spinach, mushrooms, mung sprouts, etc. should not be pressure-cooked. However, for all other vegetables, pressure cooking can be quite satisfactory if you are careful not to overcook. In fact, some nutritional experts believe that when pressure cooking is done properly it is better than steaming.

Place the vegetables in the pressure cooker. Add a small amount of water (usually about one cup of water is enough), cover the cooker, and place over high heat. When the pressure is up to maximum and the pressure regulator begins to rock, remove the pressure cooker from the heat. For vegetables that are relatively quick-cooking, such as asparagus and summer squash, or for vegetables that are cut into small pieces, cool the cooker immediately by letting cold tap water run over it. As soon as the pressure is down, remove the lid so that the vegetables stop cooking.

For slower-cooking vegetables and vegetables that are cut into larger pieces, remove the pressure cooker from the heat as soon as the pressure regulator begins to rock and let the cooker cool down on its own.

For very slow-cooking vegetables, such as whole artichokes, whole or large chunks of beets, and rutabagas, it is necessary to cook for a few minutes (about three to five minutes should be enough) with the pressure regulator rocking gently. Then remove the pressure cooker from the heat and let it cool down on its own.

If desired, a steaming rack may be placed in a pressure cooker, so that the vegetables do not touch the water. Always follow the manufacturer's instructions for your pressure cooker.

Stewing. Vegetables are slowly simmered in a broth. This can either be done on top of the stove or in the oven. Almost any vegetable can be cooked in a stew; however, it is important to cut the slower-cooking vegetables into smaller pieces and the quicker-cooking vegetables into larger pieces to assure a uniform doneness. See the recipes for *Italian Vegetable Stew*, page 235, *Ratatouille*, page 151, and *Pot au Feu*, page 235.

Stir-Frying. The vegetables are sliced into thin strips and cooked rapidly over high heat in a small amount of oil. Because of the high heat, the vegetables must be constantly stirred with a shoveling motion to keep them from scorching. Thus the term "stir-fry!"

Except for potatoes, beets, green beans, and other rather dry or hard vegetables, almost any vegetable can be stir-fried. Besides being quick, easy, and energy-efficient, stir-frying also makes good sense nutritionally, because it is one of the cooking methods that retains the largest amounts of vitamins and minerals.

Cooking a stir-fry dish is another good occasion to bring some of that "right brain" intuition that we have discussed into focus. Because the combinations of vegetables that we can use are practically unlimited, the way to go about cooking a stir-fry dish is also variable. Sometimes a stir-fry dish requires the addition of a little bit of water and some steaming. Other times it doesn't. To constantly turn out stir-fry dishes that are cooked to perfection, you must not be rigid about following fixed cooking times. You must be sensitive to the food that you are cooking. The amount of time required to cook a stir-fry dish depends on the size to which the vegetables are cut, the degree of heat used, and the quantity of

vegetables cooked. (The more vegetables being cooked, the longer it takes.)

The way that the vegetables are sliced is important. The size and the thickness of the slices should be consistent. Vegetables that are cut into strips or matchsticks cook better than those cut into cubes or rounds.

To stir-fry, heat about two tablespoons of oil in a wok or large skillet. First add the stronger-flavored and slower-cooking vegetables (onions, garlic, ginger, celery, carrots, broccoli stems, etc.) and stir over high heat for one to three minutes. Then add the vegetables that take a moderate amount of time to cook (summer squash, broccoli flowers, red or green pepper, etc.) and stir over high heat for a minute or two. Add the quick-cooking vegetables (such as mushrooms, snow peas, and mung sprouts) next. Stir for a minute. Cover and reduce the heat to low. If the vegetables are dry, it may be necessary to add a little bit of water (about one-quarter cup) before covering. Let the veggies steam for two to five minutes or until they are just barely tender.

Oilless "Stir-Frying". If you do not wish to use oil in cooking, it is possible to "stir-fry" vegetables in a small amount of water. See the recipe for *Oilless "Stir-Fried" Vegetables* on page 141.

Baking. For vegetables that lend themselves to this method of cooking, baking makes an interesting change from usual cooking procedures. It is especially nice in winter. Sweet vegetables such as winter squash, parsnips, carrots, and sweet potatoes taste even sweeter when they are baked.

Here are three different ways to bake vegetables:

1. Whole, either uncovered or covered with foil. Vegetables that can be cooked this way include: sweet potatoes, potatoes, winter squash, pumpkins, beets, and onions. When baking whole, unpeeled vegetables, always make sure that their skin is pierced in a few places with a knife or fork. If not, they may explode!

2. Sliced and baked in a dish that has been coated with a small amount of oil. For this method you can use potatoes (see *Oven-Browned Potatoes*, page 164), carrots, parsnips (see *Baked Garlic Parsnips*, page 161), turnips, or onions.

3. Baked with water or stock in a casserole or stew. Almost all vegetables can be cooked this way.

The usual oven temperature for baking vegetables is 350°F. The cooking time depends on the size of the pieces the vegetables have been cut into and the variety of the vegetables being baked.

Waterless Cooking. A fairly recent concept, this type of cooking requires no water and no fat. The vegetables gently simmer in their own juices, which makes them surprisingly more flavorful than vegetables cooked by other means. Since there is no added water to draw vitamins and minerals out of the food, and no fat to add extra calories, this is one of the best methods of cooking vegetables that I have discovered.

It is also one of the easiest methods. Just prepare the vegetables by chopping or slicing them as you would for steaming. Rinse them briefly in cold water, drain, and place them in a pan that is especially designed for waterless cooking (see page 14). Cover and cook over low heat until the vegetables are tender. Vegetables cooked in this way are so tasty that they need virtually no additional seasoning.

This chapter describes individual vegetables, with instructions and suggestions for the preparation of each vegetable. At least one recipe that features that vegetable follows. These recipes can be made into main dishes with the addition of a grain and a protein such as tofu, tempeh, or legumes.

ARTICHOKES

Worth their price, artichokes are an epicure's delight. Unlike many treats, however, they are low in calories and as healthful as they are delicious. Artichokes may be cooked whole, halved, or stuffed. Italians say that artichokes are good for the liver and they often serve them as an accompaniment to a rich meal.

To Clean: Wash the artichoke well, letting the water run down between the leaves. Cut a thin slice off the bottom of the stem. Also pull off and discard any discolored exterior leaves.

To Cook: Place the artichoke either in a steamer or in the bottom of a pan with about 1½ inches of water. Cover tightly and bring to a boil. Reduce the heat and steam until tender (about 1 hour). Check the water level from time to time, adding more water if necessary. To tell if the artichoke is done, just pull off a leaf and taste it.

To pressure-cook, let the pressure regulator rock gently for about 8 minutes (more or less depending on the size of the artichoke).

For faster cooking, cut the artichoke in half with a sharp knife. Cut out the inedible choke and cook as usual.

To Serve: Place a whole artichoke on each individual's plate and place some small individual bowls of vinaigrette or other light dressing on the table. *Lemon-Shoyu Dressing* (page 130) is great with artichokes, and so is *Avocado-Yogurt Dressing* (page 134). Artichoke hearts are marvelous in salads or in spaghetti sauce. See *Jody's Carciofi in Salsa* (Dressed Artichokes) on page 128.

To Eat: Pull the leaves off the artichoke, one by one. Dip the bottom part of the leaf in the dressing and slip it through your teeth, scraping off the fleshy part. In the center of the artichoke you will find the inedible choke, which is purple, white, and fuzzy. Discard the choke and under it you will find the delicious heart. The heart is attached to the stem, which is also good to eat.

STUFFED ARTICHOKES

Cleaning the artichokes for this recipe is a bit troublesome, but the result is well worth it.

2 large or 4 medium-sized artichokes
1 tablespoon olive oil
2 tablespoons minced onion
1½ cups finely chopped mushrooms
1 cup whole wheat bread crumbs
¼ cup grated Romano or Parmesan cheese
½ teaspoon oregano

Serves: 2–4
Time: 1½ hours

1. Slice the stem off of each artichoke so that each will stand upright. (Don't throw away the stems; they are good to eat. Either cook the stems with the artichokes or save them for a soup or broth.)

2. Using a sharp knife or scissors, cut away and discard the top ⅓ to ½ of each leaf. Spread the leaves apart with your hands, then reach down into the center of each artichoke and cut out the choke. Use a small, sharp knife to do this. Rinse the artichokes briefly under cold running water to remove any remaining pieces of the choke.

3. Heat the oil in a skillet. Add the onion and the mushrooms. Sauté until tender. Remove the skillet from the heat and stir in the bread crumbs, cheese, and oregano. Mix well.

4. Fill the center cavity of each artichoke with the stuffing mixture. Place the stuffed artichokes in a kettle (stem end down) with about 1½ inches of water. Cover and bring to a boil. Lower the heat and simmer for about 40 minutes (for medium-sized artichokes) to 1 hour (for large ones), or until tender. (You can tell when an artichoke is tender by pulling off a leaf and tasting it.) Check occasionally, adding more water if needed.

ASPARAGUS

Tender green asparagus is one of springtime's finest gifts.

To Clean: Occasionally I find a bunch of asparagus that has some sand under the little scales that are on the stem. If you find this, remove the scales as you wash the asparagus. If not, just rinse thoroughly under running water.

Break the tough part of the stalks off as far down as possible. The part of the stem that does not snap when you bend it is too tough to serve as a steamed vegetable. However, it may be used in a soup stock or blended in a cream soup.

To Cook: Steaming is the best method for cooking asparagus. It takes only a few minutes so be careful not to overcook it.

To Serve: Asparagus is wonderful plain or with a mild-flavored sauce. In addition to the following recipe, try *Asparagus Crepes* (page 219).

ASPARAGUS WITH MUSHROOMS

1 pound fresh asparagus
2 tablespoons oil
½ cup finely chopped onions
2 cups sliced mushrooms
SAUCE
¼ cup water or vegetable stock
1 tablespoon rice vinegar or lemon juice
1 tablespoon shoyu, or to taste
1½ teaspoons arrowroot

Serves: 4
Time: 20 minutes

1. Clean the asparagus and either cut the stalks into 1½ inch pieces or leave them whole, as desired. Steam until just barely tender.

2. Heat the oil in a skillet. Add the onions and sauté until they begin to get tender. Add the mushrooms and sauté until tender.

3. In a small bowl, mix together the sauce ingredients. Pour the sauce over the sautéed mushrooms and onions. Cook over medium-high heat, stirring constantly, until the mixture thickens. If the asparagus is cut into small pieces, add it to the mushrooms and sauce. Mix well. If the asparagus is whole, place it on individual serving plates and spoon the sauce over the asparagus.

BEETS

Summer or winter, crisp ruby-red beets add color and beauty to any meal.

To Clean: Most people peel beets, but it is not really necessary. Just scrub them with a vegetable brush while holding them under running water. Then cut off and discard the stem end and the root end.

To Cook: Beets may be steamed, pressure-cooked, baked, or cooked by the modified boiling method. Sliced beets take about 20 minutes (more or less, depending on the thickness of the slices and the tenderness of the beets) to steam. Modified boiling takes about the same amount of time.

Because beets take longer then some vegetables to steam, I like to pressure cook them. To pressure cook sliced beets, cook them with the pressure regulator rocking gently for 3–5 minutes. Remove the cooker from the heat and let the pressure come down on its own. The beets should be done.

Baked beets are especially sweet and flavorful. Count on one good-sized beet per person. Clean the beets and place them in a lightly oiled baking dish. Cover the baking dish and bake the beets at 350°F for one hour or more (depending on their size) until tender. They may also be wrapped in aluminum foil and baked like potatoes.

To Serve: Sliced beets are good served plain or with a little olive oil and lemon. Tarragon is a nice herb for seasoning beets. Cooked beets are good marinated and served cold with a salad (see *Easter Salad,* page 118). Serve baked beets as you would baked potatoes, but instead of using butter try serving them with olive oil or *Mock Sour Cream* (page 132). Also see the recipe for *Céline's Royal Aspic* (page 121).

BEETS WITH TOPS

4 medium beets, with their tops
1–2 tablespoons olive oil
1–2 tablespoons lemon juice
1 or more cloves garlic, pressed (optional)
½ teaspoon tarragon
Pinch of sea salt, to taste

Serves: 4
Time: 35 minutes

1. Cut the tops off of the beets and wash them in cool water. Scrub the beets with a brush and cut off the stem end and the root end. Slice the beets with a sharp knife.

2. Place the sliced beets in a pan with about 1 inch of water in the bottom. Cover and bring to a boil. Reduce the heat and simmer the beets for about 5 minutes.

3. Place the greens on top of the sliced beets. Cover and steam for about 20 minutes or until both the beets and the greens are tender. From time to time check the water level, adding more water if necessary.

4. When the vegetables are done, coarsely chop the tops and place them in a serving bowl along with the beets. Mix together the remaining ingredients and pour the mixture over the vegetables. Toss and serve.

BEETS À L'ORANGE

These orange-glazed beets add a colorful and fancy touch to a winter meal.

4 cups scrubbed and sliced beets
½ cup liquid from cooking the beets
The juice of 1 orange (about ½ cup)
The juice of ½ small lemon (about 2 tablespoons)
1½ tablespoons arrowroot
1 tablespoon grated orange peel
¼ teaspoon sea salt
1½ teaspoons honey

Serves: 4–6
Time: 35 minutes

1. Place the beets in a pan with about 1½ inches of water in the bottom. Cover and bring water to a boil. Lower the heat and simmer the beets until tender.

2. Pour the liquid from cooking the beets into a measuring cup until you have ½ cup. Discard any remaining liquid. Pour the ½ cup reserved liquid into a small saucepan.

3. In a small bowl, mix together the remaining ingredients. Add the mixture to the saucepan with the beet liquid. Bring to a boil while stirring constantly. Pour the thickened sauce over the cooked beets; mix gently and place in a serving dish. Serve immediately.

BROCCOLI

Highly nutritious, broccoli is the favorite vegetable of many. It is a good source of vitamin C and A. Broccoli is also a good source of protein (5.6 grams per medium-sized stalk) and calcium (160 milligrams per medium-sized stalk).

To Clean: Wash the broccoli under running water. To cook it whole, peel the stem, then slice the thick part of the stem up the middle twice to divide it into four sections. If bite-sized pieces are desired, peel the stem and slice it into rounds or matchsticks. Cut the top into flowerets.

To Cook: Broccoli may be steamed, pressure cooked, or stir-fried. To stir-fry, slice the peeled stem into thin matchsticks and thinly slice the flowerets also. Stir-fried broccoli takes 6 minutes or less of cooking. Whole broccoli takes about 15 minutes (or less) of steaming or modified boiling. Cut into bite-sized pieces, broccoli needs about 10 minutes or less of steaming. For pressure cooking, if the broccoli has been cut into bite-sized pieces, bring the pressure up to maximum and then cool the pressure cooker off under running water. If the broccoli is whole, let the pressure come down on its own.

To Serve: Steamed broccoli is good plain or with a mild-flavored sauce such as a *Béchamel* (page 242) or cheese sauce (try the *Easiest Cheese Sauce* on page 242). Stir-fried broccoli is good with a tamari- or shoyu-based sauce such as *Sauce Orientale* (page 245). Use broccoli in soups (*Tracey's Cream of Broccoli Soup*, page 55), casseroles (*Broccoli and Potatoes au Gratin*, page 227), mixed vegetable stir-fries (*Sweet and Sour Tempeh*, page 40), and so on. Broccoli lovers will also enjoy the recipes for *Broccoli Souffle* (page 224), *Broccoli-Tofu Quiche* (page 206), and *Broccoli and Cauliflower Salad* (page 120).

OILLESS "STIR-FRIED" VEGETABLES

Low in calories and full of flavor, this quick and easy wok dish uses broccoli and a variety of mixed vegetables.

1 cup water or vegetable stock
2–3 tablespoons tamari
A few drops roasted sesame oil (for flavor)
2 cloves garlic, minced
1 teaspoon grated ginger
1 cup sliced onion (1 medium onion)
2 stalks broccoli
1 red pepper or 1 carrot
4 cups mung bean sprouts

Serves: 2 generously
Time: 15–20 minutes

1. Place the water or stock, tamari, roasted sesame oil, garlic, and ginger in a wok.
2. Cut the broccoli flowerets into bite-sized pieces. Peel the broccoli stems and cut them into strips. Slice the pepper or carrot into strips.
3. Bring the liquid in the wok to a boil. Add the onions, broccoli, and carrot (if you are using a carrot). Stir the vegetables with a constant shoveling motion as if you were stir-frying with oil. Cook, stirring constantly, over high heat until the vegetables are beginning to get tender. (This should not take very long.) Add the pepper (if you are using a pepper) and the bean sprouts. Continue stirring until the bean sprouts shrink in size.
4. Cover the wok, reduce the heat to medium, and let steam until tender (about 3–5 minutes).

Serve over a bed of cooked rice or millet, accompanied by *Ginger Tofu* (see page 199) or *Peanut Tofu* (page 200).

NOTE: Reserve the leftover broth to use again, or to make into a sauce or a soup.

VARIATION

- Use any desired combination of vegetables that lend themselves to stir-frying (such as mushrooms, Chinese cabbage, and summer squash) to replace the ones in the recipe.

BRUSSELS SPROUTS

One cup of Brussels sprouts contains 135 milligrams of vitamin C—more than an orange. Brussels sprouts are also a surprisingly good source of protein; 1 cup contains 6.5 grams.

To Clean: Peel off the outer leaves only if they are yellow or damaged. Wash Brussels sprouts thoroughly; then cut a very thin slice off of the bottom of the stem. If the sprouts are very large, you may wish to cut them in half. If not, cut an X about 1/4–1/2 inch deep into the bottom of each.

To Cook: Brussels sprouts may be steamed, pressure-cooked, or cooked by modified boiling. Steaming or modified boiling should take 12 minutes (more or less depending on the size of the vegetables). To pressure cook, bring the pressure up to maximum, then let it cool down naturally.

To Serve: Brussels sprouts are good in all sorts of vegetable casseroles (try *Autumn Regal*, page 230), and stews (see *Brussels Sprouts Cooked in Tomato Sauce*, page 142). They are also good served plain or with a mild-flavored sauce. The sauces in this book that complement Brussels sprouts include *Béchamel Sauce* (page 242); *Cashew Béchamel* (page 243); *Easiest Cheese Sauce* (page 242); *Tahini-Miso Sauce* (page 245); and *Sauce Orientale* (page 245). Brussels sprouts can also profit from a pinch of nutmeg.

BRUSSELS SPROUTS COOKED IN TOMATO SAUCE

10 ounces fresh Brussels sprouts
2 tablespoons olive oil
1 small onion, chopped
1 small green pepper, diced
1 stalk celery, chopped
1/4 teaspoon sea salt (optional)
1 teaspoon basil
1 1/2 cups canned tomatoes, with their juice
3 tablespoons tomato paste

Serves: 4
Time: 30 minutes

1. Wash the Brussels sprouts and remove any yellow outer leaves. Cut an X about 1/2 inch deep into the bottom of the stem end of each sprout.
2. Heat the oil in a heavy kettle and sauté the onion, pepper, and celery for about 3 minutes. Add the salt, basil, canned tomatoes, and Brussels sprouts. Cover tightly and simmer over medium-low heat for about 20 minutes, or until the Brussels sprouts are tender. Then add the tomato paste, mix well, and serve.

CABBAGE

Traditionally, cabbage has been an important vegetable for winter use, because it can be naturally stored almost all winter long without freezing or canning. Cabbage keeps well in root cellars with high humidity.

Today we can still benefit from this inexpensive, low-calorie vegetable. One cup of raw cabbage provides 33 milligrams of vitamin C and only 17 calories.

To Clean: If the cabbage still has its tough, exterior leaves, you may peel off the toughest ones. If not, remove only the leaves that are brown or damaged. Wash the cabbage very thoroughly, then cut the bottom off of the stem. The core may be eaten, but it should be chopped small enough to cook as fast as the rest of the cabbage. Cabbage may be chopped, shredded, or just quartered.

To Cook: Cook by modified boiling, steaming, pressure cooking, or stir-frying. Chopped cabbage will take about 15–20 minutes to cook by modified boiling or steaming. To pressure cook, just bring the pressure up to maximum, then remove the cooker from the heat and let the pressure come down on its own. If the cabbage is quartered rather than chopped, increase the cooking time accordingly. Stir-fried cabbage takes 5–10 minutes to cook, depending on the size you chop it and the quantity you are cooking.

To Serve: Cabbage may be used raw in salads or fermented into sauerkraut (see page 144 for recipe). It is also good in soups such as *Vegetable Gumbo*, page 53, stews, and casseroles. Caraway is a classic seasoning to use with cabbage. See recipes for *Cabbage Rolls*, page 232 and *Cabbage Spaghetti*, page 226.

CABBAGE AND NEW POTATOES

A simple and hearty side dish that can easily be converted into a main dish.

1 large onion, chopped
½ medium cabbage, chopped
4 cups new potatoes, cut into chunks
1½ cups water
1 bay leaf
½ teaspoon savory
½ teaspoon caraway
2 tablespoons yellow miso

Serves: 4
Time: 30 minutes

1. Place all the ingredients except the miso in a large kettle. Cover and bring to a boil. Reduce the heat and simmer until all the vegetables are tender, stirring occasionally. This will take about 20 minutes or so, depending on the size you cut the vegetables.
2. Remove the kettle from the heat and add the miso. Mix well and serve in bowls along with the broth (the cooking water, seasoned with miso, that is left over).

VARIATION

- For a tasty, but not fancy meal, top with some crumbled feta or firm goat cheese and some sliced green olives.

SAVOY CABBAGE

Savoy cabbage resembles white cabbage but it has a crinkly, wrinkled texture. It also has a milder, sweeter flavor and cooks a little faster.

1 medium Savoy cabbage
1 teaspoon caraway seeds
2 tablespoons olive oil
Tamari or sea salt to taste

Serves: 4–6
Time: 20 minutes

1. Wash the cabbage and cut it into thin strips. Chop the core more finely than the rest of the cabbage. Place the chopped cabbage and the caraway seeds in a vegetable steamer in a pot with 1 inch or so of water in the bottom. Cover tightly and bring the water to a boil. Reduce the heat and simmer for about 15 minutes or until the cabbage is tender.
2. Place the steamed cabbage in a serving bowl. Add the olive oil and the salt or tamari. Toss and serve.

VARIATION

- Omit the salt or tamari. Blend together the olive oil and 1–2 tablespoons yellow miso, to taste. Add this to the steamed cabbage and mix well.

CABBAGE IN RED WINE
(Chou à la Bourguignonne)

4 cups red cabbage, chopped
2 large potatoes, scrubbed and cut into chunks
½ cup onions, sliced
1 cup dry red wine
1 bay leaf
½–1 teaspoon tarragon
½ teaspoon sea salt

Serves: 2–4
Time: 15 minutes

1. Place all the ingredients in a pressure cooker. (If you do not have a pressure cooker, add about ½ cup more wine or water to the recipe and cook in a regular, covered pan over medium-low heat. Stir often and add more wine or water, if necessary, to keep the vegetables from sticking.) Cook over high heat until the pressure regulator begins to gently rock back and forth. Remove the cooker from the heat; let the pressure drop on its own.
2. The wine should be absorbed and the vegetables should be tender. If the vegetables are not cooked enough, return the pressure cooker to the heat and cook for a couple of minutes more.

    This recipe is delicious served plain as a side dish, or served with *Mock Sour Cream* (page 132) as a main dish.

SAUERKRAUT

Sauerkraut is a fermented food containing beneficial bacteria. It aids digestion in the same way that yogurt does. It is also a good source of vitamin C.

This easy method of making sauerkraut is the same one that was used by both my mother and my grandmother. The best time of year to make sauerkraut is in the fall, just after the harvest. The jars should be very clean; however, sterilizing them is not necessary.

1 medium head cabbage
2–3 teaspoons sea salt
2 or more cloves garlic (optional)
1–1½ teaspoons caraway seeds (optional)
2–3 quart jars with lids

Yield: 2–3 quarts
Time: 45 minutes

1. Wash and shred the cabbage. A food processor is great for shredding.
2. If desired, place 1 or more cloves of garlic and/or ½ teaspoon caraway seeds in the bottom of each quart jar. Pack the jars with the shredded cabbage, then sprinkle 1 teaspoon sea salt over each quart of packed cabbage. Add enough water to cover the cabbage, leaving ¾-inch space at the top of the jar to allow for expansion. If you fill the jars too full, the liquid will leak out and make a mess; however, the sauerkraut will still be good.
3. Place the lids on the jars and let them sit in your cupboard for about 5 weeks. The longer the kraut sits, the more sour it becomes. Refrigerate after opening. Use sauerkraut in salads, on sandwiches, and as an accompaniment to bean dishes.

CARROTS

Carrots are probably the vegetable that I use the most. They are great in winter, because the carrots harvested in fall can be kept naturally for many months. One cup of carrots contains 15,750 I.U. of vitamin A.

Many natural foods stores sell sweet, organic carrots. They are so good that it is really worth it to buy them.

To Clean: Scrub the carrots vigorously with a vegetable brush while holding them under running water. They do not have to be peeled. Cut off the stem and the root end and slice them into chunks, rounds, matchsticks, or diagonals. An easy way to cut carrots into matchsticks is to slice them diagonally about 1/4 inch. Stack 3–4 of the diagonal slices and then slice them lengthwise. (See Figure 9.1.)

To Cook: Carrots may be steamed, stir-fried, cooked by modified boiling, pressure cooked, or baked in a stew or casserole. Stir-fried carrots take 5 minutes or more to cook, depending on the size of the slices. Steamed carrots take between 5–15 minutes and modified boiling takes about the same. To pressure cook, just bring the pressure up to maximum; then, if the carrots are thinly sliced, cool the cooker down under running water; if they are in thick slices, let the pressure come down on its own.

Figure 9.1.   Slicing Carrots into Matchsticks

To Serve: Carrots may be used raw in salads (for instance, the *Carrot-Almond Salad* on page 118) or just steamed and served plain as a side dish. They add color to stir-fried dishes such as *Sweet and Sour Tempeh* (page 40) and may also be used in soups such as the *Carrot and Rice Cream* (page 59) or *Hearty Miso Vegetable Soup* (page 54). Also see the recipes for *Carrot-Tofu Quiche* on page 206 and *Carrots, Tofu, and Hijiki in Miso Broth*, page 39.

Herbs that complement the flavor of carrots are parsley, dill, tarragon, and basil. Yellow miso is also a good seasoning for carrots.

MAPLE-GLAZED CARROTS

This makes a nice dish to accompany a Thanksgiving dinner.

4 cups sliced carrots (4 large carrots)
1 teaspoon kudzu powder or 1 1/2 teaspoons arrowroot
2 tablespoons maple syrup
1/4 cup liquid from cooking the carrots
Pinch of sea salt
1/4 teaspoon nutmeg, or to taste

Serves: 4
Time: 20 minutes

1. Cook the carrots by steaming or modified boiling until they are tender. Drain the cooked carrots and reserve 1/4 cup of the liquid from cooking them.
2. Place the 2 tablespoons of maple syrup in a cup or in a small bowl. Add the kudzu powder or the arrowroot and mix well to dissolve. (If the kudzu is in lumps, break up the lumps with the back of a spoon before adding the kudzu to the syrup.) Add the measured cooking liquid, salt, and nutmeg to the syrup mixture.
3. If you steamed the carrots, remove the wire steaming basket and place the carrots directly in the pot that they were cooked in. Pour the liquid mixture over them.
4. Bring to a boil, stirring gently. Cook until the sauce thickens.

CAULIFLOWER

Cauliflower contains only 28 calories per cup, and like other members of the cabbage family, it is a good source of vitamin C.

To Clean: Wash the cauliflower thoroughly under running water. Cut out part of the core and discard the outer leaves. Slice the core and break the flowers into flowerets. To stir-fry the cauliflower, slice the flowerets into small pieces.

To Cook: Cauliflower may be steamed, cooked by modified boiling, pressure cooked, or stir-fried. Steaming or modified boiling takes about 10 minutes (more or less, depending on the size of the pieces). To pressure cook, just bring the pressure up to maximum, then cool the cooker off under running water. Stir-fried cauliflower takes about 5 minutes.

To Serve: Because of its mild flavor, cauliflower is a good vegetable to accompany a large number of other dishes. Serve lightly cooked cauliflower plain or with a sauce. *Easiest Cheese Sauce* (page 242), *Spicy Peanut Sauce* (page 246), *Tofu and Peanut Sauce* (page 244), *Tahini-Miso Sauce* (page 245), and *Onion-Mustard Sauce* (page 244) are all good with cauliflower. Cauliflower may also be used in soups, stews, and casseroles. Thin slices of raw cauliflower are a good addition to almost any salad and larger flowerets are excellent for dipping in *Soyannaise* (page 133) or other dips.

Seasonings that complement cauliflower are parsley, chives, dill weed, tarragon, *Gomashio* (see page 247), and white or yellow miso.

CAULIFLOWER CURRY

2 tablespoons oil
1 teaspoon finely grated fresh ginger
1/2–1 teaspoon cumin
1/2 teaspoon cinnamon
1/2 teaspoon turmeric
1 large onion, chopped
1 medium-large head of cauliflower, cut into bite-sized flowerets
1/2 cup water
1/2 teaspoon sea salt
1/3 cup whole raw almonds
3–4 tablespoons raisins (optional)

Serves: 3–4
Time: 25–30 minutes

1. Heat the oil in a large skillet or heavy kettle. Add the spices and the onion. Stir over medium heat for a few minutes.
2. Add the cauliflower and stir for about 3 minutes more. Add the water and the salt. Cover, lower the heat, and simmer for about 15 minutes or until the cauliflower begins to get tender but is still crisp.
3. While the cauliflower is cooking, chop the almonds and roast them in a toaster oven or under the broiler at 350°F for 5–10 minutes or until they are light brown.
4. When the cauliflower is tender, add the toasted almonds (and the raisins, if desired).

    Serve with rice and a yogurt sauce, or with rice and beans. If you serve this curry with a bean dish, please omit the raisins.

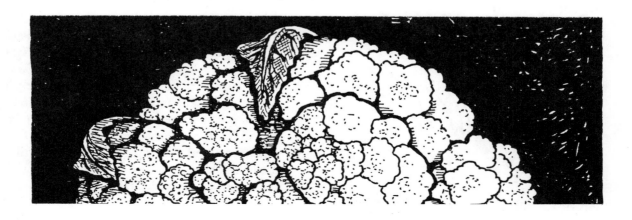

CELERY

Celery adds flavor and crispness to almost any dish without adding many calories.

To Clean: Scrub celery with a brush under running water. Chop or slice as desired. Reserve the leaves to add flavor to soups, stews, or tomato sauce.

To Cook: Celery is usually sautéed, stir-fried, or simmered in the broth of a soup or a stew. When adding it to a soup or a stew, chop it smaller than the quick-cooking vegetables. When you sauté or stir-fry celery, add it in the beginning, along with any onions.

To Serve: Raw celery may be finely chopped and added to salads, or cut into sticks and served with a dip. Celery stalks may also be stuffed with a dip or with natural peanut butter. Try stuffing celery with a half-and-half mixture of peanut butter and mashed tofu sprinkled with some veggie salt. Chopped celery may be added to almost any soup, stew, or spaghetti sauce. Sautéed celery may be added to casseroles.

CELERY-RICE CURRY

2 tablespoons oil
3 cups chopped celery
1 medium-large onion, chopped
1 teaspoon curry powder
1 teaspoon cumin
1 teaspoon fresh grated ginger
1/2 teaspoon tumeric
1/2 teaspoon mustard powder
1 cup long grain brown rice or brown basmati rice
1 3/4 cup boiling water
1/2 teaspoon sea salt (optional)
1/3 cup cashews, chopped and lightly roasted
1/3 cup raisins

Serves: 4
Time: 50 minutes

1. Heat the oil in a large skillet. Add the celery, onion, and spices. Stir over medium-high heat for 2–3 minutes. Wash and drain the rice.

Add the rice to the vegetables and stir for a minute or so.

2. Add the salt to the boiling water. Pour the water over the vegetable-rice mixture. Stir once, then cover. Lower the heat and simmer for about 40 minutes or until the water is absorbed. (Do not stir the rice while it is cooking.)

3. When the rice is done, add the nuts and raisins. (The easiest way to roast cashews is in a skillet. Place the nuts in an unoiled skillet and stir over medium heat for about 3–5 minutes, until they begin to brown. Alternatively, they may be roasted in a 350°F oven for about 10 minutes.)

4. Fluff the rice with a fork. Cover and let steam for about 5 minutes before serving.

CORN

Although corn is usually considered a vegetable, it is actually a grain. For optimal freshness, buy corn in the husk.

To Clean: Remove the husk and wash away the silks. If you wish to cut the corn away from the cob, make sure that you do not waste the nutritious germ. Run the back of your knife over the cob after you have cut away the kernels to scrape off the germ. Use the germ along with the rest of the corn.

To Cook: When corn is completely covered with water and cooked in the usual fashion, it loses both flavor and nutritional value. Therefore, steaming and modified boiling are the preferred cooking methods. After the water comes to a boil, corn only needs two to three minutes of steaming. Corn that is not very fresh may need more time.

Cream-style corn can be made by blending fresh corn in a blender. Add a little soymilk or dairy milk, some sweetener (such as honey, maple syrup, or malt) if desired, and a pinch of sea salt. Cook over medium heat, stirring constantly, for a few minutes.

To Serve: Corn on the cob is a wholesome summer tradition that everyone loves. However, the healthfulness of this wonderful fresh grain is overshadowed by harmful fat if it is drenched in butter or margarine. Try rubbing corn on the cob with an umeboshi plum (see page 11). The saltiness of the plum is an excellent complement to the sweetness of the corn.

Corn may also be cut off the cob to serve as a side dish. It may be added to almost any stew, casserole, or vegetable soup: see the recipes for *Corn and Lentil Soup* (page 52), *New Brunswick Chowder* (page 60), *Hearty Miso Vegetable Soup* (page 54), and *Vegetable Gumbo* (page 53). Also see *Golden Corn Bake* (page 177), *Vegetable Quiche* (page 225), and *Autumn Regal* (page 230).

Basil and oregano are both delicious with corn, and in some dishes a little cumin can also be good.

FRESH CORN CAKES

These are like the *Kentucky Hoe Cakes* on page 87, but they are made with fresh corn.

1³/4 cups corn, cut off the cob
2 eggs
1 teaspoon baking powder
¹/2 teaspoon sea salt
¹/2 cup cornmeal

Serves: 3–4
Time: 15 minutes

1. Place the corn, eggs, baking powder, and salt in a blender or food processor. Blend until smooth. Pour the batter into a bowl and add the cornmeal. Mix well.
2. Drop the batter by the ¹/4 cup onto a lightly oiled skillet. Cook each corn cake like a pancake over medium heat until it turns golden brown on the bottom. Turn it over and cook until done on the other side.

    Serve these in place of bread with soup or vegetables or as pancakes for breakfast.

HUMITE EN OLLA

A handsome Chilean man taught me how to make this recipe for spicy, cream-style corn. He insisted that the corn must be grated rather than blended in a blender. However, I have made it in the blender and it is still very good.

10–12 ears of corn, grated
¹/2 cup plain soymilk (you may use dairy milk instead)
1 teaspoon dry basil, or 1¹/2 tablespoons finely minced fresh basil
¹/2 teaspoon sea salt
¹/2 hot chili pepper, finely minced (or less, to taste) or a dash of cayenne
1 tablespoon olive oil
3 cloves garlic, finely minced
1 large green pepper, finely chopped
¹/2 teaspoon oregano
1 teaspoon plus 2 tablespoons malt syrup or other sweetener

Serves: 4
Time: 1 hour, 25 minutes

1. To grate the corn: place a grater in a large bowl. Grate the corn on the cob directly into the bowl, using the fine holes of the grater. If you do not wish to go to the trouble of grating the corn, just cut it off the cob and blend it in a blender or food processor.
2. Place the corn in a large, heavy kettle. Add the milk, basil, salt, and hot pepper. Cook uncovered over low heat for about 45 minutes, stirring often with a wooden spoon.
3. While the corn is cooking, heat the oil in a skillet. Add the garlic, green pepper, and oregano. Sauté until the pepper is almost tender.
4. Add this sautéed mixture to the corn. Mix well and add 1 teaspoon of malt syrup or another sweetener. Continue to cook, stirring constantly, for 15 more minutes.
5. Transfer the cooked corn mixture to a lightly oiled, shallow baking dish. Drizzle the top of the corn with the remaining sweetener and broil for a few minutes to lightly brown the top.

    Serve with a bean dish and a salad.

CREOLE CORN

3 cups corn, cut off the cob
1 cup tomato purée or canned tomatoes
1 tablespoon olive oil
1 medium onion, chopped
1 green pepper, diced
1 teaspoon basil
2 tablespoons tomato paste
1 tablespoon shoyu
1–2 teaspoons hot sauce

Serves: 4
Time: 15 minutes

1. Place the corn and tomato purée (or canned tomatoes) in a large saucepan. Bring to a boil. Cover, lower the heat, and simmer for about 5 minutes.
2. Heat the oil in a skillet. Add the onion, pepper, and basil. Sauté until the onions are tender.
3. Add the onion mixture to the corn mixture. Stir in the tomato paste, shoyu, and hot sauce.
   Serve as an accompaniment to a bean dish.

CUCUMBERS

Cucumbers. What vegetable could be more refreshing on a hot summer day? One reason for this is the cucumber's high moisture content. Cucumbers should be firm and not too large. Try to buy ones that are unwaxed.

To Clean: If the cucumber is waxed, peel it with a potato peeler. If it is unwaxed, just wash it thoroughly. Slice it any way you like: into thick or paper-thin rounds, diagonals, wedges, or sticks.

To Cook: Although cucumbers are usually eaten raw, they can be cooked like summer squash, if desired.

To Serve: A cucumber and yogurt salad is classic summer fare for vegetarians. Try the *Cucumber-Yogurt Salad* on page 117. Cucumbers are also good on sandwiches (see the *Cucumber-Watercress Sandwich*, page 66). Cut cucumbers into thick rounds, wedges, or sticks to serve with a dip; they are especially good with *Soyannaise* (page 133). Also see *Cucumber-Umeboshi Dressing*, page 130; *Creamy Cucumber Dressing*, page 134; *Marinated Cucumber Salad*, page 128; and *Chilled Cucumber Soup*, page 61.

Parsley, dill seed, dill weed, garlic, chives, and tarragon are all good seasonings for cucumbers.

REFRIGERATOR PICKLES

These pickles will keep in the refrigerator for about three weeks.

3 large unwaxed cucumbers
1 medium green pepper, chopped
1 small onion, chopped
1½ teaspoons sea salt
1 tablespoon dill seed
⅓ cup honey
½ cup cider vinegar

Serves: About 5 cups
Time: 15 minutes to prepare; 1 hour to stand;
1 day to marinate.

1. Wash the cucumbers and slice them into thin (¹⁄₁₆ of an inch) rounds. Place them in a jar (about 1½ quart size). Add the pepper and the onion. Sprinkle the vegetables with salt and dill seeds. Stir gently and let stand for about 1 hour.
2. Mix together the honey and the vinegar. Pour over the vegetables. Stir gently, cover, and refrigerate. The pickles will be ready in about one day. Store covered in the refrigerator.

DAIKON RADISH

Daikon radishes look sort of like gigantic white carrots. Widely used in Oriental cooking, the daikon radish (also called winter radish) is beginning to become popular in North America. Cooked, the daikon radish has a flavor similar to that of turnips (only daikon is juicier). Macrobiotic cooks say that daikon is good to serve as an accompaniment to tempura or other fried foods, as it helps the body to digest fat.

To Clean: Scrub the radish with a brush while holding it under running water. Discard the root end and the top end. Slice, dice, or grate.

To Cook: Daikon takes about the same amount of time to cook as carrots (maybe a little bit less). Matchstick slices of daikon may be stir-fried and sliced or cubed. Daikon may be added to soups or stews.

To Serve: Raw daikon has a fresh radish taste and is good grated and served in salads. It may be used to replace carrots, turnips, or parsnips in a vegetable soup. It may also be added to any stew that contains root vegetables, such as the *Pot au Feu* on page 235.

BAKED DAIKON WITH KOMBU AND ONIONS

2 strips kombu
2½ cups sliced daikon
1½ cups sliced onion
1 cup water
2 tablespoons tamari
½ teaspoon roasted sesame oil

Serves: 4
Time: 5 minutes to prepare; 45 minutes to bake.

1. Rinse the kombu and place it in the bottom of a baking dish. Place the sliced onion over the kombu and place the daikon over the onion. Add the water. Sprinkle with the tamari and the roasted sesame oil.
2. Cover and bake at 350°F for 30 minutes.

3. Uncover and bake for 15 minutes more, or until the vegetables are tender. Stir occasionally during the last period of baking, but don't stir up the kombu. Leave it in the bottom of the pot.
4. When the vegetables are tender, remove the kombu and slice it. Return the sliced kombu to the dish and mix it with the other vegetables.

EGGPLANT

From savory Mideastern and Indian dishes to Italian and French country-style cookery, the uses of eggplant are as varied as the countries that employ this vegetable in their traditional cuisines.

To Clean: Some people find eggplant bitter, so they peel it or sprinkle it with salt to extract its excess water. If the eggplant is very fresh, however, it is not bitter, so there is no need for peeling or salt-treating. Buy eggplant that is firm and heavy, with a smooth and unblemished skin.

Wash the eggplant well and cut off the stem end. Slice it, cube it, cut it into large chunks, or leave it whole for baking.

To Cook: This versatile vegetable may be baked, broiled, fried, sautéed, steamed, or cooked in a stew or casserole. Usually it is sautéed before it is added to a casserole. Small cubes of eggplant take about eight minutes or so of steaming or about five minutes of stir-frying. The larger the pieces, the longer the eggplant will take to cook.

To Serve: Eggplant is great with a tomato sauce, basil, and garlic, as in the following recipe for the classic French dish *Ratatouille*. The recipes for *Eggplant Roll-Ups* (page 237) and *Italian Vegetable Stew* (page 235) also feature this combination of ingredients. Eggplant may be added to any spaghetti sauce (try the *Tomato, Adzuki Bean, and Eggplant Sauce* on page 241), or thinly sliced and used as a garnish for pizza. It is equally good with curries, tahini, and chick peas. For a Mideastern flavor, try the eggplant spread *Baba Ganoui* (page 100) or *Eggplant and Chick Peas in Yogurt-Tahini Sauce* (page 39).

RATATOUILLE

Ratatouille is usually made with lots of olive oil. Here is a low-calorie version.

1 tablespoon olive oil
²/₃ cup chopped onion
2 cloves garlic, minced
½ green pepper, diced
1½ cups canned tomatoes, with their juice
1 cup sliced mushrooms
2 cups diced eggplant
2 cups sliced zucchini or summer squash
1 teaspoon basil
1 bay leaf
1 tablespoon tamari, or to taste
Pinch of cayenne, if desired

Serves: 2–4
Time: 20–30 minutes

1. Heat the oil in a large, heavy kettle. Add the onion, garlic, and pepper. Sauté for about 3 minutes.
2. Add the remaining ingredients. Cover and let simmer, stirring occasionally, until the eggplant and the zucchini are tender—about 20 minutes.

   Serve ratatouille in large, shallow soup bowls, accompanied by some whole grain bread; or serve over a bed of rice, millet, or whole grain pasta.

VARIATIONS

To turn this stew into a complete meal you may do one of the following:

- Cut about ½ pound of tofu into small cubes. Add it to the ratatouille during the last 5 minutes of cooking. Accompany with whole grain bread, pasta, or a cooked grain and a green salad.
- Add about 1 cup of cooked beans (chick peas, Great Northern beans, lima beans, etc.). Serve with whole grain bread or a cooked grain and a green salad.
- Sprinkle with grated cheese. Serve with whole grain bread or a cooked grain and a green salad.
- For a thicker stew, add as much tomato paste as you need to obtain the desired consistency.

BELGIAN ENDIVE

For some reason, many people are under the impression that Belgian endive is bitter. It isn't, not at all! It is wonderful.

To Clean: Rinse thoroughly under running water. Cut a thin slice off of the root end, and discard any wilted or damaged leaves.

To Cook: Sauté as indicated in the following recipe, or chop and eat raw in salads.

To Serve: Serve as a side dish or in a salad. See the recipe for *Belgian Endive and Walnut Salad With Goat Cheese* (see page 119). For a gourmet salad, use half endive and half watercress. Toss with your favorite dressing and serve.

GOURMET-STYLE BELGIAN ENDIVES

2 large Belgian endives
1 egg
Pinch of sea salt
¼ cup whole wheat pastry flour
2 tablespoons olive oil
2–3 sun-dried tomatoes for garnish, cut into thin strips (if desired)

Serves: 2
Time: 10 minutes

1. Wash the endives and cut them in half lengthwise. Break the egg into a shallow bowl. Add the salt and beat well.
2. Place the flour in another shallow dish. Dip each endive half in the egg mixture, then roll each one in the flour until it is well coated.
3. Heat the oil in a skillet. Place the endive halves flat side down in the skillet and sauté over medium heat until golden brown. Turn over and brown the other side. The endives should not be well cooked, just heated through, and should have a crispy crust.

   Garnish the endives with thin strips of sun-dried tomatoes, if desired. If you garnish the endives with the tomatoes, omit the salt.

FENNEL

Fern-like fennel is a plant of exquisite beauty. Its foliage is used as a garnish and to make tea. Its pungent seeds are used as a spice, and the thick, white bulb at the bottom of the plant is used as a vegetable. The fennel bulb has a texture similar to celery and a surprising licorice flavor.

To Clean: As a vegetable, use only the bottom white part. Pull the stalk apart like celery and wash it well. Chop as desired.

To Cook: Fennel may be sautéed or simmered in broth. It takes about the same amount of time as celery to cook.

To Serve: The pleasantly unusual taste of raw fennel adds a touch of sophistication to an ordinary green salad. Fennel is also good in soups. Try the recipe for *Cream of Fennel Soup* (page 56).

FENNEL AND RED PEPPER SAUTÉ

1 large bulb fennel
1 large red pepper
1 tablespoon olive oil

Serves: 3–4
Time: 8–10 minutes

1. Wash the pepper and the fennel bulb. Cut them both into julienne strips.
2. Heat the oil in a wok or skillet. Add the vegetables and sauté over high heat for 4–5 minutes, stirring constantly. Serve immediately.

GREEN BEANS

Green beans, wax beans, pole beans, scarlet runner beans, etc., can all be used in the same way. Those beans have edible pods.

Buy beans that easily snap when you break them.

To Clean: Rinse the beans thoroughly, then break off the two ends. It is rare to find beans that have strings because in recent years they have been hybridized to be stringless. Leave the green beans whole, or cut or break them into one-inch pieces.

To Cook: Steaming or pressure cooking are the best ways to cook green beans. Steaming will take about twelve minutes (less for very tender young beans and more for beans that are tough or old). To pressure cook, bring the pressure up to maximum, then remove the cooker from the heat and let it cool down on its own. For tough beans, it may be necessary to cook them under pressure for a minute before removing the cooker from the heat.

To Serve: When green beans are fresh from the garden they are wonderful unseasoned or just sprinkled with a little *Gomashio* (see page 247). They are also good topped with lightly roasted sliced almonds. Add green beans to soups (*Vegetable Gumbo*, page 53), stews (*Italian Vegetable Stew*, page 235), and casseroles (*Green Bean and Rice Casserole*, see recipe below). Among my favorite ways to use green beans are the simple *Green Bean Salad* on page 127 and the *Summer Picnic Salad* on page 127.

Rather than seasoning green beans with butter and salt, try tossing them in a little olive oil and tamari. Herbs that are good with green beans are thyme, tarragon, and savory.

GREEN BEAN AND RICE CASSEROLE

This simple casserole can be made either with or without dairy products.

1 tablespoon olive oil
1 medium onion, chopped
1½ cups sliced mushrooms
½ teaspoon thyme
2½ cups green beans, lightly steamed and broken into 1-inch pieces
2 cups cooked brown rice
1 cup of Béchamel Sauce *(page 242) or* Tahini-Miso Sauce *(page 245, made with yellow or white miso)*
½ cup grated cheese or 2 tablespoons sesame seeds

Serves: 4
Time: 50 minutes

1. Heat the oil in a skillet. Add the onions and sauté until almost tender. Add the mushrooms and the thyme. Sauté for 2–3 minutes more.
2. Place the sautéed vegetables in a large bowl. Add the cooked rice and the lightly steamed green beans.
3. Add whichever of the two sauces you choose to the vegetable-rice mixture. Mix well.
4. Place the mixture in a lightly oiled casserole dish. Sprinkle with your choice of either grated cheese or sesame seeds.
5. Bake, covered, at 350°F for 25–30 minutes. Uncover and broil for a minute to brown the top.

For a nice summer meal, serve with *Yellow Squash with Miso* (page 165) and sliced tomatoes, or with *Tomates Provencales* (page 167) and a green salad.

GREENS

The term greens encompasses all green, leafy vegetables. Greens that are usually served cooked include beet tops, Chinese cabbage, collards, dandelion greens, kale, mustard greens, spinach, Swiss chard, and turnip greens.

Vitamins A and C, calcium, iron, and other minerals are all abundant in greens. However, spinach, Swiss chard, and beet tops contain a large amount of oxalic acid, which interferes with the body's calcium use. Therefore, the greens that are the best source of calcium are kale, collards, turnip greens, and dandelion greens.

Kale is especially nutritious. For only 43 calories, 1 cup of cooked kale provides 5 grams of protein, 9,100 I.U. of vitamin A, 100 milligrams of vitamin C, 1.8 milligrams of iron, and 210 milligrams of calcium. This is over twice the vitamin C of an orange and almost as much calcium as a glass of milk.

To Clean: Fill your kitchen sink with water. Add the greens and swish them around for a minute. Remove them from the water, drain the water from the sink, and repeat, until there is no sand or dirt left in the water. Discard any yellow or blemished leaves. Chop the greens with a sharp knife before cooking, if desired.

To Cook: The amount of time required to cook greens depends on the type of greens. Spinach and dandelion cook in just a few minutes, whereas coarser greens like kale, turnip greens, etc. can take up to a half hour.

Don't forget that all types of greens will reduce dramatically in size as they cook, so make sure to cook enough. You may stir-fry, steam, or pressure cook greens.

To stir-fry, heat a small amount of oil in a large skillet or heavy kettle. Add the washed and chopped greens. Stir them over high heat until wilted. Cover, lower the heat, and steam until tender, stirring occasionally. For the coarser types of greens, it may be necessary to add about ¼ cup of water when you cover the pan.

Steam the washed and chopped greens like any other vegetable. Check them occasionally so that you will know when they are done. The tougher greens may be pressure cooked. Bring the pressure up to maximum; then remove the cooker from the heat and let the pressure come down on its own.

To Serve: Greens are good served as a side dish. Try seasoning them with your choice of the following: chopped scallions, toasted sesame seeds or gomashio, oregano, tarragon, dill, basil, chives, shoyu or tamari, lemon juice, or rice or cider vinegar.

Classic American fare from the Deep South consists of cooked greens with cornbread and beans. The beans are served in their well-seasoned cooking liquid (which thickens into a sauce after the beans are cooked for a long period of time). The beans are often poured over the cornbread, then topped with chopped scallions.

Also see the recipes for *Spinach Squares* (page 229), *Spinach and Cottage Pie* (page 227), *Potatoes and Kale a la Grecque* (page 231), *Kale, Cabbage, and White Bean Soup* (page 53), and *Fettucini with Spinach and Ricotta* (page 211).

CREAMED SPINACH (Nondairy)

1 tablespoon oil
1 small onion, chopped
10 ounces fresh spinach, washed and chopped
1 pound soft tofu
1/4 cup water
1/4 cup yellow miso
1 teaspoon basil
1/2 teaspoon oregano
1/3–1/2 cup chopped pecans or walnuts

Serves: 3–4
Time: 25 minutes

1. Heat the oil in a large, heavy kettle. Add the onion and sauté for a few minutes. Add the spinach and stir. Cover and cook over medium-low heat until the spinach is tender, stirring occasionally.
2. In a blender or food processor blend together the tofu, water, and miso until smooth and creamy. If using firm tofu, add more water as needed to achieve a sauce of the desired consistency. If using silken tofu, you may not need to add any water.
3. Add the herbs and nuts. Stir the creamed mixture into the cooked spinach. Heat, but do not cook.

    Serve over rice, millet, pasta, or toast, accompanied by a carrot salad.

JERUSALEM ARTICHOKES (SUNCHOKES)

The Jerusalem artichoke, or sunchoke, is a nonstarchy, slightly sweet tuber that belongs to the sunflower family.

To Clean: Scrub with a brush under running water. Do not peel. Slice into thin rounds.

To Cook: Thinly sliced sunchokes will take about fifteen minutes of steaming or modified boiling. They can also be sautéed or cooked in a mixed vegetable stew or soup.

To Serve: Steamed and seasoned with a little yellow miso, sunchokes make a nice side dish. Lightly steamed sunchokes may also be added to vegetable casseroles.

JERUSALEM ARTICHOKES IN COURT BOUILLON

When Jerusalem artichokes are prepared like this, they resemble globe artichoke hearts. This dish is served cold.

2 cups water
1 cup sliced onion
1 stalk celery, chopped
2 cloves garlic, minced
1 bay leaf
3 tablespoons lime or lemon juice
1 pound (approximately) Jerusalem artichokes (about 3 cups scrubbed and thinly sliced)
2 tablespoons yellow miso
1/2 lime or lemon, cut into thin slices
1 tablespoon olive oil

Serves: 4–6
Time: 30–35 minutes to prepare; refrigerate 8 hours before serving.

1. Place the water, onion, celery, garlic, bay leaf, and lime (or lemon) juice in a medium-sized pan. Cover and bring to a boil. Lower the heat and simmer for about 5–10 minutes while you prepare the artichokes.
2. Add the thinly sliced artichokes to the broth (cooking water). Cover and simmer for about 20 minutes or until they are tender.
3. Pour about 1/4 cup of the vegetable broth into a small bowl. Add the miso and mix well. Remove the pan from the heat; return the diluted miso to the pan and stir.
4. Let the broth stand for a few minutes to allow the flavors to blend. Then transfer the vegetables and broth to a bowl. Cover and refrigerate for at least 8 hours before serving.
5. Just before serving, add the olive oil and mix well. Garnish with the slices of lemon or lime.

JICAMA

Jicama (pronounced hee-ka-ma) is a root vegetable that is not very pretty to look at, but it is surprisingly sweet, juicy, and mild.

It does not seem to keep as well as other root vegetables, so use it within a week.

To Clean: Peel and slice, dice, or grate.

To Cook: Thin matchsticks of jicama can be added to mixed vegetable stir-fries. Cook jicama very briefly.

To Serve: Jicama is great served raw in salads. Try the *Sweet and Spicy Salad* on page 117—or add jicama to the salad of your choice.

JICAMA WITH ONIONS

1 tablespoon oil
1½ cups sliced onion
2 cups jicama, peeled and sliced into approximately 1-x-½-x-¼-inch strips
½ teaspoon basil

Serves: 3–4
Time: 10–15 minutes

1. Heat the oil in a large skillet. Add the onions and sauté for a minute.
2. Add the jicama. Stir for a minute or two, then cover.
3. Cook for a minute or two, stirring occasionally, until the jicama is tender but still crisp—about 5 minutes.

LEEKS

Milder than onions, leeks are a favorite of French chefs. The bottom white part and a good deal of the green part can be used.

To Clean: Leeks are always full of sand, so special care must be taken to clean them. Cut off and discard a thin slice at the root end. Then cut off the wilted or tough part of the green tops. If the leeks are to be blended into a soup, you may use the dark green part of the leaves, but if they are to be sautéed and eaten without blending, use only the white and the light green portions, which are very tender. With a sharp knife, make a deep incision in the leek starting from the bottom of the white bulb and running up to where the green leaves begin. Open the bulb with your hands and rinse it under running water.

To Cook: Leeks are usually either sautéed or simmered in the broth of a soup or stew.

To Serve: Leeks can be used in place of onions in almost any recipe. A side dish of leeks sautéed in olive oil is very good. See the recipes for *Cream of Leek Soup,* page 56, and *Crepes aux Poireaux* (Leek-Stuffed Crepes), page 221.

QUINOA WITH LEEKS AND MUSHROOMS

Simple, light, and nourishing.

½ cup quinoa
2 medium leeks (about 2½ cups chopped)
1 tablespoon oil
1 teaspoon tarragon
1 cup sliced mushrooms
Sea salt to taste (if desired)
1 cup boiling water

Serves: 2–3
Time: 20 minutes

1. Wash the quinoa and drain it through a wire strainer. Clean the leeks and chop them. (Use only the white and the light green part. Save the dark green part to blend in a soup.)
2. Heat the oil in a large skillet. Add the tarragon and the chopped leeks and stir for a few seconds. Add the quinoa and stir for about a minute more. Add the mushrooms and the salt. Stir and then add the boiling water. Cover and simmer over low heat for about 15 minutes or until the water is absorbed.

Serve with your favorite sauce and a big green salad.

MUSHROOMS

Of all the many wonderful types of mushrooms, there are only one or two varieties available in most grocery stores. However, dried mushrooms may be used to add flavor and variety to many dishes. They may be purchased in Oriental markets and natural foods stores.

To Clean: Many French chefs prefer not to wash mushrooms—they just wipe them off with a cloth. I wash them, and do not feel that it harms their flavor or texture, especially if they are washed quickly and in cold water. If the bottom of the mushroom stem has dirt clinging to it, or is shriveled, cut it off. Slice or chop as desired.

Wash dried mushrooms thoroughly and then soak them in water until they are soft. Slice or chop them as desired and add them to any recipe in which you would use fresh mushrooms. Well-soaked, dried mushrooms cook about as fast as fresh mushrooms. A few dried mushrooms go a long way.

To Cook: Mushrooms are usually sautéed or fried; however, they may also be simmered in the broth of a soup or a stew. Mushrooms cook very rapidly. Therefore, when you cook them with other vegetables, they should not be added until after the other vegetables are almost tender.

To Serve: Use mushrooms in stir-fries, soups, quiches, stews, meatless main dishes such as the *Bulghur Burgers* on page 183, casseroles, etc. Mushrooms are also good in any tomato or spaghetti sauce or as a topping for pizza. When using mushrooms in salads, make sure that they are very fresh; see *Mushroom Salad* (page 115). Also see the recipe for *Mushroom Crepes* (page 220).

Eggless Mushroom Quiche

As an experiment, I decided to try the *Creamy Onion Pie* (page 158) without looking at the recipe. The idea was to see how it would differ from the original. Never content to leave well enough alone, I added some mushrooms. We enjoyed the result, which was similar to the onion pie, but different enough to be considered a new recipe. Perhaps by comparing these two recipes you will see how you too, can change recipes to suit your own tastes and needs.

1–2 tablespoons oil, as needed
1 teaspoon thyme
1 cup chopped onions
3 cups sliced mushrooms
1 pound tofu
1/2 cup ricotta cheese
3 tablespoons tamari
1/8 teaspoon cayenne
1/2 teaspoon nutmeg
1 single crust 9-inch whole wheat pie shell, or 1 recipe Quick Bread Crumb Crust (page 94), unbaked

Yield: One 9-inch pie
Serves: 4
Time: 1 hour, 15 minutes

1. Heat the oil in a large skillet. Add the thyme and the onions. Sauté for 2–3 minutes and then add the mushrooms. Sauté for about 3 more minutes, or until the mushrooms are done.
2. In a food processor or blender, blend together the tofu, ricotta, tamari, cayenne, and nutmeg until smooth and creamy. (With a food processor this can be done all in one batch, but if you use a blender you will have to do 2–3 small batches.)
3. Combine the tofu mixture with the sautéed vegetables; mix well. Spread the mixture into an unbaked 9-inch pie shell.
4. Bake the quiche at 350°F for 45 minutes, or until set.

SEA VEGETABLES

When we are unaccustomed to a food, we tend to think of it as a "new food." In vegetarian cookery, however, all of the staples that we use have a long and proven history. Sea vegetables are no exception. The oldest known Chinese encyclopedia, dating from 300 B.C., contains writings in praise of sea vegetables. Nevertheless, it is the Japanese who make the most extensive use of these aquatic plants, serving them in the refined and imaginative manner that their cuisine is so noted for. Although we usually associate sea vegetables with Oriental food, they also have a place in the traditional Welsh, Scottish, and Irish diet. In fact, coastal-dwelling people all over the world have included sea vegetables in their diets.

The more one learns about sea vegetables, the more it becomes evident that the contributions they can make in the form of high-quality nutrition is too great to neglect. Sea vegetables are especially valuable to vegans (people who eat no animal products), because they can provide the precious calcium that a dairyless diet can be low in. One hundred grams of hijiki contain 1,400 milligrams of calcium. Other minerals are also abundant in sea vegetables. Dulse is the best natural vegetarian source of iodine.

Sea vegetables are also a good source of vitamins A, C, E, B_1, B_2, B_6, and B_{12}. In addition, they contain a high level of ergosterol, a substance that can be converted by the body into vitamin D.

As valuable a food as sea vegetables are, introducing an unfamiliar food into one's diet is not always easy. There are often prejudices to be overcome, as well as new cooking methods to learn. If you wish to include sea vegetables in your family's diet, the best way to introduce them is very slowly and discreetly. Don't make the same mistake that I did the first time I cooked hijiki.

Unaware of the fact that hijiki swells up enormously when it soaks, I placed what seemed like a reasonable amount in a bowl of water and ended up with enough seaweed to feed an army. Not wanting to waste food, I cooked it all up and placed it on the table with not much else. It took my husband almost three years before he would even consider trying hijiki again.

Some people naturally enjoy the taste of sea vegetables, but others don't, so please go easy at first. Rather than serving a dish of sea vegetables, include them in a dish where they are not the main ingredient, for example in the *Bean and Hijiki Pie* on page 189.

Following are some tips about several different types of sea vegetables.

- **Agar-agar** is usually sold in natural foods stores in the form of feather-light bars or flakes. There are two bars in a package. Agar is used as a jelling agent. Generally, 1 bar of agar can be used to jell $3\frac{1}{2}$–4 cups of liquid. One tablespoon of flakes will jell 1 cup of liquid. After trying a recipe containing agar once, you may increase or decrease the amount the next time you try it to achieve the consistency that you desire. Agar will not jell when used with wine, distilled vinegars, or foods that are high in oxalic acid, such as rhubarb, spinach, and chocolate. If you wish to keep a strict vegetarian diet, do not use the conventional gelatin sold in supermarkets, because it is derived from animal products.

- **Arame** resembles finely textured hijiki, but it is much milder-tasting. It also requires less soaking and cooking. About 5 minutes of soaking and 5–10 minutes of cooking are enough for arame. It is good in stir-fried dishes and in salads. Try the **Arame-Rice Salad** on page 118.

- **Dulse** is very easy to use; it doesn't need cooking. Just wash it carefully and add it to whatever you wish. Dulse is fairly mild-tasting and can be used as an ingredient in salads. It is also good with potato and corn dishes. This sea vegetable is high in protein, iron, vitamin A, iodine, and phosphorus.

- **Hijiki** is high in calcium and protein. It must be soaked for at least 20 minutes before you use it. When $\frac{1}{4}$ cup of dry hijiki is soaked, it will yield about 1 cup. After soaking, hijiki should be rinsed.

  Hijiki is good in bean dishes. It also nicely complements rice, carrots, onions, and tofu in stir-fried dishes. Good seasonings for both hijiki and arame are tamari or shoyu, roasted sesame oil, and rice or cider vinegar.

- **Kelp** comes in many varieties. Kombu and arame are both in the kelp family. Kelp is usually ground into a powder and used as a seasoning and nutritional supplement. Powdered kelp may be used as a salt substitute. Kelp is high in iodine and other important minerals.

- **Kombu** is sold in easy-to-use strips about 6 inches long. For quick-cooking dishes, it should be soaked about 15–20 minutes. If kombu is not soaked, it takes 40 minutes of cooking to become tender, which makes it perfect for slow cooking. Add to a pot of soup, stew, rice, or beans. With rice, kombu should be added in the beginning. Place a rinsed strip of kombu in the bottom of the pot, and when the rice is done the kombu will be done also. Remove the kombu, chop it into bite-sized pieces, and add it to the dish you are preparing. To cook kombu with beans, rinse the kombu and add it to the beans during the last 45 minutes of cooking. When both the beans and the kombu are tender, remove the kombu and chop it into bite-sized pieces. Return the chopped kombu to the pot.

  A soup or broth may be enriched by simmering a 4–6-inch strip of kombu along with the other ingredients. When the soup is done, remove the strip of kombu, slice it into bite-sized pieces, and return it to the soup. If you wish to add kombu to a dish that requires less than 40 minutes of cooking, it should be soaked for about 20 minutes before it is added.

- **Nori** is easy to use; just hold it over a candle or a gas burner for a few seconds, moving it slowly so that it doesn't burn, until it turns a dark emerald green. The toasted nori can then be cut with scissors into strips, or crumbled with your hands to be used as a garnish for grain or vegetable dishes. Pretoasted nori may be purchased in some natural foods stores. A classic and attractive way to use nori is in *Nori-Maki*, page 108.

- **Wakame**, when dried, resembles dried strands of kombu. However, wakame will become soft with less than 5 minutes of soaking, whereas kombu needs about 15 minutes. Wakame has a tough midrib that can be cut out with the tip of a sharp knife after the plant is soaked. Its flavor is mild-almost sweet. Wakame cooks rapidly; 2–3 minutes are enough. Soaked wakame may be added to soups during the last minute or so of cooking. This sea vegetable is high in protein, iron, and magnesium.

OKRA

I was once under the impression that the main criterion for appreciating this strange vegetable was being born in the Deep South. Then I learned how to cook it properly and discovered, to my great surprise, that it is really very good wherever you come from!

To Clean: Wash the pods and discard the stem ends. Slice the okra into rounds of ½-inch or less.

To Cook: See the recipe for *Cajun-Style Okra*, below.

To Serve: Cajun-Style Okra is good as a side dish to accompany grain, corn, or tomato dishes. The secret of this recipe is in first frying the okra and then baking it. Okra can also be added to soups (*Vegetable Gumbo*, page 53).

CAJUN-STYLE OKRA

2½ cups okra washed and cut into ½-inch rounds
¼ cup cornmeal
¼ teaspoon sea salt
½ teaspoon basil
2 tablespoons oil

Serves: 2–3
Time: 20 minutes

1. Place the cornmeal in a medium-sized bowl. Add the salt and the basil. Mix well. Add the okra and stir until the okra is well coated with the cornmeal mixture.
2. Heat the oil in a skillet. Add the breaded okra and sauté until the cornmeal begins to brown. If your skillet is ovenproof, place it directly in a 350°F oven. If your skillet is not ovenproof, transfer the okra to a shallow baking dish.
3. Bake at 350°F for 10–15 minutes.

ONIONS

What vegetable is more humble than the lowly onion? But what vegetable plays a more important role in providing savor and taste appeal to such a great number of dishes?

To Clean: Take a thin slice off the top and the bottom of the onion. Cut the onion in half vertically; then remove the skin. Unless the skin has been broken, there is no need to wash the onion.

See Figure 9.2 for an easy way to chop an onion.

To Cook: Onions are usually sautéed or stir-fried, but they can also be baked or stewed.

To save time when following recipes you may consider one cup of chopped onion to be equivalent to one medium-sized yellow onion. One-half of a big, sweet Bermuda or Valencia onion is also about one cup.

To Serve: I am not going to list all the recipes that contain onions because the list would include most of the recipes in this book! However, to satisfy those of you who are seeking something especially oniony, try *French Onion Soup* (page 49), *Cream of Onion Soup* (page 57), and *Creamy Onion Pie* (see recipe below).

CREAMY ONION PIE

This high-protein pie is not as rich as it tastes.

2 tablespoons oil
3 cups chopped onions
1 teaspoon thyme
1¼ cups mashed tofu
1 cup cottage cheese
3 tablespoons tamari or shoyu
¼ cup water (approximately)
½ cup sharp Cheddar cheese and/or 2 tablespoons sesame seeds
1 recipe Quick Bread Crumb Crust (page 94) or Press-In Pie Crust (page 95), or ½ recipe Whole Wheat Pie Crust (page 92), unbaked

Yield: 1 single-crust 9-inch pie
Serves: 4
Time: 1 hour, 15 minutes

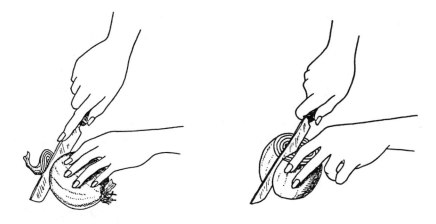

1. After peeling the onion and cutting off the top and bottom ends, cut it in half.

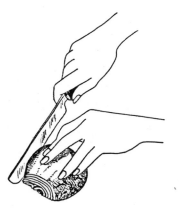

2. Then, make lengthwise slices across the onion half.

3. Turn the onion around (90°) and slice it in the other direction.

Figure 9.2.   Chopping an Onion

1. Heat the oil in a large skillet and sauté the onions and thyme over low heat until the onions are tender.
2. Place the tofu, cottage cheese, and tamari in a blender or food processor. Blend, adding as much of the water as necessary to make a sour-cream-like texture. (A soft tofu may not need any water, but a firm one may need an entire quarter-cup.)
3. Mix the tofu recipe with the sautéed onions. Spread the mixture into an unbaked pie shell and top it with the grated cheese and/or sesame seeds.
4. Bake at 375°F for 40 minutes, or until set.
    Serve with a steamed vegetable and a green salad.

PARSNIPS

Parsnips resemble white carrots in appearance, but their flavor is sweet and almost spicy. They are a very under-appreciated vegetable. Parsnips are inexpensive, easy to grow (especially in cold climates), and very versatile.

To Clean: Just scrub the parsnips with a brush under running water. There is no need to peel them. Cut off the top end and the root end. Slice as desired.

To Cook: Parsnips may be stir-fried, baked, steamed, stewed, or cooked by modified boiling. They cook a little faster than carrots.

- For mashed parsnips, clean and slice the parsnips. Cook by modified boiling or steaming for about 12 minutes or until they are good and tender. Season to taste with some yellow miso, minced parsley, and a pinch of nutmeg. Mash the parsnips with a fork or a potato masher, adding some of the liquid from cooking them if they are too dry. Serve like mashed potatoes.

- For sliced parsnips, cook and season as indicated above, but do not mash.

- Also try breaded parsnips. Simply clean and lightly steam small, whole parsnips. Dip them in beaten egg and then into finely ground, seasoned bread crumbs. Fry them in a small amount of oil.

To Serve: Use parsnips as an accompaniment to any main dish. They are good in almost any stir-fry recipe. Parsnips also add a delicate sweetness to soups or stews (see *Hearty Miso Vegetable Soup* page 54, and *Pot au Feu*, page 235).

CARROT AND PARSNIP SAUTÉ

A colorful and subtly sweet stir-fry to accompany a main dish.

1 tablespoon oil
2 medium carrots, scrubbed and cut into matchsticks
2 medium parsnips, scrubbed and cut into matchsticks
2 cloves garlic (optional)
½ teaspoon basil
Pinch of nutmeg
Pinch of sea salt
2 tablespoons chopped parsley

Serves: 2–4
Time: 12 minutes

1. Heat the oil in a skillet. Add all the ingredients except for the parsley. Stir over high heat for about 3 minutes.
2. Lower the heat. Cover and continue cooking for about 7 minutes more, or until the carrots become tender, but are still a bit crisp. Stir occasionally.

   Add the parsley and toss.

PARSNIP PATTIES

These little patties are very mild-flavored.

2 cups grated parsnips, (about 3 medium parsnips)
2 eggs, beaten
½ teaspoon sea salt, or to taste
2 tablespoons minced scallions
1 tablespoon minced parsley
½ teaspoon basil
Pinch of nutmeg

Yield: 12 small patties
Serves: 3–4
Time: 20 minutes

1. The parsnips need to be finely grated. To grate parsnips, first scrub them with a brush under running water; then, slice them and grind them in a food processor. If you do not have a food processor, leave parsnips whole and grate them on the smallest holes of a grater.
2. In a medium-sized bowl, mix together the grated parsnips and all the other ingredients.
3. Shape the mixture into 12 small patties. Heat 1–2 tablespoons of oil in a skillet and cook the patties over medium-low heat until they are brown on the bottom. Turn them over and cook them slowly on the other side.

   Serve parsnip patties plain as an accompaniment to a more strongly flavored dish, or with your favorite sauce. I always enjoy them with soup, instead of bread.

BAKED GARLIC PARSNIPS

Try this recipe when you already have the oven heated for something else.

1–2 tablespoons olive oil
4–8 small parsnips, scrubbed and sliced (2–3 cups)
3 or more cloves garlic, to taste, minced
2 tablespoons minced parsley
·Pinch of nutmeg
Pinch of sea salt (optional)

Serves: 2–4
Time: 35 minutes

1. Place the oil in a shallow baking dish. Add the parsnips and the garlic. Stir to coat with the oil.

2. Cover the dish and bake at 350°F for about 30 minutes, or until the parsnips are tender. Stir from time to time and check for doneness.

3. Uncover and broil for a couple of minutes to lightly brown the parsnips. Toss with parsley and sprinkle with nutmeg. Add a pinch of sea salt if desired.

PEAS AND SNOW PEAS

Easy to grow and difficult to find in most stores, tender, fresh peas are the preferred crop of many a backyard gardener. When peas are young and fresh, they are sweet and cook very fast. However, when they are old, they become starchy and take much longer to cook. You can tell when peas are old, because they are larger and firmer than the young ones. One pound of peas in the pod will yield about one cup after they are shelled. Snow peas, the pea pods used in Chinese-style cooking, are good even if the peas within the pod are developed, as long as they are not hard or dry.

To Clean: For green peas, simply remove the peas from the pod. For snow peas, rinse them well and break off the stem end.

To Cook: Peas are best steamed. Fresh, young peas will take only about three minutes of steaming, but older peas can take up to twenty minutes. Snow peas can either be steamed (about three minutes), or stir-fried just long enough to heat them up.

To Serve: Snow peas can be added to any mixed vegetable stir-fry (add them near the end of cooking). Raw or lightly steamed peas and snow peas are good in salads. Lightly steamed peas are delicious with potatoes. Try them in stuffed potatoes, in potato salad, or as a side dish to accompany a potato dish. Peas also make a good addition to a tomato sauce or a spaghetti sauce.

CREAMED PEAS AND MUSHROOMS

This is good served over a whole grain English muffin for a light lunch.

1 tablespoon oil
½ teaspoon savory
⅓ cup finely chopped onion
1 cup sliced mushrooms
¾ cup plain soymilk
1½ cup frozen peas
1 tablespoon arrowroot
1 tablespoon white miso
Dash of cayenne (optional)

Serves: 3
Time: 10 minutes

1. Heat the oil in a heavy saucepan. Add the onions and the savory. Sauté until the onions are almost tender. Add the mushrooms and sauté for a minute or two more. Add ½ cup of the soymilk and the peas. Cover and let simmer for two or three minutes, or until the peas are tender.
2. Place the rest of the soymilk in a small bowl. Add the arrowroot and mix until the arrowroot is dissolved.
3. When the peas are tender, add the arrowroot mixture. Stir and cook over medium heat until thickened. Add the miso, and a dash of cayenne if desired, and mix well.

BELL PEPPERS

Bell peppers (also called sweet peppers) are a good source of vitamin C. Red peppers, which are sweeter than green peppers, are also a good source of vitamin A.

To Clean: Wash the peppers, then cut them in half and remove the seeds and membranes. Slice or dice as desired.

To Cook: Usually peppers are sautéed or stir-fried, but they can also be simmered in the broth of a soup or a stew.

To Serve: Both red and green peppers can be used raw to add color and crunch to all sorts of salads. They can be used in almost any Italian or Mexican-style dish, such as in spaghetti sauce, pizza, chili, and bean dishes. See the recipe for *Mexican Stuffed Peppers* on page 231.

DOMINIQUE'S ITALIAN PIMENTOS

5 large red peppers
5 large green peppers

Yield: About 2 cups
Time: 50 minutes

1. Place the whole peppers on a shallow baking pan with about ¼ inch of water. Bake them for 40 minutes at 350°F. About halfway through the baking, turn the peppers over to assure even cooking.
2. When the peppers are well-cooked, carefully remove their skins. Slice them and discard the seeds. Serve with olive oil and pressed garlic.

POTATOES

One medium potato (2½ inches in diameter) has 104 calories—just 8 calories more than a medium-sized apple. Isn't it great that many of the misconceptions about what is "fattening" and what isn't are finally being dispelled?

To Clean: Scrub potatoes well with a vegetable brush and cut out any bad spots or eyes. Discard any potatoes that have green on their skin.

Everyone knows the importance of dietary fiber, and everyone knows the greatest concentration of vitamins and minerals in vegetables are immediately below the skin, but for some reason many people continue to peel potatoes. The only reason that I can see for this is that it is a habit. It is certainly not for flavor, because peeled potatoes are as pasty and tasteless as that fluffy white bread sold in rainbow-colored plastic bags.

To Cook: Mashed and baked are two of the most popular ways of preparing potatoes.

- Mashed Potatoes. If you wish to make mashed potatoes with unpeeled potatoes, cut them into small (½-inch) cubes before they are cooked. This way the skin will be in small pieces when the potatoes are mashed. Cook the potatoes in a tightly covered pan in about 1½ inches of water. It is not necessary to cover them with water. The small cubes will take about 15 minutes of modified boiling to become tender.

  There is nothing worse than dry, unseasoned mashed potatoes. But rather than smothering them with salt, butter, and milk, try adding as much of the liquid left over from cooking the potatoes as is necessary to yield a nice, moist consistency. Then season with yellow or white miso and mix in a generous sprinkling of finely minced fresh parsley, chives, or scallions. For a slightly piquant taste, toss in a pinch of cayenne. Your mashed potatoes will be as delicious as they are healthful, and you won't have to worry about calories.

- Baked Potatoes. Using a fork, poke a few holes into the skin of the scrubbed potatoes before placing them in the oven. Potatoes baked without any holes in the skin can explode. (This happened to me once and it's a mess!) Bake at 350°F for about 1 hour, or until tender. Instead of loading a baked potato with salt and butter, try mashing the insides with some cottage cheese—or better yet—*Mock Sour Cream* on page 132. A few drops of tamari will also add flavor to baked potatoes.

To Serve: Potatoes are an ingredient in the following soups in this book: *Cream of Leek (Nondairy)*, page 56; *Cream of Fennel,* page 56; *Soupe Provencale,* page 51; *Claire's Borscht,* page 62; and *Cream of Chestnut,* page 59. They are a satisfying base for main dishes as well—try these recipes in Chapter 10: *Potatoes and Kale a la Grecque; Gnocchi; Broccoli and Potatoes au Gratin; Shepherd's Pie; Potato Casserole Délectable; Peasant-Style Kasha and Potatoes; Potato-Tofu Bake; Pot au Feu; Seitan and Potato Pie;* and *Potato-Mushroom Kugel.*

When potatoes are used in salads they do not have to be saturated with mayonnaise! *Maritime Salad* (page 115), *Marinated Vegetable Medley* (page 122), and *Low-Fat Potato Salad* (page 114) are nice alternatives.

Leftover mashed potatoes—or the water used from cooking potatoes—can be added to bread dough and will make incredibly good bread (see *Potato Bread,* page 80). Potatoes can even be used to make tender and light pastry dough: try *Potato Pie Crust,* page 93.

Seasonings to complement potatoes are savory, dill, parsley, onions, chives, scallions, tamari, miso, sharp cheeses, etc.

MUSHROOM-AND-ONION-STUFFED POTATOES (Nondairy)

These twice-baked potatoes are filled with a creamy, low-fat stuffing. Try them when you want to make something a little special.

4 good-sized and good-looking baking potatoes
1 tablespoon olive oil
1 cup finely chopped onion
1 cup finely chopped mushrooms
1/2 teaspoon savory
1 cup soft tofu, mashed
4 tablespoons mellow white miso or yellow miso
2 tablespoons chopped parsley
Pinch of cayenne

Serves: 4
Time: About 1 1/2 hours

1. Scrub the potatoes and bake them at 350°F until they are done (about 1 hour).
2. While the potatoes are baking, prepare the other ingredients. Heat the olive oil in a skillet and add the chopped onion. Sauté very slowly over low heat until the onion is almost tender.
3. Remove 1/4 cup of onion and reserve it to use as a garnish. Add the mushrooms and the savory to the skillet containing the rest of the cooked onion. Sauté until the mushrooms are tender. Set aside.
4. When the potatoes are done, cut them in half lengthwise. Using a clean towel to keep from burning your hands, pick up the potato halves, one at a time, and scoop out their insides for use in the filling. When you scoop out each potato half, leave a shell that is about 1/4 inch thick. Set the potato halves aside while you finish the filling.

   Food Processor Method: Place the tofu, miso, and the scooped-out potato in a food processor. (Soft tofu is best; if you use firm tofu, you will probably have to add a few tablespoons of water to the blended mixture to make it creamy.) Blend until smooth and creamy. Add a few sprigs of washed parsley (it is not necessary to chop it first) and the cayenne. Con-

tinue blending until the parsley is chopped. Add the blended mixture to the skillet with the sautéed vegetables and mix well.

   Blender Method: Blend together the tofu and the miso. Add about half of the scooped-out potato and blend until smooth. Remove part of the mixture from the blender and add the remaining potato. Blend until smooth. Combine the blended mixture with the sautéed vegetables. Add the chopped parsley and the cayenne and mix well.
5. Fill the potato shells with the stuffing mixture and place them in a shallow baking dish. Top each one with some of the onion that you reserved.
6. Bake at 350°F until heated through (about 20 minutes). Turn the oven to broil for a couple of minutes to brown the top. Watch the broiling carefully so that the potatoes don't burn.

OVEN-BROWNED POTATOES

2 large or 4 small potatoes
1 medium-small onion, sliced
1/2 teaspoon savory
2 tablespoons oil
2 tablespoons tamari or shoyu
2 tablespoons minced parsley

Serves: 2–4
Time: 1 hour

1. Scrub the potatoes and cut them into halves or quarters (depending on their size). Then slice the potatoes into slices 1/4–1/2 inch thick.
2. Oil a shallow baking dish with 2 tablespoons of oil. Place the sliced potatoes, onion, and savory in the dish and stir them around to coat them lightly with the oil.
3. Bake at 350°F for 45 minutes to 1 hour, until the potatoes are tender. Stir occasionally during the baking to assure they cook evenly. If the potatoes are tender, but not brown, turn the oven to broil for a few minutes. Watch carefully so that they do not burn.
4. Remove the potatoes from the oven. Sprinkle with tamari, stirring to distribute the tamari evenly. Sprinkle with parsley and serve.

SUMMER SQUASH

Summer squashes have a thin, delicate skin and they do not keep for long periods of time like winter squash. Some varieties of summer squash are yellow squash, zucchini, and patty pan squash.

To Clean: Zucchini often has sand imbedded in its skin. Therefore, just rinsing it like other vegetables is not enough; it must be scrubbed with a brush. For the other summer squashes, it is usually sufficient to rinse them thoroughly. Slice as desired.

To Cook: Summer squash is relatively quick-cooking. If you are cooking it with other vegetables, cut it in large pieces so that it does not overcook. Summer squash may be stir-fried for about five minutes (or more, depending on the size of the slices). It may also be lightly steamed, or simmered in a soup or stew.

To Serve: All varieties of summer squash are delicious in soup; for instance, try the *Yellow Squash Soup* on page 55. Summer squash can also be added to any mixed vegetable soup. Summer squashes are good in stews, especially tomato-based stews such as the *Italian Vegetable Stew* on page 235. They are good on pizza or in a spaghetti sauce (*Garden-Fresh Spaghetti Sauce*, page 241). Summer squashes may be used in quick grain dishes such as *Bulghur with Zucchini* (page 36) and they can even be used to make desserts! (*Zucchini Cake*, page 256). Add lightly sautéed summer squash to vegetable casseroles, and try the *Golden Corn Bake*, page 177, which contains yellow squash.

Yellow miso is an excellent seasoning for yellow squash. Complementary herbs are basil, dill weed, and parsley.

YELLOW SQUASH WITH MISO

Simple as can be, this is one of my favorite dishes.

3 medium yellow summer squash (about 4 cups, sliced)
1 tablespoon oil
¼ cup finely chopped onion
1–3 cloves garlic, minced
½–1 teaspoon basil
2 tablespoons water
2 tablespoons mellow white miso or yellow miso
2 tablespoons finely chopped parsley

Serves: 3–4
Time: 15 minutes

1. Wash the squash well. Quarter them and slice into ½-inch-thick slices.
2. Heat the oil in a skillet. Add the onion and the garlic. Sauté until the onion is translucent.
3. Add the sliced squash and stir over medium-high heat for about 2 minutes. Add the basil and the water. Cover the skillet and lower the heat. Simmer for about 8 more minutes, or until the squash is cooked the way you like it.
4. Remove the skillet from the heat and add the miso. Mix well. Add the parsley; mix and serve.

This dish is a nice accompaniment to a bean and grain dish when served along with some ripe sliced tomatoes or a crisp green salad.

MEXICAN VEGGIES

I based this recipe on a mixed vegetable dish served in my favorite Mexican restaurant. The shoyu is not Mexican, of course, but it does add a lot of flavor.

2 tablespoons oil
1 medium onion, chopped
2–3 cloves garlic, minced
2 cups finely chopped cabbage
1 medium zucchini, quartered and sliced
1 medium yellow squash, quartered and sliced
1 cup corn (cut from the cob or frozen)
1 teaspoon cumin
½ teaspoon chili powder
Cayenne to taste
1 teaspoon basil
½ teaspoon oregano
2 tablespoons shoyu or tamari

Serves: 2–3
Time: 15–20 minutes

1. Heat the oil in a large skillet or wok. Add the onion, garlic, and cabbage. Stir for a minute; then reduce the heat, cover, and cook over medium-low heat until the cabbage just begins to get tender. Stir often.
2. Stir in the remaining ingredients, except the shoyu, and cover the skillet or wok. Cook until the veggies are tender, stirring often. Add the shoyu and mix well.

    Serve with *Chalupas* (page 187), or any other Mexican-style main dish.

TOMATOES

When you are cooking for people who are unfamiliar with vegetarian food, the easiest way to make a big hit is to use tomatoes and cheese.

It is worth it to get your fill of fresh, vine-ripened tomatoes when they are in season, because out-of-season tomatoes are tasteless.

Some recipes in this book call for canned tomatoes or tomato paste. If you are able to, it is best to use home-canned tomatoes. However, if you carefully read the labels on canned tomatoes in the store, it is possible to buy ones without additives.

To Clean: Wash tomatoes well. There is never any real need to peel tomatoes (except when you are canning them). Slice them any way you wish.

To Cook: Tomatoes may be stewed, baked, or briefly broiled. To lend flavor and juiciness to stir-fries, bean dishes, and grain dishes, add some raw chopped tomatoes at the last minute. Do not cook them, just heat them up.

To Serve: Serve tomatoes raw in salads, or slice them into wedges, sprinkle them with basil and olive oil, and serve as is. There are four tomato sauce recipes in Chapter 11 of this book. They are all slightly different, and all very good. Tomatoes are used in too many dishes to list them all, but in addition to the tomato sauce recipes, some tomato-based recipes include *Creamy Gazpacho*, page 61 and *Tomato Pie*, page 225.

Suggested seasonings for tomatoes are basil (of course), thyme, bay leaves, oregano, garlic, and Parmesan or Romano cheese.

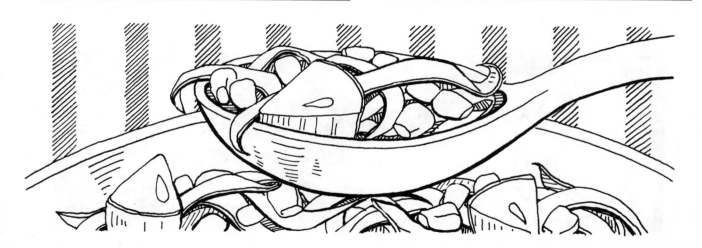

Oilless "Stir-Fried" Veggies *(page 141)* on a Bed of Brown Rice *(page 180)*.

Savory Corn-Stuffed Tomatoes *(page 167)* Make a Wholesome Side Dish.

Cauliflower Curry *(page 146)* for That Eastern Accent.

Beets à L'Orange *(page 140)* Add a Little Color to Any Meal.

CORN-STUFFED TOMATOES

A perfect combination for late summer.

4 medium tomatoes
1 tablespoon plus 1 teaspoon olive oil
1/2 cup chopped onion
2 medium ears of corn, cut off the cob
1/2 cup mashed tofu
1 tablespoon miso (dark or light as desired)
1/2 teaspoon basil
2 tablespoons minced parsley
1 slice whole grain bread
1 clove garlic, pressed

Serves: 2–4
Time: 40 minutes

1. Cut a thin slice off the top of each tomato. Using a small spoon, scoop out the pulp. Reserve the pulp for use in a soup or sauce. Set the tomato shells aside while you prepare the filling.
2. Heat 1 tablespoon of the olive oil in a skillet. Add the onion and sauté until tender. Set aside until needed.
3. Place 2/3 cup of the corn in a blender along with the tofu and the miso. Blend until smooth and creamy. If the mixture is too thick to blend, add about 1 tablespoon of water.
4. In a bowl, combine the creamed mixture with the sautéed onions. Add the remaining corn, parsley, and basil, and mix well.
5. Fill the tomato shells with this mixture. Place the stuffed tomatoes in a lightly oiled baking dish (a small cake or pie pan will do nicely).
6. Tear up the slice of bread, place it in a blender or food processor, and grind it into crumbs. While the machine is working, add the garlic and the teaspoon of olive oil. (If you are using a food processor, it is not necessary to press the clove of garlic; just remove the skin and add it whole, while the blades of the food processor are turning.)
7. Sprinkle the bread crumbs over the stuffed tomatoes. Bake at 350°F for 25 minutes.

TOMATES PROVENCALES (Broiled Tomatoes With Herbs)

1 tomato per person
Olive oil
Minced or pressed garlic
Basil
Oregano
Sea salt (optional)

Yield: 1 tomato per person
Time: 10 minutes

1. Remove the core from the tomatoes and discard a thin slice from the top and the bottom of each tomato. Cut the tomatoes in thick slices.
2. Place the slices on a cookie sheet. Brush the top of each one with olive oil. Sprinkle with minced or pressed garlic (to taste), basil, oregano, and, if desired, a pinch of salt.
3. Turn your oven to broil and place the tomatoes under the broiler until they are hot and bubbly. This will take about 5 minutes or less. Be careful not to overcook them.

Serve *Tomates Provencales* as a side dish to accompany foods of a less spicy nature, such as *Arame Rice Patties*, page 223, *Bulghur Burgers*, page 183, or a bean and grain dish.

TURNIPS AND RUTABAGAS

Turnips are purple and white. Rutabagas are big and deep yellow. While they are in the same family and can be cooked in the same ways, their flavors are quite different. Turnips have a slightly sharp taste, whereas rutabagas are sweet and mild.

To Clean: In supermarkets, rutabagas are sometimes covered with a coating of wax. These waxed rutabagas should always be peeled. However, a good scrubbing with a vegetable brush is enough for turnips and unwaxed rutabagas. Remove the root end and the top end. Slice or dice as desired.

To Cook: Rutabagas take a bit longer to cook than many other vegetables. Therefore, when cooking them in a stew with other vegetables, cut the rutabagas into smaller pieces. Steaming or modified boiling takes about 15 minutes for turnips and 20 minutes for rutabagas. Turnips and rutabagas can be baked like potatoes or cooked in a soup or stew. They can also be cut into thin matchsticks and stir-fried for 5–10 minutes.

To Serve: You can mash turnips and rutabagas like potatoes (cut them into ½-inch cubes before cooking) and season them with yellow miso, minced parsley, and a pinch of nutmeg. Or, you can leave them in cubes and season in the same way. Try combining turnips or rutabagas with carrots and potatoes; season to taste and mash.

Turnips and rutabagas are both great in vegetable soups or stews such as *Pot au Feu* on page 235. Also see the recipe for *Potato, Turnip, and Cheese Casserole* on page 229.

RUTABAGA AND SWEET POTATO CASSEROLE

My favorite dishes are often very simple. This dish is not fancy, but it is easy to make and very tasty.

1 medium rutabaga
1 large or 2 small sweet potatoes
½ large Bermuda onion, chopped
1 teaspoon tarragon
1 cup water
4 tablespoons yellow miso

Serves: 3–4
Time: 1 hour, 20 minutes

1. If the rutabaga is waxed, peel it before washing it; otherwise, just scrub the rutabaga well with a vegetable brush. Cut it into small cubes (about ½ inch).
2. Scrub the sweet potato and cut it into cubes about twice the size of the rutabaga cubes (1 inch). Place the rutabaga, sweet potato, and chopped onion in a casserole dish.
3. Sprinkle the vegetables with tarragon and add the water. Cover and bake at 350°F for about 1 hour and 15 minutes, or until the rutabaga is tender. After about 45 minutes of baking, stir and check for doneness.
4. When the rutabaga is tender, remove the casserole from the oven and add the miso. Stir until the miso dissolves and the sweet potatoes become a purée.

Serving Suggestion: For an easy and delicious meal, serve this casserole over a bed of brown rice and sprinkle with grated cheese. Accompany with a green salad. If you do not wish to eat cheese, serve this casserole with *Ginger Tofu* (page 199) instead.

WINTER SQUASH

The term "winter squash" applies to any hard-shell variety of squash that can be conserved for a long period of time without refrigeration, such as acorn, Hubbard, butternut, turban, and spaghetti squash. Pumpkins are another variety of winter squash. There are so many kinds of winter squash that I can't name them all; however, they can all be cooked in the same way.

If you are not familiar with winter squashes, you don't know what a treat you're missing! These vegetables are sweet, mild, and delicious.

To Clean: If the squash is to be cooked in a soup or stew, it must first be peeled. Peel the squash with a potato peeler, discard the seeds and the membrane, and cut the squash into cubes.

To Cook: Cubes of winter squash about ½ inch in size should take about 12 minutes to cook by steaming or modified boiling. Winter squash may also be steamed or pressure cooked in large chunks or quarters; it may be peeled either before or after cooking. Perhaps the easiest way of cooking winter squash (including pumpkins) is to bake them, unpeeled, either whole or cut in half. To bake a whole squash, just place it on a cookie sheet and poke a few holes in it with a sharp knife. Bake at 350°F until tender. Most whole squashes will take at least 1 hour to cook; a large Hubbard squash or pumpkin can take over 2 hours. If a squash is cut in half it will bake faster. Thin matchsticks of winter squash can be stir-fried; this will take about 5 minutes.

To Serve: Baked winter squash is delicious topped with grated cheese and garlic. It is also good in bean dishes. Peeled winter squash may be added (along with some chopped onions) during the last 30 minutes or so of cooking (see *Adzuki Beans With Winter Squash*, page 191, for an example of this method). Winter squash is good added to stews such as the *Pot au Feu* on page 235. Raw grated squash adds a delicious moistness to yeast breads (try *Golden Squash Bread*, page 79). Cooked and mashed or puréed squash can be made into pies (*No-Bake Pumpkin Pie*, page 263); added to soups; or seasoned with a little yellow miso, cinnamon, and nutmeg, and served as a side dish. For a main dish featuring winter squash, see the recipe on page 236, *Stuffed Spaghetti Squash*; many other recipes in Chapter 10 also utilize winter squash.

Elegant Squash Soufflés

These pretty little soufflés are very impressive. Try them for a special occasion.

2 medium acorn squash
4 eggs
2 tablespoons honey
1 teaspoon cinnamon
¼–½ teaspoon nutmeg

Serves: 4
Time: 1 hour, 30 minutes

1. Cut the squash in half. Discard the seeds and membrane.
2. Bake the squash, cut side up and uncovered, for 30 minutes or until the flesh is soft enough to easily scoop out of the shell (but not so soft that is easy to mash). Let the squash cool for about 15 minutes for easier handling.
3. Carefully scoop out the inside flesh of the squash, leaving about ½ inch around the sides. You should have about 1½ cups of squash.
4. Separate the eggs. Blend together (in the blender) the squash, egg yolks, cinnamon, nutmeg, and honey. Place the blended mixture in a bowl.
5. Beat the egg whites till stiff. Gently fold the beaten egg whites into the squash mixture.
6. Place the empty squash shells in a baking dish. Carefully spoon as much of the squash mixture into the shells as possible. Leftover filling may be baked in a small heat-resistant bowl.
7. Bake at 350°F for 30 minutes.

MAPLE-BAKED ACORN SQUASH

Simple and delicious.

1 medium acorn squash
2 teaspoons oil
2 tablespoons maple syrup
Pinch of cinnamon

Serves: 2
Time: 1 hour

1. Cut the squash in half. Remove and discard the seeds and membrane.
2. Brush the squash with the oil and pour the syrup into the cavity. Sprinkle with cinnamon.
3. Place the squash on a baking sheet and bake at 350°F until the squash is tender (1 hour or less). Baste the squash occasionally with the syrup as it is cooking.

SWEET POTATOES

Sweet potatoes are not as fattening as one might think. A medium-sized sweet potato contains 161 calories. This vegetable is also an excellent source of vitamin A, with an average of about 9,230 I.U. per potato.

To Clean: Scrub sweet potatoes with a brush under running water and cut out any bad spots with a sharp knife. Leave the sweet potatoes whole for baking; cut them into chunks for stew, or slice them into cubes for steaming or modified boiling. Do not peel.

To Cook: Cubes of sweet potato (about ½ inch in size) take about 12–15 minutes to cook by steaming or modified boiling. A medium-sized sweet potato will take at least 1 hour to bake.

To Serve: Sometimes I like to base a whole meal around a baked sweet potato, serving it with a steamed green vegetable and a salad. Also see the recipes for *Sweet Potato and Cheese Soup* (page 58) and *Pot au Feu* (page 235).

BAKED SWEET POTATOES WITH CHEESE

When someone asked what I most like to cook, I was embarrassed to admit that I do not especially like to cook. The reason that I cook is to eat well, feel good, and be healthy. My favorite food to cook is baked sweet potatoes because they cook all by themselves! You do not have to do anything but eat them, and they are so good! When they are cooked like this with melted cheese, they make a real feast.

1 medium sweet potato per person (try to find the Red Garnet variety, as they are the best)
Two thick slices of cheese per person (Cheddar, Jarlsberg, Havarti, etc.)

Yield: Varies
Time: 1 hour, 15 minutes

1. Scrub the potatoes and pierce holes in them with a fork. Place them on a baking sheet and bake at 350°F for about 1 hour (the exact time will depend on the size of the potatoes). They are done when they are very soft inside and bubbling with sweet syrup.
2. Cut the potatoes in half and place them, cut side up, on the baking sheet. Push a thick slice of cheese into the center of each potato half. Return them to the oven and bake for about 15 minutes more to melt the cheese. If you wish, broil for a minute to brown the tops.

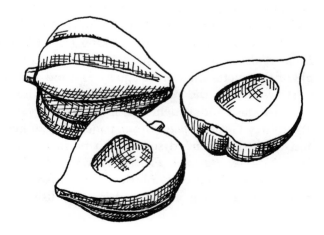

10. *MAIN DISHES*

Many people are under the impression that vegetarians subsist on vegetables alone. Of course, there are some rather extreme vegetarians who do. However, most vegetarians have a varied diet, of which vegetables are only a part. A vegetarian diet is not simply a standard North American diet minus the meat. It is much more.

The good vegetarian cook uses a variety of grains, legumes, soyfoods, and vegetables so creatively that the number of dishes that appear in the typical vegetarian household is truly outstanding. In lacto-ovo-vegetarian cooking, (which is exemplified in this book), moderate use is also made of dairy products and eggs. This adds still more diversity to our diet. However, I have taken great care not to overuse these foods. Many beginning vegetarian cooks make the mistake of relying far too heavily on dairy products and eggs for protein; this can cause even a meatless diet to be excessively high in saturated fat.

Most individuals seriously considering a vegetarian diet are concerned primarily about having adequate nutrition. There are some nutrients that have a reputation for being difficult to obtain on a vegetarian diet—protein, calcium, iron, zinc, and vitamin B_{12}. However, a balanced vegetarian diet generously supplies all the nutrients that the body needs.

Today it is understood that a lack of protein is not a problem in a balanced and varied vegetarian diet. Frances Moore Lappe, who popularized the concept of complementary proteins, emphasizes in the new revised edition of *Diet for a Small Planet* (Ballantine Books) that with a whole foods vegetarian diet containing sufficient calories, it is practically impossible to lack protein.

The average American eats far more protein than the body can use. For example, a Kentucky

Fried Chicken dinner contains fifty-two grams of protein.[1] This one meal surpasses the RDA (Recommended Daily Allowance) for protein for women and is just four grams under the RDA for men. Imagine how much excess protein (not to mention fat, calories, and sodium) one would be getting with two more high-protein meals each day!

Almost all foods contain some protein. The best vegetarian sources of protein are legumes, soy products (tofu, tempeh, T.V.P., and soymilk), grains, nuts, and seeds. Some vegetables, especially greens and vegetables of the cabbage family, also contain protein.

Just as there are different types of fat, there are many kinds of protein. All protein, however, is made up of "building blocks" known as amino acids. There are twenty-two amino acids naturally occurring in our food. Most of these amino acids can be manufactured by the human body. However, eight of them cannot, and these *must* be procured through our food. Thus, they are called the eight essential amino acids. Vegetable proteins were once thought to be inferior to animal proteins because they do not contain all of the eight essential amino acids. Meat contains the eight essential amino acids—and so do dairy products and eggs. But we do not need to rely on these animal products for our essential amino acids.

Using complementary proteins means matching foods that are deficient in certain amino acids with others that are high in those particular amino acids to create a dish or a meal that contains all of the eight essential amino acids. To put it more simply—eating beans and rice together! Grains and legumes are complementary proteins. In most countries where little or no meat is eaten, the traditional diet is based on mixed grain and legume dishes.

Today, many vegetarians believe that it is not absolutely necessary to mix complementary proteins in the same meal. However, grains and legumes (or grains and soy or dairy products) taste better and are more satisfying when eaten together. Furthermore, using complementary proteins is easy, so why take chances? The main dishes in this chapter use complementary proteins, and they are all good quality protein sources for a meal.

With a lacto-ovo-vegetarian diet, calcium is not a problem either. It is when all dairy products are eliminated that more care must be taken. Sea vegetables are the best nondairy sources of calcium and should be eaten daily by persons who do not eat dairy products. Dark green leafy vegetables such as kale, collards, broccoli, and turnip greens are also excellent sources of calcium. Spinach, Swiss chard, beet tops, wild poke, and rhubarb contain oxalic acid, which interferes with the body's calcium absorption, and makes them poor sources of calcium even though they contain high amounts.

As we have seen, many North Americans eat too much protein. Yet when one's diet is not excessively high in protein, calcium is much more easily absorbed into the system. Agatha Moody Thrash, M.D. notes in her book *Nutrition for Vegetarians:*

> For adults with a protein intake as low as the current RDA (56 grams for men, 46 grams for women), many nutritionists believe 350 mg of calcium daily would be adequate, rather than the allowance of 800 mg per day recommended in 1968. (This recommended level of calcium is well above that of Canada, the United Kingdom, and FAO/WHO.)[2]

Therefore, a good way to help prevent calcium deficiency and osteoporosis (weakening of the bones due to calcium deficiency) would be not only to eat foods providing sufficient calcium, but also to keep one's protein intake at a reasonable level so that the calcium can be utilized.

Many women are slightly deficient in iron. It is not something that is peculiar to vegetarians. Having good general health practices and eating foods that are rich in iron will prevent iron-deficiency anemia. Vegetarian sources of dietary iron include green leafy vegetables, legumes, prunes (especially prune juice), dried apricots, raisins, nuts, and whole grains.

Whole grains and beans are both high in zinc. But both of these foods contain phytates, which are substances that inhibit zinc absorption. This is why vegetarians are said to be prone to zinc deficiency. Nevertheless, when a study was done on fifty-seven long-term vegetarian women, they did not have reduced levels of iron or zinc.[3]

The nutritional availability of zinc in grains is increased by leavening. Therefore, yeast-leavened whole grain bread, or better yet, sourdough whole grain bread, should be a regular part of the vegetarian diet.

Dairy products and eggs are good sources of vitamin B_{12}; so are tempeh and sea vegetables. So, if any of these foods are regularly included in a well-balanced vegetarian diet, there will be no problem of a B_{12} deficiency.

In their book *Nutrition for Vegetarians*, Agatha Moody Thrash, M.D. and Calvin L. Thrash, Jr., M.D. say that the major dietary problems in the Western world do not come from a lack of vitamins and minerals. They stem from excesses in fat, protein, sodium, and refined carbohydrates, not to mention the chemical additives, residues, hormones, and antibiotics which are so abundant in the standard American diet. When problems develop on a meatless diet it is usually because the individual has severely limited his or her diet either in variety or in calories. In other words, if you eat a varied diet consisting of whole grains, vegetables, legumes, soy products, fruits, and nuts, don't worry. You are doing just fine!

GRAINS

Since the development of agriculture, grains have been humanity's most important food. In the industrialized nations, however, we have made the sad mistake of feeding the largest part of our grains to animals for the privilege of eating the animals in return. The high-fat and high-protein diet that results from this practice was once considered a sign of an improved standard of living. However, the epidemic of heart disease and other illnesses that have arisen from this affluent diet has recently taken away a great deal of its prestige.

The desire for good health has motivated many people to eat fewer animal products and more fruits and vegetables, but for some reason, grains are still largely neglected. Perhaps this is because many people continue to associate grains with the refined, starchy products that health-conscious or weight-conscious individuals have learned to avoid. To prove that natural, whole grains are not fattening, one has only to look at people who live in parts of the world where a traditional grain-based diet is still the norm.

Whole grains provide us with complex carbohydrates, B vitamins, minerals, and fiber. These grains are also a good source of protein, especially when combined with foods that contain complementary amino acids (legumes, seeds, dairy products, and even some vegetables).

Just as grains are of utmost importance in a traditional diet, they are a key component of the modern vegetarian diet (which is in essence a traditional diet). In the pages that follow I will give a brief description of different grains with ways to cook and serve them.

Before listing the grains, here's a practical note on their storage. Grains that have been split, cracked, rolled, or ground (such as flours, rolled oats, bulghur wheat, cornmeal, etc.), should be kept in airtight containers in the refrigerator. The reason for this is that when grains are in their whole, unbroken form, the natural oils that they contain are protected. However, when the grains are split, ground, or broken, the oils become exposed to oxygen, and therefore can rapidly become rancid. The germ of grains (such as wheat germ or corn germ) is especially susceptible to rancidity. For whole, unbroken grains such as rice, buckwheat, millet, and barley, a tightly closed glass jar in your cupboard is adequate. Store each variety in its own jar.

Some grains, especially those bought in bins at natural foods stores or organic groceries, may need to be cleaned. Grains that need to be cleaned should be placed in a bowl of water, swished around, and drained through a wire mesh strainer. Some grains may need to be rinsed more than once.

AMARANTH

Before Columbus came to America, amaranth was a popular grain in the western parts of what is now North and South America. Now it is grown only in some parts of Mexico, Central America, and South America, although it is now also being utilized in parts of Asia.

Amaranth is not a true grain, but it is classified by use as a grain. The plants that are grown for their seed are called "grain amaranth." Grain amaranth contains 16 percent protein, which is more than corn or rice, and is high in the amino acid lysine.

Amaranth grains can be popped, milled into flour and used to make flatbreads (it does not make a light yeast bread), and prepared as porridge. It can be bought in natural foods stores in the form of cereals and crackers.

---

[1]Eva May Nunnelley and Eleanor Noss Whitney, *Nutrition Concepts and Controversies* (St. Paul, Minnesota: West Publishing Company, 1979), 527.
[2]Agatha Moody Thrash, M.D. and Calvin L. Thrash Jr., M.D., *Nutrition for Vegetarians* (Seale, Alabama: Thrash Publications, 1982), 72–73.
[3]Ibid, page 73.

AMARANTH PANCAKES

1 cup amaranth cereal (can be purchased in a natural foods store)
¼ cup whole wheat pastry flour
1 teaspoon baking powder
1 egg
¾ cup milk (soy or dairy)

Serves: 2
Time: 10 minutes

1. In a medium-sized bowl, mix together the cereal, flour, and baking powder. Add the egg and mix again. Pour the milk over the mixture and beat with a spoon until the ingredients are well combined. If the batter is too thick, you may add a little more milk.
2. Drop the batter by the ¼ cup into a hot, oiled skillet and cook over medium-high until bubbles begin to appear on the tops of the pancakes. Turn them over and cook until done.

BARLEY

Barley has been popular in the Eastern Hemisphere for hundreds of years and was used for a long time as the chief grain. It is a hearty, filling grain.

To cook barley, wash 1 cup of barley and place it in a pan with 3 cups of water. Cover the pan and bring to a boil. Reduce the heat and simmer, without stirring, for 1 hour or until the water is absorbed. This will yield 3½ cups of cooked barley.

Barley (about ¼ cup) can be added to any soup, and will thicken it and add flavor, body, and texture. Since barley takes so long to cook, it is a good idea to simmer it in the soup broth for about 45 minutes before adding the vegetables, or you will end up with a soup of overcooked vegetables and undercooked barley.

Barley-and-Almond-Stuffed Squash (page 175) is a wonderful way to use barley; so is the *Barley and Vegetable Pie*, see recipe below. Barley flour can be used in cakes, breads, and muffins. Try the *Barley and Malt Cake* recipe on page 252.

BARLEY AND VEGETABLE PIE

This is a good recipe for fall or winter.

1 cup barley
3 cups water
1 medium onion
2 medium carrots
2 medium parsnips
2 cups chopped cabbage
½ cup water from cooking the vegetables
¼ cup tahini
2 tablespoons tamari
2 tablespoons nutritional yeast
1 teaspoon thyme
¼ teaspoon caraway seeds
1 egg, beaten
1 double-crust 10-inch whole wheat pie shell, unbaked

Yield: 1 double-crust 10-inch pie
Serves: 4–6
Time: 1 hour to cook barley; 1 hour, 25 minutes for pie.

1. Wash the barley, place it in a large kettle with the water, and bring to a boil. Lower heat, cover, and simmer for 1 hour, or until the water is absorbed.
2. While the barley is cooking, prepare the vegetables: chop the onion and slice the carrots and parsnips, and steam them, along with the cabbage, until they are tender-crisp.
3. Mix together the cooked barley and vegetables. Add the remaining ingredients. If the mixture is very hot, let it cool for a few minutes before adding the egg. Mix well.
4. Spread the mixture into an uncooked 10-inch pie shell. Cover with the top crust. Cut a hole into the top crust to let steam escape.
5. Bake at 375°F for 35 minutes, or until the crust is golden brown.

BARLEY-AND-ALMOND-STUFFED SQUASH

The right combination of pure and simple ingredients makes this easy recipe very special. I enjoy this stuffed squash plain, but it is also good with the *Easiest Cheese Sauce* on page 242. Accompany it with a steamed vegetable such as green beans and a nice big salad. For a grain side dish, follow the above recipe but omit the squash.

1 medium-small acorn squash (about 1½ pounds), or another winter squash of a similar size
⅓ cup chopped almonds
1 tablespoon olive oil
1½ cups chopped onions
½ teaspoon thyme
1 cup cooked barley (see page 174 for how to cook barley)
1 tablespoon tamari

Serves: 2
Time: 1 hour, 15 minutes

1. Cut the squash in half lengthwise. Discard the seeds and membrane and place the squash cut-side down on a lightly oiled baking dish. Bake at 350°F until the squash is still firm, but tender enough to easily scoop out with a spoon (about 45 minutes).
2. After the squash has been baking about 25 minutes, place the chopped almonds in a pie tin or another small ovenproof container and bake until they turn a toasty light brown (10–15 minutes). Check both the almonds and the squash occasionally so you will know when they are done.
3. Heat the olive oil in a large skillet. Add the onions and the thyme. Sauté over low heat until the onions are well done. Add the cooked barley, tamari, and toasted almonds to the sautéed onions.
4. Using a small spoon, scoop bite-sized chunks out of the cooked squash, leaving enough flesh around the shell so that it stays strong enough to hold its shape. Add the scooped-out squash to the barley mixture. Mix well.

Fill the empty squash shells with this mixture, mounding it as high as possible.
5. Place the stuffed squash in a baking dish. Cover with aluminum foil and bake at 350°F for about 20 minutes.

BUCKWHEAT

Buckwheat is a highly nutritious grain and is really worth getting to know. Whole, untoasted buckwheat is called buckwheat groats; cracked buckwheat is called buckwheat grits.

To obtain about 2½ cups of cooked buckwheat, start with 1 cup of untoasted buckwheat groats and 2 cups of boiling water. Wash and drain the buckwheat. Place it in an unoiled skillet over medium-high heat. Stir until the buckwheat emits a fragrant, nutty odor and becomes a toasty brown (about 5 or more minutes). Remove the skillet from the heat and pour in the boiling water. Cover the skillet and return it to the heat. Simmer over low heat, without stirring, for 20 minutes, or until the water is absorbed. Fluff with a fork before serving.

Kasha, or pretoasted buckwheat, may be cooked in the same way. Rather than toasting it for 5 minutes, just stir it over medium-high heat for a minute or two before adding the boiling water.

For instructions on cooking buckwheat grits, see *Corn and Buckwheat Porridge*, page 25.

Buckwheat is good with cabbage, potatoes, and wintery vegetables (see *Peasant-Style Kasha and Potatoes*, page 176). It makes a nice bed for stir-fried vegetables or *Ginger Tofu* (page 199) instead of the usual rice or millet. Also see the recipe for *Tofu and Buckwheat Pie* (page 204). Buckwheat flour makes wonderfully flavorful pancakes or crepes; try the *Buckwheat Crepes* recipe on page 30.

FLUFFY KASHA

When buckwheat is cooked in this way, it is light and not sticky.

1 cup kasha (whole, toasted buckwheat groats)
2 tablespoons olive oil
1 small onion
1 egg, beaten
2 cups boiling water
Pinch of sea salt

Serves: About 3 cups
Time: About 25 minutes

1. Wash and drain the kasha. Set it aside.
2. Heat the oil in a large skillet. Add the onion and sauté for 2–3 minutes. Add the kasha and stir for a few minutes more.
3. Remove the skillet from the heat and stir in the beaten egg. Return the skillet to the heat and stir until the buckwheat grains no longer stick together (about 3 minutes).
4. Remove the skillet from the heat; pour in the boiling water.
5. Cover, return the skillet to the heat, reduce the heat to low, and simmer for about 20 minutes, or until the water is absorbed. Fluff with a fork before serving.

    Serve the kasha as a bed for vegetables, tofu, seitan, tempeh, etc.

PEASANT-STYLE KASHA AND POTATOES

A hearty and easy-to-prepare dish for winter.

1 tablespoon oil
1 medium onion, chopped
2–4 cloves garlic, minced
1 teaspoon thyme
1 cup buckwheat
2 cups boiling water
2 medium potatoes, scrubbed and diced
1 recipe Tahini-Miso Sauce (page 245) or Tofu and Peanut Sauce (page 244)

Serves: 3
Time: 30 minutes

1. Cook the diced potatoes by modified boiling (see page 163) or by cooking them in a pressure cooker until they are tender. Keep warm until needed.
2. While the potatoes are cooking, heat the oil in a large skillet. Add the onion, garlic, and thyme. Sauté for 2–3 minutes.
3. Wash and drain the buckwheat; then add it to the skillet with the onions. Stir constantly for about 3 minutes.
4. Remove the skillet from the heat and pour the boiling water over the buckwheat. Then cover the skillet, return it to the heat, and simmer over low heat until the water is absorbed (about 20 minutes).
5. Add the hot, cooked potatoes and toss lightly.
6. Place each portion on an individual serving plate and cover it with sauce. Garnish with chopped parsley, if desired.

VARIATIONS

- Add about 1 pound of tofu, cut into small cubes, along with the potatoes. This addition goes best with the *Tahini Miso Sauce.*
- Serve with *Ginger Tofu* (page 199) and replace the *Tahini-Miso Sauce* or the *Tofu and Peanut Sauce* with the sauce from the *Ginger Tofu* recipe.

CORN

Corn is America's native grain. Dried corn is usually ground into flour or meal. Sometimes it is first cooked in water to which a small amount of powdered lime is added, and then ground to make tortillas.

It is definitely best to buy cornmeal from natural foods stores because the cornmeals sold in supermarkets have been degermed (they are not made from whole corn). In addition, they sometimes contain additives. This is especially true of the self-rising varieties. Yellow and white varieties of cornmeal are similar nutritionally, except that yellow cornmeal contains more vitamin A. There is even a blue variety of cornmeal. All the different types can be used interchangeably in recipes.

Cornmeal and corn flour (which is finely ground cornmeal) are used in baking. Follow the directions in the recipe you are using. Some suggestions are listed below.

Use cornmeal in muffins (*Corny Corn Muffins*, page 89); breads (*Southern Cornbread*, page 85); pancakes (*Orange-Banana Corn Cakes*, page 27, *Hoe Cakes*, page 87); and breakfast porridge (*Corn and Buckwheat Porridge*, page 25). For a finer texture, corn flour may be used to replace cornmeal in breads or muffins. You can even use fresh corn for this purpose (see *Fresh Corn Cakes*, page 148). If you have a slow-cooking electric pot, try the *Slow-Cooking Spoon Bread* recipe on page 85.

Good-quality corn tortillas can be purchased in natural foods stores. They are used in *Chalupas*, page 187, and as a wrapper for *Refried Beans*, page 44.

GOLDEN CORN BAKE

This recipe has been a big hit every time I've made it.

1 tablespoon oil
1 medium onion, chopped
3 medium yellow squash, sliced
2 cups sliced mushrooms
4 cups corn, cut off the cob
6 eggs
1 teaspoon sea salt
1 teaspoon basil
2 cups grated cheese
1½ cups bread crumbs

Serves: 6
Time: 1 hour, 15 minutes

1. Heat the oil in a large skillet. Add the onions and sauté for 2–3 minutes. Add the squash and stir for a minute. Add the mushrooms; stir, cover the skillet, and cook for about 5 minutes more.
2. While the vegetables are cooking, place the corn, eggs, salt, and basil in a blender or food processor. Blend till smooth and creamy.
3. Place the sautéed vegetables in the bottom of a 7-x-11-inch baking dish. Pour the corn mixture over the vegetables. Top with grated cheese and sprinkle with bread crumbs.
4. Bake at 350°F for 45 minutes, or until set. If necessary, place the casserole under the broiler for a minute to brown the top.

VARIATIONS

- Substitute lightly steamed broccoli for the yellow squash. Do not sauté.
- Place the steamed broccoli in the bottom of the baking dish along with the onion and mushrooms.

MILLET

Light, fluffy, and mild-tasting, millet can be substituted for rice in almost any recipe. Use hulled millet for cooking.

Millet can be used either toasted or untoasted. For toasted millet, use 1 cup of millet and 2½ cups of boiling water or vegetable stock. Place the millet that is wet from being washed in an unoiled skillet and stir over high heat until it is dry. Continue stirring until it begins to give off a nutty aroma. Remove the skillet from the heat and pour in the boiling water. Cover the skillet and return it to the heat. Simmer, without stirring, over medium-low for 20 minutes, or until the water is absorbed. Fluff the millet with a fork before serving.

To cook untoasted millet (I call this *Easy Millet*), wash 1 cup of millet and place it in a pan with 3 cups of water. Cover and bring to a boil. Lower the heat and simmer, without stirring, for 20 minutes, or until the water is absorbed. This yields about 3 cups.

Toasted millet is dry and fluffy; it is ideal as a bed for stir-fried vegetables, baked tofu in a sauce, beans, etc. Millet cooked by the easy method is moist and sticky. Use it for casseroles, pies, patties, loaves, and so on.

Uncooked millet can be ground for use in pancakes or crepes (*Millet Flour Pancakes*, page 27) or as a breakfast cereal (*Millet Cream*, page 26). Cooked millet or millet cream can be blended in a blender with a little soup stock and used to thicken soups. Leftover cooked millet is good with fruit and yogurt or soymilk for breakfast.

Also see the recipes for *Apple-Millet Pie* (page 258), *Millet Cheese Balls* (page 64), *Tourtière au Millet* (see recipe on right), and *Summer Grain Pilaf* (page 35).

TOURTIÈRE AU MILLET

As the legend goes, there once was a species of a bird that lived in the province of Quebec called a tourt (I don't know its English name). This bird was the main ingredient in a special type of meat pie called a tourtière. The tourtière was traditionally served only around Christmastime. However, during the Depression, when most people were very poor, they took advantage of this supposedly delicious bird and they began eating it all the time. Today the tourt is extinct, but the tourtière is still made, and other meats are substituted for the tourt. Since vegetarians are especially talented in making the traditional dishes of their culture without meat, the "tourtière au millet" was a natural development. It's a favorite among French-Canadian vegetarians.

1 tablespoon oil
1 medium onion, chopped
8–10 ounces sliced fresh mushrooms
1 teaspoon thyme
3 cups cooked millet (see left column)
¼ cup nutritional yeast
¼ cup tamari
2 tablespoons water
1 egg, beaten
1 unbaked 9-inch double-crust, whole wheat pie shell (see recipe on page 92)

Yield: 1 double-crust 9-inch pie
Serves: 4–6
Time: 1 hour

1. Heat the oil in a large skillet. Add the onion and sauté until almost tender. Add the mushrooms and the thyme. Sauté for a few minutes more, until the mushrooms are cooked.

2. Add the millet and the nutritional yeast to the sautéed onions and mushrooms. Mix well. Add the tamari and the water and mix again. (Real wheat-free tamari is better than shoyu in this recipe.) If the mixture is hot, let it cool slightly; then add the egg. Mix well.

3. Transfer the mixture to an unbaked pie shell. Cover the pie with the top crust. Flute the edges and cut some holes in the top of the crust to allow the steam to escape. Bake at 375°F for 40–45 minutes, or until the crust is done.

VARIATION

- If desired, substitute another grain such as bulghur or buckwheat for part of the millet.

OATS

Oats are becoming more popular every day, and people are also discovering oat bran. Oats are usually used in sweet dishes such as porridges, cookies, granolas, and desserts. But there is no need to stop there. Oats are a great filler for meatless loaves, patties, and other vegetable main dishes. In fact, it is surprising just how many ways they can be used.

Oat flour can be used in pancakes, muffins, and breads. To make oat flour, just grind some oats in a blender.

Chapter 2 contains directions on how to cook oatmeal porridge. Other recipes in this book that use oats are *Oatmeal Burgers Deluxe* (the recipe is on this page). They are really good. The *Black-Eyed Pea and Oat Casserole* (page 45) and the *Sweet Potato, Oatmeal, and Cashew Loaf* (page 222) are also very tasty. Some other recipes that contain oats or oatmeal are the *Oatmeal Pie Crust* (page 96), *Coconut Pie Crust* (page 95), *Wildflower Apple Crisp* (page 264), *Polynesian Bars* (page 270), *Fruit and Oat Squares* (page 268), *Maple-Walnut Cookies* (page 266), *Apple, Date, and Oatmeal Muffins* (page 88), *Oat Crepes* (page 30), and *Maple Oat Bran Granola* (page 31).

OATMEAL BURGERS DELUXE

This is one of my husband Claude's favorite recipes. You could easily trick a skeptic into believing that it is made out of meat.

BURGERS
1 cup rolled oats
¾ cup grated cheese (sharp Cheddar is good)
¼ cup sesame seeds
1 small onion, finely chopped
3 cloves garlic, pressed
½ teaspoon sage
2 tablespoons tamari
3 eggs, beaten

SAUCE
2 tablespoons whole wheat pastry flour
½ cup tomato juice
½ cup water
1 tablespoon tamari
1 cup sliced mushrooms

Serves: 2–3
Time: 25 minutes

1. Mix together the burger ingredients. Set the mixture aside while you prepare the ingredients for the sauce.
2. Place the flour in a small bowl. Stir a little bit of tomato juice into the flour to make a paste. Gradually stir in the remaining juice. Add the tamari and mushrooms.
3. Heat the oil in a heavy skillet, and drop the oat mixture into the skillet to make 4–6 large patties. (The patties will hold together as they cook.) Cook the patties over medium heat until brown on the bottom, then turn them over to brown on the other side.
4. Remove the skillet from the heat. Remove the patties and pour the sauce into the skillet. Stir, then place the patties in the sauce. Cover and simmer for about 10 minutes, or the time it takes to make a quick salad.

QUINOA

Although quinoa (pronounced "keenwa") is difficult to find and relatively expensive, it is worth seeking out because of its nutritional value and delicious, mild flavor. This grain was popular in South America thousands of years ago and now it is grown in Colorado. Quinoa is high in protein, calcium, and iron. If you cannot find it in your local natural foods store, write to the Quinoa Corporation, P. O. Box 7114, Boulder, Colorado 80306 for information.

To make 3 cups of cooked quinoa, bring 2 cups of water to boil in a medium-sized saucepan. Add 1 cup of quinoa and cover. Reduce the heat to low and simmer, without stirring, for about 15 minutes, or until the water is absorbed.

Quinoa can be used in the same ways that rice or millet are used in recipes. Try it!

QUINOA, LEEK, AND TOFU CASSEROLE*

1½ cups tofu
2 teaspoons sesame oil
1 clove garlic, pressed
1 leek, chopped
2 cups cooked quinoa
1 teaspoon sea salt or 2 teaspoons shoyu
Dash black pepper
1 cup whole wheat bread crumbs
1 cup soymilk
½ cup cheese, grated (optional)

Serves: 5
Time: About 1 hour

1. Preheat oven to 350°F. Working with ½ cup tofu at a time, squeeze out water with your hands. Set aside.
2. Heat a large skillet or wok and add the oil. Add the garlic and the leek. Sauté until lightly browned. Add quinoa, then tofu, sautéing for 2 minutes after each addition. Add seasonings.

3. Oil a casserole dish. Add ½ cup bread crumbs and rotate the casserole dish to coat evenly.
4. Gently add the quinoa mixture. Press a well in the center of the quinoa and pour in the soymilk. Cover with the remaining bread crumbs and cheese.
5. Cover and bake for 20 minutes. Remove the cover and continue to bake until the cheese is nicely browned.

*Reprinted from *Shopper's Guide to Natural Foods*, from the Editors of East West Journal, Avery Publishing Group, 1987.

RICE

Need I say that the rice I use is whole, unpolished brown rice? Not only is it more nourishing than white rice—it tastes better as well.

In the large natural foods stores there are many varieties of unpolished rice. These include long grain brown rice, medium grain brown rice, short grain brown rice, sweet rice, brown basmati rice, wehani rice, and wild rice. Brown rice flour is widely available.

There are also organic and nonorganic varieties of rice. Organic rice is more expensive, but it is also cleaner, containing fewer hulls.

Except for wild rice, all varieties of rice may be cooked in the same fashion. They can even be mixed, if desired. Below are three different methods for cooking brown rice.

- *Fluffy rice.* Place rice in an unoiled skillet and stir it over medium-high heat until it begins to emit a fragrant, nutty odor. Remove the skillet from the heat and pour in 2 cups of boiling water. Stir once. Cover the skillet and simmer over low heat, without stirring, for 35–40 minutes, or until the water is absorbed. If you are not sure if the rice is done, open the lid quickly and poke a knife down to the bottom of the pot to see if there is any water left. This will make about 3 cups of cooked rice.
- *Easy rice.* Place 1 cup of brown rice in a pan containing 2 cups of cold water. Cover and bring to a boil; then lower the heat and simmer, without stirring, for about 35–40 minutes, or until the water is absorbed. Rice cooked by this method will not be fluffy. Use it in casseroles, puddings, etc. This will yield about 3 cups of cooked rice.

- *Baked rice.* Place 1 cup of brown rice in a casserole dish. Pour in 2 cups of boiling water. Cover the casserole and bake at 350°F for 45 minutes or until the water is absorbed. This will make about 3 cups of fluffy baked rice.

Use rice in stuffings, loaves, patties, casseroles, breakfast porridges, desserts, salads, and soups. (Does that cover everything?) In addition to the *Eggplant and Rice Casserole* below, some recipes in this book that use rice are: *Nori-Maki* (page 108), *Cauliflower Curry*, (page 146), *Celery-Rice Curry* (page 147), *Winter Squash and Rice Squares* (page 228), *Carrot and Rice Cream* (page 59), *Arame Rice Patties* (page 223), *Tempeh, Carrot, and Rice Loaf* (page 217), *Green Bean and Rice Casserole* (page 152), *Rice Cream* (page 26)—and I'm sure you will find some others. Rice flour is used in *Rice Flour Crepes* (page 29), *Almond and Date Cookies* (page 265), *Maple Walnut Cookies* (page 266), and *Tempura* (page 234).

EGGPLANT AND RICE CASSEROLE

If you have some leftover rice, this casserole takes no time to make.

2 tablespoons olive oil
1 medium onion, chopped
3 cloves garlic, minced
1 medium eggplant, quartered and sliced
1 teaspoon basil
2 cups cooked brown rice
1/3 cup tomato paste
2 tablespoons shoyu
1 cup ricotta or cottage cheese
1 cup (or less) grated provolone cheese

Serves: 3
Time: 35–45 minutes

1. Heat the oil in a large skillet. Add onion and garlic. Sauté for a minute or two; then add the eggplant and basil. Stir, then cover and cook over medium-low heat until the eggplant is tender. Stir occasionally.
2. Remove the skillet from the heat. Add the rice, tomato paste, shoyu, and ricotta, and mix well. If you have an ovenproof skillet, leave the mixture in the skillet. Otherwise, transfer it to an oiled baking dish.
3. Sprinkle with the grated provolone and bake at 350°F until the cheese is melted and the casserole is thoroughly heated (about 15–20 minutes).
   Serve with a big green salad.

VARIATIONS

- This is one of those simple, basic recipes that may be easily varied to suit the ingredients in your refrigerator. Some suggested additions are: 1 cup sliced mushrooms, 1 sliced green pepper, 1 small sliced zucchini, or 1/4 cup sliced black olives. Cook these added ingredients along with the eggplant.

WILD RICE

1 cup wild rice
3 cups water

Yield: Approximately 4 cups
Time: 1 hour, 35 minutes

1. Wash the rice in cold water and drain it in a wire strainer.
2. Bring the water to a boil and add the rice. Cover, reduce the heat, and gently boil for 5 minutes. Remove the pan from the heat and let it stand for 1 hour.
3. Return the rice to the heat and simmer for 30 minutes, or until the water is absorbed.

RYE

Although rye berries (whole grains of rye) are usually ground into flour, they can also be cooked. In my opinion, there is nothing better than a dark and pungent loaf of sourdough rye bread made from whole rye flour. Rye flour can be (and usually is, unless otherwise stated) just as refined as white flour. Therefore, buy your rye flour from a natural foods store and carefully read the labels on rye breads and crackers.

Natural foods stores sell rye flakes, which may be cooked like oatmeal. See page 25 in Chapter 2 for directions.

There are not many recipes that use whole rye berries, but the following recipe, *Fried Wheat and Rye*, uses both whole soaked rye berries and wheat berries.

Try the *Sourdough Rye* bread on page 83; it is very easy to make and has a fantastic flavor. The *Wheatless Onion Quick Bread* on page 86 is good, too. Rye grains can also be sprouted to make *Essene Bread* (page 91). Just substitute rye sprouts for the wheat sprouts. (See the inset on pages 124–125 for information about sprouting.)

FRIED WHEAT AND RYE

1 cup whole wheat berries, soaked 6–8 hours
1/4 cup rye berries, soaked 6–8 hours
1 1/2–2 cups water
Pinch of sea salt
1 tablespoon chopped scallion
1/2 cup onions, diced
1/4 cup celery, diced
1/2 cup carrots, diced
Dark sesame oil
Tamari

Serves: 4–6
Time: Soak 6–8 hours; cook about 1 1/2 hours.

1. Place wheat and rye berries in a pressure cooker with water and sea salt. Pressure cook for 50 minutes. Remove from heat and allow to cool.

2. Heat a small amount of dark sesame oil in a skillet. Sauté the scallion and onion for 1–2 minutes, then add the celery and carrots and sauté for 1 minute.

3. Add the cooked wheat and rye berries, sprinkle a little tamari on top, and cover. Reduce the heat to low and cook until the vegetables are tender.

4. Season the dish with a little more tamari, if desired, and mix. Sauté 1–2 minutes more. Remove from heat and place in a serving bowl. Serve while hot.

WHEAT

Wheat products that are available in natural foods stores include bran, bulghur, and couscous, among others. Wheat is the grain most commonly used in North America today. It surpasses all other grains with its versatility. Whole wheat berries can be sprouted, cooked, or ground into flour. The endless variety of breads, cakes, pastries, pastas, and other items that can be made with wheat flour is astounding. The recipes in this book will show you many ways to cook wheat and wheat products. A very convincing mock meat dish called *Seitan* (see page 193) is also made out of wheat flour.

To cook whole wheat berries, place 1 cup of soft wheat berries in a pot with 3 cups of water. Cover the pot and bring the water to a boil. Reduce the heat and simmer for 1 hour, or until the wheat is tender and the water is absorbed. This will yield about 3 cups.

The following recipe, *Basic Bulghur*, makes a quick entrée when you add some cooked beans or top it with grated cheese. Other recipes using bulghur are *Bulghur with Spinach* (page 36), *Bulghur with Zucchini* (page 36), *Bulghur-Peanut Pilaf* (page 37), and *Bulghur Burgers* (page 183). Other recipes using wheat include *Miller's Pancakes* (page 29), *Easy Cooked Wheat,* (page 26), and *Wheat and Lima Beans* (page 43). There are also many recipes in this book using wheat flour. (See Chapter 5, starting on page 69). For information on sprouting wheat, see the inset on pages 124–125.

BASIC BULGHUR

1 tablespoon oil
1 small onion, chopped
1 clove garlic, minced
1 cup bulghur wheat
2 cups boiling water
1 tablespoon tamari

Serves: 4
Time: 15 minutes

1. Heat the oil in a large skillet. Add the onion and garlic. Sauté for 2–3 minutes.
2. Add the bulghur and stir. Remove the skillet from the heat and pour in the boiling water. Cover the skillet, return it to the heat, and simmer over low heat for 10 minutes or until the water is absorbed.
3. Season to taste with tamari.

VARIATION

- Sauté other vegetables with the onion, such as green or red peppers, celery, or mushrooms. Add your choice of herbs or seasonings. If desired, add one or two chopped fresh tomatoes after the bulghur is cooked. Do not cook the tomatoes, just let them get warm.

BULGHUR BURGERS

1 cup cooked bulghur wheat
1 cup dry whole grain bread crumbs
3 eggs
1 or more cloves garlic, pressed
¼ cup finely chopped mushrooms
⅔ cup grated cheese
2 tablespoons tamari, or less to taste
½ teaspoon thyme
Oil as needed

Yield: About 6 patties
Serves: 3
Time: 20 minutes

1. Place all the ingredients in a large bowl and mix well.
2. Drop the mixture by the heaping tablespoon onto a hot, well-oiled skillet. Using your spoon, shape the mixture into patties. Cook over medium-low heat until the patties are brown on the bottom. The patties will hold together as they cook. Carefully turn them over and cook until firm and brown.

These patties can be served plain or with a sauce. Accompany them with a green salad and a steamed vegetable.

DRIED LEGUMES

The virtues of dried legumes (beans and peas) are many. They are one of the most nourishing and least expensive kinds of foods that exist. Their protein content is especially high and they are a good source of iron and many other nutrients. In contrast to the protein derived from animal sources, legumes contain no cholesterol or saturated fat. There is also great diversity among legumes. I once bought a sample of each kind of bean that was available in Montreal and ended up with twenty-three varieties! Each variety has its own distinctive flavor, shape, and color. And as an added bonus, legumes taste good!

Despite their many virtues, one thing has greatly limited the popularity of legumes. This is, of course, that they are difficult to digest and have a tendency to cause flatulence. However, with a little bit of care in eating habits, food combinations, and cooking methods, most people can eat and enjoy legumes without experiencing the unpleasantness that is often associated with beans.

In fact, a little attention to menu planning and eating habits can help assure you of good digestion of all your meals. The following list contains some general suggestions as well as some tips on cooking beans to render them more digestible.

- Make sure that your meals are spaced far enough apart. Nibbling in between meals slows down the digestion of previously eaten foods, giving them time to ferment in the digestive system, causing gas and discomfort.
- Drinking with meals also inhibits digestion to some extent. When we drink with our meals, the time that the food spends in our mouth is much shorter. Less saliva is produced and the food is less thoroughly chewed. Digestive enzymes in the mouth, stomach, and intestines are diluted by beverages taken with meals; thus, digestion is delayed. Also, the stomach must make more acid to retain the proper environment for digestion. All of these factors increase the likelihood of fermentation and gas in the digestive system.
- Keep your meals simple. When you have legumes, don't eat potatoes, fruit, sweeteners (such as molasses with baked beans), or desserts in the same meal. Also, don't combine too many different types of food in the same meal. An ideal meal centered on beans would consist of the beans, a grain or bread, a simple green salad, and a cooked vegetable.
- Eat beans in small amounts, especially to begin with. Many people who cannot tolerate a large quantity of legumes have no difficulty when eating small portions (1/2 cup or less). A good ratio of beans to grains in a meal is about 1/3 beans to 2/3 grains. When beans are a regular part of the diet, our systems adapt to them and digestion becomes easier.
- Beans must be well cooked. Long, slow cooking, such as in an electric, slow-cooking pot, is ideal.
- Add salt (or tamari) only near the end of cooking.
- A tablespoon or so of vinegar added to a pot of beans as they are cooking is said to make them easier to digest. It also enhances their flavor.
- Miso, sauerkraut, and yogurt are good to serve in the same meal with beans, because they are foods that aid digestion.
- Seasoning a bean dish with savory or summer savory also seems to help.
- Fennel tea (unsweetened) relieves gas and aids digestion, which makes it a nice beverage to serve after a meal containing beans. It has a fresh, anise-like flavor.
- Soaking dried legumes before cooking them improves their digestibility (see page 185).
- Do not cook dried beans in the water used for soaking them. Discard the water or use it to water your plants.
- The best way I know of to make beans easy to digest is to sprout them a little bit before cooking them. The sprouts do not have to be as long as the mung sprouts used in Chinese cooking. A 1/4-inch sprout is enough to make a difference. Sprouting beans, even just slightly, also makes them cook faster. See pages 124–125 for how to sprout beans. It is really easy!

HOW TO COOK DRIED LEGUMES

The cooking method for all types of dried legumes is the same. It is only the cooking time that varies. Even if the legumes have been sprouted for 1–3 days, the cooking method is still identical; however, they will cook faster. (Note: If you let the beans sprout 1–3 days, they will be beans with a small sprout growing from them. If you let them sprout 3–5 days, as in the inset on pages 124–125, you will have a longer sprout—more sprouts than bean, hence the label "sprouts.")

Although soaking is not essential for every type of legume, they all profit from it. Soaking shortens the cooking time and improves their digestibility. Going one step further and sprouting the beans increases their digestibility and shortens their cooking time even more. The list below outlines how to soak and cook dried legumes. For instructions on cooking beans in an electric slow-cooking pot, see page 186.

1. Wash and pick over the beans (or peas). Be careful, because sometimes dirt and small stones are mixed in with dry beans.
2. Place the washed beans in a bowl and cover them with water (about 1½ cups water is enough to soak 1 cup of dried beans). They will double in size as they soak, so make sure that your bowl is big enough. Soak the beans eight hours or overnight. After soaking, you may either cook them immediately, or sprout them, as desired.
3. Drain the beans, place them in a large kettle, and cover them with about 1½ inches of fresh water (or 2–2½ cups of water for each cup of beans). The important thing is to make sure that the beans are covered with water.
4. Cover the kettle and bring the water to a boil. Reduce the heat and slowly simmer the beans until they are tender.
5. As the beans cook, stir them occasionally and add more water, if needed.
6. When the beans are well cooked, they will be very tender and the cooking liquid will have thickened into a flavorful sauce.

Tips and Suggestions

- Bear in mind that 1 cup of dried beans yields 2½–3 cups cooked. It is a good idea to cook more than you will need for one meal; however, it is easy to go overboard and cook more than you will be able to use.
- If you cook more beans than you need, they can be frozen. See page 34 in Chapter 3, "Fast-Food Vegetarian Style."
- A strip of kombu (see page 6) added to a pot of beans adds minerals and a pleasant flavor.
- Vegetables and seasonings may be added to a kettle of beans during the last 30 minutes of cooking.
- Good seasonings for beans include tamari, miso, vinegar, lemon, bay leaves, garlic, savory, cayenne, basil, chili powder, cumin, parsley, and scallions.

COOKING TIMES FOR LEGUMES

Here is a list of approximate cooking times for some of the most commonly used beans. Times will vary depending on the freshness of the beans (fresh beans cook more quickly) and the water that you use. Beans cooked in hard water take longer to become tender.

- *Adzuki beans* (also called aduki or azuki). Unsoaked, 1 hour or more; soaked overnight, 40 minutes; sprouted 2–3 days, 30 minutes or less.
- *Black beans.* Unsoaked, not recommended; soaked overnight, 2–3 hours; sprouted 2–3 days, 1½–2 hours.
- *Black-eyed peas.* Unsoaked, 1½ hours; soaked overnight, 1 hour or less; sprouted 2–3 days, 30 minutes.
- *Chick peas* (garbanzos). Unsoaked, not recommended; soaked overnight, 2–3 hours; sprouted 2–3 days, 1 hour or more.
- *Kidney beans.* Unsoaked, 1½–2 hours; soaked overnight, 1 hour; sprouted 2–3 days, 30 minutes or more.
- *Lentils.* Unsoaked, 1 hour or less; soaked overnight, 30 minutes; sprouted 2–3 days, 10 minutes.
- *Pinto beans.* Unsoaked, 3 hours; soaked overnight, 2 hours; sprouted 2–3 days, 30 minutes or more.
- *Soybeans.* Unsoaked, not recommended; soaked overnight, 3–4 hours; sprouted 2–3 days, 1½ hours or more.

COOKING BEANS IN A SLOW-COOKER

Wash and pick over the desired amount of beans. For the average household, 1–2 cups of beans is probably enough. Remember that 1 cup of dry beans will yield about 3 cups cooked.

Place the beans in a bowl that gives them room to more than double in size. Add enough water to cover the beans by about 1½ inches and let them soak overnight (8–10 hours).

Drain and rinse the soaked beans and place them in an electric slow-cooker. Add enough water to cover them by 1 inch. Cover the pot and turn it on high. Let the beans cook for 1–2 hours. Turn the pot to low and let the beans continue to cook until they are very tender (8–12 hours, depending on the type of bean).

During the last hour of cooking you may add seasonings such as tamari, vinegar, bay leaves, savory or other herbs, or garlic. When the beans are finished cooking, you may add a tablespoon of olive oil, some fresh parsley, or minced scallions. A 6-inch strip of kombu may also be added during the last hour or two of cooking. If the beans become too dry near the end of cooking, add a little more water.

BEANS AND DUMPLINGS

Here's an old Southern dish that is both simple and satisfying. Almost any type of bean can be used for this recipe, but great northern or pinto beans are especially good.

1 cup dried beans
3 cups water
1 medium onion, chopped
2 bay leaves
1 teaspoon savory
1 recipe Sigi's Bread Dumplings *(page 64)*, Yogurt Dumplings *(page 63)*, Tofu Dumplings *(page 63)*, or Millet Cheese Balls *(page 64)*
2–4 scallions, chopped

Serves: 3
Time: Soak beans for 8 hours; 1–3 hours to cook, depending on type of beans.

1. Wash and pick over the beans. Place the beans in a medium-sized bowl with water to cover, and soak them for about 8 hours.

2. Drain and rinse the beans. If you wish, sprout the beans for 1–2 days before cooking. (See pages 124–125 for details on sprouting.)

3. Place the soaked (or soaked and sprouted) beans in a large pot with 3 cups of water. Cover and bring to a boil. Reduce the heat and simmer until the beans are just barely tender.

4. Add the chopped onion, bay leaves, savory, and tamari. Simmer until both the beans and the onion are tender.

5. While the beans and onion are cooking, prepare your chosen dumpling recipe. If the liquid from cooking the beans evaporates during the cooking, add a little more water so that the beans are "juicy."

6. Drop the dumplings into the pot of simmering beans, and cook according to the dumpling recipe.

7. Top with the chopped scallions just before serving. Serve with a steamed vegetable and a salad.

VARIATION

- If you have some precooked beans, this dish is quick to make. Simply place 3 cups of cooked beans in a large kettle with enough water to make them juicy. Add the onion, herbs, and tamari, and simmer until the onion is done. Add the dumplings and cook according to the dumpling recipe. Garnish and serve.

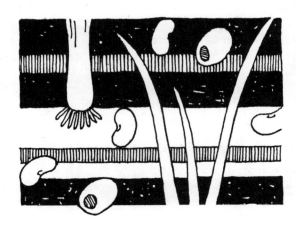

CHALUPAS

The perfect dish for a Mexican fiesta!

6 corn tortillas
Oil as needed
3 cups cooked pinto or red kidney beans
¼ cup water from cooking the beans (approximately)
1 teaspoon cumin
1 teaspoon chili powder
1 teaspoon basil
½ teaspoon oregano
Cayenne to taste
¼ cup tomato paste
2 tablespoons shoyu or tamari
½ cup grated cheese
1 medium avocado
2 tablespoons lemon juice
2–3 cloves garlic, pressed
2 ripe tomatoes, chopped
Shredded lettuce

Serves: 3–6
Time: 30 minutes

1. Brush the tortillas with a small amount of oil, then toast them in a toaster oven or under the broiler until crispy. This takes just a couple of minutes so be careful not to burn them.
2. Set the toasted tortillas aside and make the topping.
3. Mash the beans with enough of the water from cooking them to obtain a spreadable consistency. Mix the mashed beans with the herbs, spices, tomato paste, and shoyu.
4. Generously spread the toasted tortillas with the bean mixture and sprinkle with the grated cheese.
5. Place the tortillas on a cookie sheet and bake them at 400°F for about 10–15 minutes, or until they are thoroughly heated and the cheese is melted.
6. While the chalupas are cooking, mash together the avocado, lemon juice, and garlic.
7. Top the hot chalupas with shredded lettuce and chopped tomato. Garnish with a big spoonful of the avocado mixture.

CORNBREAD 'N' BEANS

1 tablespoon oil
1 cup chopped onion
1 green pepper, diced
1 teaspoon cumin
1 teaspoon basil
1 teaspoon chili powder
½ teaspoon oregano
2 cups cooked pinto or red kidney beans
½ cup liquid from cooking beans
1 tablespoon tamari
⅓ cup black or green olives, sliced (I use Jalapeno-stuffed green olives)
2 tablespoons tomato paste
1 recipe Southern Cornbread (page 85)

Serves: 4
Time: 50 minutes

1. Heat the oil in a large skillet. Add the onion and sauté for about 3 minutes. Add the green pepper, cumin, basil, chili powder, and oregano. Sauté until the vegetables are almost tender.
2. Add the beans, ½ cup of the liquid from the beans, tamari, olives, and tomato paste. Mix well. Evenly distribute the bean mixture over the bottom of an oiled, 11-x-17-inch baking dish. (If you bake this recipe in a dish that is too deep and small, the cornbread will be too thick and will not cook well.) Set the baking dish aside while you prepare the batter for *Southern Cornbread*.
3. When the batter is mixed, spread it over the beans. Bake at 375°F for 25 minutes, or until the cornbread is done.

VARIATION

• Chopped celery may be sautéed with the onions, if you wish. Another good addition is about ⅓ cup of soaked hijiki or arame. Add it at the same time you add the olives. A dash of cayenne or hot sauce could also be added. If you wish to omit the olives, add 1 tablespoon of tamari to the recipe.

SPICY PINTO SPROUTS WITH GREEN OLIVES

3 cups pinto bean sprouts (1 cup of dry pinto beans, soaked overnight and sprouted for 2–3 days, will yield about 3 cups of sprouts. See pages 124–125.)
2 cups water (approximately)
1 tablespoon olive oil
1 medium onion, chopped
1 green pepper, chopped
½ teaspoon cumin
½ teaspoon chili powder
1 teaspoon basil
Cayenne to taste
2 medium tomatoes
½ cup sliced green olives
3–4 scallions, chopped

Serves: 4
Time: 35 minutes

1. Place the beans and the water in a large kettle, cover, and bring to a boil. Reduce the heat to medium-low and simmer until tender (about 30 minutes). Add a little more water if necessary to keep the beans from drying out.
2. While the beans are cooking, heat the oil in a large skillet. Add the onion and sauté for a few minutes. Add the green pepper, cumin, chili powder, basil, and cayenne. Sauté until the onion and the pepper are almost tender.
3. Chop one of the tomatoes and put it in a blender along with ½ cup of the cooked beans. Blend until smooth.
4. Place the cooked beans, the bean and tomato purée, and the sliced olives in the skillet with the sautéed vegetables. Simmer for a few minutes to blend the flavors.
5. Chop the remaining tomato and add it just before serving. Continue cooking just long enough to heat the tomato. Garnish with the chopped scallions and serve over rice or millet, accompanied by a big green salad.

VARIATION

• Instead of serving the sprouts over a bed of rice or millet, make the dish into a casserole with tortillas. Place a layer of torn-up corn tortillas in a casserole dish. Cover the tortillas with half of the sprout mixture. Add another layer of tortillas; top with the remaining bean mixture. Bake at 350°F for 15–20 minutes. (This variation needs only one tomato, for the purée.)

MEXICAN BEAN AND RICE CASSEROLE

1 tablespoon oil
1 large onion, chopped
2 stalks celery, chopped
1 red bell pepper, diced
3 cups cooked red kidney beans
Enough liquid from cooking the beans to make a purée
6 ounces tomato paste
1 teaspoon cumin
1 teaspoon chili powder
1 teaspoon basil
½ teaspoon oregano
Pinch of cayenne, if desired
3 tablespoons shoyu or tamari
1 cup soaked arame (optional)
4 cups cooked brown rice
½ cup chopped parsley
3 ripe large tomatoes, sliced
4–5 cloves garlic, pressed

Serves: 6
Time: 1 hour, 15 minutes

1. Heat the oil in a large skillet and sauté the onion, celery, and red pepper till almost tender.
2. Blend together the beans, a small amount of the liquid from cooking them (about ¼ cup), the tomato paste, the spices, and the shoyu or tamari in a blender or food processor to make a purée. Transfer the purée to a large bowl.
3. Add the sautéed vegetables and the soaked arame (if desired) to the bean purée and mix well.
4. In a separate bowl, mix the rice and parsley together.

5. Oil a large, deep baking dish. Place half of the rice in the bottom of the dish. Spread half of the bean mixture over the rice, top it with half of the sliced tomatoes, and then distribute half of the pressed garlic evenly over the tomatoes. Repeat the layers.
6. Bake at 350°F for 45 minutes.

   This casserole is delicious with steamed artichokes and a big green salad.

BEAN PIE WITH MILLET CRUST

CRUST
3 cups cooked millet
2 tablespoons oil
1 egg, beaten
1/4 teaspoon sea salt (optional)

FILLING
2 cups red kidney beans or pinto beans, cooked and drained
1 egg
1–2 tablespoons shoyu or tamari, to taste
1 teaspoon cumin
1 teaspoon chili powder
1/4 teaspoon cayenne, or your favorite hot sauce (to taste)

GARNISH
1–2 large tomatoes, cut in thick slices
1 teaspoon oregano
4 tablespoons grated Parmesan (optional)
3/4 cup grated Cheddar cheese (optional)

Serves: 4
Time: 1 hour

1. To make the pie crust, mix together the millet, oil, and egg. Press the mixture into an oiled 7-x-11-inch baking dish, covering the bottom and halfway up the sides.
2. To make the filling, blend together the beans, egg, shoyu, and spices in a blender or food processor. Fill the millet crust with the bean mixture and arrange the sliced tomatoes attractively on top. Sprinkle the pie with the oregano, and top with the grated cheese (if desired).
3. Bake at 350°F for 40 minutes or until the pie is firm enough to slice.

   Serve with *Guacamole* (page 102) and a big green salad.

BEAN AND HIJIKI PIE

This is a good recipe to introduce sea vegetables to your family. You can use dried pinto or kidney beans that have been soaked, or canned beans.

2 cups cooked and drained pinto or red kidney beans
1/3 cup tomato paste
2 tablespoons shoyu or tamari
1 egg
1 teaspoon basil
1 teaspoon oregano
1/2 teaspoon cumin
Cayenne to taste
3 cloves garlic, pressed
1/3 cup soaked and chopped hijiki
1 cup cooked brown rice
1 recipe Press-In Pie Crust (page 95) or 1/2 recipe Whole Wheat Pie Crust (page 92), unbaked
1/2 cup sharp Cheddar cheese, or 2 tablespoons sesame seeds
Thin slices of green pepper or fresh tomato

Yield: 1 single-crust 9-inch pie
Serves: 4
Time: 1 hour, 15 minutes

1. Place the cooked beans, tomato paste, shoyu (or tamari) and egg in a blender or food processor. Blend until smooth.
2. Transfer the blended mixture to a large bowl. Add the basil, oregano, cumin, cayenne, garlic, hijiki, and rice. Mix well.
3. Spread the mixture to fill an unbaked 9-inch pie shell. Top with slices of green pepper or tomato and sprinkle with cheese or sesame seeds.
4. Bake at 350°F for 40–45 minutes.

LENTIL-CARROT LOAF

3 cups carrots, cut into 1/3-inch slices
1 1/2 cups lentils, cooked and drained
1/2 cup finely chopped onions
1/2 teaspoon sage
1 teaspoon curry powder
2 tablespoons shoyu or tamari
1 cup rolled oats
1/2 cup chopped walnuts or pecans
2 tablespoons finely chopped parsley

Serves: 4
Time: 1 hour

1. Steam the carrots until tender. Drain the carrots, and, if desired, reserve the water to make a sauce to serve with the loaf.
2. Mix together the cooked carrots and lentils. Mash them coarsely with a potato masher. Add the remaining ingredients and mix well.
3. Pack the mixture into a well-oiled loaf pan. Decorate the top of the loaf with nut halves if desired.
4. Bake at 350°F for 35–40 minutes, or until firm and golden brown.
5. After baking, let the loaf stand for about 5 minutes and then unmold it onto a serving platter. For an attractive presentation, surround the unmolded loaf with sliced ripe tomatoes, or any other colorful vegetable.
   Serve with the sauce of your choice.

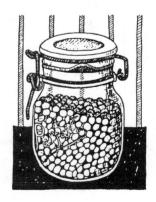

LENTIL PIE

1 1/2 cups uncooked lentils
3 cups water
1 tablespoon oil
1 stalk celery, chopped
1 medium onion, chopped
1 teaspoon thyme
1 teaspoon cinnamon
1/4 teaspoon cloves
3/4 cup Brazil nuts, finely chopped
1/4 cup tamari
1/4 cup tomato paste
1 double-crust 9-inch whole wheat pie shell, unbaked (page 92)

Yield: 1 double-crust 9-inch pie
Time: 1 hour, 35 minutes

1. Wash the lentils and place then in a pan with the water. Cover and cook for about 40 minutes, or until the water is absorbed.
2. Heat the oil in a skillet; add the celery, onion, thyme, cinnamon, and cloves. Sauté until the celery is just barely tender.
3. Add the cooked lentils to the celery-onion mixture; then add the remaining ingredients. Mix well. Spread the mixture into an unbaked pie shell. Cover with the top crust. Flute the edges and cut a hole into the top crust to allow steam to escape.
4. Bake at 375°F for 40 minutes, or until the crust is golden brown.
   Serve with a steamed vegetable and a green salad. The lentil pie is also good with a sauce or some homemade relish.

BABY LIMA BEANS IN TAHINI SAUCE

This recipe is easy, versatile, and very good.

1 cup dried baby lima beans
3 cups water
3 bay leaves
1/3 cup tahini
2 tablespoons arrowroot
1 teaspoon tarragon
3 tablespoons tamari
1 tablespoon cider or rice vinegar
Cayenne to taste
Finely chopped parsley and scallions

Serves: 4
Time: Soak overnight;1 hour, 40 minutes to
  prepare.

1. Wash the beans well and soak them overnight in water to cover. Drain.
2. Place the soaked beans in a large kettle with the water and the bay leaves. Cover, bring to a boil, reduce the heat, and simmer until very tender (about 1 hour and 30 minutes).
3. In a small bowl, mix together the tahini and arrowroot. Add the mixture to the kettle of cooked beans. Mix well. Add the tarragon, tamari, vinegar, and cayenne. Simmer, stirring constantly, until the sauce thickens. If the sauce becomes too thick, add some water.

   Serve over a bed of rice or millet and garnish with finely chopped scallions and parsley.

NOTE: This recipe can also be very good with Great Northern beans, white kidney beans, or black-eyed peas. However, you may have to adjust the amount of liquid and/or arrowroot to obtain the proper consistency for the sauce. The cooking time will also vary with the type of beans used.

VARIATION

- After the beans have cooked for 45–60 minutes, add some chopped onion, celery, and carrots. Simmer until both the beans and the vegetables are tender. Season and make the sauce as indicated above.

ADZUKI BEANS WITH WINTER SQUASH

This is an adaptation of a classic macrobiotic recipe.

1 cup uncooked (dried) adzuki beans
4 cups water
1 medium acorn squash, or 3–4 cups of any other kind of winter squash, cut into cubes
1 large onion, chopped
1 teaspoon savory
1/2 teaspoon thyme
4 tablespoons miso (use a dark barley or rice miso)
2 tablespoons chopped parsley

Serves: 4
Time: 1 hour, 20 minutes

1. Wash and pick over the beans.
2. Place the washed beans in a large kettle with the 4 cups of water. Cover and bring to a boil. Reduce the heat and simmer the beans over low heat for about 1 hour, or until they are tender.
3. While the beans are simmering, peel the squash and cut it into cubes. When the beans are almost tender, add the squash, chopped onion, savory, and thyme. Continue to simmer until the vegetables are tender (about 20 minutes more).
4. Remove the kettle from the heat; add the miso and mix well. If the stew becomes too dry, add a little more water. Serve over a bed of cooked rice or millet and garnish with some chopped parsley. Accompany with a green salad.

VARIATIONS

- To make this stew into a delicious soup, just add enough water to yield the desired consistency.
- Add about 1/4 cup of washed and soaked hijiki to the stew at the same time as the squash.

SEITAN AND GLUTEN

Seitan and gluten are meat analogues made from wheat protein. Like many other vegetarian foods, gluten and seitan are new to most North Americans, but they have been used in the Orient for centuries. Seitan is the Japanese name for wheat gluten that has been cut into small pieces and cooked in a seasoned broth. Gluten is the English name for any products made from wheat gluten. However, many people use the word seitan to refer to any gluten product.

According to *The Gluten Book* by Lee Arta Moulton, gluten and seitan are very high-protein foods; one cup of raw gluten contains 72 grams of protein. You can make your own gluten or seitan in fairly large quantities and freeze it. The frozen seitan may be used as needed to supplement other protein foods such as beans, soy products, or dairy products. One cup of raw gluten combined with ¼ cup of T.V.P. (see page 11) provides 82 grams of supplemented (or "complete") protein.

The first time you make seitan or gluten you may feel that the work involved is greater than the results. However, after you discover how many quick, delicious, and inexpensive meals you can produce from one recipe of raw gluten, I think you will change your mind. If your family is still eating meat, you may add gluten to your favorite meat-based recipes (reducing the quantity of meat, of course) without anyone ever suspecting. Since gluten contains no cholesterol or saturated fats, this little bit of culinary trickery could be a real health-saver for a stubborn meat-eater.

What most cooks object to is the 20 minutes of kneading involved in making gluten. I love it! Think of it as exercise. Put on your favorite dance music and get a good workout while you knead! With gluten making, as with any other skill, the more you practice, the faster and easier it becomes. Of course, if you have a food processor that can knead bread, or an electric bread maker, making gluten is easy.

The pages that follow contain detailed instructions for making and using gluten and seitan. Happy kneading!

STARCH WATER

Raw gluten (see recipe below) is the first step in making seitan and other gluten products. The by-product of gluten making is about 1 gallon of cloudy water. This water contains the starch of the wheat, along with some of the bran and many of the vitamins. Therefore it is a shame to throw it out. Below are some suggested ways of using the starch water.

- In baking breads, muffins, cookies, pancakes, cakes, etc., in place of clear water or milk.
- In soups, sauces, or stews (it will thicken as it cooks).
- Cover the bowl or jar containing the water and leave it overnight in the refrigerator. In the morning, pour off the clear liquid and use it to water your plants. Save the thick starch to thicken sauces and gravies (keep it in a covered jar in the refrigerator). To thicken 1 cup of water for a sauce, use 2 tablespoons of this thick starch.

RAW GLUTEN

3 cups water

7 cups whole wheat bread flour (approximately)

Yield: 1½–2 cups
Time: 45 minutes

1. Pour the water into a large bowl. Add about 3 cups of the flour and mix well. Beat the dough for about 100 strokes, or until it becomes elastic. Gradually add enough of the remaining flour to make a kneadable dough.
2. Turn the dough out onto a generously floured surface and knead in enough flour to make a firm and nonsticky dough. (See page 72 in the bread making chapter for information on how to knead.) Knead the dough vigorously for 20 minutes. If kneading becomes too difficult for you, try pounding the dough with a rolling pin or with your fists.

3. Continue kneading and/or pounding the dough until it becomes very smooth and elastic. To make sure that the dough is kneaded enough, break off a small piece and wash it. If it is sufficiently kneaded, the starch will wash away, leaving the elastic gluten.

4. The next step is washing (rinsing) the dough. Fill a large bowl with room-temperature water (use the same bowl you used to mix the dough). Place the bowl in the sink and place the dough in the bowl. Work the dough by rubbing it and squeezing it between your hands with a motion similar to that of washing clothes. Don't worry if the dough falls apart, because it will come back together as it is washed.

5. When the water becomes very cloudy, pour it (with the dough) through a colander. If you want to save the starch water (see page 192), place an empty bowl under the colander to catch it. Repeat this squeezing and rinsing process until the rinse water is practically clear and the dough resembles a large, elastic wad of chewing gum. You now have raw gluten.

   Use the raw gluten to make *Seitan* (see recipe below), *Seitan with Beans* (page 195), and *Ground Seitan* (page 195).

SEITAN

1 recipe Raw Gluten *(page 192)*
2 tablespoons oil
1 teaspoon roasted sesame oil
1 onion, chopped
8–10 cloves garlic, minced (or less, if desired)
1–2 teaspoons fresh grated ginger
1 teaspoon thyme
4 cups water or vegetable broth
¼ cup tamari

Yield: Approximately 4 cups seitan
Time: 45 minutes to prepare raw gluten; 1 hour to prepare seitan.

1. Follow the recipe for the preparation of raw gluten. Set the raw gluten aside while you prepare the broth.

2. Heat both kinds of oil together in a large, heavy kettle. Add the onion, garlic, ginger, and thyme. Sauté over low heat until the onion is tender.

3. Add the water and the tamari. Cover the kettle and let the broth simmer over low heat while you roll out the gluten.

4. Using your hands and/or a rolling pin, roll out and stretch the gluten to a ¼–½–inch thickness. This takes a little bit of patience because the gluten has a tendency to spring back to its original shape.

5. Using a sharp knife or scissors, cut your thin slab of gluten into ¼–½-inch pieces.

6. To cook the seitan, reduce the heat under the broth, if necessary, so that it is just barely simmering. (If the broth is too hot the seitan will become spongy, which is undesirable.) Drop the pieces of raw gluten into the broth. Cover and cook over *low* heat for about 45 minutes, or until the seitan is firm. Check occasionally during the cooking to make sure that the broth is just barely simmering and not boiling.

   Seitan may be used in place of meat in any stir-fry dish. It is also a delicious addition to a vegetable stew such as the *Pot au Feu* on page 235.

   The broth used to cook the seitan may be thickened with arrowroot, cornstarch, flour, or the wheat starch from the starch water. The thickened broth makes a delicious sauce to serve with the seitan or over grain dishes.

   Seitan may be frozen in an airtight plastic container, either with or without its broth.

VARIATION

• Before cooking the seitan, cut the thin slabs of raw gluten into large, steak-like pieces instead of small bite-sized pieces. Cook in the broth until firm, as described above (adjust the cooking time if necessary). These seitan "steaks" may be breaded and fried until brown on both sides. Serve them with a sauce.

SEITAN WITH RED AND GREEN PEPPERS

¼ cup whole wheat pastry flour
½ teaspoon garlic powder
2 cups seitan, cut into thin, bite-sized pieces
3 tablespoons oil
1 large onion, sliced
1 red pepper, sliced
1 green pepper, sliced
2 cups mushrooms, sliced
1½ tablespoons arrowroot
1½ cups broth from cooking seitan

Serves: 4–6
Time: 25 minutes

1. Mix together the flour and the garlic powder. Dredge the pieces of seitan in the flour to coat them on both sides.
2. Heat 2 tablespoons of the oil in a skillet and fry the pieces of seitan until they are brown and crispy. Set aside the fried seitan and keep it warm while you cook the vegetables.
3. Heat the remaining tablespoon of oil (use the same skillet that you used to cook the seitan). Add the onion and sauté for 2–3 minutes. Add the peppers and sauté for a few minutes more; then add the mushrooms and about ½ cup (one-third) of the seitan broth. Cover and simmer until the vegetables are tender, but still a bit crisp.
4. Dissolve the arrowroot in the remaining broth (if the broth is hot, dissolve the arrowroot in ¼ cup of cold water first, then add it to the broth). Pour the arrowroot broth into the skillet with the vegetables. Mix well.
5. Raise the heat and cook, stirring constantly, until the sauce thickens.
   Serve the vegetables in their sauce over a bed of rice, millet, buckwheat, or pasta. Top with the pieces of seitan.

WHEAT LOAF

If you cook for someone who is less than enthusiastic about vegetarian cuisine, make this dish a few times before you tell him (or her) what it is made of!

2 cups Ground Seitan Mix (see page 197)
½ cup T.V.P. (textured vegetable protein)
2 eggs, beaten
½ cup finely grated carrots (lightly packed into the cup)
¼ cup plus 2 tablespoons tomato paste

Serves: 4
Time: 40 minutes

1. Mix together all the ingredients except for the 2 tablespoons of tomato paste.
2. Pack the mixture into a loaf pan and spread the top of the loaf with the 2 tablespoons tomato paste.
3. Bake at 350°F for 35 minutes, or until firm.
   Serve with whole grain bread, a cooked vegetable, and a salad.

SEITAN WITH BEANS

What would you serve a group of hungry skiers or other athletes? *Seitan With Beans* is ideal. It's high in protein and very satisfying. In addition, the beans and wheat gluten are complementary proteins, so all the essential amino acids are provided. And this dish is economical—the protein ingredients are not expensive. But, best of all, seitan is absolutely delicious when cooked in a slowly simmering pot of well-seasoned beans.

1½ cups dried uncooked beans *(Great Northern or pinto are good)*
1 cup (or about ½ of the recipe) Raw Gluten *(page 192)*
Water for cooking the beans
1 large onion, chopped
2 stalks celery, chopped
2 small carrots, sliced
4 bay leaves
1 teaspoon thyme
¼ teaspoon celery seed
4–5 tablespoons tamari, to taste
2 tablespoons olive oil
4 cloves garlic, pressed
¼ cup chopped parsley

Serves: 6
Time: Soak beans overnight; 45 minutes to make raw gluten (while beans are cooking); 2 hours, 40 minutes to cook.

1. Wash the beans and soak them overnight in water to cover.
2. Drain the beans, discarding the water used for soaking them. Put beans in a large kettle with fresh water to cover. Place a lid on the kettle and simmer until the beans are tender (about 2 hours). Stir occasionally and add more water if necessary. (See page 185 for more specific information on cooking dried beans.)
3. Roll out or stretch the raw gluten until it is about ½ inch thick. Using a sharp knife or scissors, cut the gluten into bite-sized pieces.
4. When the beans are tender, measure the cooking liquid that remains. Add more water if necessary to obtain at least 1½ cups. Return the liquid to the kettle with the beans. Add the vegetables, bay leaves, thyme, celery seed, and tamari. Also add the pieces of raw gluten.
5. Cover and simmer *very slowly* over low heat for about 40 minutes, or until the seitan is firm and the veggies are tender. If the seitan is cooked over heat that is too high, it will become spongy. Stir occasionally during the cooking.
6. Add the olive oil, garlic, and parsley.
   Serve with whole grain bread, or over a bed of rice or millet.

NOTE: If you have seitan that has already been cooked in its broth, you can just add it to a pot of cooked beans!

GROUND SEITAN

A food processor or a meat grinder is needed to make ground seitan.

1 recipe Raw Gluten *(page 192)*

Yield: About 4 cups ground seitan
Serves: 8–10 when used in a recipe
Time: 45 minutes to make raw gluten; 40–45 minutes for ground gluten.

1. Place the raw gluten on a well-oiled cookie sheet. Using your hands and/or a rolling pin, flatten the gluten out to a slab that is about ½ inch thick. Bake at 350°F for about 15 minutes.
2. After 15 minutes or more of baking, the gluten should begin to puff up and form air pockets. Poke these bubbles with a fork to let the air escape and allow for more even cooking. Bake the gluten for 15–20 minutes more.
3. Remove the gluten from the oven and from the cookie sheet. Fold it in half and cover it with a large inverted bowl. Let the gluten stand, covered, for about 10 minutes to soften the crust.
4. Tear or cut the baked gluten into pieces and place it in the food processor. Briefly grind it to obtain a ground-beef-like texture. If you prefer, you may run the gluten through a meat grinder instead of a food processor.
   Use the ground gluten to make *Ground-Seitan Mix* (page 197). Or use it in any recipe that is traditionally made with ground beef

(adjusting the seasoning to taste). Also try the recipe for *Wheatballs*, on page 196. *Ground Seitan* may be frozen in an airtight plastic bag or airtight container.

WHEATBALLS

These mock meatballs fool those who say that they don't like vegetarian food.

1 recipe Ground Seitan *(page 195)*
¹/₃ cup minced onion
2–3 cloves garlic, pressed
¹/₄ teaspoon celery seed
³/₄ teaspoon oregano
1 teaspoon basil
1 teaspoon thyme
4 tablespoons tamari (not shoyu)
2 tablespoons olive oil
3 tablespoons nutritional yeast
¹/₄ cup whole wheat flour
¹/₄ cup peanut butter

Yield: About 45 1-inch wheatballs
Time: 45 minutes to make ground gluten; 35 minutes for wheatballs.

1. Follow the recipe for ground gluten.
2. Place the ground gluten in a large bowl and add the remaining ingredients. Mix well.
3. Using your hands, shape the mixture into 1-inch balls. Place them on a well-oiled cookie sheet and bake at 350°F for 25 minutes. Turn the wheatballs over once during the baking to assure even browning.

    Serve the wheatballs with a tomato sauce and spaghetti or in a vegetable stew. Wheatballs can be frozen for later use as needed. Store in freezer in an airtight plastic bag or another container that is airtight.

CHILI CON SEITAN

A Mexican dish with some Japanese ingredients and American imagination, it's even better than the real thing!

2 tablespoons olive oil
1 large onion, chopped
2 stalks celery, chopped
4 cloves garlic, minced
1 green pepper, chopped
2 cups Ground Seitan *(page 195)*
1 teaspoon basil
¹/₂ teaspoon oregano
1 teaspoon cumin
1 teaspoon chili powder
¹/₄ teaspoon ground cloves
Cayenne or hot sauce, to taste
2 cups cooked red kidney beans
¹/₂ cup liquid from cooking the beans
4 cups canned tomatoes
Tamari to taste

Serves: 4–6
Time: 20 minutes

1. Heat the oil in a large, heavy kettle. Add the onion and celery. Sauté until almost tender. Add the garlic, green pepper, gluten, and spices. Sauté for a few minutes more.
2. Add the beans, cooking liquid, and tomatoes. Cover and simmer for about 10 minutes. Add tamari to taste.

    Serve with cornbread or tortillas and a big green salad.

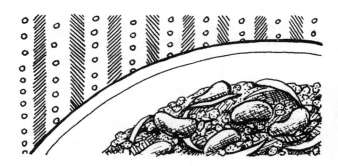

GROUND SEITAN MIX

Use this mix in any recipe that ordinarily calls for ground beef.

1 recipe Ground Seitan *(page 195)*
2 tablespoons oil
1 teaspoon roasted sesame oil
2 cups chopped onion
4–6 cloves garlic, minced
1 teaspoon thyme
1 teaspoon basil
½ teaspoon celery seed
2 tablespoons nutritional yeast
4 tablespoons tamari, or to taste

Serves: 4 cups
Time: 45 minutes to make ground seitan; 15 minutes for ground seitan mix.

1. Follow the recipe for ground seitan. Set the ground seitan aside while you sauté the onions and garlic.
2. Heat both kinds of oil together in a large skillet. Add the onion, garlic, and herbs. Sauté until the onion is tender. Add the ground gluten and stir for a couple of minutes.
3. Remove the skillet from the heat and stir in the yeast. Slowly stir in the tamari and mix well.

    This mix will keep well in the refrigerator for at least one week. It may also be frozen for longer storage.

VARIATIONS

Ground seitan mix can be the basis of all delicious dishes. If you keep some on hand it allows you to turn out a great meal at a moment's notice.

- Combine ground seitan mix with cooked brown rice; adjust the seasoning to taste. Use this to stuff cabbage leaves or peppers. Serve with a tomato sauce.
- Use in spaghetti sauce. Sauté the veggies for your sauce as usual, then add the ground seitan mix. Sauté for a couple of minutes more; then add the tomatoes.
- Use as a topping for pizza.
- Use in place of the pressed tofu mixture in the *Shepherd's Pie* on page 205.
- Add to soups or chili.

SEITAN AND POTATO PIE

A tasty mock meat pie.

2 cups (½ recipe) Ground Seitan Mix *(see left)*
3 medium baking potatoes, scrubbed and cut into ½-inch cubes (about 4 cups)
½ cup chopped parsley
¼ teaspoon ground cloves
½ teaspoon savory
1 tablespoon tamari, or to taste
2 eggs, beaten
1 recipe Whole Wheat Pie Crust *(page 92)*

Yield: 1 double-crust 9-inch pie
Serves: 4–6
Time: 1 hour, 10 minutes

1. Place the 2 cups of seasoned seitan mix in a large bowl.
2. Cook the potatoes in a small amount of water until tender. Drain the potatoes (reserving the water for future use) and add them to the ground gluten mixture. Add the parsley, cloves, savory, tamari, and beaten eggs. Mix well.
3. Place the mixture in an unbaked 9-inch pie shell. Cover the pie with the top crust. Flute the edges of the crust and cut some holes in the top to allow the steam to escape.
4. Bake at 350°F for 45 minutes, or until the crust is golden brown.

    This dish is good accompanied with some homemade catsup or dill pickles. It is also good with a sauce. Serve with a steamed vegetable and a green salad.

NOTE: To heat up leftovers, cover the pie with aluminum foil and bake for about 20 minutes. Remove the foil and bake for about 5 minutes more.

TOFU

Tofu is soybean curd. In Japan it is used in just about every way you can think of. Tofu has no cholesterol, lots of B vitamins, and plenty of protein.

There are several kinds of tofu. I use firm (Chinese-style) tofu most often, and when a recipe calls for crumbled tofu, firm tofu should be used. Firm tofu is good for frying, grilling, stir-frying, and in sandwiches.

Silken and soft (Japanese-style) tofu are also available. Soft tofu has an almost creamy texture and silken tofu is extra-soft and smooth.

Soft tofu is not suitable for many of the recipes in this book. It can be used in recipes that call for blended tofu. However, if the recipe calls for water that is added when the tofu is blended, the water should be omitted.

Silken tofu is very mild and delicious. It is great in desserts or used to make sauces. Silken tofu contains more water and less protein than the other types. It is good to use in sauces, but is not good for frying and grilling. Most of the recipes in this book were not designed for silken tofu, and if it is used, the texture of the finished product will be different than what was intended.

PRESSED TOFU MIX

Whenever you have a little extra time for cooking, make up a batch or two of this mix. It freezes well and can be used in recipes instead of ground beef.

2 pounds tofu
8 cups boiling water
2 tablespoons oil
1 cup chopped onion
4 cloves garlic
1/2 teaspoon thyme
1 teaspoon basil
1/4 teaspoon celery seed
1/2 teaspoon sage
4 tablespoons tamari
2 tablespoons tomato paste
2 tablespoons nutritional yeast
1/4 cup water

Serves: 4–6
Time: 20–25 minutes

1. Crumble the tofu and drop it into a large kettle of boiling water. Bring the water back to a boil and cook for 1 minute.
2. Drain the tofu through a colander lined with a clean dishtowel as shown in Step 1 of Figure 10.1.
3. Run some cold water over the tofu to cool it off for easier handling. Twist the towel and press the tofu to expel the excess water (see Step 2 in Figure 10.1). Continue pressing the tofu until it has a firm, ground-beef-like texture; then set it aside.
4. Heat the oil in a large skillet. Add the onion, garlic, thyme, basil, celery seed, and sage. Sauté until the onion is tender.
5. Add the pressed tofu and sauté, stirring occasionally, for 5–10 minutes more. Add the tamari, tomato paste, nutritional yeast, and water. Mix well.

Use this mix in casseroles, spaghetti sauces, chili, pizza toppings, etc.

Fresh Tomato Pizza *(page 214)* with Assorted Veggie Toppings.

Tofu Loaf *(page 203)* with Mushrooms and Dill for a Change of Pace.

Parmesan-Topped Fettucini with Spinach and Ricotta *(page 211).*

1. Draining the tofu.

2. Squeezing out excess water.

Figure 10.1.   Pressing Tofu

GINGER TOFU

This basic recipe can be used in hundreds of different ways.

1 pound firm tofu
1½ teaspoons fresh grated ginger
1 teaspoon roasted sesame oil
1 or more cloves garlic, pressed
2 tablespoons tamari, or more to taste
1¼ cups water
1½ tablespoons arrowroot

Serves: 2–3
Time: 5 minutes to prepare; 30 minutes or more to marinate; 35–40 minutes to bake.

1. Slice the tofu into small rectangles of ¼–½-inch thickness and place them in a shallow dish or baking pan.
2. Mix together the ginger, sesame oil, garlic, tamari, and water. Pour this mixture over the tofu and let it marinate for at least 30 minutes. (If desired, the tofu may be placed in the refrigerator to marinate for several hours or overnight.)
3. Remove the marinated tofu from the liquid, reserving the liquid to make the sauce. Place the tofu on a well-oiled cookie sheet and bake at 375°F for 35–40 minutes, or until the desired crispness is reached (the longer the tofu bakes the firmer and crisper it becomes).
4. To make the sauce, mix the arrowroot with the marinade. Place the mixture in a small saucepan and bring to a boil. Cook, stirring constantly, until thickened.

    Ginger Tofu may be served with or without the sauce. With the sauce, serve it over a bed of rice, millet, buckwheat, or pasta. Add your favorite stir-fried veggies and you have a colorful and nutritious meal. Use many varieties of grains and vegetables to create your own, individual recipes. Without the sauce, serve slices of *Ginger Tofu* as hors d'oeuvres, or use them in sandwiches. *Ginger Tofu* may also be added to a vegetable stew.

BAKED PEANUT TOFU

Most children really like tofu when it is prepared this way.

1 pound firm tofu
4 tablespoons peanut butter
2 tablespoons tamari, or more to taste
1 or more cloves garlic, pressed
1 cup water
1½ tablespoons arrowroot

Serves: 2–3
Time: 5 minutes to prepare; 30 minutes or more to marinate; 30–45 minutes to bake.

1. Cut the tofu into small rectangles that are about ¼–½ inch thick.
2. In a small bowl, mix together the peanut butter, tamari, and garlic. Slowly stir in the water. Mix well.
3. Place the tofu slices in a shallow dish and pour the liquid over it. Let the tofu marinate for at least 30 minutes. If desired, you may leave it for several hours or overnight. In this case, keep it refrigerated while it is marinating.
4. When you are ready to cook, remove the pieces of tofu from the marinade and place them on a well-oiled cookie sheet. Reserve the liquid to make the sauce.
5. Bake at 375°F for 30–45 minutes, or until the desired crispness is reached (the longer the tofu bakes, the crisper it becomes).
6. Mix the arrowroot with the remaining marinade. Place the mixture in a saucepan and cook over high heat, stirring constantly until the sauce thickens.
7. Place the baked tofu on a bed of cooked grain (rice, millet, buckwheat, or even pasta). Cover with the sauce.
    Serve with steamed or stir-fried vegetables and a salad.

TOFU "FISH" STICKS

These "fish sticks" probably do not really taste like fish, but they look like fish sticks and are crisp and tasty.

1 strip kombu, 6 inches long
½ cup water
2 tablespoons lemon juice
2 tablespoons lime juice
2 tablespoons tamari
1 teaspoon tarragon
2 tablespoons grated onion
10 ounces firm tofu
3 slices whole grain bread
2 cloves garlic
4 sprigs parsley
2 eggs, beaten

Serves: 2–3
Time: 15 minutes to prepare; 30 minutes or more to marinate; 30 minutes to bake.

1. Wash the kombu and place it in a small saucepan with ½ cup of water. Bring the water to a boil. Cover, reduce the heat, and simmer for about 10 minutes.
2. Remove the kombu from the broth and add the lemon juice, lime juice, tamari, tarragon, and onion to the broth.
3. Slice the tofu into 6 slabs about ¼–½ inch thick and about the size of fish sticks.
4. Place the tofu in a shallow dish. Pour the broth over the tofu, trying to distribute the onions evenly. Let this marinate for at least 30 minutes. If desired, you may let the tofu marinate for several hours in the refrigerator.
5. Tear the slices of bread into pieces and place them in a blender or food processor. Grind the bread into fine crumbs. If you are using a food processor, you may grind the garlic and the parsley in the food processor along with the bread. However, if you are using a blender, you will probably find it necessary to press the garlic and mince the parsley; then add them to the crumbs and mix well.

6. Place the seasoned bread crumbs in a plate or shallow bowl. Remove the tofu from the marinade (the liquid may be reserved to add to soups, sauces, or to marinate more tofu). Dip the tofu first into the beaten egg and then into the bread crumbs.

7. Place the breaded tofu on a well-oiled cookie sheet. Bake at 350°F for 30 minutes or until it is brown and crispy.

    Serve these tofu sticks with a salad and a steamed vegetable. They are also good in sandwiches with some horseradish, lettuce, and a slice of tomato, or with some of the "natural imitation" catsup that is sold in health food stores.

VARIATION

• For a simpler version of this recipe, do not marinate the tofu. Just brush it generously with tamari. Then bread it and bake as indicated above.

TOFU BOURGUIGNON

Please even your most difficult meat-eating friends with this richly flavored gourmet-style stew!

2 pounds firm tofu, cut into 1-inch squares of ½-inch thickness
1½ cups dry red wine
¼ cup tamari (real tamari is better than shoyu in this recipe)
4 cloves garlic, pressed
Water as needed
2 tablespoons olive oil
2 cups sliced onions
4 cups sliced mushrooms
4 bay leaves
1 teaspoon thyme
1 teaspoon tarragon
4 tablespoons whole wheat pastry flour

Serves: 4–6
Time: 1 hour or more to marinate; 50 minutes to prepare.

1. Place the pieces of tofu in a large, shallow dish.

2. Mix together the wine, tamari, and garlic. Pour the mixture over the tofu, add water as needed to cover it, and let it marinate for at least 1 hour. If the tofu is going to marinate for more than an hour, place it in the refrigerator.

3. Place the marinated tofu on a well-oiled cookie sheet, reserving the marinade.

4. Bake at 375°F for 35–45 minutes or until crispy and brown. Turn the tofu over once during the baking so that it browns on both sides.

5. While the tofu bakes, heat the oil in a large pan, and slowly sauté the onions. When the onions are almost tender, add the mushrooms and the herbs. Sauté for a few minutes more.

6. Add the flour and mix well. Remove the pan from the heat and stir in a little of the marinade. Continue stirring until a paste is formed. Return the pan to the heat and slowly add the remaining marinade, stirring constantly.

7. Add the baked tofu, and simmer until thickened.

    Serve over pasta, rice, or millet.

POTATO-TOFU BAKE

3 large baking potatoes
1 onion, thinly sliced
1 pound tofu, cut into 1/3-inch slabs
1 teaspoon savory
1 cup whole grain bread crumbs
3 tablespoons tahini
2 tablespoons shoyu
3 tablespoons nutritional yeast
1 1/2 cups water or vegetable stock

Serves: 3–4
Time: 1 hour, 15 minutes

1. Scrub the potatoes and slice them very thinly.
2. Place half of the sliced potatoes in the bottom of an oiled baking dish. On top of the potatoes, place half of the onion slices. Cover the onions with half of the slabs of tofu, and sprinkle the tofu with 1/2 teaspoon of savory.
3. Repeat the layers and top the casserole with the bread crumbs.
4. Mix together the tahini, shoyu, and yeast. Gradually stir in the water or stock. Mix till smooth. Slowly pour the liquid mixture over the bread crumbs.
5. Bake the casserole at 350°F for 1 hour, or until the potatoes are cooked and the excess liquid is gone.

TOFU "MEAT" BALLS

These could easily be passed off as the real thing!

6–8 cups boiling water
5 cups crumbled tofu (just under 3 pounds)
1 cup whole grain bread crumbs
1/4 cup tamari (do not use shoyu)
1/4 cup nutritional yeast
1/4 cup peanut butter
1 egg
1/2 cup finely chopped onion
3–4 cloves garlic, pressed
1 teaspoon thyme
1 teaspoon basil
1/4 teaspoon celery seed
1/4 teaspoon ground cloves

Serves: 6
Time: 40 minutes

1. Drop all but 1 cup of the crumbled tofu into the boiling water. Bring the water back to a boil and cook for 1 minute.
2. Drain the tofu into a colander lined with a clean dishtowel. Run cold water over the hot tofu to cool it off for easier handling.
3. Twist the dishtowel and press the tofu to squeeze out the excess water (see Figure 10.1 on page 199). The pressed tofu should have a firm, ground-beef-like texture.
4. Put the pressed tofu in a bowl and add the remaining ingredients to the pressed tofu and mix well (use your hands for mixing). Shape the mixture into walnut-sized balls and place them on a well-oiled cookie sheet.
5. Bake at 350°F for 20–25 minutes or until the balls are firm and brown. Turn them over once during the baking if necessary.

Serve tofu "meat" balls with your favorite tomato sauce and whole wheat spaghetti. Tofu "meat" balls freeze very well, so make more than you need. They may be reheated by dropping them into a simmering sauce or stew.

BAKED TOFU AND RICE PATTIES

1 cup mashed tofu
1 cup cooked brown rice
1/2 cup minced celery
1–2 cloves garlic, minced
1 tablespoon nutritional yeast
1 tablespoon peanut butter
2 tablespoons shoyu or tamari
1/2 teaspoon roasted sesame oil (optional)
1/2 teaspoon sage
2–4 tablespoons whole wheat pastry flour, as needed

Yield: 6 patties
Serves: 2–3
Time: 40 minutes

1. Place all the ingredients, except for the flour, in a medium-sized bowl and mix well. Using your hands, shape the mixture into 6 patties. Press firmly so that the patties hold together well.
2. Dredge both sides of each patty in the flour and place them on a well-oiled cookie sheet.
3. Bake the patties at 400°F for 25–30 minutes, or until they are golden brown. Turn the patties over halfway through the baking.

   Serve them with the sauce of your choice (the *Onion-Mustard Sauce* on page 244 is good), accompanied with a steamed vegetable and a salad.

TOFU LOAF

2 cups mashed tofu
1 cup chopped onion
1 cup rolled oats
1/2 cup chopped walnuts
3 tablespoons peanut butter
4 tablespoons tamari (not shoyu)
1–2 cloves garlic, pressed
1/2 teaspoon sage

Serves: 4
Time: 1 hour, 10 minutes

1. Place all the ingredients in a large bowl. Mix well, using your hands if necessary.
2. Press the mixture into a well-oiled loaf pan. Bake at 350°F for 55–60 minutes.
3. Run a knife around the edges of the pan and unmold the loaf onto a serving platter. Surround the platter with colorful steamed vegetables and serve with a sauce. The *Sauce Orientale* on page 245 is good.

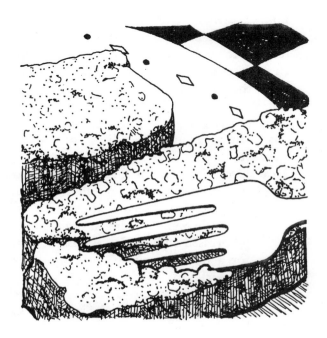

TOFU AND BUCKWHEAT PIE

This is a type of mock meat pie that our friends in Quebec enjoy.

3 cups crumbled tofu
6 cups boiling water
2 tablespoons vegetable oil
1 teaspoon roasted sesame oil
1 medium onion, chopped
8 ounces fresh mushrooms
1 teaspoon thyme
¼ teaspoon celery seed
¼ teaspoon ground cloves
2 cups cooked buckwheat
¼ cup tamari (not shoyu)
2 tablespoons nutritional yeast
2 tablespoons whole wheat flour
1 double-crust 10-inch whole wheat pie shell, unbaked (see recipe on page 92)

Yield: 1 double-crust 10-inch pie
Serves: 6
Time: 1 hour, 45 minutes

1. Drop the tofu into a large kettle of boiling water. Bring the water back to a boil and cook for a minute.
2. Line a colander with a clean dishtowel and drain the tofu into the colander. Run cold water over the tofu to cool it for easier handling. Bring the edges of the towel together and twist the towel to squeeze the excess water out of the tofu (see Figure 10.1 on page 199). Continue twisting and pressing until the tofu has a firm, ground-beef-like consistency; then set it aside.
3. Heat the oils in a large skillet. Sauté the onion for a few minutes and then add the mushrooms, thyme, celery seed, and cloves. Cook until the mushrooms are almost done.
4. Add the pressed tofu to the skillet. Stir and cook for a minute or two. Add the buckwheat, tamari, yeast, and flour. Mix well.
5. Turn the mixture out into a unbaked 10-inch pie shell. Cover the pie with the top crust and flute the edges.

6. Cut some holes in the top crust to allow steam to escape and bake at 375°F for 40–45 minutes.

This recipe is good accompanied with homemade relish or catsup. Also serve the pie with a green salad and steamed vegetable.

TOFU-VEGETABLE CASSEROLE

8 cups mixed raw vegetables, cut into ½-inch cubes or slices
1 pound tofu
¼ cup chopped onion
⅓ cup water or vegetable stock
4 tablespoons yellow miso
1 teaspoon Dijon mustard
Cayenne to taste
1 teaspoon tarragon
1 cup whole grain bread crumbs

Serves: 3–4
Time: 1 hour

1. Steam or pressure cook the vegetables until they are just barely tender. One of my favorite combinations of vegetables is: 1 onion, 2 carrots, ¼ of a Savoy cabbage, 1 potato, and 1 turnip. Add about ½ cup of frozen peas after the other vegetables are cooked.
2. While the vegetables are cooking, place the tofu, onion, water, miso, mustard, cayenne, and tarragon in a blender or food processor and blend until smooth and creamy. (This may have to be done in two batches in a blender.)
3. When the vegetables are done, drain them and mix them with the tofu cream. Transfer the mixture to a lightly oiled casserole dish.
4. Sprinkle the bread crumbs over the top of the casserole. Lightly press the bread crumbs so that they sink into the surface of the casserole slightly.
5. Bake at 350°F for 20–30 minutes.

Serve with a green salad and (if you want to serve a bigger meal) some fresh corn on the cob.

SHEPHERD'S PIE

The French call this dish *paté chinois*, which means Chinese paté. However, I have never figured out what is Chinese about it. It is a great family dish that almost everyone loves and is a good way to use up leftover mashed potatoes. You don't have to peel the potatoes if you cut them into very small cubes; this way, they can be mashed with their vitamin-filled skins.

3 cups crumbled tofu
6–8 cups boiling water
1 medium onion, chopped
1 stalk celery, chopped
1 teaspoon savory
1 teaspoon thyme
1/2 teaspoon sage
1/4 teaspoon celery seed
1/4 cup tamari (not shoyu)
2 tablespoons nutritional yeast
1/4 cup liquid from cooking the vegetables
3 cups lightly cooked mixed vegetables (peas and corn are traditional)
3–4 cups mashed potatoes, seasoned to taste (use very little salt)
1/2–1 cup grated cheese

Serves: 6
Time: 40 minutes

1. Drop the crumbled tofu into the boiling water. Bring the water back to a boil and cook for a minute.
2. Drain the tofu into a colander lined with a clean dishtowel. Run cold water over the tofu to cool it down; then twist the towel and press the tofu to squeeze out the excess water (see Figure 10.1 on page 199 for illustrations on how to press tofu). When the tofu is well-pressed, it should have a firm, ground-beef-like texture.
3. Sauté the onions and celery until they are almost tender. Add the herbs and the pressed tofu. Cook over medium heat for about 10 minutes, stirring occasionally.
4. Add the tamari, the yeast, and the liquid from cooking the vegetables to the tofu. Mix well.
5. Lightly oil a 7-x-11-inch baking dish and spread the tofu mixture in an even layer in the bottom of the dish.
6. Top the tofu with an even layer of the cooked vegetables. Spread the mashed potatoes over the veggies and sprinkle with grated cheese.
7. Bake at 350°F for 15–20 minutes, or until the casserole is thoroughly heated and the cheese topping is golden brown. If necessary, place the dish under the broiler for a few minutes to brown the top.

NOTE: This dish may be assembled in advance and baked just before serving. If the ingredients are cold, cover the dish and bake for 30 minutes. Uncover and bake 10 minutes more.

VARIATION

- Replace the pressed and seasoned tofu (the tofu mixed with onions, celery, herbs, tamari, yeast, and cooking water) with 2 1/2–3 cups *Ground Seitan Mix* on page 197.

CARROT-TOFU QUICHE

This eggless quiche is as pretty as it is delicious.

4 cups sliced carrots
2 cups mashed tofu
¼ cup water from cooking the carrots (approximately)
1 teaspoon sea salt
1 small onion, minced
½ teaspoon dill seed
2 tablespoons chopped parsley
1 recipe Quick Bread Crumb Crust *(page 94), or a whole wheat crust of your choice*
2 tablespoons sesame seeds

Serves: 4–6
Time: 1 hour, 10 minutes

1. Steam the carrots until tender.
2. Blend together the tofu, water, and salt. Use enough water to obtain a thick, creamy consistency like that of mayonnaise or pudding. (The amount of water you use will depend on the moisture content of the tofu.)
3. Add the onion, dill, and parsley to the tofu cream. Mix well.
4. Coarsely mash the carrots and add them to the tofu mixture. Mix well.
5. Spread the tofu-carrot mixture over the crust in a 7-x-11-inch baking dish. Sprinkle with sesame seeds and bake at 350°F for 35–45 minutes, or until set.

BROCCOLI-TOFU QUICHE

Light and nourishing! If you are in a hurry and do not want to make a pie crust, try the *Quick Bread Crumb Crust* on page 94.

3 cups finely chopped broccoli
1 pound tofu
¼ cup yellow miso
1 egg
1 tablespoon Dijon mustard
Cayenne to taste
⅓ cup chopped onion
1 single-crust 9-inch whole wheat pie shell, unbaked
2 tablespoons sesame seeds, or ½–1 cup grated cheese

Yield: 1 single 9-inch crust
Serves: 4
Time: 1 hour

1. To prepare the broccoli, wash it well, peel the stems, and chop it into small pieces.
2. Steam the chopped broccoli for a few minutes until it just begins to become tender, but is still crisp.
3. While the broccoli is cooking, blend together the tofu, miso, egg, mustard, cayenne, and onion in a blender or food processor until it is smooth and creamy. If the tofu that you are using is very firm, it may be necessary to add a tablespoon or two of water to the mixture in order to blend it.
4. Add the lightly cooked broccoli to the creamed mixture (make sure the broccoli is well drained). Mix well.
5. Transfer the mixture into an unbaked 9-inch pie shell. Spread the filling mixture against the sides of the shell so that it does not shrink away from the crust as it bakes. Top the pie with the sesame seeds or the cheese.
6. Bake on the bottom rack of the oven at 350°F for 40 minutes, or until firm.

PASTA

Pasta offers the vegetarian cook a multitude of delightful culinary possibilities. Besides being nutritious and economical, it is one food that just about everybody likes, especially children.

Need I say that eating pasta made from bleached white flour is not much different from eating spongy white bread? If one begins to eat good-quality whole grain pasta, it becomes impossible to enjoy the pasty white commercial stuff.

If you care about the quality of the food you eat, make sure to read the label when you are buying pasta. Even in natural foods stores, the pasta is often made with a good portion of white flour and sometimes contains only enough whole wheat flour, buckwheat flour, or dried vegetables to make it *look* "natural." If you buy bulk pasta out of a bin, and the ingredients are not listed, ask a store employee. Usually the people who work in natural foods stores are pretty knowledgeable and they will not mind answering your questions. The best pasta to buy is made from 100 percent organically grown whole grains.

Good-quality store-bought pasta does have its advantages, but taste-wise it cannot compete with fresh, homemade pasta. There really is a difference. Pasta making, like bread making, however, is surrounded by a certain mystique. Most ordinary non-Italian mortals seem to believe that it is beyond their reach. It is either thought of as something too difficult and time-consuming or something that requires expensive equipment.

On the contrary! Pasta making is not difficult. It is a fun and relaxing activity that can be pleasantly shared with children or friends. Without a machine I am able to make about eight servings of pasta in less than one hour. Of course, your first attempt may take longer, but as with anything else, the more you practice the more efficient you become.

If you are not yet confident in your ability to become a creative cook, a pasta dish is one of the best places to start.

A good vegetarian pasta entrée can be very simple. It consists of the pasta, of course, one or more types of vegetables, a sauce, and a protein complement.

The Pasta: Make the *Whole Wheat Egg Noodle* recipe on page 208, or choose from any of the many interesting varieties of whole grain pasta that are available in natural foods stores. One pound of pasta yields about eight cups cooked and can serve four to six persons. Simply cook the pasta in a large kettle of boiling water, drain it, and assemble it with the other ingredients in a way that you find appealing.

The Vegetables: What do you have on hand? It is usually not necessary to run out and buy special ingredients every time you wish to make a special dish. The best traditional recipes probably stem from a desire to make something good out of a limited supply of ingredients. Pick out a few vegetables that you enjoy together and steam or stir-fry them to the degree of doneness that you like.

The Sauce: Tomato sauce is undisputedly wonderful with pasta, but don't limit yourself. Be a little daring. *Velvet Tofu-Mushroom Sauce* (page 243), *Spicy Peanut Sauce* (page 246), *Tahini-Miso Sauce* (page 245), and *Tofu and Peanut Sauce* (page 244) all have the ability to turn a pasta dish into a delectably exotic experience. For something more conventional, try the *Easiest Cheese Sauce* (page 242), or the *Béchamel Sauce* (page 242). For homemade pasta, which is a taste treat to begin with, a simple dressing of olive oil, herbs, and garlic may be enough.

The Protein Complement: This can be tofu (marinated, cooked, or uncooked) cubed, crumbled, or made into "meat" balls (see page 202). Or it can be cooked tempeh, grated cheese, *Main-Dish Nut Balls* (page 222)—or even cooked beans. If the sauce you are using with the pasta is high in protein, such as the *Veggie Deluxe Spaghetti Sauce* (page 240), *Spicy Peanut Sauce* (page 246), or *Velvet Tofu-Mushroom Sauce* (page 243), it is not necessary to add an additional source of protein.

As you assemble your creation, be aware of the texture of the dish as well as the flavor. Make sure that you have enough sauce and vegetables to go with the pasta, so as to not have a dry or pasty dish. Garnish your pasta so it looks as good as it tastes—and Enjoy!

WHOLE WHEAT EGG NOODLES

You do not need any special equipment to make these great-tasting wholesome noodles.

---

2 eggs

1½ cups whole wheat bread flour (approximately)

Serves: 4
Time: 50 minutes

---

1. Break the eggs into a medium-sized bowl and beat them with a fork. Slowly stir in the flour, adding enough flour to make a kneadable dough. The amount of flour needed will depend on the size of the eggs and the moisture content of the flour. The dough should be firm, but not hard.

2. Turn the dough out onto a lightly floured work surface and knead for about 10 minutes. Knead in enough flour to make a dough that is smooth, elastic, and does not stick to your hands or to the work surface. (See page 72 for instructions on kneading.) Cover the kneaded dough with an inverted bowl and let it rest for 5–10 minutes.

3. Cut the dough into 4 pieces of equal size. You will be rolling out 1 piece of dough at a time, so keep the other 3 pieces covered with the inverted bowl to prevent them from drying out.

4. To roll out the dough, first lightly sprinkle your work surface with flour. Then sprinkle flour over the top of the piece of dough you will be rolling out to keep it from sticking to the rolling pin. Roll the dough out into a thin rectangle. Turn it over occasionally and sprinkle your work surface with more flour to keep the dough from sticking, if necessary. Take your time and carefully try to roll the dough out as thin as possible. It should be almost translucent when you hold it up to the light, and thin, like a piece of watercolor paper. Set the sheet of dough aside and roll out the remaining 3 pieces.

5. When all four pieces of dough have been rolled out, it is time to cut them into noodles. Start with the first piece of dough that you rolled out. By now it should be slightly dry and have a leather-like consistency. Beginning at one end, roll it up like a jelly-roll. (See Figure 10.2, Step 1.) With a sharp knife, slice the rolled-up dough. Make the slices the same width that you want the noodles to be. (See Step 2.) Unroll the dough—and voilà, you have made pasta!

6. This pasta may be cooked immediately or, if desired, partially dried for future use. To dry the pasta you may drape it over the backs of your kitchen chairs; over a horizontally fixed

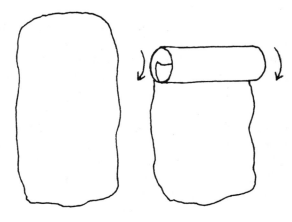

1. Rolling the dough.

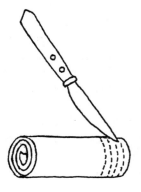

2. Slicing the dough.

Figure 10.2.   Slicing Whole Wheat Egg Noodles

broom handle (set the broom on a table with the handle extended and weigh the broom end down with a book), on a makeshift clothesline, or anything else you can rig up. Let the pasta dry for 1–2 hours and then put it into plastic bags. Refrigerated, the partially dried pasta will keep for about 1 week. Frozen, it will keep indefinitely.

To cook the noodles, bring a large kettle of water to a boil. Add the pasta and simmer for about 3–5 minutes, or until tender (al dente). Drain through a strainer and serve with your favorite sauce.

NOTE: This recipe may be easily doubled if desired.

VARIATION

- *Lasagna:* Follow the above recipe. Then, cut the dough into large lasagna-shaped noodles, and use them in your favorite lasagna recipe.

SPAGHETTI WITH TOFU

Pasta with garlic, mushrooms, wine, and tofu.

2½ cups crumbled tofu
8 cups boiling water
2 tablespoons olive oil
1 large onion, chopped
5 cloves garlic, minced
1 teaspoon thyme
1 teaspoon basil
½ teaspoon oregano
¼ teaspoon celery seed
⅛ teaspoon ground cloves
2 cups mushrooms, sliced
4 tablespoons tamari
8 ounces whole wheat spaghetti
½ cup dry red wine
¼ cup minced parsley

Serves: 2–4
Time: 35 minutes

1. Drop the tofu into a large kettle of boiling water. Bring the water back to a boil and cook for 1 minute.
2. Line a colander with a clean dishtowel and drain the tofu in the colander. Rinse the tofu under cold water to cool it off for easier handling. Bring the edges of the towel together, twist the towel, and press the excess water out of the tofu. (See Figure 10.1 on page 199.) Continue pressing the tofu until it has a firm ground-beef-like texture; then set it aside.
3. Heat the oil in a large skillet. Add the onion, garlic, thyme, basil, oregano, celery seed, and cloves. Sauté over low heat until the onion is almost tender. Add the mushrooms and cook until they are done.
4. Add the pressed tofu to the sautéed mixture. Stir in the tamari and mix well. Set the skillet aside while you prepare the spaghetti.
5. Boil a large kettle of water and cook the spaghetti until it is tender. Drain the cooked spaghetti and add it to the skillet with the tofu mixture. Add the wine and the parsley; mix well.

Serve with a big green salad.

VARIATION

- Add 1 cup of fresh or frozen peas along with the onion.

VEGETARIAN SPAGHETTI

Please your friends or family with a big pot of Italian-style spaghetti.

2½ quarts of water (approximately)
12 ounces–1 pound whole wheat spaghetti, or 1 recipe Whole Wheat Egg Noodles *(page 208)*
1 teaspoon oil

Serves: 4
Time: 5–10 minutes to cook pasta.

1. Place the water in a large kettle and bring it to a boil. Add the oil and the spaghetti. Stir once. Partially cover the kettle, leaving the lid slightly ajar, and reduce the heat to a simmer. Cook the spaghetti until it is tender but not mushy (al dente). This will take about 3 minutes for fresh pasta and 5–10 minutes for dry pasta (or according to the package directions).
2. Drain the cooked pasta through a colander or a wire strainer.
3. Place the pasta on individual serving plates. Top with one of the variations suggested below and serve immediately.

VARIATIONS

Top the spaghetti with the ingredients of your choice. Here are a few suggestions:
- *Veggie Deluxe Spaghetti Sauce* (page 240).
- *Garden-Fresh Spaghetti Sauce* (page 241) sprinkled generously with grated Romano, Parmesan, or provolone cheese.
- *Tofu "Meat" Balls* (page 202) or *Wheatballs* (page 196) served with either the *Garden-Fresh Spaghetti Sauce* (page 241) or the *Quick and Easy Tomato Sauce* (page 240). Sprinkle with a little Parmesan cheese, if desired.

TOFU-STUFFED PASTA SHELLS

This dish is best if you use a sauce with lots of nice chunks of vegetables in it.

20 large whole wheat pasta shells
2 cups mashed tofu
⅓ cup grated Parmesan cheese
3–4 cloves garlic
½ teaspoon oregano
1 egg
¼ teaspoon sea salt
¼ cup dried onion flakes
5 cups spaghetti sauce (See Quick and Easy Tomato Sauce *on page 240;* Veggie Deluxe Spaghetti Sauce *on page 240;* or Garden-Fresh Spaghetti Sauce *on page 241.)*

Serves: 4
Time: 1 hour, 10 minutes

1. Put on a large kettle of water to boil the pasta. Drop the pasta in the boiling water and cook until almost but not quite tender (the shells will finish cooking in the oven). Drain the shells through a colander, then rinse them with cold water.
2. While the pasta is cooking, blend together the tofu, Parmesan, garlic, oregano, egg, and salt in the blender or food processor. Add the onion flakes and mix well.
3. Stuff each of the shells with the tofu mixture.
4. Cover the bottom of a baking dish with about 2 cups of the sauce. Place the stuffed shells on top of the sauce, then pour more sauce over the shells. Repeat the layers if necessary (depending on your baking dish).
5. Bake at 350°F for 45–50 minutes or until the sauce is bubbly hot and the stuffing mixture becomes firm.

Serve with a steamed vegetable and a large green salad.

FETTUCINI WITH SPINACH AND RICOTTA

The first time I made this dish it was with spinach and basil from the garden and homemade pasta. It was divine! Since then I have made it with store-bought ingredients and it is still very good. It's quick to make, too.

6 ounces whole wheat fettucini
2 tablespoons olive oil
10 ounces fresh spinach
1¼ cups fresh ricotta cheese
¼–⅓ cup chopped walnuts
½ teaspoon sea salt, or to taste
4 scallions, chopped
The leaves from 2 stems of fresh basil, minced, or 1 teaspoon dry basil
½ teaspoon oregano

GARNISH

¼ cup chopped fresh parsley
Grated Parmesan, as desired

Serves: 2–3
Time: 35 minutes

1. Boil a large kettle of water to cook the fettucini.
2. While you are waiting for the water to boil, wash and chop the spinach. Heat the olive oil in a large skillet or heavy kettle and add the spinach. Stir, cover, and reduce the heat to medium-low.
3. Cook the spinach until tender, stirring occasionally. Meanwhile, cook the pasta until it is done (al dente).
4. When the spinach is ready, stir in the ricotta, walnuts, salt, scallions, basil, and oregano. Heat the mixture thoroughly, but do not boil it.
5. Drain the fettucini and place it on individual plates. Top it with the spinach mixture and sprinkle with the parsley and Parmesan. Serve immediately, accompanied by a carrot salad.

GNOCCHI

A hearty, traditional Italian dish. Gnocchi are sort of in between potato dumplings and pasta. This is one of my favorites!

2 medium potatoes (about 1 pound)
1 large egg, beaten
1½ cups whole wheat pastry flour
¼ teaspoon sea salt
Pinch of nutmeg

Serves: 4
Time: 40 minutes

1. Scrub the potatoes and dice them.
2. Place the potatoes in a pot with about 1½ inches of water. Cover and cook until tender. Drain the potatoes, reserving the water, if desired, for use in making bread or soup.
3. Return the potatoes to the pot and stir them over high heat for a few minutes to dry them off. Mash the potatoes with a potato masher. If they are still hot, let them cool slightly.
4. After the potatoes have cooled, add the egg to the mashed potatoes and mix well. Add the flour, salt, and nutmeg. Mix well.
5. Turn the dough out onto a floured surface and knead it a few times. Divide the dough into 3–4 equal portions. Using your hands, roll each portion of dough into a long, snake-like strand about ½ inch thick. Cut the strands into 1-inch pieces. Press your finger into the center of each piece of dough to form a dimple and to make the dough curve slightly.
6. Drop the gnocchi, a few at a time, into a large kettle of gently boiling water. Cook for about 3–5 minutes, until they rise to the surface. Lift the gnocchi out of the water with a slotted spoon, and keep them warm until they are all cooked.

   Serve with tomato sauce or pesto sauce (or both). Sprinkle with grated Parmesan cheese and/or a milder grated cheese. Include a big green salad in your meal.

JOHANNA'S VEGETARIAN LASAGNA

Johanna's vegetarian lasagna is lighter and less rich than most lasagna recipes.

8 ounces whole wheat lasagna noodles (or slightly less as needed)
4 cups well-seasoned spaghetti sauce (see Quick and Easy Tomato Sauce on page 240; Veggie Deluxe Spaghetti Sauce on page 240; or Garden-Fresh Spaghetti Sauce on page 241.)
½ cup T.V.P. (textured vegetable protein)
1½ cups mashed tofu
3 cloves garlic
⅓ cup plus 2 tablespoons grated Parmesan or Romano cheese
1 egg
1 cup frozen peas (optional)
1½ cups grated mozzarella cheese

Serves: 6
Time: 1 hour

1. In a large pot, heat water for cooking pasta. Use enough water to cover the pasta while it cooks. While you are waiting, mix together the spaghetti sauce and the T.V.P. and let the mixture sit for about 15 minutes.
2. Blend together the tofu, garlic, ⅓ cup grated Parmesan (or Romano) cheese, and egg in a blender or food processor until smooth and creamy. Set aside.
3. Cook the lasagna noodles until they are just barely tender (al dente). Drain the noodles and rinse them with cold water.
4. Spread about 1 cup of the sauce in the bottom of a 7-x-11-inch baking dish. Cover the sauce with a layer of the cooked lasagna noodles, placing them lengthwise in the baking dish. Then, spread the pasta with a layer of half of the tofu mixture (¾ cup), a layer of half of the peas (they don't have to be cooked first), and then a layer of half of the mozzarella (¾ cup). Spread the mozzarella with one cup of the sauce, then make another layer of pasta, placing it in the opposite direction of the first layer. Finish layering the lasagna in the following manner: tofu mixture, peas,

sauce, and mozzarella. Sprinkle the top with the remaining Parmesan.
5. Bake at 350°F for 25 minutes. Let the lasagna cool for 10 minutes before slicing.

MUSHROOM-NOODLE CASSEROLE

6 ounces whole wheat fettucini noodles
Boiling water
1 tablespoon oil
1 medium onion, chopped
2½ cups sliced mushrooms
1 teaspoon thyme
1 cup cottage cheese
1½ cups mashed tofu
1 egg
2 tablespoons shoyu, or tamari
1 cup fresh or frozen peas (optional)
½ cup whole wheat bread crumbs
2 teaspoons oil

Serves: 3–4
Time: 45 minutes

1. Cook the pasta in boiling water till done (al dente), then drain.
2. Heat the oil in a skillet. Sauté the onion for a couple of minutes, then add the mushrooms and thyme. Cook for a few minutes more.
3. Place the cottage cheese, tofu, egg, and shoyu in a blender or food processor. Soft tofu is best to use. If your tofu is firm, add 2–4 tablespoons of water to the mixture in the blender or food processor. Blend until smooth and creamy.
4. Mix together the cooked and drained pasta, the sautéed vegetables, the tofu mixture, and the peas. Place in an oiled baking dish. Top with the bread crumbs and drizzle with the 2 teaspoons oil.
5. Bake at 350°F for 20 minutes.
   Serve with a steamed vegetable and a raw salad.

PIZZA

Like pasta or crepes, pizza is something that nearly everyone likes. It also offers us a chance to play the role of the creative chef. Tomato and cheese pizza is great, but some people do not eat tomatoes or cheese. This is why I developed the *Tempeh, Onion, and Olive Pizza* on page 215. I'm sure that you, too, will be able to come up with other types of good, dairyless pizzas if you wish. A cook at a vegetarian restaurant where I once worked used to make a macrobiotic pizza. (Persons following the macrobiotic diet do not eat cheese or tomatoes.) He made the sauce from beets and carrots that were cooked, seasoned, and blended together to look and taste similar to tomato sauce. Then he garnished the pizza with mushrooms and onions and topped it with tofu!

My favorite pizza is so simple that I didn't even write a recipe for it. It has a thick, soft, rectangular-shaped bread dough crust with an unpretentious topping of tomato sauce, herbs, garlic, and olive oil. It does not even have a garnish or a cheese topping. It is the kind of pizza that Italian bakeries and short-order restaurants in Montreal sell to take home. I like to make this kind of pizza when I made bread. Just save some of your bread dough (the *Basic Bread* recipe on page 76 is good for this). Roll it out onto an oiled cookie sheet to a thickness of about ½ inch and let it rise until it is almost doubled in bulk. Spread with tomato sauce; top with basil, oregano, and minced garlic. Drizzle with olive oil and bake at 375°F for about 20 minutes, or until the crust is done.

After trying my pizza recipes, have fun creating some of your own!

WHOLE WHEAT PIZZA CRUST

½ cup warm water
2 tablespoons oil
1 teaspoon honey
2 teaspoons dry active yeast
1¼ cups whole wheat flour (bread or pastry flour may be used)

Yield: 1 round 12½-inch crust
Time: 1 hour 15 minutes to prepare; 15–30 minutes to bake.

1. Combine the water, oil, honey, and yeast in a medium-sized bowl and let the mixture stand for about 10 minutes to dissolve the yeast.
2. Add 1 cup of the flour and mix well. Knead in the remaining flour. The dough will be soft and slightly sticky.

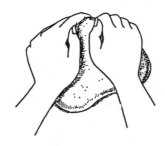

3. Place the dough in a lightly oiled bowl. Turn the dough over so that it is oiled on both sides; then cover it with a damp cloth and let it rise in a warm place until it doubles in bulk (45 minutes to 1 hour).

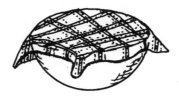

4. Transfer the dough to an oiled pizza sheet. Using your hands, flatten and stretch the dough till it covers the pan in an even thickness.

5. Cover the dough with the desired topping. Place it on the bottom rack of an oven and bake according to the topping recipe (depending on the oven temperature, it will generally take from 15–30 minutes for the toppings to cook and the crust to brown).

NOTE: This pizza dough can also be shaped on an oiled rectangular pan (cookie sheet). If you use a 9-x-12-inch baking sheet, there may be a little bit left over if you do not like thick dough. Use this leftover dough for a small "individual" pizza, or freeze it in an airtight container for later use.

FRESH TOMATO PIZZA

The fresh tomatoes are a nice addition to this pizza.

1 recipe Whole Wheat Pizza Crust *(page 213)*
1 cup tomato sauce
2 small tomatoes, chopped

YOUR CHOICE OF GARNISH
1½ cups grated low-fat mozzarella cheese (more or less as desired)
¼ cup grated Romano cheese, or to taste
Sliced mushrooms
Pitted black or green olives
Thin slices of red or green pepper
Eggplant, thinly sliced and quartered
Thin rounds of zucchini
Finely chopped broccoli flowerets
Thinly sliced or chopped onion
Just about anything else you like

Serves: 4
Time: 1 hour 15 minutes for crust; 15 minutes to assemble; 15–20 minutes to bake.

1. Follow the recipe for the pizza crust and let it rise in a warm place while you prepare the topping.
2. Transfer the dough to an oiled pizza sheet. With your hands, flatten and stretch the dough until it covers the pan in an even thickness.
3. Spread the crust with the sauce and then distribute the fresh tomatoes over the sauce.
4. Add the garnishes of your choice. Top with the two cheeses and bake at 400°F for 15–20 minutes.

VARIATION

• Omit the fresh tomatoes and increase the amount of sauce from 1 cup to 1½–2 cups, as desired. Proceed as indicated above.

SPINACH AND COTTAGE CHEESE PIZZA

When I had a natural foods store I used to sell a pizza similar to this and it was quite popular.

1 recipe Whole Wheat Pizza Crust *(page 213)*
2 tablespoons olive oil
1 medium onion, finely chopped
10 ounces fresh spinach, washed and drained
1 teaspoon basil
½ teaspoon oregano
¼ teaspoon dill seed
1½ cups low-fat cottage cheese
1 egg, beaten
¼ teaspoon sea salt
½ cup grated cheese (Cheddar, mozzarella, Jarlsberg, provolone, Parmesan), or more to taste
2 tablespoons grated Romano cheese (optional)
2 tablespoons sesame seeds

Serves: 4
Time: 1 hour, 15 minutes for crust; 20 minutes to assemble; 30 minutes to bake.

1. Follow the recipe for the crust and let it rise in a warm place while you make the filling.
2. Heat the olive oil in a large, heavy kettle and sauté the onion for a couple of minutes. Add the spinach; cover and cook for about 5 minutes, stirring occasionally.
3. Place the cooked spinach in a colander and press it lightly to expel some of the excess liquid. Chop the spinach with a sharp knife. Place it in a bowl. Add the basil, oregano, dill, cottage cheese, egg, and salt. Mix well.
4. Arrange the pizza crust in the pan and cover it with the spinach mixture. Sprinkle with the grated cheeses and the sesame seeds.
5. Bake on the bottom rack of the oven at 350°F for 30 minutes, or until the crust is done on the bottom.

TEMPEH, ONION, AND OLIVE PIZZA

This unusual pizza contains no dairy products or tomatoes.

1 recipe Whole Wheat Pizza Crust *(page 213)*
½ pound tempeh, cut into tiny cubes
1–2 teaspoons plus 1 tablespoon olive oil
2 cups chopped onion
4 cloves garlic, minced
1 can (3½ ounces) pitted black olives
½ teaspoon thyme
1 teaspoon basil
½ teaspoon oregano
2 tablespoons tamari
¼ cup water
2 tablespoons nutritional yeast

Serves: 4
Time: Crust: 1 hour, 15 minutes; Topping: 20 minutes; 25 minutes to bake.

1. Follow the pizza crust recipe and let the dough rise in a warm place while you make the filling.
2. Place the tempeh in a vegetable steamer and steam over boiling water for about 10 minutes.
3. While the tempeh is steaming, sauté the onion and garlic in 1–2 teaspoons olive oil till tender.
4. In a large bowl, combine the steamed tempeh, sliced olives, sautéed onion and garlic, herbs, tamari, water, and yeast. Mix well and slightly mash the tempeh with a fork.
5. Stretch the pizza crust to fit the pan and top it with the tempeh mixture. Drizzle with the tablespoon of olive oil. Bake for 25 minutes at 375°F.

TEMPEH

Tempeh is a traditional Indonesian soyfood made from split soybeans, water, and beneficial bacteria. It is rich in protein and vitamin B_{12}.

Because tempeh is fermented, it takes only about 15 minutes to cook. It can be bought in natural foods stores, and is available in rectangular cakes and patties and in precooked preparations.

Many people enjoy tempeh when it is pan-fried. To pan-fry tempeh, heat a small amount of oil in a frying pan and place slices of tempeh in the pan. Brown on each side for about 8 minutes.

The following recipes are varied and delicious ways of using tempeh.

TEMPEH-NUT PIE

This is really a variation of the *Savory Nut Pie With a Potato Crust* recipe on page 226. The addition of tempeh creates a slightly larger pie, so you will need to roll out the *Potato Pie Crust* dough to make a 10-inch pie.

1 tablespoon oil
2 cups chopped onion
2 cups chopped celery
1 teaspoon rosemary
1 teaspoon thyme
8 ounces tempeh, chopped into small cubes
1 cup pecans or walnuts, chopped
2 tablespoons tamari or shoyu
2 eggs, beaten
¼ cup water or vegetable broth
1 recipe Potato Pie Crust (page 93)

Yield: 1 single-crust, 10-inch pie
Serves: 4–6
Time: 1 hour, 20 minutes

1. Heat the oil in a large skillet. Sauté the onions and celery for a minute or two and then add the tempeh. Sauté for 2–3 minutes more.

2. Let the tempeh-vegetable mixture cool slightly and then add the nuts, tamari, eggs, and water or broth. Mix well.

3. Roll the potato pie dough crust out to make a 10-inch crust.

4. Pour the mixture into the crust. Place the pie on the bottom rack of a 350°F oven and bake for 40 minutes, or until the crust is brown and the filling is set.

TEMPEH PATTIES

½ pound tempeh, chopped into small cubes
1 small onion, minced
1 small stalk celery, finely chopped
1–2 cloves garlic, pressed
2 tablespoons tamari
⅔ cup dry, toasted whole grain bread crumbs, or cracker crumbs
½ teaspoon thyme
½ teaspoon sage
¼ teaspoon celery seed
½ cup ground walnuts
1 egg

Serves: 4
Time: 35 minutes

1. Place the tempeh in a vegetable steamer and steam over boiling water for 20 minutes.

2. Transfer the steamed tempeh to a large bowl and mash it with a fork. Add the remaining ingredients and mix well. Use your hands for the mixing.

3. Shape the mixture into 4 patties. Heat a small amount of oil in a skillet and brown the patties on both sides.

Serve with a sauce—or on whole grain hamburger buns with all the trimmings!

TEMPEH LOAF

½ pound tempeh
⅓ cup almonds
2 cups whole grain bread crumbs, lightly packed into the cup (from about 4 slices of bread)
1 egg
1¼ cups tomato purée (use canned tomato purée or blend 2 small tomatoes in a blender or food processor to make 1¼ cups of purée)
⅓ cup grated celery
½ cup finely chopped onion
1 teaspoon sage
3 tablespoons tamari

Serves: 3–4
Time: 1 hour, 15 minutes

1. If tempeh is frozen, thaw it out. Break the tempeh into chunks and grind it, along with the almonds, in a food processor or blender. In a food processor this can be done all at one time, but in a blender it will have to be done in about 3 small batches.
2. Transfer the mixture to a large bowl. Add the remaining ingredients and mix well.
3. Pack the mixture firmly into a well-oiled loaf pan. Bake at 350°F for about 1 hour, or until firm and brown.

   Serve like meat loaf, plain or with a sauce. Accompany with a steamed vegetable and a green salad. Leftovers can be used in sandwiches.

TEMPEH, CARROT, AND RICE LOAF

2 cups carrots, cut into ½-inch slices
1 tablespoon oil
½ teaspoon roasted sesame oil
½ pound tempeh, cut into very small cubes
½ teaspoon sage
1 small onion, chopped
2–3 cloves garlic, minced
2 tablespoons shoyu or tamari
1 cup cooked brown rice
⅓ cup sunflower seeds
1 egg, beaten

Serves: 3–4
Time: 1 hour

1. Cook the carrots until tender. If desired, reserve the liquid for use in making a sauce.
2. Heat the oils in a skillet. Add the tempeh and stir over medium heat for about 10 minutes, or until the tempeh begins to brown. Add the sage, onion, and garlic. Cook, stirring occasionally, for a few minutes more. Remove the skillet from the heat and stir in the one tablespoon of shoyu or tamari. Mix well.
3. Coarsely mash the carrots and mix them with the cooked tempeh and onion. Add the remaining ingredients, including the remaining tablespoon of shoyu, and mix well.
4. Pack the mixture into an oiled loaf pan (to keep the loaf from sticking, you may sprinkle the pan with cornmeal). Bake at 350°F for 25–30 minutes or until the loaf is firm and golden brown.

   Serve with your favorite sauce and a green salad.

CREATIVE MAIN-DISH CREPES

Crepes are incredibly versatile. The French make a type of crepe called the "crepe Bretagne." These crepes are paper-thin and about 3 feet in diameter. A special griddle of enormous proportions is needed to make this kind of crepe. Many Canadian creperies (restaurants serving only crepes) offer the choice between wheat-batter crepes and buckwheat crepes. But the fun is in choosing the fillings. It is not unusual for a creperie to have 30 or more different types of fillings on its menu. There is a crepe to suit everyone's taste. There are sweet dessert or breakfast crepes (for breakfast crepe recipes, see Chapter 2), served with maple syrup, and savory dinner crepes that are usually served with béchamel sauce. At home it is impossible to make crepes as big as the "crepe Bretagne," but it is possible to make them just as thin, tasty, and versatile.

Crepe making requires a bit of skill. But don't let this stop you, because you can easily learn this skill before a single batch of batter is used up! The first crepe in a batch usually does not turn out well. The next one, however, will be better. Here are some general guidelines.

- If you do not have a large crepe pan, don't use much more than ¼ cup of batter for each crepe, or you may end up with crepes that are too thick.
- When you pour the batter into the skillet or crepe pan, pick the pan up by its handle and rotate it. While you are rotating the pan, tilt it at a 30° angle to distribute the batter in a thin, even coat over the bottom of the pan. When the batter is evenly distributed, set the pan back down on the burner. Cook the crepe until it is set on the top, and lightly browned on the bottom. Using a spatula, flip the crepe over and cook it briefly on the other side.
- Stack the cooked crepes on a plate. Cover them with a clean dishtowel to keep them warm until you are ready to fill them. The crepes may be made a day in advance and refrigerated until needed.

In this book there are three different types of crepe batters: *Rice Flour Crepes* on page 29, *Buckwheat Crepes* on page 30, and *Oat Crepes* on page 30. Take your pick and try your hand at different types of fillings. Below are some of my suggestions for crepe fillings. Try making some of your own. Crepe cookery really gives you a chance to be a culinary artist. So don't be timid; have fun!

SAVORY CREPES

In addition to making the *Asparagus Crepes* on page 219, the *Crepes aux Poireaux* (Leek-Stuffed Crepes) on page 221, and the *Mushroom Crepes* on page 220, try various combinations of sauces and fillings.

Sauce Suggestions

Sauce Orientale (page 245), *Pecan Sauce* (page 244), *Béchamel Sauce* (page 242), *Quick and Easy Tomato Sauce* (page 240), and *Easiest Cheese Sauce* (page 242).

Fillings

The possibilities are limitless! Here are some basic themes you may wish to elaborate on.

- Tiny cubes of stir-fried tofu or tempeh with any of your favorite cooked vegetables. Choose a sauce and mix a little bit of it in with the filling ingredients; reserve the rest to pour over the top of the crepes.
- Lightly steamed broccoli, chopped into bite-sized pieces and mixed with a béchamel sauce (page 242). Sprinkle with grated cheese and reserve extra béchamel to pour over the top of the crepes. Bake the crepes at 350°F for about 10 minutes to melt the cheese.
- *Refried Beans* (page 44). Sprinkle with grated cheese, if desired; roll up the crepes and top them with tomato sauce.
- Any kind of lightly cooked vegetables in a compatible sauce may be used for dinner crepes. This is a good way to use up leftovers.
- Steamed asparagus and sautéed mushrooms mixed with a little bit of cheese sauce (see *Easiest Cheese Sauce*, page 242). Bake at 350°F for about 10 minutes. Pour extra cheese sauce over the crepes just before serving. Garnish with finely chopped scallions.

If you want to try sweet crepes with fruit fillings, see the crepe recipes in Chapter 12.

ASPARAGUS CREPES

An elegant dish with a refined and delicate flavor. These crepes may be made a day in advance, covered, and stored in the refrigerator.

CREPES

¾ cup brown rice flour
⅓ cup whole wheat pastry flour
5 eggs
¾ cup milk or water
Oil as needed

Yield: 12 crepes
Serves: 4–6
Time: About 1 hour

1. In a medium-sized bowl, mix together the two flours. Add the eggs and beat. Add the milk or water and continue to beat until the batter is smooth.
2. Drop a little less than ¼ cup of batter at a time onto a hot, lightly oiled skillet or crepe pan. Tilt and rotate the skillet to evenly distribute the batter over the bottom of the pan. Cook the crepe until it is done on the bottom. (You can tell when the crepe is done by carefully lifting it up by the edge. The bottom should be lightly flecked with brown.) Turn the crepe over and cook briefly on the other side. Repeat this process with the remaining batter, oiling the skillet as necessary.

   Crepe batter has a tendency to thicken. Therefore, as you are making the crepes, it may be necessary to occasionally add a little extra milk or water to thin it.
3. Stack the cooked crepes one on top of the other until you are ready to fill them.

FILLING

3 cups fresh asparagus, cut into 1-inch pieces
1 cup fresh or frozen peas
1 pound tofu
6 cups boiling water
½ teaspoon sea salt
1 teaspoon tarragon
4 scallions, finely chopped

1. Steam the asparagus and the peas until they are tender, but still crisp. Set aside.
2. Crumble the tofu and drop it into the boiling water. Bring the water back to a boil. Drain the tofu in a colander, but do not press it.
3. Mix together the steamed vegetables, tofu, salt, tarragon, and finely chopped scallions. Set the mixture aside while you make the sauce.

SAUCE

2¼ cups water (use any water that is left over from steaming the vegetables)
4 tablespoons arrowroot
2 tablespoons lemon juice
2 tablespoons shoyu or tamari, or more to taste
3 bay leaves
1 cup sliced mushrooms
2–3 scallions, chopped

1. Dissolve the arrowroot in the water. (If the water is hot, first dissolve the arrowroot in ¼ cup of cold water and then add it to the hot water.) Add the lemon juice, shoyu or tamari, bay leaves, and mushrooms.
2. Pour the mixture into a saucepan and bring to a boil. Cook, stirring constantly, until the sauce thickens. Remove the bay leaves and the scallions.

To Assemble

1. Mix ½ cup of the sauce with the filling. If the mixture is not warm, heat it in a small pan.
2. Place about ¼ cup of filling in the center of each crepe and roll up the crepes. Place them on individual serving plates and pour some sauce over each crepe. Serve.

NOTE: If you have made the crepes in advance, and they are cold, place the unfilled crepes in a cake pan, cover them with aluminum foil, and bake them at 350°F for a few minutes until heated through.

VARIATION

- If desired, use all rice flour or all wheat flour to make the crepe batter.

MUSHROOM CREPES

A nice light dish for when you want to make something special. Serve as part of the main course, or as an appetizer.

CREPES

1 recipe Rice Flour Crepes, *omitting the vanilla and maple syrup (page 29)*

Serves: 3 as a main dish; 6 as an appetizer
Time: Soak mushrooms 1 hour; about 1 hour to prepare.
Yield: 6 crepes

1. Follow the recipe, omitting the vanilla and maple syrup. It should make about 6 crepes.
2. Set the crepes aside while you make the filling.

FILLING

1/2 cup dried shiitake mushrooms
2 tablespoons olive oil
1 cup finely chopped onion
3 cloves garlic
2 bay leaves
4 cups finely chopped fresh mushrooms
1 teaspoon tarragon
2 tablespoons whole wheat pastry flour
1/3 cup dry red wine
1–2 tablespoons tamari, to taste
Cayenne, to taste

1. Place the shiitake mushrooms in a bowl. Cover them with water and let them soak for at least 1 hour. Discard the stems and finely chop the mushrooms. Set aside.
2. Heat the oil in a skillet. Add the onion, garlic, and bay leaves. Sauté over low heat until the onions are translucent. Add the shiitake mushrooms, the fresh mushrooms, and the tarragon. Cook until the mushrooms are done.
3. Stir in the flour and mix well. Pour in the wine while continuing to stir. Cook until the mixture thickens. Add the tamari and cayenne to taste. Set the filling aside while you make the sauce.

SAUCE

1 cup water or mild vegetable stock
1 1/2 tablespoons arrowroot or 2 teaspoons kudzu powder
2 tablespoons dry red wine
1 tablespoon tamari, or more to taste

Dissolve the arrowroot or kudzu in the water. Add the wine. Cook in a small saucepan over high heat, stirring constantly, until the sauce thickens. This is not supposed to be a very thick sauce, so do not overcook it. Add the tamari to taste and mix well.

To Assemble

1. If the filling mixture has cooled down, heat it by returning the skillet to the stove and stirring the mixture over medium-high heat until it is hot.
2. Place about 1/4 cup of filling in the center of each crepe and roll up the crepes.
3. Place the crepes on individual serving plates. Pour some of the sauce over each crepe and serve.

NOTE: If you made the crepes earlier and want to heat them up, place the unfilled crepes in a cake pan, cover them with aluminum foil, and bake them at 350°F until heated through.

CREPES AUX POIREAUX
(Leek-Stuffed Crepes)

This recipe is a testimonial to creative cooking. A few years ago, I had planned to make the *Asparagus Crepes* (page 219) in my cooking class and at the last minute I realized that there was no asparagus to be found. In fact, the only vegetables that looked halfway fresh were the leeks. Some quick improvisation, and voilà! Leek crepes. The whole class loved them.

Yield: 12 crepes
Serves: 6
Time: About 1 hour

CREPES
Crepe batter from Asparagus Crepes—*Follow the recipe on page 219.*

FILLING
1–2 tablespoons olive oil
3½ cups chopped leeks (Use only the tender, light green part. See page 155.)
1½ cups sliced mushrooms
½ teaspoon thyme
1 teaspoon tarragon

Heat the oil in a large skillet. Add the leeks and sauté them until they are almost tender. Add the mushrooms, thyme, and tarragon. Sauté until the mushrooms are tender. Set the mixture aside while you make the sauce.

SAUCE
2 cups skim milk
2 cups grated sharp Cheddar cheese
3 tablespoons whole wheat pastry flour
1 cup finely chopped mushrooms
2 teaspoons Dijon mustard
1 tablespoon mellow white miso

1. Heat the milk in a saucepan. Mix together the flour and the grated cheese and add it to the hot milk. Add the mushrooms.
2. Stirring constantly, cook the mixture over medium-high heat until the cheese melts and the sauce thickens. Remove the saucepan from the heat; add the mustard and the miso and mix well.

To Assemble

1. Mix 1 cup of the sauce with the sautéed leeks. If the mixture has cooled down, stir it over medium-high heat until it is warm.
2. Place about ¼ cup of filling in the center of each crepe and roll up each one.
3. Place the crepes on individual serving plates, pour some of the sauce over them, and serve.

OTHER MAIN-DISH RECIPES

The following recipes are the result of a little right-side creativity. Most of them use vegetables as a main ingredients, and some include nuts as a protein-rich main ingredient.

Once you become used to cooking with vegetables, grains, tofu, seitan, tempeh, and the other staples of a vegetarian diet, you can begin creating your own delicious main dishes.

SWEET POTATO, OATMEAL, AND CASHEW LOAF

This loaf has a very nice flavor.

½ cup cashews
1½ cups rolled oats
1½ cups grated sweet potato
½ cup finely chopped onion
1 cup water
2 tablespoons tamari
2 cloves garlic, pressed
2 tablespoons nutritional yeast
2 eggs, beaten

Serves: 3–4
Time: 55 minutes

1. Grind the cashews in a blender.
2. Place the ground cashews in a large bowl. Add the remaining ingredients and mix well.
3. Generously oil a loaf pan and sprinkle it with additional rolled oats to keep the loaf from sticking. Pack the loaf mixture into the pan.
4. Bake at 350°F for about 45 minutes, or until firm and brown.

    Serve with your favorite sauce, a salad, and a steamed vegetable.

MAIN-DISH NUT BALLS

Easy to make mock meatballs.

½ cup sunflower seeds
¼ cup chopped cashews
¼ cup unsalted peanuts
1 cup dry whole grain bread crumbs
3 eggs, beaten
2 cloves garlic, pressed
1 tablespoon tamari
¼ teaspoon celery seed
½ teaspoon basil
4 cups tomato sauce or spaghetti sauce (any of the recipes in this book, or your own)

Serves: 4
Time: 25 minutes

1. Place the sunflower seeds, cashews, and peanuts in a blender and grind them. The size of the ground pieces is not very important, but make sure they are not too big.
2. Place the ground nuts in a medium-sized bowl and add the bread crumbs, eggs, garlic, tamari, celery seed, and basil. Mix well and shape the mixture into walnut-sized balls.
3. Place the tomato sauce in a large kettle and bring to a gentle simmer. Drop the balls into the sauce. Cover and let simmer for about 15 minutes.

    Serve with whole grain spaghetti and a big green salad.

ARAME RICE PATTIES

These patties are crisp and mild-flavored. The small strands of arame create an attractive pattern throughout each patty.

1½ cups cooked brown rice
1 egg, beaten
1½ cups whole grain bread crumbs
⅓ cup finely chopped onion
⅓ cup soaked arame (About ¼ cup dry arame will make ⅓ cup soaked. See page 157.)
2 tablespoons natto miso (Can be found in most natural foods stores. If desired, another type of miso may be substituted.)
1 teaspoon thyme
2 tablespoons tahini

Yield: 6 patties
Serves: 2–3
Time: 20 minutes

1. Place all the ingredients in a large bowl. Mix well, using your hands if necessary.
2. Shape the mixture into 6 small patties, using your hands to firmly press the mixture together.
3. Heat a small amount of oil in a skillet. Place the patties in the skillet and cook over medium heat until they are brown on the bottom. Turn the patties over and brown them on the other side.

   Serve these patties with soup, in place of bread, or with a bean or tofu dish.

POTATO-NUT PATTIES

4 cups unseasoned mashed potatoes
¼ cup minced onion
¾ cup filberts, ground in a blender
½ cup whole wheat bread crumbs
½ teaspoon sage
1 teaspoon savory
3 tablespoons miso
3 tablespoons parsley
⅓ cup whole wheat pastry flour (approximately)
Oil as needed

Serves: 4
Time: 20 minutes

1. Make sure the nuts are ground into small pieces. Place the potatoes, onion, ground filberts, bread crumbs, sage, savory, miso, and parsley in a large bowl. Mix well.
2. Shape the mixture into hamburger-sized patties of about ½-inch thickness.
3. Dredge both sides of each patty in the flour. Heat a small amount of oil in a large skillet and brown the patties on both sides.

   These patties are good plain or accompanied by a sauce. If desired, place a thin slice of cheese on top of each patty; place them on a cookie sheet and broil to melt the cheese.

ALMOND LOAF

This recipe is an old favorite at our house.

1½ cups almonds
2 cups whole grain bread crumbs
2 eggs
1 cup canned tomatoes, with their juice
½ cup finely chopped onion
2 cloves garlic, pressed
1–2 tablespoons tamari
½ teaspoon ginger
3 tablespoons minced parsley

Serves: 4–6
Time: 40 minutes

1. Grind the almonds in a blender.
2. Place the almonds in a large bowl. Add the remaining ingredients and mix well.
3. Pack the mixture into a well-oiled loaf pan. Bake at 350°F for about 30 minutes.
4. Unmold the loaf and serve.

This loaf would be good with sauce, a steamed vegetable, and a green salad. Sauces that are good with this recipe include the *Quick and Easy Tomato Sauce* (page 240), *Yeast Gravy* (page 246), *Onion-Mustard Sauce* (page 244), and *Easiest Cheese Sauce* (page 242).

BROCCOLI SOUFFLÉ

4–5 slices whole grain bread
2 tablespoons oil
4 tablespoons whole wheat pastry flour
1⅓ cups skim milk
1 teaspoon sea salt
1 teaspoon Dijon mustard
Pinch of cayenne
⅔ cup grated cheese (sharp Cheddar is good)
2 cups broccoli flowerets, chopped very finely
2 tablespoons minced onion
5 eggs, separated

Serves: 4
Time: 1 hour, 25 minutes

1. Line the sides and the bottom of a soufflé dish with the slices of bread. If you do not have a soufflé dish, use a deep casserole dish.
2. In a small saucepan, mix together the oil and flour. Over medium heat, slowly stir in the milk. Cook, stirring constantly, until the sauce is thick. Add the salt, mustard, and cayenne. Mix well.
3. Remove the sauce from the heat and add the grated cheese. Stir until the cheese is melted. Pour the sauce into a large bowl and add the chopped broccoli and the minced onion. Let the mixture cool for about 5 minutes.
4. Add the egg yolks, one by one, to the broccoli-sauce mixture, beating between each addition. Let the mixture stand while you beat the egg whites. Beat the egg whites with an eggbeater or a wire whisk until they stand up in firm peaks. Take a large spoonful of the stiffly beaten egg whites and gently fold it into the broccoli-sauce mixture. Using a gentle folding motion, incorporate the remaining egg whites into the broccoli mixture.
5. Carefully turn the mixture into the prepared soufflé dish. Bake in a preheated oven at 350°F for 50–55 minutes. Do not open the oven door while the soufflé is baking.

VEGETABLE QUICHE

Because this quiche only contains 2 eggs, it is not as rich as most quiche recipes.

1 recipe Potato Pie Crust *(page 93), unbaked (You can use another pie crust, but this one is especially good.)*
2 cups corn, cut off the cob
2 eggs
2 tablespoons yellow miso
1 tablespoon olive oil
1/2 cup chopped onion
1/2 cup finely chopped celery
1/2 green pepper, diced
1 teaspoon basil
2 cups sliced mushrooms
1 cup grated cheese (Jarlsberg and Emmenthal are especially good)

Yield: 1 single-crust 9-inch pie
Serves: 4
Time: 1 hour, 15 minutes

1. Follow the recipe for the pie crust using a 9-inch pie pan. Do not bake the crust; simply set aside while you make the filling.
2. Place the corn, eggs, and miso in a blender or a food processor and blend until creamy. Set aside.
3. Heat 1 tablespoon of oil in a skillet. Add the onion and the celery. Sauté for a couple of minutes and add the green pepper. Sauté until the vegetables are almost tender. Place the sautéed vegetables in the bottom of the unbaked pie crust. Pour the creamed corn mixture over the sautéed vegetables.
4. Lightly sauté the mushrooms in the skillet that you used to sauté the other vegetables (add a little more oil if necessary). Distribute the lightly sautéed mushrooms over the quiche. Sprinkle the top with the grated cheese.
5. Bake on the bottom rack of the oven at 350°F for 35 minutes, or until the center is set and slightly puffed and the crust and top are golden.

   For a great summer meal, serve this quiche with lightly steamed green beans and sliced tomatoes.

TOMATO PIE

If you like tomatoes, you will love this flavorful and juicy pie.

1 recipe Whole Wheat Pie Crust *(page 92)*
1–1 1/2 cups grated cheese (Gruyère, Jarlsberg, Cheddar, etc.)
1/4 cup arrowroot
1/2 teaspoon cinnamon
1/8 teaspoon ground cloves
1 teaspoon basil
1/2 teaspoon sea salt
5–6 ripe tomatoes, cut into 1/4-inch-thick slices and quartered
3–5 cloves garlic, minced
1 tablespoon honey or malt syrup

Yield: 1 double-crust 9-inch pie
Serves: 4–6
Time: 1 hour, 25 minutes

1. Follow the recipe for the pie crust. Roll out the bottom crust and line a pie pan with it. Reserve the top crust for later. Sprinkle 1/3 of the grated cheese over the bottom crust.
2. Mix together the arrowroot, cinnamon, cloves, basil, and salt. Sprinkle 1/3 of this mixture over the grated cheese in the crust.
3. Make a thick layer of the sliced tomatoes. Evenly distribute 1/2 of the garlic over the tomatoes. Top with 1/2 of the remaining cheese and sprinkle with 1/2 of the remaining arrowroot mixture.

   Make another layer of tomatoes, using enough tomatoes to generously fill the pie shell and make a rounded top.

   Sprinkle with the remaining garlic and arrowroot. Drizzle with honey or malt syrup and top with the remaining cheese.
4. Cover the pie with the top crust. Flute the edges of the crust and cut some holes in the top to allow steam to escape.
5. Bake at 375°F on the bottom rack of the oven for 10 minutes. Reduce the heat and bake at 350°F for 40–45 minutes more.

   This tomato pie is delicious with steamed broccoli and a salad of Belgian endive.

CABBAGE SPAGHETTI

Thin strips of cabbage are used instead of pasta in this easy recipe. Don't laugh until you've tried it, because it's good!

½ of a medium-small cabbage (4–5 cups after it is cut into strips)
2 cups homemade spaghetti sauce*
Finely grated cheese (optional)

Serves: 2
Time: 25 minutes

1. Wash the cabbage and cut it in half from top to bottom. Cut out the core of the cabbage and discard it. Place the cabbage, with the cut side down, on a chopping board. With a sharp knife, cut the cabbage (lengthwise) into thin strips. Steam the strips of cabbage until they are tender (15–20 minutes).
2. Place a generous serving (a spaghetti-sized serving) of the steamed cabbage on individual serving plates. Top the cabbage with the sauce (sauce and cabbage should both be warm). Sprinkle some finely grated cheese, to taste, over the sauce.
    Serve with hot garlic bread.

NOTE: *You can use any of the spaghetti sauce recipes in this book. However, if you wish to use little or no cheese, choose one of the sauces that contains a protein source, such as the *Tomato, Adzuki Bean, and Eggplant Sauce* on page 241 or the *Veggie Deluxe Spaghetti Sauce* on page 240. See *Quick and Easy Tomato Sauce* on page 240; or *Garden-Fresh Spaghetti Sauce* on page 241.

SAVORY NUT PIE WITH A POTATO CRUST

This is a nice dish to serve to guests. This recipe may be partially baked in advance. Bake the pie for about 25 minutes; let it cool slightly and then refrigerate it until shortly before serving time. Before serving, bake the pie for 15–20 minutes more, or until it is hot and the crust is brown.

1 tablespoon oil
2 cups chopped onion
2 cups chopped celery
1 teaspoon rosemary
1 teaspoon thyme
1 cup pecans or walnuts, chopped
2 tablespoons tamari or shoyu
2 eggs, beaten
¼ cup water or vegetable broth
1 recipe Potato Pie Crust *(page 93), unbaked*

Yield: 1 single-crust 9-inch pie
Serves: 4
Time: 1 hour, 15 minutes

1. Heat the oil in a large skillet. Add the onion and celery. Sauté until almost tender.
2. Let the vegetables cool slightly and then add the nuts, tamari, eggs, and water or broth. Mix well.
3. Pour the mixture into an unbaked 9-inch potato pie crust.
4. Place the pie on the bottom rack of a 375°F oven and bake for 40 minutes, or until the crust is brown and the filling is set.

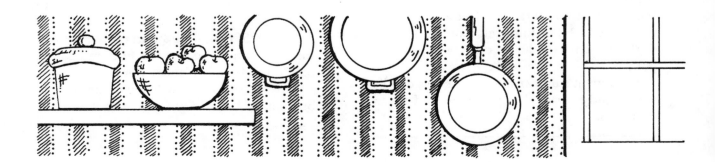

SPINACH AND COTTAGE PIE

This pie is especially delicious with the *Parmesan Pie Crust* on page 94. The *Whole Wheat Pie Crust* on page 92 is also good with this, but you will need to divide the recipe in half (or bake two single crusts and save one).

10 ounces fresh spinach
1 pound cottage cheese
2 eggs
¼ cup dried onion flakes
¾ teaspoon sea salt
½ teaspoon dill seed
½ teaspoon oregano
½ teaspoon basil
2 tablespoons whole wheat pastry flour
1 single 9-inch Parmesan Pie Crust, unbaked (see recipe on page 94)

Yield: 1 single 9-inch crust
Serves: 4
Time: 1 hour, 20 minutes

1. Wash and chop the spinach. Place it in a large kettle and cook it, without adding water, until it wilts. Drain the spinach and press out the excess liquid.
2. Beat together the remaining ingredients in a large bowl. Add the cooked spinach and mix well.
3. Transfer the mixture to an unbaked pie shell.
4. Bake at 350°F for 50 minutes or until firm.

BROCCOLI AND POTATOES AU GRATIN

This is a very satisfying nondairy dish. The words "au gratin" in the name of this recipe refer to the bread crumb topping.

5 cups broccoli, stems peeled and sliced into bite-sized pieces, and flowerets cut into bite-sized pieces
2 large potatoes, sliced and cooked (leftover baked potatoes are good)
1 tablespoon oil (plus 1 additional tablespoon oil, if desired)
1 medium onion, chopped
⅓ cup tahini
2 tablespoons barley or rice miso
2 tablespoons nutritional yeast
2 cups water (use water left from cooking vegetables)
3 tablespoons arrowroot
1 teaspoon savory
½ cup whole grain bread crumbs

Serves: 4
Time: 45 minutes

1. Lightly steam the broccoli until it is just barely tender.
2. Cook the potatoes (unless you are using leftover baked potatoes).
3. Heat the oil in a skillet, and sauté the onion.
4. Blend together the tahini, miso, yeast, water, arrowroot, and savory. Pour the sauce mixture into the skillet with the onions, and simmer until thick.
5. Mix the potatoes and broccoli with the sauce, and place the mixture in an oiled baking dish. Top with the bread crumbs. Drizzle with 1 tablespoon oil, if desired.
6. Bake at 350°F for 15 minutes; then broil for a minute or two to brown the top.

VARIATION

- If you wish to add protein, 1 block of tofu, cut into small pieces, may be mixed with the veggies, or the casserole may be topped with grated cheese.

POTATO CASSEROLE DÉLECTABLE

1 cup tomato paste
1³⁄₄ cups buttermilk
4 large potatoes, scrubbed and sliced very thinly
1 large onion, sliced very thinly
1 pound tofu, cut into ¹⁄₄-inch slices
¹⁄₂ cup grated Parmesan or Romano cheese
2 teaspoons basil
1 cup whole grain bread crumbs

Serves: 6
Time: 1 hour, 45 minutes

1. Oil a large casserole dish. Mix together the tomato paste and the buttermilk to make a sauce.
2. Make a layer consisting of ¹⁄₃ of the potatoes in the bottom of the baking dish. Top the potatoes with ¹⁄₃ of the onion and ¹⁄₃ of the sliced tofu. Spread ¹⁄₃ of the tomato sauce over the tofu and sprinkle this with ¹⁄₃ of the Parmesan and ¹⁄₃ of the basil.
3. Repeat the layers two more times. Sprinkle the last layer with bread crumbs.
4. Cover the casserole and bake it at 350°F for 1¹⁄₂ hours, or until the potatoes are tender. Uncover it and broil for a few minutes to brown the top, if necessary.

    Serve with steamed green beans or another vegetable and a salad.

WINTER SQUASH AND RICE SQUARES

This casserole has a nice golden color.

1 tablespoon oil
1 small onion, chopped
2 stalks celery, chopped
2¹⁄₂ cups cooked brown rice
1 teaspoon tarragon
¹⁄₂ teaspoon sea salt
4 eggs
2 cups baked acorn squash (1 medium acorn squash) or another baked winter squash
2 tablespoons light yellow miso
¹⁄₂ cup grated cheese or 2 tablespoons sesame seeds (or both)

Serves: 4
Time: 45 minutes

1. Heat the oil in a small skillet and sauté the onions and celery until they start to become tender, but still remain a bit crisp.
2. Place the sautéed vegetables in a large bowl along with the cooked rice, tarragon, salt, and 3 of the eggs (if the rice is hot, let it cool slightly before adding the eggs). Mix well.
3. Press one-half of the rice mixture into the bottom of a lightly oiled 7-x-11-inch baking dish.
4. Peel the cooked squash and place it in a bowl. Mash the squash, add the miso and the remaining egg, and mix well.
5. Spread the squash over the layer of rice in the baking dish. Top the squash with an even layer of the remaining rice. Sprinkle with the cheese and/or sesame seeds.
6. Bake at 350°F for 25 minutes; then broil for a minute or two to brown the top.

    Serve with a salad and a steamed vegetable such as green beans.

POTATO, TURNIP, AND CHEESE CASSEROLE

Even people who usually do not like turnips will probably like them this way!

1½ cups potatoes, scrubbed and cut into paper-thin slices
1½ cups turnips or rutabagas, scrubbed and cut into paper-thin slices
1 medium onion, sliced very thinly and separated into rings
Sea salt (optional)
½ teaspoon savory
2 tablespoons minced parsley
2 cups grated cheese (Jarlsberg is good)
1 cup whole grain bread crumbs
1 cup skim milk

Serves: 4
Time: About 1 hour

1. Oil a casserole dish. Place half of the potatoes in the bottom of the dish, cover the potatoes with half of the turnips, and cover the turnips with half of the onions. Sprinkle with a little salt, if desired. Then sprinkle with half of the parsley and ¼ teaspoon of savory. Cover with 1 cup of the cheese.
2. Repeat the layers.
3. Top the casserole with the bread crumbs. Pour the milk over the crumbs and bake, uncovered, at 350°F for 45 minutes, or until the vegetables are tender.

    Serve with a steamed vegetable such as broccoli or green beans and a salad.

SPINACH SQUARES

This is a dish that is high in protein and low in calories. One serving contains 23 grams of protein and only 178 calories. It's easy to make, too.

10 ounces fresh spinach (1 bag)
1 pound low-fat cottage cheese or farmer's cheese (the brick-style cottage is best)
2 eggs
½ teaspoon sea salt, or to taste
2 tablespoons sesame seeds

Serves: 4
Time: 45 minutes

1. Wash the spinach well. Drain it and dry it either with towels or in a salad spinner. Chop or tear the spinach into bite-sized pieces.
2. Place the cheese, eggs, and salt in a large bowl. Using a fork, cream together the cheese and eggs. Add the chopped spinach. Mix well, using your hands.
3. Oil a 7-x-11-inch baking dish and evenly press the spinach mixture into the dish. Sprinkle it with the sesame seeds.
4. Bake at 350°F for about 30 minutes. Place baking dish under the broiler for a few seconds to brown the sesame seeds, if desired. Cut into squares to serve.

    Serve with a cooked vegetable (such as a baked potato or steamed parsnips) and a carrot salad.

AUTUMN REGAL

A simple yet delightful casserole to share with someone special on a cool and quiet evening.

12 chestnuts, shelled and skinned
10 ounces Brussels sprouts
1 tablespoon oil
2 cups chopped Bermuda onion
2 cups fresh corn, cut off the cob
1/2 teaspoon sea salt
1 teaspoon basil
1/2 cup grated cheese (Jarlsberg is good)
1/2 cup whole grain bread crumbs

Serves: 2 (generously)
Time: 35 minutes

1. Boil or steam the chestnuts until tender.
2. Wash and trim the Brussels sprouts, cutting the large ones in half. Steam until just barely tender.
3. Heat the oil in a skillet and sauté the onion until tender.
4. Blend the corn in the blender until creamy. Add the salt and basil. Mix well. Mix together all the ingredients except for the cheese and bread crumbs.
5. Place the mixture in a lightly oiled baking dish. Top with the cheese and the bread crumbs.
6. Bake at 350°F for 15 minutes, then place under the broiler for a few minutes to lightly brown the top.

POTATO-MUSHROOM KUGEL

This soufflé-like casserole is very tasty as well as nourishing.

1 tablespoon oil
1/2 cup finely chopped onion
1 1/4 cups finely chopped mushrooms
2 cups unseasoned mashed potatoes
2/3 cup grated Parmesan cheese
3 egg yolks
3 egg whites

Serves: 3
Time: 1 hour, 5 minutes

1. Heat the oil in a skillet. Add the onion and sauté for a few minutes. Add the mushrooms and sauté until tender.
2. Mix together the mashed potatoes and the Parmesan. (If the potatoes are hot, first let them cool for a few minutes.) Beat in the egg yolks. Add the sautéed vegetables to the potato mixture and mix well.
3. Beat the egg whites until stiff. Fold the beaten egg whites into the potato mixture. Transfer the mixture to an oiled soufflé dish or casserole dish with high sides.
4. Bake at 350°F for 40–45 minutes.

   Serve with a steamed vegetable (such as green beans or broccoli) and a salad.

For a Light Meal, Try Mushroom Crepes *(page 220)*.

Tempura and Dipping Sauce *(page 234)* for an Oriental Flair.

Festive Mexican Stuffed Peppers *(page 231)* Can Make Your Meal.

Quick and Easy Tomato Sauce *(page 240)* on Whole Grain Spaghetti.

POTATOES AND KALE À LA GRECQUE

This is a very light but extremely nutritious dish.

3 baking potatoes
10 ounces fresh kale
2 cups water (approximately)
½ teaspoon basil
¼ teaspoon oregano
½ teaspoon dill seed
¼ cup finely chopped onion, or to taste
1 cup crumbled feta cheese, or to taste
2 tablespoons olive oil (optional)

Serves: 3–4
Time: 40 minutes

1. Scrub the potatoes and cut them into 1-inch chunks.
2. Wash the kale. Cut the stems into ¼-inch pieces; chop the leaves more coarsely.
3. Place the potatoes and kale in a large kettle with the water, basil, oregano, and dill seed. (The potatoes and kale may be cooked in a pressure cooker, if desired.) Cover and bring to a boil. Reduce the heat and simmer, stirring occasionally, until the potatoes are tender (about 30 minutes or less). Check the kettle occasionally and add more water if necessary. By the time that the veggies are tender, most of the water should be gone.
4. Using a slotted spoon, remove the potatoes and kale from the kettle and place them on individual serving plates. Top each serving with chopped onion to taste. Sprinkle generously with feta cheese and if desired, drizzle with olive oil.

   Serve with slices of fresh, ripe tomato and avocado, or some nice black olives.

MEXICAN STUFFED PEPPERS

This is a nice dish to make for a casual dinner party. It is especially attractive when made with red peppers.

I have used both beans cooked in the standard way and beans that have been sprouted for 2–3 days in this recipe.

4 large red or green sweet peppers
1 tablespoon olive oil
1 cup chopped onion
2 stalks celery, diced
1 teaspoon cumin
1 teaspoon chili powder
1 teaspoon basil
½ teaspoon oregano
2 cups cooked brown rice
1½ cups cooked and drained red kidney beans
2 tablespoons tamari or shoyu
Cayenne to taste
1½ cup canned tomatoes, with their juice
1 small can (6 ounces) tomato paste
6 thin slices of cheese (optional)

Serves: 4
Time: 1 hour

1. Wash the peppers and cut them in half lengthwise. Remove the seeds.
2. Place the peppers, cut side facing down, on a rack above boiling water. Cover the pot and steam for about 10 minutes, or until the peppers are just beginning to get soft. To ensure even doneness, do not stack the peppers on top of each other; keep them in a single layer. If you have a wok with a steaming rack, all the peppers can be steamed at the same time. If not, do them in two batches.
3. Heat the olive oil in a large skillet. Add the onions, celery, cumin, chili powder, basil, and oregano. Sauté until the onions are almost tender.
4. Add the cooked rice and beans. Mix well; then add the shoyu or tamari and the cayenne to taste. Mix again.
5. Lightly oil a shallow 7-x-11-inch baking dish. Fill each pepper with the bean and rice mixture and place the peppers side by side in

6. Mix together the canned tomatoes and the tomato paste. If the tomatoes are whole, chop them or break them up with a fork.

7. Pour the tomato mixture over the stuffed peppers. Cover the baking dish with aluminum foil and bake at 350°F for 30 minutes.

8. Uncover the dish and top each pepper with a thin slice of cheese, if desired. Return the dish to the oven and bake about 5 minutes more to melt the cheese.

   Serve with a big green salad and slices of ripe avocado.

VARIATION

• Use 2 cups of tomato sauce instead of the canned tomatoes mixed with tomato paste.

STUFFED ACORN SQUASH

1 medium acorn squash
1 tablespoon oil
1/2 cup chopped onion
1/2 cup chopped celery
1 or more cloves garlic
1/4–1/2 teaspoon rosemary
1/2 cup ricotta cheese
1/2 cup cooked brown rice
1/4 teaspoon sea salt
1/3 cup frozen peas
1/4 cup grated cheese such as Jarlsberg

Serves: 2
Time: 1 hour, 10 minutes

1. Cut the squash in half. Using a spoon, scoop out the seeds and membrane.

2. Place the cleaned squash on a baking sheet, cut side up. Bake at 350°F for about 50 minutes, or until tender, but not mushy. When the squash is done you can let it cool, if desired, for easier handling.

3. Carefully scoop out the flesh, leaving at least 1/4 inch around the edges to give strength to the shell. Mash the cooked squash with a fork.

4. While the squash is baking, heat the oil in a skillet and sauté the onions, celery, garlic, and rosemary until almost tender.

5. Mix the sautéed vegetables with the mashed squash. Add the ricotta, rice, salt, and peas. Mix well.

6. Fill the squash shells with the stuffing mixture. Top with the grated cheese. Bake at 350°F for about 20 minutes.

   Serve the stuffed squash with a steamed vegetable (fresh asparagus is great!) and a salad.

CABBAGE ROLLS

Making these cabbage rolls is a bit time-consuming—but they are so delicious that it's well worth it.

1 medium head cabbage
2 1/2 cups crumbled tofu
6–8 cups boiling water
2 tablespoons olive oil
1 medium-large onion, chopped
1 stalk celery, chopped
1 teaspoon basil
1 teaspoon thyme
1/2 teaspoon cinnamon
1/4 teaspoon cloves
1/4 teaspoon celery seed
4 tablespoons tamari
1/2 cup tomato paste
2 cups cooked brown rice
1/2 cup chopped nuts (optional)
16 ounces canned tomatoes, with their juice
10 ounces sauerkraut

Serves: 6
Time: 1 hour, 45 minutes

1. Cut the core out of the cabbage and discard it. Place the cabbage, stem end down, in a large kettle. Place about 1 inch of water in the bottom of the kettle. Cover and bring the water to a boil. Reduce the heat to a simmer and steam the cabbage for about 10 minutes.

1. Cut away the tough part of each leaf.

2. Drop one tablespoon of filling into the center of each leaf.

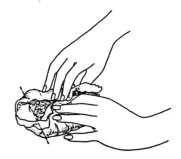

3. Fold both top and bottom of the large leaf over the filling, then fold the two sides over the seam.

4. Place the cabbage rolls seam side down in the baking dish.

Figure 10.3.   Making Cabbage Rolls

2. Remove the cabbage and let it cool for easier handling. Save the remaining water for use in soups or stews, if desired.

3. While the cabbage cools, drop the crumbled tofu into the 6–8 cups boiling water. Bring the water back to a boil and let the tofu cook for 1 minute. Drain the tofu through a colander lined with a clean dishtowel. Run cold water over the tofu to cool it off for easier handling. Twist the towel containing the tofu and press it to squeeze out the excess water (see Figure 10.1 on page 199). The pressed tofu should have a firm, ground-beef-like texture. Set the tofu aside while you prepare the remaining ingredients.

4. Heat the olive oil in a large skillet. Add the onion, celery, herbs, and spices. Sauté until the onions begin to get tender. Add the pressed tofu to the sautéed vegetables and stir over medium heat for a couple of minutes. Add the tamari, tomato paste, rice, and nuts. Mix well and remove from heat.

5. Carefully peel the leaves away from the steamed cabbage. Inside each of the larger leaves, place one small leaf. Cut away the thick, tough part of the leaves (see Step 1 in Figure 10.3).

6. Drop one heaping tablespoon of the tofu-rice filling into the center of each small leaf (see Step 2). Fold both the top and the bottom of the large leaf over the filling, then fold the two sides over the seam (refer to Step 3 in Figure 10.3). Place the cabbage rolls seam side down on your table or countertop.

7. Mix together the tomatoes and sauerkraut and place half of the mixture in the bottom of a large, shallow baking dish or in two 7-x-11-inch baking dishes. Set the cabbage rolls seam side down on top of the tomato-sauerkraut mixture as seen in Step 4. Pour the remaining tomato-sauerkraut mixture over the cabbage rolls.

8. Cover the baking dish(es) with aluminum foil and bake at 350°F for 45–60 minutes, or until the cabbage is tender. Uncover the cabbage rolls during the last 10 minutes of baking.

TEMPURA

Once or twice a year, I break my rule of not eating deep-fried foods and make a wonderful tempura.

BATTER

1 cup whole wheat pastry flour
1/4 cup brown rice flour and 1/4 cup corn meal or 1/2 cup of either
1/4 teaspoon sea salt (optional)
2 teaspoons dry mustard
1 1/2 cups cold water (more as needed)
About 6 cups tofu or prepared vegetables (your choice): Carrot (diagonal slices, about 1/4 inch thick), parsnip (diagonal slices, about 1/4 inch thick), broccoli flowerets, slices of sweet potato (half-rounds about 1/4-inch thick), onion rings, whole mushrooms, zucchini slices (rounds or diagonals, a little thicker than the carrots), cubes of tofu

ADDITIONAL

Flour for dredging the vegetables
Oil for deep frying (peanut or sesame)

Serves: 3–4
Time: 1 hour

1. To make the batter, place the flours, salt, and mustard in a medium-sized bowl. Add the cold water and mix. Don't worry if there are lumps; it's not important.
2. Chill the batter for at least 30 minutes while you prepare the vegetables, tofu, and dipping sauce (see right).
3. After the batter is chilled and everything else is ready, heat about 2 inches of oil in a wok, deep-fryer, or large kettle. To make a good tempura the oil must be at the proper temperature. If the oil is too hot it will smoke and burn the tempura, and if it is not hot enough the food will become saturated with oil. To test the temperature, drop a small amount of batter into the oil. If the batter sinks to the bottom, the oil is not hot enough. If it does not sink at all, but sizzles on the surface of the oil, it is too hot. The ideal condition is when the batter sinks just a little, then quickly returns to the surface and browns in less than 1 minute.
4. To prepare the vegetables, first dredge 4–5 pieces of the vegetables and/or tofu in flour; then dip them in the batter (which should remain cold). The bowl of batter may be set inside a bowl of ice to keep it cold, if desired. When the batter is good and cold, it clings to the vegetables better. If the batter becomes too thick from sitting, add a little more cold water as needed.
5. Drop the batter-coated vegetables into the hot oil (4–5 pieces at a time) and cook them until they turn golden. Remove the tempura from the oil with a slotted spoon, and drain them on paper towels. Continue this procedure with the remaining vegetables and/or tofu until the batter is used up.
6. Serve the tempura hot and as promptly as possible. Accompany it with dipping sauce (below), *Daikon Condiment* (page 247), and perhaps some *Nori-Maki* (page 108).

DIPPING SAUCE FOR TEMPURA

1/4 cup shoyu or tamari
3/4 cup water
1 teaspoon freshly grated ginger
1 teaspoon grated orange peel
1 teaspoon honey
1 teaspoon Dijon mustard
1 finely chopped scallion

Yield: 1 cup
Time: 5 minutes

Mix together all ingredients. Serve the dipping sauce in small individual bowls.

ITALIAN VEGETABLE STEW

A colorful dish that is easy to make and always well received.

3 cups green beans, broken into 1-inch pieces
1 small eggplant, quartered and cut into thick slices
2 zucchini or yellow squash, cut into thick slices
1 cup water
2 tablespoons olive oil
1 medium onion, chopped
4 cloves garlic, minced
1 teaspoon basil
1/2 teaspoon oregano
1 teaspoon thyme
1/2 teaspoon celery seed
1 1/2 cups cooked chick peas, white kidney beans, or lima beans (canned beans may be used)
1/2 cup tomato paste
1 tablespoon shoyu or tamari
2 fresh, ripe tomatoes (optional)
Grated Parmesan cheese (optional)

Serves: 4
Time: 30 minutes

1. Place the green beans in a large kettle. Top with the sliced eggplant and squash. Add the water. Cover, bring to a boil, and then lower the heat and simmer until the vegetables are just beginning to get tender, yet are still a bit crisp. Stir after about 10 minutes of cooking.
2. While the vegetables are simmering, heat the oil in a skillet and sauté the onion, garlic, and herbs until the onion is tender.
3. Add the sautéed onion to the veggies along with the beans, tomato paste, and shoyu. Simmer for a couple of minutes. Add fresh chopped tomatoes if desired; cook until just heated through.

   Serve with hot, crusty, whole grain bread, or over rice, millet, or pasta. Sprinkle with Parmesan, if desired.

POT AU FEU
(Baked Vegetable Stew)

This is a delicious warm dish for a cold winter evening.

1 large baking potato
1 large sweet potato
1 small rutabaga or 2 small white turnips
2 large carrots
3–4 small parsnips
3 1/2 cups chopped onion
3 bay leaves
1/4 cup shoyu or tamari
2 cups water or vegetable stock

SAUCE
2 tablespoons oil
4 tablespoons whole wheat flour
1 teaspoon curry powder
1 teaspoon tarragon
1/3 cup water

Serves: 4
Time: 1 hour, 45 minutes

1. Scrub the potatoes, rutabaga or turnips, carrots, and parsnips. Cut them into medium-sized chunks. Place the vegetables in a large, deep baking dish along with the chopped onion, bay leaves, shoyu, and water. A cast iron Dutch oven is ideal for baking this stew.
2. Cover the baking dish and bake at 350°F for about 1 1/2 hours, or until the vegetables are tender. When the vegetables are almost tender, prepare the sauce.
3. To make the sauce, heat the oil in a small saucepan. Add the flour, curry, and tarragon. Stir the flour mixture over medium-high heat until the flour browns and begins to give off a nutty aroma. Remove the saucepan from the heat and stir in the 1/3 cup water. Stir vigorously until a smooth paste is formed.
4. Add the flour paste to the stew and mix well. If the sauce is too thin, bake the stew, uncovered, for a few minutes until it thickens. If it is too thick, add a little water.

Serve over rice, or millet, or with some good whole grain bread. *Pot au Feu* is also delicious with *Ginger Tofu* (page 199) or *Tofu "Meat" Balls* (page 202).

VARIATIONS

- Cabbage, celery, and/or winter squash may be added to or substituted for some of the vegetables in the recipe.
- Add 1 recipe *Tofu "Meat" Balls* (page 202), *Wheatballs* (page 196) or *Main-Dish Nut Balls* (page 222) to *Pot au Feu*. After "meat" balls, wheatballs, or nut balls are cooked, drop as many as desired into the cooked stew. *Pot au Feu* recipe will expand to feed 6.

STUFFED SPAGHETTI SQUASH

Usually spaghetti squash is served with tomato sauce and cheese. For a delicious change, try it this way.

1 medium spaghetti squash
1 tablespoon and one teaspoon olive oil
1 large onion, chopped
1 green pepper, diced
2 cups mushrooms, sliced
1/2 teaspoon rosemary
1 teaspoon basil
1 cup mashed tofu
1/4 cup yellow miso
1/4 cup water (or more, depending on the consistency of the tofu)
1/3 cup chopped walnuts
1/3 cup sliced black olives
1/4 cup minced parsley
3 slices whole grain bread
2–3 cloves garlic

Serves: 4
Time: 1 hour

1. Cut the squash in half. Scoop out the seeds and the membrane and discard them. Place the squash, cut side down, on a lightly oiled cookie sheet.

2. Bake at 350°F for about 35 minutes, or until the shell can be easily pierced with a fork. Be careful not to over-bake the squash; if you do, it will get mushy. After baking, let the squash cool slightly for easier handling.

3. While the squash is baking, heat 1 tablespoon of the oil in a skillet. Add the onion and sauté for a few minutes. Add the green pepper and sauté until just tender. Then add the mushrooms, rosemary, and basil. Sauté for about 3–5 minutes, or until the mushrooms are done.

4. Place the tofu, miso, and water in a food processor or blender, and blend until smooth and creamy. Add a little more water if necessary to give the purée a whipped-cream consistency.

5. Add the tofu cream to the sautéed vegetables. Also add the chopped walnuts, olives, and parsley, and mix well.

6. Scoop the spaghetti-like flesh out of the squash, leaving enough around the edges of the shell to keep it strong enough to stuff.

7. Combine the scooped-out squash with the tofu-vegetable mixture and mix well. Fill the squash shells with this mixture.

8. Tear up the bread and place it in a blender or food processor, along with the garlic. Grind to fine crumbs. Add the remaining 1 teaspoon of oil and blend well.

9. Top the stuffed squash with the bread crumb mixture. Place the squash in a shallow, lightly oiled baking dish and bake at 350°F for about 20 minutes, or until thoroughly heated. Serve directly from the shell.

VARIATION

- Substitute 2 thinly sliced carrots for the mushrooms. Sauté them at the same time as the onion, then proceed as described above. If you do not wish to serve the squash in the shell, scoop out all the flesh and combine it with the tofu-vegetable mixture. Place the squash in a lightly oiled casserole dish, top with bread crumbs, and bake as directed above.

EGGPLANT ROLL-UPS

1 medium eggplant
1 cup mashed tofu
⅓ cup grated Parmesan or Romano cheese
1 or more cloves garlic, to taste
¼ cup chopped onion
¼ cup chopped parsley
2 cups cooked brown rice
2 cups tomato sauce (see Quick and Easy Tomato Sauce, *page 240)*
½–1 cup grated cheese (optional)

Serves: 3–4
Time: 1 hour

1. Cut off the stem and the bottom of the eggplant. (See Figure 10.4, Step 1.) The slices should be cut lengthwise and on opposite sides of the eggplant. This is to remove part of the peel and to make a flat surface. Then slice the eggplant into 6–8 slices, about ½ inch thick. Place these slices in a steamer or in a colander. (The steaming rack of a wok works best.)

2. Steam the eggplant for a few minutes, or until it is tender. If your steamer is small, steam only a few slices at a time. Turn the slices over after about 3 minutes of steaming so that they cook evenly. Be careful not to overcook them. The steamed eggplant should be tender but not mushy, and still hold its shape well.

3. While the eggplant is steaming, place the tofu, grated cheese, garlic, and onion in a food processor or blender. Blend until creamy. Add the parsley and mix well.

4. Oil a 7-x-11-inch baking dish and cover the bottom of the dish with an even layer of cooked rice. Generously spread each of the eggplant slices with the tofu mixture. Roll up the eggplant slices in jelly-roll fashion. (See Step 2 in Figure 10.4.) Place the roll-ups on top of the rice in the baking dish, seam side down.

5. Pour the tomato sauce over the eggplant roll-ups. Sprinkle with grated cheese, if desired. Cover the baking dish with aluminum foil

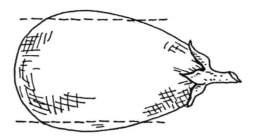

1. Cutting slices from the sides of the eggplant.

2. Rolling up the eggplant slices.

Figure 10.4.   Making Eggplant Rollups

and bake for 35 minutes at 350°F. Dish up the rice along with the roll-ups. Garnish with extra grated cheese if desired.

Serve with a big green salad.

INDIVIDUAL POTATO PASTRIES

1 recipe Potato Pie Crust *(page 93)*
1 recipe Savory Nut Pie *(page 226), filling only*

Yield: 12 mini pie crusts
Time: 1 hour

Follow the recipe for the potato pie crust but instead of rolling out the dough divide it into 12 equal-sized pieces. Press the dough into the bottom and partway up the sides of the muffin tins. Fill the pastries with the savory nut filling and bake at 375°F for about 20 minutes.

11. SAUCES & CONDIMENTS

Do you think of sauces as a high-calorie indulgence that you are better off without? You don't have to think that way, because when a sauce is made with the right ingredients, it can add as much nutritional value to a meal as it adds pleasure.

The absence of butter, cream, and animal fat in these sauces is made up for by the addition of such nutritious ingredients as tahini and nuts. Some recipes employ small amounts of vegetable oil and a few use milk. Sinfully creamy textures can be achieved by using blended tofu, and marvelously rich flavors can be created with the help of tamari, nutritional yeast, and the different varieties of miso.

Learning to master sauces will help you become a more creative cook. By combining one of the high-protein sauces in this chapter with a cooked grain or pasta and your choice of vegetables, you can invent a limitless amount of meals. Simply cook up a pot of rice, millet, buckwheat, or pasta. While the grain is cooking, steam or stir-fry your choice of seasonal vegetables and make the high-protein sauce that you think best complements the other ingredients. The high-protein sauces that can be used in this manner are: *Velvet Tofu-Mushroom Sauce* (page 243), *Easiest Cheese Sauce* (page 242, *Tofu and Peanut Sauce* (page 244), *Spicy Peanut Sauce* (page 246), *Veggie Deluxe Spaghetti Sauce* (page 240—you don't even need to cook extra vegetables to go with this one!) and *Tomato, Adzuki Bean, and Eggplant Sauce* (page 241).

Place a portion of cooked grain on each individual serving plate. Generously top the grain with an attractive arrangement of cooked vegetables.

Pour the sauce over the vegetables. Serve this dish along with a salad, and you have a quick custom-made meal of your own invention.

If you wish to create a meal around one of the other sauces in this book, it is best to add a little more protein such as some tofu, cooked beans, cooked tempeh, or cheese.

Here's a creative cooking tip: almost any sauce can be made into a mushroom sauce. For flour-thickened sauce, sauté about 1 cup of sliced mushrooms in the oil before adding the flour, and proceed as usual. For sauces that will be thickened with arrowroot, cornstarch, or kudzu, add about 1 cup of sliced mushrooms to the broth and simmer for a few minutes. Add the thickening agent according to the recipe, and simmer to the desired consistency.

VEGGIE DELUXE SPAGHETTI SAUCE

The tofu and the sunflower seeds in this sauce make it high in protein.

2 cups mashed tofu
5–6 cups boiling water
2–3 tablespoons olive oil
1 medium onion, chopped
1 cup thinly sliced carrots
1 cup sliced broccoli (flowerets cut into bite-sized pieces and stems peeled and sliced)
1 cup sliced zucchini
1 cup sliced mushrooms
3–4 cloves garlic, minced
1 teaspoon basil
1 teaspoon thyme
1/2 teaspoon oregano
1/4 teaspoon celery seed
1/4 teaspoon ground cloves
1/2 cup sunflower seeds, coarsely ground
2 tablespoons tamari (not shoyu)
1 pound canned tomatoes
1/2 cup tomato paste
1 tablespoon honey

Serves: 4
Time: 40 minutes

1. Drop the tofu into the boiling water. Bring the water back to a boil and cook for 1 minute.
2. Drain the tofu into a colander that has been lined with a clean dishtowel. Run cold water over the tofu to cool it off for easier handling. Twist the dishtowel and press the tofu to squeeze out the excess water (see Figure 10.2 on page 199). When the tofu has been adequately pressed, it should have a firm, ground-beef-like texture.
3. Heat the oil in a large, heavy kettle. Add the onion, carrots, and broccoli. Stir-fry for about 5 minutes.
4. Add the zucchini, mushrooms, garlic, herbs, and spices. Stir for a couple of minutes, then cover the kettle and cook over medium heat until the vegetables are tender, but still crisp. Stir occasionally.
5. Add the pressed tofu, sunflower seeds, and tamari. Stir for a minute over medium heat.
6. Add the remaining ingredients and simmer for 2–3 minutes.

    Serve this sauce over whole grain pasta, accompanied by a big green salad.

QUICK AND EASY TOMATO SAUCE

The only thing quicker would be to open up a can of ready-made sauce!

1 tablespoon olive oil
1/2 cup chopped onion
1 or more cloves garlic, minced
1 large can (28 ounces) tomatoes
1 teaspoon basil
1/2 teaspoon honey
1 tablespoon tamari
1 small can (5 1/2 ounces) tomato paste

Yield: About 4 cups
Time: 10–15 minutes

1. Heat the olive oil in a large skillet. Add the onion and the garlic. Sauté until tender.
2. Add the canned tomatoes, basil, honey, and tamari to the sautéed onions. Simmer for about 5 minutes.
3. Add the tomato paste and mix well.

    This is good with pasta, veggie burgers, and meatless loaves.

VARIATION

- Other vegetables, such as mushrooms, celery, peppers, and summer squash may be sautéed with the onions. It may be necessary to add another tablespoon of oil.

GARDEN-FRESH SPAGHETTI SAUCE

Because this sauce cooks only briefly, it has an exceptionally fresh taste.

2 tablespoons olive oil
1 large onion, chopped
3 cloves garlic, minced
2 small zucchinis, scrubbed and sliced
3 cups sliced mushrooms
1 teaspoon thyme
2 teaspoons basil
1/2 teaspoon oregano
3 bay leaves
1/4 teaspoon ground cloves
5 medium tomatoes
1 cup fresh or frozen peas
1 tablespoon honey
1 tablespoon tamari
1/2 cup tomato paste (or more as needed)

Serves: 4–6
Time: 20 minutes

1. Heat the oil in a large, heavy kettle. Add the onion and the garlic. Sauté for 2–3 minutes. Add the zucchini; cover the kettle, and cook, stirring occasionally, until the zucchini begins to get tender.
2. Add the mushrooms, thyme, basil, oregano, bay leaves, and cloves. Cook for a few minutes more until the mushrooms are done.
3. Cut the tomatoes into large chunks. Place the chopped tomatoes in a blender or food processor. Blend to a purée.
4. Add the tomato purée, the peas, the honey, and the tamari to the sautéed vegetables. Bring the sauce to a boil, stirring often.
5. Add 1/2 cup of tomato paste and mix well. If the sauce is still too thin, add as much tomato paste as needed to thicken it to the desired consistency.

For a real treat, try this sauce with whole grain pasta and some *Tofu "Meat" Balls* (page 202).

TOMATO, ADZUKI BEAN, AND EGGPLANT SAUCE

This is another of my "East meets West" recipes.

2 tablespoons olive oil
1 cup chopped onion
2–3 cloves garlic, minced
1 green pepper, diced
1 1/2 cups grated eggplant
1 1/2 cups sliced mushrooms
1 teaspoon basil
4 medium-sized ripe tomatoes, chopped into large pieces
1 tablespoon kudzu
2 tablespoons tamari
1 teaspoon honey
1 cup cooked adzuki beans (about 1/2 cup uncooked) (Lentils or any other cooked beans can be substitutes. See page 185 for how to cook legumes.)

Serves: 4–6
Time: 20 minutes

1. Heat the oil in a large skillet. Add the onion and the garlic and sauté for about 3 minutes. Add the green pepper and the grated eggplant. Stir and continue to cook until the vegetables are almost tender; then add the sliced mushrooms and cook until they become tender.
2. Place the tomatoes, kudzu, tamari, and honey in a food processor or blender. Blend to a purée.
3. Pour the purée into the skillet with the sautéed vegetables. Add the adzuki beans and bring the sauce to a boil, stirring constantly. Reduce the heat and stir over low heat until the sauce thickens.

Serve over pasta or over cooked grains such as rice, millet, or buckwheat.

EASIEST CHEESE SAUCE

For a quick meal, serve *Easiest Cheese Sauce* over a bed of rice, millet, bulghur, or pasta topped with a fresh steamed vegetable such as broccoli, cauliflower, or green beans. Accompany with a green salad.

1 cup skim milk
1½ cups grated cheese (Cheddar, Jarlsberg, Swiss, etc.)
2 tablespoons whole wheat pastry flour
Pinch of sea salt (optional)
1 teaspoon Dijon mustard (optional)
Pinch of tarragon (optional)
Pinch of cayenne (optional)

Yield: 1½ cups
Time: 10 minutes

1. Heat the milk in a small saucepan.
2. Mix together the grated cheese and the flour. Slowly stir the cheese into the hot milk. Cook over medium heat, stirring constantly, until the cheese is melted.
3. Season to taste.
    Serve cheese sauce over vegetables, grains, or veggie loaves or burgers.

VARIATIONS

*   *Onion Cheese Sauce:* Sauté 1 cup chopped onions in 1 tablespoon of oil until tender. Add the milk. Heat and proceed as indicated above.
*   *Mushroom Cheese Sauce:* Sauté 1 cup sliced mushrooms in 1 tablespoon of oil until tender. Add the milk. Heat and proceed as indicated above.

BÉCHAMEL SAUCE

The classic French white sauce, minus the butter and cream.

2 tablespoons mild-flavored oil (such as sunflower or safflower oil)
3 tablespoons whole wheat pastry flour
1 cup skim milk
¼ teaspoon sea salt
Pinch of nutmeg

Yield: 1 cup
Time: 10 minutes

1. Heat the oil in a small saucepan over medium-high heat. Sprinkle in the flour and mix well.
2. Remove the pan from the heat and add a small amount of the milk while stirring vigorously to form a paste. Return the pan to the heat and add a little more milk, stirring vigorously all the time. Continue stirring and adding milk until all the milk is used up and the sauce is thick.
3. Add the salt and the nutmeg to taste.

VARIATIONS

*   *Béchamel aux Fines Herbes:* When the sauce is returned to the heat the second time, add some finely minced fresh parsley, chives, tarragon, rosemary, etc., to the sauce along with the milk.
*   *Béchamel Piquante:* Add ½ teaspoon dry mustard or 1 teaspoon Dijon-style mustard to the sauce along with the milk. A pinch of cayenne is also good.
*   *Mushroom Béchamel:* Sauté 1 cup of sliced mushrooms in the oil before adding the flour. Mix well and proceed as indicated above.
*   *Soymilk Béchamel:* Replace the skim milk with unsweetened soymilk.

CASHEW BÉCHAMEL

This is a rich and creamy white sauce that does not contain dairy products.

¼ cup whole raw cashews
2 tablespoons whole wheat pastry flour
1 cup water or vegetable stock
¼ teaspoon sea salt, or to taste
Pinch of cayenne
¼ cup finely minced parsley

Yield: About 1¼ cups
Time: 10 minutes

1. Place the cashews, flour, water or stock, salt, and cayenne in a blender (a food processor will not work as well). Blend until very smooth and creamy.
2. Pour the mixture into a small saucepan. Bring to a boil over high heat, stirring constantly. Add the parsley and mix.

    Serve over steamed vegetables such as broccoli or cauliflower.

VELVET TOFU-MUSHROOM SAUCE

1 tablespoon oil
½ cup chopped onions
1 cup sliced mushrooms
1 cup mashed tofu
⅓ cup water or vegetable stock (approximately)
3 tablespoons tamari, or to taste

Serves: 2–4
Time: 15 minutes

1. Heat the oil in a skillet and sauté the onions. When the onions are almost tender, add the mushrooms and sauté until tender.
2. While the vegetables are cooking, place the tofu, water or stock, and tamari in a blender or food processor. Blend until very smooth and creamy. Add as much water as is necessary to yield a sauce of the desired consistency.
3. Add the tofu cream to the sautéed vegetables and stir the sauce over medium heat until it is warm, but do not bring it to a boil.

    This sauce is delicious served over vegetables or grain dishes.

PECAN SAUCE

This sauce has a delicious, refined flavor and a wonderfully creamy texture.

1/3 cup pecan halves
1 tablespoon whole wheat pastry flour
1 cup water or vegetable stock
2 tablespoons miso

Yield: About 1 1/3 cups
Time: 12 minutes

1. Place the pecans in a hot, unoiled skillet or saucepan and stir them over medium-high heat for 2–3 minutes. Add the flour and continue to stir until the mixture gives off a nutty aroma.
2. Place the lightly roasted nuts and flour in a blender with the water or broth and blend until the mixture is very smooth and creamy.
3. Pour the mixture into a small saucepan. Bring to a boil while stirring constantly. Reduce the heat and simmer, stirring often, until the sauce thickens. Remove the saucepan from the heat and add the miso. Stir well to blend.

   This sauce is particularly good over vegetable-stuffed crepes and veggie burgers—in fact, it can enhance almost any grain or vegetable dish.

ONION-MUSTARD SAUCE

2 tablespoons oil
1 1/2–2 cups chopped onions
1 teaspoon tarragon
3 tablespoons whole wheat pastry flour
1 1/2 cups water or vegetable stock
1–2 teaspoons Dijon mustard
2 tablespoons tamari

Yield: About 2 cups
Time: 15 minutes

1. Heat the oil in a skillet and sauté the onions over low heat until they are tender. Cooking the onions very slowly will bring out their sweetness.
2. Add the tarragon and the flour to the onions. Stir for a minute or two.
3. Add a small amount of the water and stir vigorously. Continue to add the remaining water a little at a time, stirring constantly. Cook until the sauce thickens.
4. Add the mustard and the tamari and mix well.

   Serve with a mild-flavored vegetable such as cauliflower. *Onion-Mustard Sauce* is also good over veggie burgers or meatless loaves.

TOFU AND PEANUT SAUCE

This sauce is light and very creamy.

1/4 cup peanut butter
14 ounces tofu
1 cup water or unseasoned vegetable stock (approximately)
1 or more cloves garlic
3 tablespoons tamari
Pinch of cayenne or your favorite hot sauce (optional)

Serves: 3–4
Time: 10 minutes

1. In a blender or food processor, blend together all the ingredients until smooth and creamy. If the sauce is too thick, add a little extra water.
2. Pour the sauce into a skillet or saucepan and stir over medium heat until it is thoroughly heated.

   Serve over grains such as buckwheat, millet, or rice, or over pasta.

SAUCE ORIENTALE

This is a light sauce to serve over stir-fried vegetables, meatless loaves, croquettes, etc.

1 cup cold or room-temperature water or vegetable stock
1½ tablespoons arrowroot
½ teaspoon honey
½ teaspoon roasted sesame oil
2 tablespoons tamari

Yield: About 1 cup
Time: 10 minutes

Combine all the ingredients in a small saucepan. Stir to dissolve the arrowroot. Stirring constantly, bring the mixture to a boil. Cook for 1–2 minutes (always stirring), until the sauce thickens.

(Hot liquid will not mix with arrowroot. Therefore, if you wish to use hot stock [water that was just used for cooking vegetables] for the sauce, first dilute the arrowroot in about ¼ cup cold water and use only ¾ cup stock.)

VARIATIONS

- *Sweet and Sour Sauce:* Follow the above recipe but make the following changes: increase the honey to 2 teaspoons and add 1½–2 tablespoons rice or cider vinegar.
- *Light Mushroom Sauce:* Follow the above recipe but make the following changes: omit the honey and add 1 cup of sliced mushrooms to the saucepan along with the other ingredients.

TAHINI-MISO SAUCE

A richly flavored sauce that is good over grains, tofu, tempeh, or mild vegetables.

1 tablespoon oil
3 tablespoons whole wheat pastry flour
¼ cup tahini
1¼ cups water or vegetable stock
2 tablespoons miso (barley or white miso are good)

Yield: About 1¾ cups
Time: 10 minutes

1. Heat the oil in a small saucepan. Add the flour and cook, stirring constantly, until the flour is lightly browned and begins to give off a nutty aroma.
2. Remove the pan from the heat and stir in the tahini. Add a small amount of water and stir vigorously to form a paste.
3. Return the pan to the heat and slowly add the remaining water. Stirring continuously, cook the sauce until the desired consistency is reached. (If the sauce is too thick, add a little water.)
4. Remove the saucepan from the heat and add the miso. Mix well.

VARIATION

- Sauté ½ cup of finely chopped onion in the oil before adding the flour. Mix well and proceed as indicated above.

SPICY PEANUT SAUCE

Spicy peanut sauce is traditionally Indonesian. This recipe is delicious served over tempeh, tofu, beans, rice, and vegetables.

⅓ cup unsalted peanut butter
3 tablespoons lemon juice
1 tablespoon shoyu or tamari
1–2 cloves garlic, pressed
Pinch of cayenne or a dash of your favorite hot sauce, to taste
¾ cup water

Yield: About 1½ cups
Time: 10 minutes

1. Cream together all the ingredients except for the water.
2. Slowly stir in the water.
3. Place the mixture in a saucepan and cook, stirring constantly with a wire whisk, until the sauce thickens.

YEAST GRAVY

A tasty way to get your B vitamins.

2 tablespoons oil
4 tablespoons whole wheat pastry flour
1½ cups water or vegetable stock
¼ cup nutritional yeast
2 tablespoons miso or tamari to taste

Yield: About 1½ cups
Time: 10 minutes

1. Heat the oil in a saucepan. Stir in the flour and cook over medium-high heat, stirring constantly, until the flour is lightly toasted.
2. Remove the saucepan from the heat and stir in a little water or vegetable stock. Stir vigorously to form a paste. Then return the saucepan to the heat and slowly add the remaining water, stirring constantly. Add the yeast. Mix well and simmer until the sauce thickens.
3. Remove from heat and add miso or shoyu. Mix well.

   Serve this gravy with vegetables, grain dishes, veggie burgers, and meatless loaves.

ARAME CONDIMENT

If you are not a sea vegetable lover, you will be surprised at how good arame tastes prepared in this way.

1 cup arame
2 tablespoons tamari
2 tablespoons water
1 teaspoon roasted sesame oil

Yield: 1 cup
Time: 15 minutes

1. Soak the arame for about 5 minutes, or until soft. Drain and rinse.
2. Place the arame in a small saucepan along with the remaining ingredients. Simmer uncovered over medium heat for 5–10 minutes.
3. Store arame condiment in a covered container in the refrigerator. It will keep very well for at least 1 week. This condiment may be used to add flavor and nutritional value to salads, soups, grain dishes, and vegetables.

DAIKON CONDIMENT

1½ cups grated daikon radish
2 tablespoons lemon juice
1 tablespoon shoyu or tamari
¼ teaspoon roasted sesame oil (optional)

Yield: About 1¼ cups
Time: 5 minutes to prepare; 30 minutes to chill.

Mix together all the ingredients. Chill for about 30 minutes before serving. Use this condiment as an accompaniment to tempura, grain dishes, or any fried foods.

GOMASHIO

Rather than keep a salt shaker on the table, put a small pot of gomashio there instead. It will give you more flavor for less sodium.

½ cup sesame seeds
2 teaspoons sea salt

Yield: About ½ cup
Time: 8 minutes

1. Place the sesame seeds and the salt in a skillet. Stir over medium-high heat until the seeds begin to brown. When they are almost done, they will begin to make popping noises and emit a fragrant, nutty aroma. When this starts to happen the seeds will brown very fast, so be careful not to burn them.
2. Place the lightly browned sesame seeds in a blender and whiz them briefly. There is no need to finely grind the seeds. Let the gomashio cool and place it in an airtight container in the refrigerator.

    Use gomashio instead of salt on salads, steamed vegetables, grains, and beans.

BONNIE'S MARINATED HIJIKI

My friend Bonnie is a very busy artist and teacher. She loves exotic foods, and although she does not have much time for cooking, she always has a big jar of this marinated hijiki in her refrigerator. Apart from being an unusual garnish, it is an easy way to add minerals, vitamins, and flavor to all sorts of dishes.

1 cup dry hijiki (not packed into the cup)
5 tablespoons rice or cider vinegar
1 cup water
1 tablespoon shoyu or tamari
3 cloves garlic, minced

Yield: About 2 cups
Time: 45 minutes to prepare; marinate overnight.

1. Soak the hijiki in water to cover for at least 30 minutes. Drain the soaked hijiki through a wire strainer and rinse it well. Place the hijiki in a vegetable steamer and steam it for about 10 minutes.
2. Place the cooked hijiki in a wide-mouthed jar or ceramic bowl. Add the remaining ingredients. Mix well, cover the container, and refrigerate.
3. Let the hijiki marinate overnight before serving. Marinated hijiki keeps well, so make more than you need for one time.

    Use this as a condiment or garnish with tofu dishes, stir-fries, salads, etc.

ORANGE DATE SAUCE

1 cup freshly squeezed orange juice
1½ tablespoons arrowroot
1 tablespoon grated orange peel
¼ cup chopped dates

Yield: 1 cup
Time: 5 minutes

Place all the ingredients in a saucepan and stir until the arrowroot is dissolved. Stirring constantly, bring the mixture to a boil and cook until thickened.

Serve warm over pancakes or crepes.

APPLE AND RAISIN PANCAKE SAUCE

Instead of using syrup or honey on pancakes, try using this fruit-sweetened sauce.

1 cup apple juice
¼ cup raisins
1½ tablespoons arrowroot
1 tablespoon lemon juice
½ teaspoon cinnamon
Pinch of cloves

Yield: 1 cup
Time: 5 minutes

Place all the ingredients in a saucepan and stir until the arrowroot is dissolved. Bring the mixture to a boil, stirring constantly until thickened.

To serve, pour the warm sauce over pancakes or crepes.

MARIE-HÉLÈNE'S SUNNY CITRUS SAUCE

½ cup sunflower seeds
½ cup water
2 tablespoons honey
2 teaspoons grated orange peel
½ cup freshly squeezed orange juice
2 tablespoons lemon juice

Yield: Approximately 1¼ cups sauce
Time: Soak overnight; prepare in 5 minutes.

1. Place the sunflower seeds and the water in a small bowl. Cover and let soak overnight.
2. Place the soaked seeds and any remaining water in a blender. Blend until smooth and creamy, adding a little extra water if necessary.
3. Add the honey, the orange peel, and a little of the orange juice. Blend again. Continue to blend while slowly adding the remaining orange and lemon juice.

This sauce is wonderful over fruit salad. It can also be served over mochi or over hot cereal in place of yogurt.

VARIATION

- Substitute 3–4 soft dates for the honey.

APPLE-TAHINI SAUCE

This light and creamy sauce is great over pan-fried or baked mochi or on cereal in place of yogurt.

1 small apple, washed and cut into chunks
2 soft dates
2 tablespoons tahini
1/4 cup water or apple juice (approximately)

Serves: 1–2
Time: 5 minutes

Blend together all ingredients in the blender. Add as much additional water as necessary to obtain a creamy consistency.

Serve over fruit, cereal, or pancakes. For a real treat, sprinkle with 1 teaspoon bee pollen.

VARIATIONS

• Make breakfast sauces using a pear in place of the apple; almond butter or peanut butter in place of the tahini; or prunes, apricots, or raisins in place of the dates.

PRUNE AND DATE SAUCE

1/2 cup water
5 pitted dates
5 pitted prunes

Yield: Approximately 1 cup
Time: Soak overnight; prepare in 3–5 minutes.

1. Place the dates, prunes, and water in a small bowl. Cover and let the fruit soak overnight.
2. Place the soaked fruit and any remaining water in a blender and blend till smooth.

Serve over sliced bananas, pancakes, mochi, or toast.

CREAMY CASHEW SAUCE

1/2 cup raw cashews
1 cup apple juice

Yield: About 1 1/4 cups
Time: Soak overnight; prepare in 3–5 minutes.

1. Place the cashews in a small bowl. Pour the apple juice over the cashews and let them soak overnight.
2. Place the soaked cashews along with any remaining juice in a blender. Blend until smooth and creamy.

Serve the sauce over fruit or on hot cereal in place of milk or yogurt.

12. DESSERTS

Since desserts are for pleasure, the two main considerations when making desserts are, of course, taste and appearance. In this book, these are not the only considerations; nutrition is important as well. Compare a few of these recipes with the recipes in any standard cookbook, and you will find that they are much lower in fat and sugar. You will also find that the types of fat and sugar are different. The sweeteners used in these recipes are honey, maple syrup, malt, and fruit. Because these sweeteners are only slightly refined (and some, especially fruit, are not refined at all), they have nutritional value. White sugar and other refined sweeteners lack nutritional value, so are "empty" calories. The fats in these recipes are vegetable oils and nuts—and in only a few recipes a little butter. A number of the desserts in this chapter are also wheatless, dairyless, or eggless, so that they can be enjoyed by persons who have allergies to these foods.

Always use whole wheat pastry flour instead of whole wheat bread flour in desserts. The result will be lighter and more tender. I never use unbleached white flour, but if you are unaccustomed to using whole grains and wish to gradually adjust your taste, you may substitute part or all unbleached white flour for the whole wheat pastry flour in a recipe.

Of the sweeteners used in these recipes, honey is the sweetest. It is much sweeter than sugar, which is why it is used in fairly small quantities. Maple syrup is the next most concentrated sweetener, while malt and fruit are the least concentrated. If you wish to substitute one type of sweetener for another, you may have to slightly adjust the amount of sweetener to taste.

In a cake recipe, you may substitute two egg whites for one egg, if desired. In any recipe, dairy milk can be replaced by soymilk, or vice versa.

To make your desserts look enticing, decorate them with fresh and dried fruits, nuts, sesame and sunflower seeds, shredded coconut, and even fresh flowers. The way you garnish your dishes can make all the difference. On a cake with cream cheese icing, I like to design little flowers made of tiny black currants. Thin slivers of orange or lemon peel can also be shaped to create pretty petals. Cream cheese icing can even be forced through a pastry bag, like sugar icing, to give your cakes a professional look. There is no need to rely on sugared, artificially colored garnishes when there is such a wealth of color and beauty in natural ingredients.

Perhaps the nicest thing about making desserts from wholesome ingredients is that they are so well appreciated. A dessert can be the perfect gentle introduction into the world of natural foods.

Fussy teenagers who refuse to taste tofu, or spouses who insist on snow-white commercially processed bread, may find themselves asking for a second helping of tofu cheese cake with whole grain crust before they realize what they're doing!

SIMPLE WHOLE WHEAT CAKE

This simple cake is good as is, but if you wish to "dress it up," a little imagination can make it into something special.

1½ cups whole wheat pastry flour
2 teaspoons baking powder
⅓ cup oil
⅓ cup maple syrup
1 egg
1 teaspoon vanilla
½ cup buttermilk

Yield: One 8-x-8-inch cake
Time: 45 minutes

1. Sift together the flour and the baking powder.
2. In a large bowl, beat together the oil, maple syrup, egg, vanilla, and buttermilk.
3. Gradually stir the flour mixture into the liquid mixture. Beat just enough to mix well.
4. Pour the batter into a well-oiled and floured 8-x-8-inch cake pan. Bake at 350°F for 20–25 minutes, or until a toothpick inserted into the center of the cake comes out clean.

VARIATION

• *Fancy Birthday Cake:*
Double the above recipe and bake it in 2 pans. Remove the cake from the pans and let it cool.

1. Make a double recipe of *Cream Cheese Icing* (page 274).
2. Place one of the cakes on a pretty serving plate. Place pieces of wax paper just under the edges of the bottom of the cake (to keep the plate clean).
3. Generously spread both layers of the cake

with cream cheese icing. Now comes the time to be creative! Top the bottom layer with sliced peaches, strawberries, blueberries, bananas, or chopped nuts, etc. Place the other cake on top and cover it with as much of the remaining icing as needed. Remove the wax paper. Decorate the top of the cake and around the base with additional sliced fruit and or chopped nuts.

BARLEY AND MALT CAKE

A light and tender wheatless cake that is sweetened with malt and dates.

1 cup barley flour
¾ cup malt powder
3 teaspoons baking powder
¼ cup oil
2 eggs
½ cup milk or water
1 cup chopped pitted dates

Yield: One 8-x-8-inch cake
Time: 45 minutes

1. Sift together the flour, malt powder, and baking powder into a bowl.
2. In another large bowl, beat together the oil, eggs, and milk. Gradually stir in the dry mixture. Beat just enough to mix well. Fold in the dates.
3. Pour the mixture into an oiled and floured 8-x-8-inch cake pan. Bake at 350°F for 25 minutes, or until a toothpick inserted into the center of the cake comes out clean.

ROLLED-UP BERRY CAKE

A rolled berry cake that creates a pink spiral pattern when you slice it. The French name for this recipe is "Gâteau Roule."

FILLING

2 cups raspberries or sliced strawberries
1/3 cup honey
2 tablespoons arrowroot
1 cup finely grated unsweetened coconut

CAKE

1 cup whole wheat pastry flour
1 teaspoon baking powder
5 eggs, separated
1/4 cup honey
1 teaspoon vanilla

Serves: 8–10
Time: 1 hour

1. Combine the filling ingredients in a saucepan. Cook over high heat, stirring constantly, until the mixture thickens. Let it cool to room temperature before spreading it on the cake.
2. Sift together the flour and the baking powder. In a separate large mixing bowl, beat together the egg yolks, honey, and vanilla.
3. Beat the egg whites in a small bowl until they stand in stiff peaks.
4. Stir the flour mixture into the egg yolk mixture and beat just enough to mix well. Gently fold in the egg whites.
5. Spread the batter onto a 17-x-11-inch cookie sheet that has been lined with oiled wax paper. Bake the cake at 375°F for about 10 minutes, or until firm.
6. When the cake is baked, transfer it to a clean dishtowel. Carefully peel off the wax paper. Roll the cake up in the towel, starting from one of the shorter ends. Leave the cake rolled up in the towel for 10 minutes. Then unroll it and spread it with an even coat of the berry filling. Roll the cake back up (without the towel!) and place it, seam side down, on a serving plate. Let it stand for at least 1 hour before serving.

Top each slice with a spoonful of *Tofu and Cashew Cream*, page 274.

YOGURT-RAISIN CAKE

2 cups whole wheat pastry flour
2 teaspoons baking powder
1 teaspoon baking soda
1/2 teaspoon nutmeg
1/3 cup oil
1/2 cup maple syrup
2 eggs
1 cup plain yogurt
1 teaspoon vanilla
1 1/2 teaspoons finely grated orange peel
1 cup raisins

Yield: 1 round 10-inch cake
Time: 55 minutes

1. Sift the flour, baking powder, soda, and nutmeg into a large bowl. In another bowl, beat together the oil, maple syrup, eggs, yogurt, vanilla, and orange peel.
2. Stir the flour mixture into the liquid mixture and beat just enough to mix well. Fold in the raisins.
3. Pour the batter into a well-oiled and floured 10-inch cast iron skillet. Bake at 350°F for 35 minutes, or until a toothpick inserted into the center of the cake comes out clean.

   Serve plain, with *Cream Cheese Icing* (page 274), or with *Orange Date Sauce* (page 248).

VARIATION

- For a layer cake, pour the batter evenly into 2 well-oiled and floured 8-x-8-inch cake pans. Bake the cake at 350°F for 20 minutes or until done. Let it cool and spread it with *Cream Cheese Icing*, page 274. To generously cover the cake with icing, you will need about 1 1/2 recipes of icing.

BLUEBERRY UPSIDE-DOWN CAKE

TOPPING

1/3 cup mild-flavored oil such as safflower or sunflower oil

1/4 cup honey

2 1/2 cups blueberries, washed and drained

1 tablespoon arrowroot

BATTER

1 1/2 cups whole wheat pastry flour

3 teaspoons baking powder

1/4 cup mild-flavored oil such as safflower or sunflower oil

1/3 cup maple syrup

2 eggs

1/4 cup water, milk, or soymilk

Yield: 1 round 10-inch cake
Time: 55 minutes

1. To make the topping, mix together 1/3 cup of oil and 1/4 cup of honey in the bottom of an 10-inch cast iron skillet. In a bowl, mix together the blueberries and the arrowroot. Distribute the blueberry mixture, in an even layer, over the honey-oil mixture in the bottom of the pan. Set this aside while you make the batter.
2. Sift together the flour and the baking powder. In another bowl, beat together the oil, maple syrup, eggs, and water or milk. Stir the flour mixture into the liquid mixture and beat just enough to mix well. Don't overbeat.
3. Pour the batter evenly over the blueberries. Bake in the skillet at 350°F for 30–35 minutes or until the cake springs back when touched or a toothpick inserted into the center of the cake comes out clean.
4. Let the cake cool for about 10 minutes, then loosen it from the edges of the pan with a knife. Turn the cake over onto a serving platter. Or, if desired, serve the cake right out of the pan.

PEACH UPSIDE-DOWN CAKE

TOPPING

1/4 cup butter

1/4 cup honey

1 teaspoon cinnamon

1/4 teaspoon nutmeg

2 cups sliced peaches

BATTER

1 cup whole wheat pastry flour

2 teaspoons baking powder

1/3 cup maple syrup

1/4 cup oil

1 egg

3 tablespoons milk, water, or soymilk

1 teaspoon vanilla

1 teaspoon finely grated lemon peel

Yield: One 8-x-8-inch cake
Time: 1 hour

1. Place the butter, honey, cinnamon, and nutmeg in a small saucepan. Stir over medium heat until the butter is melted.
2. Pour the mixture into the bottom of an 8-inch square cake pan. Make an even layer of peaches over the honey-butter mixture. Set the pan aside while you make the batter.
3. Sift together the flour and the baking powder. In another bowl, beat together the maple syrup, oil, egg, milk or water, vanilla, and lemon peel.
4. Stir the flour mixture into the liquid mixture. Beat just enough to mix well; take care not to overbeat. Evenly pour the batter over the peaches.
5. Bake the cake at 350°F for 30 minutes, or until it springs back when touched. Let the cake cool for about 5 minutes, then loosen it from the edges of the pan with a knife. Turn it over onto a serving platter. It may be served warm or chilled.

CAROBANANA CAKE

This is one of my favorites!

3 cups whole wheat pastry flour
1/4 cup carob powder
3 teaspoons baking powder
2 ripe medium bananas
1/2 cup oil
1/2 cup maple syrup
3 eggs
3/4 cup milk or water
3/4 cup chopped walnuts

Yield: One 7-x-11-inch cake
Serves: 8–10
Time: 1 hour, 5 minutes

1. Sift together the flour, carob powder, and baking powder.
2. Mash the bananas. Add the oil, milk, and maple syrup, and beat well. Beat in 1 egg at a time, beating well between each addition.
3. Gradually beat the dry ingredients into the wet ingredients. Beat until the batter is well mixed.
4. Fold in the walnuts.
5. Pour the batter into an oiled and floured 7-x-11-inch cake pan. Bake at 350°F for 40–45 minutes, or until a toothpick inserted into the center of the cake comes out clean.

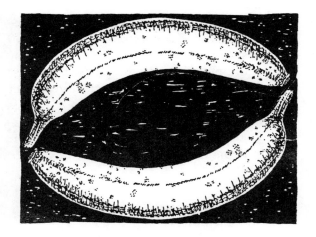

DATE AND BRAZIL NUT LOAF

This cake uses whole dates and nuts. They aren't chopped until you slice the cake, and they create a beautiful pattern when you slice it.

1 cup whole wheat pastry flour
2 teaspoons baking powder
1 teaspoon cinnamon
1/3 cup oil
1/4 cup honey
4 eggs
2 cups whole, shelled Brazil nuts
2 cups whole, pitted dates

Yield: 1 loaf
Time: 1 hour, 20 minutes

1. Sift together the flour, baking powder, and cinnamon into a bowl.
2. In another bowl, beat together the oil, honey, and eggs.
3. Mix the nuts and dates with flour. (Occasionally, a package of pitted dates contains a date or two that still has a pit; therefore, it is a good idea to carefully examine each date to make sure that the pit is removed.)
4. Combine the liquid mixture with the flour-date mixture and mix well. Line a 4½-x-8½-x-2½-inch or similar size loaf pan with three thicknesses of wax paper. Oil the wax paper. Pour the batter into the paper-lined pan and bake at 350°F for 60 minutes, or until a toothpick inserted into the center of the cake comes out clean. Let the cake cool in the pan for about 5 minutes; then remove it and peel off the wax paper. Let the loaf cool before slicing.

This cake stores very well. Wrap it in foil and keep it in the refrigerator until needed.

ZUCCHINI CAKE

2 cups whole wheat pastry flour
3 teaspoons baking powder
1/2 teaspoon baking soda
1 teaspoon allspice
1/3 cup oil
1/2 cup maple syrup
2 eggs
1/4 cup milk or soymilk
1 cup grated zucchini
1 cup raisins
1/2 cup chopped walnuts or pecans

Yield: 1 round 10-inch cake
Time: 50 minutes

1. Into a bowl, sift together the flour, baking powder, soda, and allspice.
2. In another large bowl, beat together the oil, syrup, eggs, and the milk or soymilk.
3. Gradually stir the flour mixture into the liquid mixture. Beat just enough to mix well. Fold in the grated zucchini, raisins, and nuts.
4. Pour the batter into a well-oiled 10-inch cast iron skillet. Bake at 350°F for 30 minutes, or until a toothpick inserted into the center of the cake comes out clean.

    Serve zucchini cake plain while it is still warm, or let it cool and frost it with *Cream Cheese Icing* (page 274).

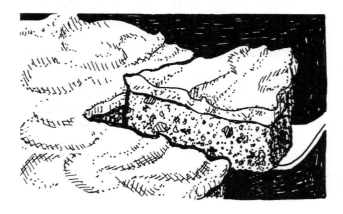

STRAWBERRY TOPPED TOFU CHEESECAKE

A nondairy cheesecake that is not too sweet.

1 recipe Oatmeal Pie Crust (page 96), Maple Pecan Pie Crust (page 97), or Coconut Pie Crust (page 95)
1 teaspoon cinnamon
1 cup cashews
1 cup mashed tofu (use tofu that is very fresh)
1/2 cup honey
1 cup soymilk
1 1/2 tablespoons arrowroot
1 1/2 teaspoons vanilla
2 teaspoons lemon juice
2 teaspoons grated lemon peel

TOPPING
2 cups sliced strawberries
1/4 cup water
3 tablespoons honey
1 tablespoon agar flakes

Serves: 1 round 9-inch cake
Time: 1 hour

1. Follow the recipe for the pie crust, adding 1 teaspoon cinnamon to the flour-oat mixture. Do not bake the crust until it is filled.
2. Place the cashews, tofu, honey, soymilk, arrowroot, vanilla, lemon juice, and grated lemon peel in a food processor. Blend until very smooth and creamy. If you do not have a food processor, you can use a blender; the mixture will have to be blended in small batches.
3. Pour this tofu-cashew cream into the unbaked pie crust. Bake the pie at 350°F for 30 minutes, or until set. Chill.
4. When the pie is thoroughly chilled, arrange 1 1/2 cups of the strawberries attractively over the top. Place the remaining 1/2 cup of berries in a small saucepan, along with 1/4 cup of water, 3 tablespoons of honey, and the agar flakes. Bring the mixture to a boil. Lower the

heat and simmer until the agar is completely dissolved (about 5 minutes). Pour the mixture into a blender and blend to a purée.

5. Chill the purée for about 5 minutes. Then pour it over the cheesecake and chill until set.

VARIATION

- Substitute blueberries or sliced peaches for the strawberries.

TOFU-CAROB BROWNIES

These brownies have a marvelous spongy texture. Don't tell anyone what they are made of.

1/2 cup mashed tofu
1/2 cup maple syrup
1 teaspoon vanilla
2 tablespoons oil
2 tablespoons carob powder
2/3 cup whole wheat pastry flour
1 teaspoon baking powder
1/2 cup chopped pecans

Yield: 16 brownies, 2 inches square
Time: 45 minutes

1. Place the mashed tofu, maple syrup, vanilla, oil, and carob powder in a blender or food processor. Blend until smooth and creamy. Transfer the cream to a large or medium-sized bowl.
2. In another bowl, sift together the flour and the baking powder. Add the pecans and mix well. Stir the flour mixture into the tofu-carob cream and mix well.
3. Spread the batter into a well-oiled 8-x-8-inch cake pan. Bake at 350°F for 20 minutes, or until the brownies spring back when touched.
4. Let the brownies stand for about 5 minutes after they are removed from the oven, then cut them into squares and remove them from the pan.

DATE AND APPLE BROWNIES

These brownies are dense and chewy.

1 cup whole wheat pastry flour
1 teaspoon baking powder
1/4 cup carob powder
1/3 cup oil
1/4 cup malt syrup or honey
1 egg
2 tablespoons water
1 cup chopped dates
3/4 cup grated apple (1 medium apple)
1/4 cup chopped pecans or walnuts

Yield: 16 brownies, 2 inches square
Time: 35 minutes

1. Sift together the flour, baking powder, and the carob powder into a bowl.
2. In a separate large bowl, beat together the oil, malt or honey, egg, and water.
3. Stir the flour mixture into the liquid mixture and beat just enough to blend. Add the dates and the grated apple. Mix well.
4. Spread the mixture into a well-oiled 8-x-8-inch cake pan. Sprinkle it with the nuts. Press the chopped nuts into the batter. Bake at 350°F for about 15 minutes, or until firm. Let the cake cool slightly and cut it into squares.

STRAWBERRY PIE

A scrumptious but light dessert made with fresh raw strawberries.

1 recipe Oatmeal Pie Crust *(page 96)*
1½–2 pints fresh strawberries (as needed to fill the pie crust)
1 cup water
¾ bar agar, torn into small pieces
¼ cup mild-flavored honey or maple syrup

Yield: 1 single-crust 9-inch pie
Time: 25 minutes for crust; 15 minutes for filling;
2 hours to chill.

1. Bake the pie crust according to the recipe on page 96 and let it cool.
2. Clean and slice the strawberries. Fill the baked and cooled pie crust with the sliced berries, reserving about 1 cup of berries to cook with the agar. Place the berry-filled crust in the refrigerator while preparing the remaining ingredients.
3. Put the water, the agar, and 1 cup of the sliced berries in a small saucepan. Bring the mixture to a boil. Reduce the heat and simmer for about 10 minutes, or until the agar is completely dissolved.
4. Place the dissolved agar mixture in a blender along with the honey or maple syrup. Blend for a few seconds. Pour the agar mixture into a bowl and place it in the refrigerator to let it cool for about 15 minutes—just until it begins to reach the jelling point. If the agar is poured into the crust when it is extremely hot, it will cause the crust to become soggy.
5. When the agar mixture has cooled sufficiently, pour it over the sliced strawberries in the crust. Chill the pie for about 2 hours before slicing.

NOTE: For added color, blend a ½-inch cube of raw beet in the blender with the cooked agar-strawberry mixture.

APPLE-MILLET PIE

There are many recipes for apple pie, but this is one of my favorites.

½ cup millet
1½ cups water
⅔ cup maple syrup
⅓ cup yogurt
5 cups sliced apples (tart apples are best)
Cinnamon (optional)
1 double-crust 10-inch whole wheat pie shell, unbaked

Yield: 1 double-crust 10-inch pie
Time: 1 hour, 20 minutes

1. Wash the millet and put it in a saucepan with the water. Bring to a boil. Lower the heat and simmer the millet until the water is absorbed (about 20 minutes).
2. Blend the cooked millet, maple syrup, and yogurt together in a blender or food processor, until smooth and creamy.
3. Mix the sliced apples with the millet cream and place the mixture in an unbaked 10-inch pie shell. Sprinkle with cinnamon, if desired, and cover it with the top crust. Cut some holes in the top crust to allow steam to escape.
4. Bake the pie at 400°F for 10 minutes, then lower the heat to 350°F and bake for 35 minutes more, or until the crust is golden.

PEANUT BUTTER CREAM PIE

For peanut butter lovers! If you really like peanuts, then you'll like the *Peanut Butter Pie Crust* with this.

1 recipe Oatmeal Pie Crust *(page 96)*, Maple Pecan Pie Crust *(page 97)*, *or* Peanut Butter Pie Crust *(page 96)*
⅓ bar agar, broken into small pieces
1½ cups water
¾ cup peanut butter
½ cup mashed tofu
⅓ cup maple syrup
1–2 bananas (optional) (Use bananas only if the pie is going to eaten within 24 hours; if kept longer, they will turn brown.)
2 tablespoons chopped peanuts

Yield: 1 single-crust 9-inch pie
Time: 25 minutes for crust; 15 minutes for filling; chill 2 hours.

1. Follow the recipe for the pie crust. Let it cool while you make the filling.
2. Put the agar and the water in a saucepan. Bring the water to a boil, then reduce the heat and simmer until the agar is completely dissolved.
3. In a blender or food processor, blend together the peanut butter, tofu, and maple syrup until smooth and creamy. Add the dissolved agar mixture and continue to blend until the two mixtures are well combined.

4. Line the bottom of the baked pie crust with the sliced bananas. Pour the filling over the bananas. Garnish with chopped peanuts and chill for at least 2 hours before serving.

CALIFORNIA DATE AND ORANGE PIE

This pie is simply marvelous, and it is sweetened with fruit.

1 recipe Oatmeal Pie Crust *(page 96)*, Coconut Pie Crust *(page 95)*, *or* Maple Pecan Pie Crust *(page 97)*
1½ cups pitted dates
2½ cups freshly squeezed orange juice
1 tablespoon finely grated orange peel
¾ of a bar of agar, torn into small pieces
½ cup chopped pecans

Yield: 1 single-crust 9-inch pie
Time: 25 minutes for crust; 15 minutes for filling; chill for 2 hours.

1. Follow the recipe for the pie crust, and let it cool while you make the filling.
2. Put the dates, orange juice, orange peel, and agar in a medium-sized saucepan. Bring the juice to a boil. Lower the heat and simmer, stirring occasionally, until the agar is completely dissolved (about 5 minutes).
3. Place the cooked date mixture in a blender or food processor and blend to a purée. Pour the purée into a bowl and refrigerate it for about 5 minutes to cool it slightly. Be careful not to let it cool completely, or it will jell.
4. Pour the slightly cooled purée into the baked pie crust. Sprinkle with pecans and refrigerate until set (about 2 hours).

VARIATION

- Replace the chopped pecans with finely grated coconut, if desired.

COCONUT CREAM PIE

This pie is like the one my mother used to make, only better. It's hard to believe that it contains no milk or cream.

1 recipe Coconut Pie Crust *(page 95)*
¹/₃ cup honey
3 tablespoons arrowroot
2 cups cashew milk
3 slightly beaten egg yolks
1 cup finely grated unsweetened coconut (available in natural foods stores)
1 teaspoon vanilla

MERINGUE
3 egg whites
¹/₄ teaspoon cream of tartar
¹/₂ teaspoon vanilla
2 tablespoons honey

Yield: 1 single-crust 9-inch pie
Time: 25 minutes for crust; 35 minutes for filling; chill 2 hours.

1. Follow the recipe for the *Coconut Pie Crust*. Let the crust cool while you make the filling.
2. In a medium-sized saucepan, combine the honey, arrowroot, and cashew milk. To make cashew milk, blend together ¹/₂ cup cashews and 2 cups water in a blender until smooth and creamy.
3. Mix well and cook over medium heat, stirring constantly, until the mixture thickens and boils. Continue stirring and cook for 2 minutes longer.
4. Remove the saucepan from the heat. Stir a small amount of the hot mixture into the egg yolks; then immediately pour the egg yolk mixture into the saucepan. Cook for 2 minutes, stirring constantly.
5. Remove the pan from the heat and add the coconut and vanilla. If you wish to lightly toast the coconut, you will improve its flavor. To toast it, place it in an unoiled skillet and stir over medium-high heat until it becomes golden brown. Mix well and pour the mixture into the baked 9-inch pie shell.
6. Place the egg whites, the cream of tartar, and the vanilla in a medium-sized bowl. Beat with an eggbeater or wire whisk until the egg whites stand up in firm peaks. Slowly add the honey, while continuing to beat. Continue beating until the honey is well incorporated into the mixture. Then spread the meringue over the pie. Make sure to spread it all the way to the edges. Bake at 350°F for about 12 minutes, or until golden. Chill before serving.

VARIATION

- Sliced bananas may be used to replace the coconut if desired.

PINEAPPLE-YOGURT PIE

Use this luscious pie to convince your favorite "junk food junkie" how wonderful natural foods really are.

1 recipe Coconut Pie Crust *(page 95)*
¹/₃ cup mild-flavored honey (clover honey is good)
4 tablespoons arrowroot
One 20-ounce can crushed unsweetened pineapple (in its own juice)
1 cup yogurt
1 tablespoon lemon juice
2 slightly beaten egg yolks

MERINGUE
2 egg whites
¹/₄ teaspoon cream of tartar
¹/₂ teaspoon vanilla
2 tablespoons honey

Yield: 1 single-crust 9-inch pie
Time: 25 minutes for crust; 35 minutes for filling; chill 2 hours.

1. Follow the recipe on page 95 for the *Coconut Pie Crust*. Let the crust cool while you make the following.
2. In a saucepan, combine the honey and the arrowroot. Stir in the pineapple, yogurt, and lemon juice, and mix well. Cook, stirring constantly, until the mixture thickens and comes to a boil. Cook for 2 minutes more, stirring constantly.
3. Stir a small amount of the hot mixture in with

the egg yolks. Then add the egg yolk mixture to the saucepan containing the hot mixture. Cook for 2 more minutes, stirring constantly. Spoon the mixture into the cooled pie shell.

4. To make the meringue, place the egg whites, the cream of tartar, and the vanilla in a medium-sized bowl. Beat with an eggbeater or a wire whisk until the egg whites stand up in firm peaks. Slowly add the honey, while continuing to beat. Continue beating until the honey is incorporated into the mixture. Spread the meringue over the pie, making sure to spread it all the way to the edges.

5. Bake at 350°F for about 12 minutes, or until the meringue is golden. Chill the pie before serving.

NO-BAKE BLUEBERRY PIE

Wholesome, easy, and very good.

1 recipe Coconut Pie Crust *(page 95),* Oatmeal Pie Crust, *(page 96), or* Maple Pecan Pie Crust *(page 97), baked and cooled*
3 cups blueberries, washed and drained
½ bar agar, torn into small pieces
¾ cup water
¼ cup honey

Yield: 1 single-crust 9-inch pie
Time: 25 minutes for crust; 15 minutes for filling; chill 2 hours.

1. Follow the recipe for the pie crust. Let the crust cool while you make the filling.

2. Place 1 cup of the blueberries, the agar, and the water in a saucepan. Bring to a boil. Reduce the heat and simmer for 5–10 minutes, or until the agar is completely dissolved.

3. While the blueberry mixture is cooking, place the remaining blueberries in the pie crust.

4. When the agar is dissolved, place the mixture in a blender, add the honey, and purée. Pour the puréed mixture over the blueberries in the pie crust. Chill for at least 2 hours to set.

    Serve with *Tofu and Cashew Cream* (page 274), if desired.

STEPHAN'S NO-BAKE APPLESAUCE PIE

Easy, light, and not too sweet. If you wish, you can replace the honey with maple syrup, rice syrup, or malt syrup to taste.

1 recipe Oatmeal Pie Crust *(page 96) or* Maple Pecan Pie Crust *(page 97), baked*
5–6 medium apples, washed and sliced
½ bar of agar, torn into small pieces
¼ cup honey
½ cup currants or raisins
½ teaspoon cinnamon
Sliced almonds

Yield: 1 single-crust 9-inch pie
Time: 25 minutes for crust; 25 minutes for filling; chill 2 hours.

1. Follow the recipe for the pie crust. Let the crust cool while you make the filling.

2. Put the sliced apples, agar, and honey in a medium-sized saucepan and cook over medium heat, stirring often, until the agar is completely dissolved. (About 10–15 minutes.)

3. Put the cooked apple-agar mixture in a blender or food processor and blend to a purée. Pour the apple purée into a bowl, add the currants or raisins and the cinnamon, and mix well.

4. Transfer the mixture to a baked and cooled pie crust. Sprinkle with the sliced almonds. Chill for at least 2 hours before serving.

CAROB BANANA CREAM PIE

A very creamy but not-too-rich pie. The bananas in this pie cause it to turn brown rather rapidly; however, this does not affect their delicious flavor. If you do not have a 10-inch pie pan, you may use a 9-inch pan; however, some filling will be left over.

1 recipe Coconut Pie Crust (page 95)
1 cup water
2/3 bar agar, broken into small pieces
4 medium bananas
1 cup soft tofu, mashed
1/2 cup honey
1 teaspoon vanilla
3 tablespoons carob powder
Finely grated coconut or chopped nuts

Yield: 1 single-crust 10-inch pie
Time: 25 minutes for crust; 20 minutes for filling; chill 2 hours.

1. Follow the recipe for the *Coconut Pie Crust.* Bake the crust and allow it to cool.
2. Put the water and the agar in a small saucepan. Bring to a boil; then reduce the heat and simmer until the agar is completely dissolved. This will take about 5–10 minutes. Stir occasionally while the mixture is cooking.
3. Blend together 2 bananas, the tofu, honey, vanilla, and carob powder in a blender or food processor until very smooth and creamy. Add the dissolved agar mixture and continue to blend for a few seconds more, until well mixed.
4. Line the pie crust with the remaining sliced bananas. Pour the tofu mixture over the bananas. Sprinkle the pie with finely grated coconut or chopped nuts. Chill for about 2 hours to set.

VARIATION

- *Banana Cream Pie:* Follow the above recipe, but omit the carob powder and substitute 2 tablespoons lemon juice.

CAROB CREAM PIE

A creamy and mild-flavored pie that is made without dairy products.

1 cup water
3/4 bar agar, or 3 tablespoons agar flakes
1 cup cashews
1 1/2 cup water or soymilk
1/2 cup maple syrup
1 teaspoon vanilla
1/4 cup carob powder
1 single-crust 9-inch pie shell, baked and cooled

Yield: 1 single-crust 9-inch pie
Time: 25 minutes for crust; 15 minutes for filling; chill 2 hours.

1. Place 1 cup of water in a small saucepan. Add the agar. If you are using agar in the bar form, tear it into small pieces before adding it to the water. Bring the water to a boil; then lower the heat and simmer until the agar is completely dissolved.
2. Place the remaining ingredients in a blender. Blend until smooth and creamy. (A food processor does not work as well as a blender for this.)
3. Add the agar mixture and blend again. Pour the cream into the baked pie crust. Chill for about 2 hours before serving.

VARIATION

- Follow the above recipe, but before filling the pie shell, line it with slices of banana.

Mouth-Watering Peach Upside-Down Cake *(page 254)* Will Have Them Asking for Seconds.

Irresistible Date and Apple Brownies *(page 257)* Will Bring Smiles to Their Faces.

Cool Off with Fruit-Filled Kanten *(page 272)* on Any Hot Day.

Strawberry-Topped Tofu Cheesecake *(page 256)* **Will Be a Just Dessert.**

CREAMY PEACH OR NECTARINE PIE

1 recipe Coconut Pie Crust *(page 95)*, Oatmeal Pie Crust *(page 96)*, or Maple Pecan Pie Crust *(page 97)*, baked
³/₄ cup mashed soft tofu
8 small peaches or nectarines (or about 5 large ones), washed or peeled, and sliced
¹/₃ cup honey
1 teaspoon vanilla
³/₄ cup orange juice
2¹/₂ tablespoons agar flakes

Yield: 1 single-crust 9-inch pie
Time: 25 minutes for crust; 20 minutes for filling; chill 2 hours.

1. Follow the recipe for the pie crust (if desired, add 1 teaspoon of cinnamon). Bake the crust and let it cool while you make the filling.
2. Place the mashed tofu, 2 large or 3 small peaches or nectarines, the honey, and the vanilla in a blender or food processor. Blend until smooth and creamy. (In a blender, this may have to be done in more than one batch.)
3. Place the orange juice and the agar flakes in a small saucepan. Bring to a boil. Lower the heat and let the mixture simmer until the agar is thoroughly dissolved (about 5 minutes).
4. Line the bottom of the pie crust with a layer of sliced peaches (reserving enough to decorate the top). Blend the dissolved agar mixture with the tofu mixture. Pour the filling into the crust. Decorate the top with the remaining sliced peaches and chill the pie for at least 2 hours before serving. The filling will become firm when it is well chilled.

NO-BAKE PUMPKIN PIE

This pie contains no eggs or dairy products.

1 single-crust 9-inch pie (the Maple Pecan Pie Crust, *page 97, is good)*
3 cups cooked and drained pumpkin (see page 169 for how to cook pumpkin)
3 tablespoons agar flakes
³/₄ cup maple syrup, or less to taste
¹/₂ teaspoon cinnamon
¹/₂ teaspoon mace
¹/₄ teaspoon ground cloves
¹/₂ cup raisins
¹/₃ cup pecan halves

Yield: 1 single-crust 9-inch pie
Time: 25 minutes for crust; 15 minutes for filling; chill 2 hours.

1. Follow the recipe for the pie crust. Bake it and let it cool while you make the filling.
2. Place the cooked pumpkin, agar flakes, maple syrup, and spices in a large saucepan. Bring the mixture to a boil. Reduce the heat and simmer until the agar is completely dissolved (about 5–10 minutes).
3. Place the mixture in a blender or food processor and blend until smooth. Add the raisins and mix well.
4. Pour the purée into the pie shell. Top with the pecan halves and chill until set (about 2 hours).

PECAN TARTS

Sinfully delicious and picture perfect, these tarts should be reserved for special occasions.

CRUST
½ cup butter, at room temperature
3 tablespoons cream cheese
1 cup whole wheat pastry flour

FILLING
1 egg
⅔ cup maple syrup
¾ cup chopped pecans
2 tablespoons whole wheat pastry flour

GARNISH
24 pecan halves

Yield: 24 small tarts
Time: 40 minutes

1. Make the crust first. If you have a food processor, place the butter, cream cheese, and flour in the processor and, using the blending blade, blend until well mixed. If you are working by hand, cream together the butter and cheese, then work the flour into the butter mixture using a fork. Mix well.
2. Shape the dough into 24 small balls. Place each ball of dough in the bottom of a muffin tin and carefully press it down, covering the bottom of the tin and about halfway up the sides.
3. To make the filling, beat together the egg, maple syrup, pecans, and flour. Place 1 tablespoon of the mixture in each pastry shell. Top each tart with a pecan half.
4. Bake at 350°F for 12–15 minutes, or until the filling is set and the crust is golden brown. Remove them from the oven and let cool about 5 minutes; then carefully remove them from the tins using a small knife.

WILDFLOWER APPLE CRISP

I used to make this recipe for "macrobiotic night" when I worked at the Wildflower vegetarian restaurant in Sarasota, Florida.

4 cups sliced apples (about 5 medium apples)
2 tablespoons lemon juice
1 cup raisins
1 teaspoon vanilla
1 teaspoon cinnamon

TOPPING
1¼ cups rolled oats
¾ cup whole wheat pastry flour
⅓ cup oil
⅓ cup barley malt syrup or maple syrup

Serves: 4–6
Time: 1 hour

1. Place the sliced apples, lemon juice, raisins, and vanilla in a bowl. Mix well. Transfer the mixture to a shallow baking dish (I use a 9-inch round dish that is 1½ inches deep). Sprinkle with cinnamon.
2. Place the oats, flour, and oil in a bowl. Mix with a fork to incorporate the oil. Add the syrup and mix well.
3. Spread this mixture on top of the apple mixture, but do not spread it all the way to the sides of the dish. Leave about ¼ inch of space around the edges for steam to escape.
4. Bake at 350°F for 40–45 minutes, or until crispy brown.

   This apple crisp is good served plain, either warm or cold. It is also good hot from the oven with vanilla soymilk poured over it.

STEWED RHUBARB

We used to have rhubarb growing in our yard. It appears in very early spring, as soon as the snow is gone. If you are used to cooking rhubarb with lots of sugar or honey, you will probably be surprised to see how sweet and delicious it is when it is sweetened only with raisins. We enjoy it as a healthful dessert, or topped with yogurt for breakfast.

5 cups rhubarb (stalks), cut into ¹/₂-inch pieces
1¹/₂ cups raisins
2 tablespoons grated orange peel (optional)
1 teaspoon cinnamon
1 teaspoon vanilla
¹/₄ cup water or apple juice (approximately)

Serves: 4–6
Time: 40 minutes

Place all the ingredients in a heavy, medium-sized pan. Cover and cook over low heat, stirring occasionally, for about 30 minutes, or until the rhubarb is tender. It may be necessary to add a small amount of water or juice during the cooking. Do not add more than is needed to keep the rhubarb from sticking to the bottom of the pan. Chill before serving.

VARIATION

- *Rhubarb Crisp*: Omit the water or apple juice in the above recipe. Mix all the other ingredients, but instead of cooking, place them in the bottom of a shallow baking dish. Spread the topping from the *Wildflower Apple Crisp* (page 264) over the rhubarb mixture and bake at 350°F for 40–45 minutes. Serve either chilled or at room temperature.

ALMOND-DATE COOKIES

The sweetener in these cookies is the dates and the shortening is the almonds. When you taste them it is hard to believe how simple they are to make.

¹/₂ cup whole, raw almonds plus 16 whole almonds for garnish
¹/₂ cup pitted dates (packed into the cup)
¹/₂ cup brown rice flour
1 teaspoon vanilla or almond extract
1 large egg

Yield: Sixteen 2-inch cookies
Time: 30 minutes

1. Place the almonds, dates, and flour in a food processor and grind as finely as possible. (If you prefer, you can grind the almonds in a blender and chop the dates as finely as possible with a sharp knife.) Add the extract and the egg. Mix well. (Use your hands for mixing if necessary.)
2. Press the mixture into the bottom of a lightly oiled 8-x-8-inch cake pan. Score the dough with a knife to mark off 2-inch squares. Press an almond into the center of each square.
3. Bake on the top rack of the oven at 350°F for 15 minutes. If the tops of the cookies do not brown, turn your oven to broil (but do not raise the heat) and continue baking for a couple of minutes more, until the cookies are golden-brown. Cut the cookies on the scored lines and remove them from the pan.

NOTE: Because the moisture content of dates varies, you may find that you have to add a small amount of water to the dough to get it to stick together. If so, add the water by the teaspoon and don't add more than necessary.

MAPLE-WALNUT COOKIES

Light and crisp.

1 1/4 cups walnuts
3/4 cups rolled oats
1/2 cup brown rice flour
1/4 cup oil
1/3 cup maple syrup

Yield: Approximately 35 small cookies
Time: 30 minutes

1. *Food Processor Method*: Place the walnuts, oats and rice flour in the food processor. Using the blending blade, grind the ingredients to a flour. Add the oil to the flour-nut mixture; place in a food processor and blend briefly until it is evenly distributed. Add the maple syrup and mix well.

   Blender Method: Grind the walnuts (about 1/2 cup at a time) in a blender. Then grind the oats. Place the ground walnuts and oats in a bowl. Add the rice flour and mix well.

   Add the oil to the flour-nut mixture and stir with a fork until it is evenly distributed. Add the maple syrup and mix well.

2. After the dough is mixed, oil a cookie sheet. Drop the dough by the teaspoon onto the cookie sheet. The dough should be rather thick—you will have to push it off the spoon.

Flatten each cookie by pressing it with a fork. Dip the fork into cold water to keep the dough from sticking.

3. Bake on the top rack of the oven at 375°F for about 15 minutes, or until the cookies are golden. They will be soft when hot, but will become crisp as they cool.

ONE-TWO-THREE MAPLE PEANUT COOKIES

Nothing could be easier. Children can have fun making these simple cookies.

1/2 cup peanut butter
1/3 cup maple syrup
1/2 cup whole wheat pastry flour

Yield: About 20 small cookies
Time: 25 minutes

1. In a medium-sized mixing bowl, cream together the peanut butter and maple syrup. Add the flour and mix well.

2. Drop the batter by the heaping teaspoon onto a well-oiled cookie sheet. Flatten the cookies by pressing each one twice with a fork, as shown in Figure 12.1. (Dip the fork into cold water to keep it from sticking.)

3. Bake at 375°F for about 12 minutes.

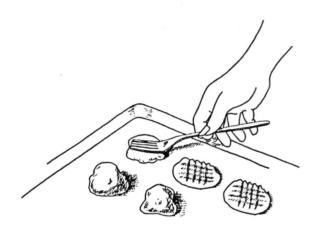
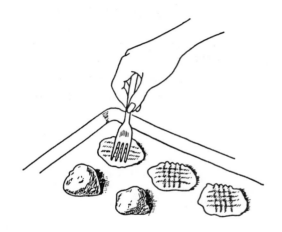

Figure 12.1.   Pressing cookies with a fork.

ALMOND BUTTER AND JAM COOKIES

A food processor is needed to make these sweet and tender cookies. When I make these, I use a honey-sweetened plum jam, but any jam or jelly would work well. However, if you prefer a cookie that is sweetened entirely with fruit, use unsweetened apple butter.

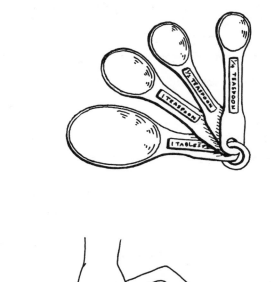

½ cup smooth almond butter
½ cup raisins
½ cup whole wheat pastry flour
2 tablespoons water (approximately)
⅓ cup naturally sweetened jam or jelly

Yield: About 14 cookies
Time: 30 minutes

1. Place the almond butter, raisins, and pastry flour in a food processor. Mix with blending blade until the raisins are finely ground. Gradually add as much water as needed to make a dough that will hold together when you press it.
2. Shape the dough into about 14 walnut-sized balls and place them on an oiled cookie sheet. Make a well in the center of each ball of dough. If desired, shape the outer edges of the cookies with your fingers (as shown in Step 1 of Figure 12.2) to get rid of cracks in the dough and to give the cookies a more regular form. Drop about ½ teaspoon of jam into the indented center of each cookie (see Step 2).
3. Bake at 350°F on the top rack of the oven for 12 minutes. Carefully remove the cookies with a spatula. They will become more firm as they cool.

1. Shaping the cookies.

2. Filling the cookies.

Figure 12.2.   Filling the Cookies.

DATE-FILLED TAHINI COOKIES

These cookies are delicious.

FILLING

½ cup pitted dates
⅓ cup water
2 tablespoons maple syrup

DOUGH

½ cup tahini
2 tablespoons oil
¼ cup maple syrup
1 teaspoon vanilla
1 cup whole wheat pastry flour

Yield: 18–20 cookies
Time: 30 minutes

1. Make the filling first. Place the dates and the water in a small saucepan and cook over medium heat for about 10 minutes. Add the maple syrup and blend the mixture in the blender. Set the filling aside until it is needed.
2. In a mixing bowl, cream together the tahini, oil, maple syrup, and vanilla. Slowly mix in the flour to form a stiff dough. Mix with your hands and knead the dough a few times, if necessary, to make it hold together.
3. Roll the dough into 18–20 balls the size of small walnuts. Place the balls of dough on an oiled cookie sheet. Make a "well" in the center of each cookie by pressing it with your thumb. If you wish, you can shape the well with your fingers as in Step 1 of Figure 12.2. Drop 1 teaspoon of filling into each well (see Step 2 of Figure 12.2).
4. Bake at 350°F for 15 minutes on the top rack of the oven. If the cookies are not cooked on the top, turn your oven to broil (without raising the temperature) and cook for a couple of minutes more. Watch closely so they do not burn.

FRUIT AND OAT SQUARES

1½ cups rolled oats
½ cup whole wheat pastry flour
⅓ cup finely grated unsweetened coconut
1 cup chopped pitted dates
½ cup raisins
½ cup oil
¾ cup mashed banana

Yield: Sixteen 2-inch squares
Time: 30 minutes

1. In a medium-sized bowl, combine all the ingredients in the order they are listed above. Mix well, using your hands if necessary.
2. Oil an 8-x-8-inch cake pan. Transfer the oat mixture to the pan. Press it with your hands to obtain an even thickness. Bake at 350°F for 20 minutes or until the cookies turn golden.
3. While the cookies are still hot, cut them into squares. Let them cool before removing them from the pan.

FIG BARS

These cookies taste even better than the commercially available fig bars. In fact, I used to sell these when I had a natural foods store! This recipe makes a large quantity, so you may wish to cut it in half. However, for a large party or a bake sale, it is great just the way it is.

FILLING
3 pounds figs
1½ cups water plus ¼ cup or more additional water if necessary

DOUGH
3 cups whole wheat pastry flour
2 cups rice flour
1 teaspoon nutmeg
¾ cup oil
1 egg
½ cup honey
2 teaspoons vanilla

Yield: 40 bars
Time: 1 hour

1. To prepare the filling, place the figs and the water in a large kettle. Cover the kettle and cook the figs till they are soft, stirring often.
2. Purée the cooked figs in a food processor or blender (a little at a time). Add additional water if necessary to obtain a consistency similar to that of jam or apple butter. Set the filling aside while you make the dough.
3. Mix together the flours and nutmeg. Work in the oil with your hands. In a separate bowl, beat together the egg, honey, and vanilla. Then, using a fork, work the honey mixture into the flour mixture to make a stiff dough.
4. Divide the dough in half. Roll one half of the dough directly onto an unoiled 11½-x-17½-inch cookie sheet. Spread the filling over the dough.
5. Roll the remaining dough out between two sheets of wax paper to make an 11½-x-17½-inch rectangle. Carefully peel off the top sheet of wax paper. Pick up the dough by the bottom paper and place it over the filling. Peel off the wax paper.
6. Cut the top dough into 3-x-1½-inch bars, then prick each bar three times with the tines of a fork. Place on the middle rack of the oven and bake at 350°F for 20 minutes.
7. When the bars are baked, cut them all the way through, but don't remove them from the pan until they have cooled.

CHEWY TAHINI MALT COOKIES

½ cup tahini
½ cup barley malt syrup
½ cup finely chopped walnuts
½ cup plus 1 tablespoon whole wheat pastry flour
1 teaspoon baking powder

Yield: About 16 cookies
Time: 25 minutes

1. In a medium-sized bowl, cream together the tahini and malt. Add the walnuts and mix well.
2. In another bowl, mix together the flour and baking powder. Add the flour mixture to the tahini mixture. Using your hands, knead the flour into the dough. (There is no need to take the dough out of the bowl to knead it. Be careful not to knead it too much; just enough to mix in the flour.)
3. Shape the dough into walnut-sized balls. Place them on a well-oiled cookie sheet. Make sure to leave some space between the cookies, because they will flatten out as they bake. Bake on the top rack of the oven at 350°F for 12–14 minutes.

MACRO MAMA'S BIG OATMEAL COOKIES

These cookies are not crisp and fancy. They are big, chewy, and very satisfying. Make them for your kids, or for the kid in you!

2 cups rolled oats
3/4 cup whole wheat pastry flour
1 cup raisins
1/3 cup oil
1/4 cup malt syrup
1/4 cup water, or as needed

Yield: 8 big cookies
Time: 30 minutes

1. In a large bowl, mix together the oats, flour, and raisins. Gradually stir in the oil and mix well. Add the malt syrup and mix again (you will probably have to use your hands for mixing). Add as much water as you need to make the dough hold together. Mix with your hands and shape the dough into a large mass.
2. Cover a cookie sheet with wax paper. Oil the wax paper. Using a 1/4 cup measuring cup or an ice cream scoop (an ice cream scoop works better), scoop up about 1/4 cup of firmly packed dough. Turn the dough out onto the cookie sheet. If you are using a measuring cup, turn the cup upside down and tap one side of the rim of the cup firmly against the cookie sheet until the dough falls out. Continue scooping the dough onto the cookie sheet until it is all used up. Using the palms of your hands, flatten the mounds of dough into cookies that are about 1/4 inch thick and 4 inches in diameter.
3. Place the cookies on the top rack of the oven and bake at 350°F for about 15 minutes. Carefully remove the cookies from the cookie sheet with a spatula and let them cool on a rack.

VARIATION

- You can, of course, make small cookies instead of large ones if you desire. Small cookies will bake a little bit faster than the big ones, so watch them carefully. You may also want to substitute chopped nuts or coconut for half of the raisins; or add some cinnamon, nutmeg, ginger, or cloves if desired.

POLYNESIAN BARS

2 cups chopped dates
1 cup raisins
One 20-ounce can unsweetened crushed pineapple (in its own juice)
3/4 cup water
1 teaspoon vanilla
1 1/2 cups whole wheat pastry flour
1 1/2 cups rolled oats
1/2 cup coconut
1/2 cup chopped nuts
3/4 cup oil

Yield: 16 bars, approximately 2x3 inches each
Time: 50 minutes

1. Combine the dates, raisins, pineapple, water, and vanilla in a pan. Bring to a boil, reduce the heat to low, and simmer (uncovered) until the mixture is thick. Stir occasionally while cooking. Once the mixture thickens, remove it from the heat and set it aside.
2. In a bowl, mix together the flour, oats, coconut, and chopped nuts. Add the oil and mix with your hands until well-blended. Evenly press half of the mixture into the bottom of a 7-x-11-inch baking dish. Spread the date mixture over this crust, then sprinkle the rest of the flour mixture on top.
3. Bake at 350°F for 30 minutes. Cut into bars. Let the bars cool before removing them from the pan.

FRUIT AND NUT BARS

A delicious and nutritious candy that takes only minutes to make in a food processor.

1 cup whole raw almonds
1 cup raisins
1 cup pitted dates
1 teaspoon grated lemon peel
1/3 cup finely grated unsweetened coconut (as needed)

Yield: 32 bars
Time: 15–20 minutes

1. Place the almonds, raisins, dates, and lemon peel in a food processor. Using the blending blade, process the mixture, grinding it as finely as possible.
2. Sprinkle the bottom of an 8-x-8-inch cake pan with half of the coconut. Using your hands, evenly press the fruit-nut mixture over the coconut to cover the bottom of the pan. To keep the candy from sticking to your hands, sprinkle the remaining coconut over the top as you press it.
3. Chill the candy for about 2 hours and then cut it into bars. If desired, you may wrap each bar individually in wax paper. Store the candy in the refrigerator until you're ready for a treat!

NOTE: If the dates and raisins are extremely dry, add a very small amount of fruit juice or homemade jam to the mixture to make it stick together.

VARIATION

- *Blender Method*: Grind the almonds in the blender. Remove the ground almonds from the blender and add 1/2 cup of raisins. Blend the raisins to a sticky paste. Remove this paste, then add the remaining 1/2 cup of raisins and blend again to obtain a sticky paste. Chop the dates as finely as possible with a sharp knife. Using your hands, mix together the ground almonds, raisins, dates, and lemon peel. Follow the above directions for pressing, chilling, and cutting.

Rather than making bars, you may shape the candy into small balls. Roll each ball in coconut or sesame seeds.

HAWAIIAN SNOW

A light and refreshing pineapple sherbet. This recipe may be made the day before you wish to serve it.

2 cups buttermilk
1/4 cup honey
1 cup unsweetened crushed pineapple, drained
1 teaspoon vanilla
2 egg whites

Serves: 4–6
Time: 15 minutes to prepare; freeze for 3 hours.

1. In a medium-sized plastic or metal bowl, mix together the buttermilk, honey, pineapple, and vanilla.
2. Place the mixture in the freezer until it is frozen around the edges of the bowl (about 1 hour). Remove the bowl from the freezer and beat the mixture well with a spoon. Return the bowl to the freezer and freeze until the pineapple has the consistency of slushy snow.
3. Beat the egg whites until they stand up in stiff peaks. Fold the egg whites into the slushy mixture and freeze until firm. Remove the sherbet from the freezer about 1/2 hour before serving.

MELON SHERBET

This sherbet has a beautiful pastel color. Don't let its simplicity fool you; it is a light and luscious dessert that makes the perfect ending to an elegant dinner.

1 medium cantaloupe or similar melon
1 teaspoon grated lime peel
2 tablespoons honey, or more to taste

Serves: 4
Time: 15 minutes to prepare; freeze overnight.

1. Cut the melon in half; remove and discard the seeds and membrane. Cut the fruit away from the rind and cut it into chunks. Place the chunks in a plastic bag. Close the bag with a twist tie and freeze overnight or until the melon is very solid.
2. Remove the bag from the freezer. Hit the bag of frozen melon against a countertop a few times to separate the pieces.
3. Place the frozen melon in a food processor with the blending blade. Add the lime peel and the honey. Blend. It may be necessary to stop the machine occasionally and stir the mixture to assure thorough blending. Continue blending until the sherbet becomes smooth and fluffy.
4. Pile the mixture into sherbet glasses and serve immediately. If necessary, this sherbet can be made just before the meal, then returned to the freezer to keep until dessert time.

KANTEN

Kanten is the Japanese version of gelatin. The main difference between kanten and commercially produced brands of gelatin is that kanten is very good for you. This recipe makes a wonderful light dessert and is a great medium for culinary artistry. It lends itself to almost limitless possibilities. Any type of sweet-tasting fruit juice may be used to make this kanten. Grape, orange, and apple are all excellent; however, for a special occasion you may wish to try one of the more exotic juices that are sold in health food stores, such as pineapple-coconut, black cherry, papaya, etc.

1 bar agar
3 cups unsweetened fruit juice

Serves: 4
Time: 15 minutes to prepare; chill for 2 hours.

1. Break the agar into small pieces and place it in a saucepan along with the fruit juice. Bring the juice to a boil; then lower the heat and simmer until the agar is dissolved. Pour the kanten into a mold. If you use a simple mold such as a rectangular baking dish, dip the dish briefly into cold water before pouring in the kanten. However, if you use a fancy mold, it is better to lightly oil the mold before you pour in the kanten.
2. Chill the kanten until it is firm (about 2 hours). If you are using a square or rectangular mold, cut the gel into squares and remove it from the mold with a spatula. If you are using a fancy mold, unmold it onto a serving platter.

VARIATION

*   Slices of fresh fruit, chopped dried fruit, or nuts may be added to the kanten to add interest and flavor. To make additions; let the kanten chill and become partially set, then fold in the fruit or nuts. If unsweetened fruit juice is not sweet enough for you, add undiluted fruit juice concentrate or a little honey (to taste) to the dissolved agar mixture.

GRAPE GEL

Very wholesome and easy to make.

3 cups good-quality unsweetened grape juice
1 bar agar
1½ cups mixed fruit, in bite-sized pieces

Serves: 4–6
Time: 10–15 minutes to prepare; chill for 2 hours.

1. Place the juice in a medium-sized saucepan. Tear the agar into small pieces and add it to the grape juice. Bring to a boil. Reduce the heat to medium-low and simmer until the agar is completely dissolved (about 5–10 minutes).
2. Choose an appropriate bowl, mold, cake pan, etc., to contain the gelatin, and dip it into cold water. (This will keep the gel from sticking.) Then pour in the dissolved agar-juice mixture.
3. Chill until the mixture just begins to set (about 45 minutes or less); then fold in the fruit. Chill until completely set.

     Serve plain or with *Tofu and Cashew Cream* (page 274).

PEAR AND BERRY GEL

The raspberries add a touch of elegance to this simple, low-calorie dessert.

3 cups pear nectar
1 bar agar
1½ cups blueberries
1 cup raspberries

Serves: 6
Time: 15 minutes to prepare; chill 2 hours.

1. Break the bar of agar into small pieces, and place it in a saucepan with the pear nectar. Bring the pear nectar to a boil. Lower the heat and simmer until the agar is completely dissolved (about 5–10 minutes).
2. Dip an 8-x-8-inch cake pan into cold water,

then pour the pear-agar mixture into the pan. Refrigerate the mixture until it begins to set (at least 30 minutes). Then fold in the berries, and chill until firm (about 1 hour).

     To serve this dessert, cut it into squares. Top each serving with a whipped topping, if desired.

FRUIT AND NUT VELOUTÉ

This dessert is light, elegant, and easy to prepare.

1 recipe Kanten *(page 272)*
1 recipe Tofu and Cashew Cream *(page 274)*

Serves: 4
Time: 15 minutes to prepare *Kanten*; chill for 2 hours; 10 minutes to prepare *Tofu and Cashew Cream.*

1. Choose either a dark or a bright-colored juice for the kanten, such as red grape, orange, apple-strawberry, etc. Follow the recipe for the kanten and place it in a rectangular mold to jell. When the kanten is set, cut it into tiny (about ½ inch) cubes.
2. Distribute half of the cubes evenly among 4 sherbet glasses. Top with half of the tofu cream. Repeat the layers.

     Garnish each glass with a cherry, strawberry, orange twist, etc. Serve chilled.

AVOCADO MOUSSE

This simple dessert looks and tastes so elegant that it is hard to believe how easy it is to prepare. Do not make this dessert too far in advance, because the avocado will turn brown.

1 small Florida avocado, or 2 small California avocados
¼ cup soymilk
¼ cup honey
2 tablespoons lemon juice
Fresh strawberries or raspberries
Finely grated coconut

Serves: 4
Time: 10 minutes

1. Cut the avocado or avocados in half lengthwise. Remove the pit and scoop out the flesh. Place the flesh in a blender along with the soymilk, honey, and lemon juice. Blend until smooth and creamy.
2. Put the mousse in chilled sherbet glasses. Top with the strawberries or raspberries and sprinkle with a little grated coconut. Chill until ready to serve.

CREAM CHEESE ICING

Simple and delicious.

8 ounces cream cheese (1 package)
¼ cup honey, or less to taste
1 teaspoon vanilla
1 teaspoon finely grated lemon peel

Yield: Enough for a 4½-x-8½-x-2½-inch loaf
      cake or a 7-x-11-inch cake
Time: 10–15 minutes

Using a fork, wire whisk, or hand mixer, cream together all the ingredients. Spread the icing over a cooled cake. If the cake is not to be eaten immediately, refrigerate it.

TOFU AND CASHEW CREAM

Use this whipped topping over jelled desserts or fruit salads. It is also good on a plain cake or a fruit pie.

1 cup mashed soft tofu
¼ cup whole raw cashews
⅓ cup honey, or less to taste
1 teaspoon vanilla
Water (as needed)

Yield: About 2 cups
Time: 10 minutes

Blend together all ingredients in a blender till smooth and creamy, using a rubber spatula to push the mixture down toward the blades.

NOTE: If you use firm tofu, you may have to add about ¼ cup of water to the cream to achieve the desired consistency. If the cream is going to be chilled before serving, it will thicken slightly, so adjust the amount of water you add accordingly.

PEANUT BUTTER ICING

½ cup cream cheese
½ cup peanut butter
1 teaspoon vanilla
¼ cup honey
2 tablespoons milk (approximately)

Yield: Enough to cover a 7-x-11-inch cake
Time: 10–15 minutes

Mix together the cream cheese, peanut butter, and vanilla. Gradually cream in the honey. Add enough milk to reach the desired spreading consistency. Spread the icing on cooled *Carobanana Cake* (page 255) or on any other cake of your choice.

STUFFED FIGS

Here's a nourishing and exotic dessert—or a gourmet treat to carry in your backpack on a ski or hiking trip.

18–20 large brown dried figs
Water or apple juice to cover (optional)
1 cup ground pecans
¼ cup finely grated unsweetened coconut
2–3 tablespoons honey
1 teaspoon coriander
18–20 pecan halves

Yield: 18–20 stuffed figs
Time: 20 minutes

1. If the figs are soft and fresh they may be stuffed without soaking. However, if they are hard, soak them overnight, or until soft, in water or apple juice to cover. Cut the stem end off the figs. Using your fingers, open up the figs to form a pouch.
2. Mix together the ground pecans, coconut, honey, and coriander.
3. Stuff the figs with the nut mixture and top each with a pecan half.

ROASTED CHESTNUTS

Yield: As many chestnuts as you wish to roast
Time: About 25 minutes

Subtly sweet, roasted chestnuts make an ordinary winter meal a warm and festive occasion. They may be served as an accompaniment to a main dish, or afterwards as a healthful dessert.

Punch a hole into the shell of each chestnut with a sharp knife. If you forget to do this, the chestnuts will explode! Follow one of these three roasting methods:

1. Place the chestnuts in a heavy skillet over medium heat. Cover the skillet and cook the chestnuts for about 20 minutes, stirring often.
2. Place the chestnuts on an unoiled cookie sheet or in an ovenproof dish. Bake them at 375°F for about 20 minutes, stirring occasionally.
3. Wrap the chestnuts in a sheet of aluminum foil and place them directly over the hot coals in your fireplace, barbecue, campfire, or wood stove. The cooking time will depend on the heat, so check them after about 10 minutes and turn them over to prevent burning.

Index